Blaze

Blaze:
Discourse on Art, Women and Feminism

Edited by

Karen Frostig and Kathy A. Halamka

CAMBRIDGE
SCHOLARS
PUBLISHING

Blaze: Discourse on Art, Women and Feminism, Edited by Karen Frostig and Kathy A. Halamka

This book first published 2007. The present binding first published 2009.

Cambridge Scholars Publishing

12 Back Chapman Street, Newcastle upon Tyne, NE6 2XX, UK

British Library Cataloguing in Publication Data
A catalogue record for this book is available from the British Library

ISBN (10): 1-4438-0239-5, ISBN (13): 978-1-4438-0239-0

Dedication

American Feminist, Activist and Writer,

Betty Friedan (1921–2006)

Civil Rights and Equal Rights Activist,

Coretta Scott King (1907-2006)

Feminist Art Activist and Writer, Critic and Curator,

Arlene Raven (1944-2006)

Feminist Art Activist, Artist, Writer, and Critic,

Tee Corinne (1943-2006)

Feminist and Environmental Art Activist, Writer and Curator,

Jo Hanson (1918-2007)

TABLE OF CONTENTS

List of Images

PREFACE

Blaze: Discourse on Art, Women, and Feminism is a feminist anthology comprised of second-wave and third-wave feminist artists, art historians, critics, journalists, curators, interdisciplinary artists, and arts administrators of diverse backgrounds, living across the United States. We developed this book from our open call for essays for the 2006 Annual National Women's Caucus for Art (WCA) conference, held at the Sheraton Hotel in Boston, Massachusetts.

Founded in 1972, the WCA is a volunteer, non-profit organization. Its mission statement to "increase opportunities, visibility, and recognition for women in the arts" has been at the core of every action at the WCA. An elected president, representative officers, and a national volunteer board governed by a code of by-laws, all support 29 independent chapters across the United States. Each chapter is governed by the consensus of a steering committee. Conferences typically reflect this configuration, often featuring national voices, as well as local leadership in the arts, largely determined by the hosting chapter.[1]

The conference co-chairs, Karen Frostig, Kathy A. Halamka, and Cynthia Runge, all worked in concert with the Boston chapter steering committee to develop a title for the 2006 National Conference *Digging Deeper to Build New Paradigms.* The title began as a sly play with words about Boston's famous "Big Dig" public works project. However, this title quickly turned into a framework for addressing the emerging constructive discourse between second-wave and third-wave feminists. This illuminated shared concerns, as well as divergent approaches and positions.

Past WCA Boston Chapter president, Cynthia Runge, developed a network of relationships while researching what was needed to successfully host the conference: booking venues, negotiating rates, and creating contracts. Kathy A. Halamka focused on keeping all the disparate elements in focus, and on crafting the various visual exhibitions, including the 2006 National Exhibition. The national exhibition was held at the Kniznick Gallery, within the Women's Studies Research Center (WSRC) of Brandeis University in Waltham, Massachusetts. The jurors for this nationwide call for artists were Wendy Tarlow Kaplan, curator of the Kniznick Gallery, and Raphaela Platow, curator of the Rose Art Museum,

Waltham. The exhibition, Vital Voices: Women's Visions, joined the WSRC's mission, "Where Research Art and Activism Converge"[2] with the mission of the WCA. Karen Frostig contributed to the overall development of the conference, while devoting her primary attention to the panel program.

Our initial open call for conference papers was advertised in numerous venues, as well as posted on the national and local Web sites of the WCA. As chair of the conference panel program, Frostig was deeply committed to broadening the general scope of the conference, raising the bar for engaging discourse, and to developing fresh dialog between second-wave and third-wave feminists. In order to supplement the slim response to the original call, she developed an outreach initiative. Frostig contacted numerous art professionals from across the United States. Recognizing the instrumental nature of networking, she was keenly aware of the historic record whereby privilege and omission determined professional success or failure. It was important not to impose a privileged system of representation onto the development of the panel program.

Intuitively, Frostig began this process by returning to the period when she first joined the Boston chapter of the WCA in 1988. She contacted the leaders of this chapter from that time: Susan Schwalb, Patricia Johnston, Patricia Hills, and Alicia Faxon. All of these women had remained active in the art world and many of them held key positions of leadership at various universities in the area. From these conversations, she accrued names of arts professionals working in a variety of contexts. These names were added to a growing resource list of feminist artists, academics, and activists, as well as community arts activists working outside of established institutions. It was critical to spark the participatory interest of feminist artists and art historians, as well as other leaders of the feminist art movement represented in a number of recent publications. All possibilities, from national to local, were under scrutiny.

The networking prism became the mechanism to expand this conference. These conversations opened up a panorama of ideas and issues on the minds of many women across the country. The serendipitous nature of how one conversation led to the next, added a measure of adventure to the process.

Although this process skewed to some degree the open nature of conference panel development, the end result reflected countless conversations and input from hundreds of women who recommended many of the speakers at the 2006 conference. In part, because of how the panel program developed, there were many friendships and mentoring relationships represented on the various panels. Overall, the panels could be seen as an expression of women admiring the work of women. The feeling of a "homecoming" was palpable. In addition, presenters were not required to submit official abstracts in advance, which expanded the possible presentations to both the academic and the personal.

Many of the panelists participating in the conference had either prominent national or local reputations, had the financial means to attend a conference in Boston, and were engaged in work that promoted feminist concerns framed by critical discourse. The conference panel program was comprised of 16 panels and 70 presenters, representing a range of topics: women's organizations and camaraderie to feminist scholarship and mentorship; issues of domesticity and performance to spiritual forays and ritual practice; fictional narratives to narrative memory; activism in the public sphere to ecofeminism; and dialogue between second-wave and third-wave feminists to economic strategies and critical analysis of the art world. Panel diversity, represented by race, age, class, and sexual orientation, was actively pursued, but not as fully achieved as had been desired.

Overcoming these constraints, the 2006 Conference received enthusiastic reviews. The conference reflected the extensive collaboration between the three conference co-chairs, the local membership, the New Hampshire and Central Massachusetts chapters, and members on the National Board. Our invited conference keynote speaker was Coco Fusco, an internationally acclaimed performance artist and author, and professor in the School of the Arts at Columbia University, New York. Fusco's address fanned the heat of controversy, as she discussed her latest project,[3] detailing an underreported scheme of sexual exploitation in a branch of women in the military. This address followed the truly unique and critically important WCA Annual Lifetime Achievement Award Honoree Ceremony. Awardees for 2006 included Eleanor Antin, Marisol Escobar, Elinor Gadon, and Yayoi Kusama.[4] In addition, the conference included Femlink,[5] a juried international festival of video shorts, five national and regional visual art exhibitions, pre-conference off-site academic panels, and a book fair. Significantly, for the first time at a WCA National Conference, audio-visual engineers and a team of interns produced a twenty-five hour audio-visual recording of the entire conference for posterity.[6] Immediately prior to the start of the conference, we received an invitation from the publisher, Cambridge Scholars Publishing (UK). We were presented the welcome opportunity to create a manuscript of enhanced conference proceedings for book publication. We were well aware of our complementary styles, so it was natural that we decided to work collaboratively together on this project. Our call for essays was inserted that night into the attendees and presenters conference program packets. With no conference abstracts in hand, we were essentially starting from scratch. Since the book was also wedded by design to the distinctive timeframe and location of our 2006 National WCA Conference, we had certain parameters to keep in mind as we sought our writers. To enlarge our pool of exceptional writers, we approached conference attendees, conference honorees, exhibition jurors and curators, pre-conference panelists, and numerous potential panelists, who were unable in the end to attend the conference.

Throughout the hot summer that followed our National Conference, cyberspace sizzled with the traffic of e-mails solidifying the essay abstracts. Essays encompassed an array of topics, emanating outward, from the personal to the public, from the historic to the fresh and new. Many essays also reflected the movement from individual to collaborative projects. *Blaze: Discourse on Art, Women, and Feminism* takes on a political positioning, supporting a feminist framework. Our Table of Contents is divided into four sections: Leadership, Criticism, Collaboration, and The Work. Although every essay contains aspects of all four categories, we believe that this organization highlights key ideas within each essay. The four categories also name different methods of cultural intervention. In addition, Blaze also features 14 new histories about feminist organizations, journalism, second-wave and third-wave feminism, Chicana/Latina artists, and issues of representation, new media, ecofeminism, performance art, and the handling of the nude. These embedded histories are further animated by ideas about leadership, criticism and collaboration.

Blaze conjures up images of light, fury and transformation. The text goes to great length to examine the political underpinnings of various problems followed by transformative solutions that promote social change. In this way, our diverse book of essays, which became *Blaze* in the heat of that summer after the conference, forges new ideas about contemporary feminist issues in the arts.

---

[1] Detailed information on conferences is maintained by National Administrator Karin Luner on the National WCA Web site at http://www.nationalwca.org/Framesets/conferframeset.htm. Access date June 10, 2007.

[2] The mission of the WSRC is described fully at the Web site http://www.brandeis.edu/centers/wsrc/. Access date June 10, 2007.

[3] Fusco's project is described at length on her personal Web site "Coco Fusco's Virtual Laboratory" at http://www.cocofusco.com/. Access date June 10, 2007.

[4] Dena Muller and Susan King Obarski eds., *Women's Caucus for Art, Honor Awards for Lifetime Achievement in the Visual Arts: Honor Awards 2006*. (New York: WCA Publishing, 2006), i.
[5] Femlink is fully documented at its Web site http://www.femlink.org/. Access date June 10, 2007.
[6] An edited two-hour disc of these panel tapes is described on the National WCA Web site. http://www.nationalwca.org. Access date June 10, 2007.

Works Cited

Dena Muller and Susan King Obarski eds. *Women's Caucus for Art, Honor Awards for Lifetime Achievement in the Visual Arts: Honor Awards 2006.* New York: WCA Publishing, 2006.

ACKNOWLEDGMENTS

Our appreciation first goes out to the many lively participants of the 2006 National Women's Caucus for Art (WCA) conference whose enthusiasm seeded this project. A large number of conference presenters became contributors to Blaze. Over the course of three years, many of our writers maintained close communication with us, becoming collaborators as well as contributors. The complexity of everyone's life became part and parcel of the work and the conversations about feminism.

Special thanks goes to the WCA board, which supported and funded the original initiative to tape and publish the disc of conference proceedings. Mark Buchanan and his fabulous team of conference video interns, as well as Joseph Douillette and Kerry Molloy from Eggrock Media, video editors extraordinaire, worked together to create the conference disc. We also want to recognize the efforts of members of the Boston WCA chapter; Laura Morrison, president of the New Hampshire chapter; and C.M. Judge, founding president of the central Mass chapter, who were instrumental in contributing to the success of the conference. The bookstore at Simmons College provided us with a conference book table to celebrate our many published presenters. All of these coordinated efforts set the stage for Blaze to emerge as a formal publication.

We would also like to acknowledge the support and interest extended to this project by past and present WCA presidents. Judith K. Brodsky, Noreen Dresser and Jennifer Colby provided timely input, as did Carol Becker, Ruth Weisberg, Paul Von Blum, and Phyllis Holman Weisbard.

We are especially indebted to Cynthia Runge, former president of the Boston chapter and 2006 WCA conference co-chair. Her legal counsel and expertise in international copyright law for artists and authors was indispensable. We have valued her support and relied on her talent since the very beginning. We also had the good fortune to hire Heather Dubnick as our proofreader, copyeditor, and indexer, whose detailed knowledge and resourcefulness was key in carrying the book through to completion.

We would also like to thank our publisher, Dr. Andy Nercessian at Cambridge Scholars Publishing (CSP), who first saw the spark in the concept for this book. We are grateful to Amanda Millar, Editor for CSP, who provided us with ongoing support, Vlatka Kolic for assistance in designing a dust jacket, and Carol Koulikourdi, who facilitated prompt responses to all of our questions, helping us to move through the various phases of production with great ease.

From Karen Frostig:

Special appreciation goes to my college-bound son, Kabren Levinson, political technologist, musician, and artist. His faith in "the people" and "open source" systems reminded me again and again of where we are headed. My husband, Brent Levinson's enduring presence and ongoing support helped sustain me through many long nights at the computer. Nanette Levinson's boundless encouragement and willingness to read a short draft came at a critical moment. Suzi Gablik, my long-time mentor and friend, provided me with heartfelt guidance. I wish to thank my colleagues: Lisa Donovan, division director; Julia Halevy, dean of the graduate school of the arts and sciences; as well as the academic affairs committee, who generously awarded me with a fellowship for this project from Lesley University's Center for Research Fellowship Program. I am also thoroughly indebted to Shulamit Reinharz, Founding Director of the Hadassah-Brandeis Institute, who had the vision to create an environment where women mingle over scholarship and creative pursuits, and to include me in this vision as a research associate.

Finally, my expression of gratitude goes to Kathy Halamka, editorial partner and friend. Over the course of working together on the conference and this book, we discovered that our skills were remarkably complementary. My respect for Kathy's ability to stay balanced, kind, and always collaborative in the midst of managing multiple deadlines and projects continues to grow. She is a superb communicator. Her talent as a creative thinker, fine writer, and detailed editor is meticulously evidenced throughout the volume. I especially appreciated the rare opportunity to think together, to converse about ideas, and to reach toward a vision of a more inclusive world. The mix of pleasure and hard work was always present.

From Kathy A. Halamka:

I want to thank my talented daughter, Lara Halamka, and her unending support and love that make this all possible. She always knows when her smile and a few words of encouragement were just what I need. It is for Lara, and this generation of young women artists, that this feminist dialog must remain prominent. Since the day we met, my husband, John D. Halamka, has always been my very best model for acting with thoughtful consideration, kindness, patience, and remembering the value of the golden rule. His love and compassion are my sanctuary.

My father, Harold E. Greene, has been a wellspring of quiet and unquestioned belief in me all my life. He has always been there to help in any way possible, no matter how large or how small. So very much of my visual art and writing are in loving memory of my mother, Susan Eunja Greene. I will always admire her fateful decision to emigrate in the name of love, and make a new life here in the United States. And John E. and Dagmar Halamka have been unfailingly kind and supportive, thank you for sharing John D. with me all these years

My co-editor, Karen Frostig, has a marvelous ability to make the impossible, possible. She created true magic with her ideas for Blaze. Deeply intelligent and seemingly tireless, she managed to also have solo exhibits to showcase those considerable talents, while simultaneously crafting this book. Our work synergy makes it often seem as if we are thinking as one—the very best in collaboration.

INTRODUCTION

How has feminism matured over the years? What are the pressing agendas for today's feminists working in the arts? How do women make sense of an increasingly interconnected world, where local and national concerns interact with a new set of global realities?

Destabilization of systems and hybridization of ideas, both highlight this period as an unusually rich nexus of opportunity. Unorthodox processes abound, and risk has become a highly valued commodity. *Blaze: Discourse on Art, Women, and Feminism*, emerges as a navigational text, celebrating past victories while charting new directions for today's second wave and third wave feminists.

In developing a feminist framework for *Blaze*, the editors asked writers to consider the different waves of feminism in relationship to their own evolving practice and scholarship, as artists, art historians, critics, curators, and arts administrators. We sought clarifying dialogue about the waves while being careful not to reinforce existing, nor to invent new, feminist stereotypes. The incendiary word, "blaze" connotes both hot and new, in addition to trail blazing. It signifies that the experiences of women and feminists are anything but static, tame, or marginal, while the term "discourse" grounded the text in a degree of formal, critical analysis.

We first established a number of specific objectives for this book. It was imperative that the book should honor the historic, as well as palpably discern the current pulse of the feminist art movement. We hoped our writers would map the loci of anger, yearning, fear, comfort, doubt, and concern that women artists, historians, and critics activate in their work. We were also specifically interested in examining how women defined success and meaning at this juncture in history, as well as how they contemplated changing cultural attitudes about the body, power, authority, and vulnerability. We warmly welcomed narratives that disrupted conventional timelines, and consciously looked for multiple threads of narrative, rather than a single account of any one period. Finally, we particularly hoped the book would shed light on new models of criticism, new methods of integrating theory with practice, and new forms of conceptualization, both of the problems and the solutions.

We provided writers with this vision for the book, and then encouraged *Blaze* writers to articulate their personal concerns, social agendas, and political aspirations. It was important for the breadth of the essays to present a rich array of honest and thoughtful experiences.

Writers for *Blaze* come from all regions of the United States and represent seasoned, as well as emerging, voices. Blaze features celebrated authors, scholars and artists: former and current presidents of national arts organization, editors of leading professional art journals, founders and curators of new museums, galleries and artists' slide registries, and former and current university department chairs and professors. The text also includes new voices from artists, activists, and academics as first-time authors. We felt committed to this combination, which we believe emulates the current mix of second-wave and third-wave feminist artists and scholars shaping contemporary feminist discourse in the arts. Many of these writers feel equally at home in cyberspace, and they regularly work on international projects and collaborations.

The book spotlights 14 detailed and well-documented feminist histories that narrate a number of pertinent strands of activism regarding feminist art, scholarship, organizational development and community initiatives. In developing new historical narratives, it behooves writers and readers alike to ask themselves: Whose history is it? Who is empowered to tell this history? Have there been any omissions? These questions, first asked by feminists in the 1970s, also enrich the readings of contemporary feminist histories, deepening the critical analysis of these histories. These core questions reoccur in Blaze with persistence and relevance.

The context of the Women's Caucus for Art (WCA) conference, and this organization's enormously influential history, is given prominent attention within this book. Eleanor Dickinson's detailed report on the history of the WCA, Patricia Hills's close look at the development of the WCA Boston chapter, and Susan King's rich discussion of the exceptional WCA Honoree Lifetime Achievement Awards all provide readers with multiple viewpoints on a number of important historical moments within the life of this remarkable organization.

A number of new histories, freshly experienced, are also contained in *Blaze.* Jeanne Philipp creates an account of the history of new media and feminism. Joan Marter chronicles feminist art journalism over a 30-year period, noting the rise and fall of various important journals during that time, and some of which continues to thrive. Maria Elena Buszek and Dena Muller define and deliver charged portraits of second-wave and third-wave feminists. Patricia Rodriguez provides a critical review of institutionalized exclusions of Latina and Chicana feminist artists. She places the spotlight on surprising continuing exclusions. Cynthia Fowler comments on the disappearing nude, and the significance of its recent return to prominence. Aviva Rahmani and Anna Shapiro produce examples of timely ecofeminist activisms, contextualized within the broader feminist movement. Harriet Senie imparts a sobering and fresh feminist reading of New York City's public works memorials, and Christina Lanzl presents a partial history of Boston's public works projects, examining the power of collaboration. Finally, Anna Wexler and Janet Gillespie provide the reader with a historically derived, cross-cultural analysis of feminist performance art.

Within this confluence of vibrant histories, particular themes begin to emerge around issues of representation. Teaching and exhibiting, in addition to the rise of new divisions and alliances between the waves, play a key role. Other essays address topics derived from the feminist histories. For example, what does the explosive number of public works projects, launched by feminist artists in recent years, indicate about feminist concerns and interests in the public domain? Ann Rosenthal and Ruth Wallen provide further examples of ecofeminist activism and leadership, which reflects the timely values of global interdependency. Pam Allara, Ellen Driscoll, and Mags Harries discuss public works project development with a particular concern for its relationship to the marketplace, the gallery system, and tenuous regard within higher education. Noreen Dean Dresser and Laurie Elizabeth Talbot Hall use different perspectives to analyze economic implications for art-based professionals, picking up on pertinent issues related to arts' economies; and Ruth von Jahnke Waters shares with us her own insider's story as the first feminist founder of a regional museum of art.

Another subject receiving due attention in these essays is the importance of innovative approaches to scholarship. Jennifer Hall and Ellen Ginsburg join to introduce new models of collaboration and interdisciplinary research, creating a vital dialogue between art and science. Jennifer Colby looks closely at art-based feminist scholarship, while Elinor Gadon addresses the clear need for new forms of mentoring relationships between women. Susan Siskin and Cher Krause Knight discuss new pedagogies, and interactions with students, and Joan Ryan examines the peculiar and persistent effects of popular culture on aesthetic development, questioning the role of kitsch in the feminist realm and general art perceptions.

The issue of "invisibility," which has followed women persistently, comes home to roost in these essays from our third-wave feminists, Maria Elena Buszek and Dena Muller. They independently chose to open their essays with a short vignette: these vignettes ironically place both of the writers in an audience comprised largely of second-wave feminists, asking, "Where are the third-wave feminists?" Buszek retorts that they are right there "next to you," while Muller notes that the third-wave has developed methods of circumventing the old paradigms.

Problematic issues of invisibility can also surface concerning employment opportunities, or lack thereof. This tension creates a new generational divide. With hundreds of new PhD and MFA graduates receiving degrees each year, there are growing numbers of third-wave feminists pounding the pavements, looking for academic and curatorial positions as well as exhibition opportunities. Despite increases in college student enrollments, new positions and new lines for studio arts and art history professorships have been agonizingly slow to materialize in U.S. universities and colleges. In addition, many second-wave feminist academics feel that they are just entering their prime, and that retirement is still years away. A new waiting game is being played out between the waves.

Concurrently, the opposite trend is unfolding within the art market. With the market's emphasis on fresh ideas and youth culture, the power of accumulated experience and knowledge of institutional history have lost their power and relevance. The horizontal thrust of web-based communications, and the dismantling of hierarchy and privilege, further amplify this trend. Museums and commercial galleries tend to show the same circuit of second-wave artists over and over again, while relative "no-name" third-wave feminists and other women artists not identifying as feminists, are being ushered into exhibition halls and hot new alternative spaces in droves, under the trendy catch phrase, "emerging artists." As Patricia Hills remarked at the 2006 WCA conference, many second-wave feminist artists have been "erased" from history.[1] Are we entering a new paradigm of opportunity, whereby second-wave feminists hold the academic positions and third-wave feminists obtain exhibition preferences?

A twist on issues of invisibility can be found in Mira Schor's essay about blogging, in Laurie Beth Clark's essay about truth-telling and what one's perception of truth might be, and also in THINK AGAIN's collaborative project to examine links between the flow of international capital, minority women, and violence. It is timely to observe that by introducing blogging as a legitimate feminist practice, Mira Schor touches provocatively upon a host of related topics that trigger new divisions between women, sometimes correlated with age. These topics include different preferences for selecting communication formats, publication protocols, and patterns of organizational affiliations. In general, spunky third-wave feminists tend to "travel light" and are inclined to invent non-restrictive rules, rather than subscribe to legal codes that curtail movement and impede collaboration. Preferring e-mail to "snail mail" (instant versus time-based), creative commons licenses to copyrights (sharing versus ownership), and listservs to formal memberships in non-profits (platforms versus organizations), these feminists tend to select flexible systems of affiliation, virtual or otherwise. Tallied returns, regarding advantages for each group, are still coming in. Spontaneous, specific, short-term alliances, versus in-depth, face-to-face, ongoing memberships, seem to be a matter of preference, and one not clearly determined simply by chronological age.

On a different track, some of the writers here, including Thea Paneth, Simone Alter-Müri and Denise Malis, CoachTV and C.M. Judge, link a discussion of intimate relationships with new models of collaboration. These intimate relationships are often familial in form, but the definition of family continues to expand. Geography holds little to discourage collaboration in our connected, cross-cultural modern world. L'Merchie Frazier, Catherine McGregor, and Mari Novotny-Jones look at performance and ritual practices, also within a cross-cultural framework. The physical, spiritual, and metaphysical dimensions ripple through this group of essays. The emphasis here is on the inherent creative value of collaboration.

After reviewing the essays, the editors asked once again: "What characterizes this writing as feminist?" Previous historians have credited second-wave feminists of the 1960s and 1970s with establishing the feminist art movement. Inspired by the civil rights movement and the women's liberation movement of the 1960s, women were incensed by gendered issues of power and privilege. The paramount focus of these times was on the persistence of patriarchy, and the complete omission of all women from the history of art. Institutionalized sexism was revealed. These questions rose again: Whose history? Who is included and who is omitted? Who has the power to represent this history?

Third-wave feminists emerged in the 1980s and 1990s. This group differed from second-wave feminists by representing a broader reach of inclusiveness. Third-wave feminists identified with a variety of subgroups, and positioned themselves along a continuum of political engagement. A critical examination of power and exclusionary practices continued.

Where does this leave feminists at this moment in time? Are we at a new crossroads? Although the 2006 WCA conference was focused on local and national discussions of feminism, new alliances between the local and the global seem to be more pronounced a year after the conference, than in 2004, when the conference was first taking shape. This is particularly true of transnational feminism and global social justice initiatives linked in spirit to third-wave feminist activism.

No longer exclusively focused on power struggles between men and women, feminists are now examining the power differentials between, and among, women. These conversations engage myriad groups of women: second wave to third wave; third wave to second wave; second wave to second wave; third wave to other women who do not even identify themselves as feminists. Similar to the situation at the start of the feminist movement, issues of representation and work claim center stage.

As we return to the longstanding issue of representation within the history of the feminist art movement, we seem to be at a new junction. Having accrued substantial power in recent years, second-wave and third-wave feminists demand that any history, written by or about women, must take into account, multiple voices, and multiple points of view. This contemporary feminist history, which represents 35 tumultuous years of passionate fury, sacrifice, and camaraderie between women, is also embodied in the complex history of the WCA.

In writing her report on the history of the WCA, Eleanor Dickinson relentlessly pursued factual data from all sources. Getting it right required extensive collaboration between large numbers of women who were active in the movement for many years. In the final reading, the persistent question "What characterizes this writing as feminist?" evolved into "What makes this book relevant to feminists today?" The artistic fervor of feminists working together across differences, captured so profoundly in the writing of the history of the WCA and manifested in the writing *throughout* this text, makes this book a feminist project. In this world filled with strife, it is this form of engagement—one that is closest to the hearts of many—that inspires continued activism.

---

[1] Patricia Hills, "Reflections: Art and Feminism in Boston, the 80s and Today" (panel presentation at the 2006 National Women's Caucus for Art Conference, Boston, Massachusetts, 2006).

PART I: LEADERSHIP

PERSONAL RECOLLECTIONS OF THE EARLY YEARS OF THE WOMEN'S CAUCUS FOR ART IN BOSTON

PATRICIA HILLS

The Founding of the Boston WCA

The idea of founding a Boston, Massachusetts chapter of the Women's Caucus for Art (BWCA) was first broached to me in 1981, when Patricia Johnston suggested that we start a chapter.[1] I thought that forming a chapter would be a splendid idea. Vermont had a chapter, but no organization in Boston brought together women artists and art historians.[2]

I felt it was about time for me to "get active" as a feminist in Boston, where I had moved to in 1978 to teach my own specialty—American art—at Boston University (BU). In 1972, while still a graduate student living in New York, I had attended the meeting of the College Art Association (CAA) in San Francisco, California, at the time the National WCA was launched with art historian Ann Sutherland Harris as first president. I recall standing in the back of a crowded overheated hotel ballroom and admiring Harris for speaking out on women's issues in academia, with Linda Nochlin, Muriel Magenta, Joyce Kozloff, and others commenting from the panel table. It was an exciting moment—when women artists, critics, and art historians saw the necessity for coming together to work for the common goal of redressing the gender inequities in the art studios, in museums, and in academia.[3]

By then—the early 1970s—I considered myself both a leftist and a feminist. I was not alone. Many of my generation of young, urban mothers working or attending school part-time, involving themselves in their communities, and above all struggling to find an identity other than that of "mother" or "wife" were radicalized by the Civil Rights Movement and the protests against the Vietnam War. Although never active in the New York WCA chapter, I had been in two New York consciousness-raising groups from 1970 to 1972; first with neighbors in my Upper West Side building—almost all mothers with professional husbands—then with artists and other artworkers, some single and some parents, who met in our various Manhattan apartments.[4] While still a graduate student at the Institute of Fine Arts, I had also been active in founding the New Art Association in New York, which grew out of the protests against the shootings of student anti-war demonstrators at Kent State on May 4, 1970. I also became active in the Museum Workers' Association, a loose organization formed in the mid-1970s when the Professional and Staff Association of the Museum of Modern Art went on strike.[5]

In retrospect, it is clear that the Boston University Art Gallery (BUAG), at 855 Commonwealth Avenue, Boston, played an important role in the success of the BWCA in the early years. Soon after I had joined the BU faculty, I was given the departmental task of assessing the possibilities for the BUAG, previously under the control of the studio art department.[6] When the Art History Department took charge of the BUAG, during the 1979–80 academic year, I was assigned to supervise art history graduate students and plan exhibitions.[7]

For the first fall exhibition after the restructuring of the BUAG, I proposed a show of the recent paintings of Alice Neel, whom I had known in New York. The show, Alice Neel: Paintings of Two Decades, opened on October 9, 1980. Neel came and delivered one of her funny, peppery, and egocentric two-hour slide shows. For the spring of 1981, gallery manager Amy Lighthill mounted two other exhibitions of the work of women: Massachusetts Quiltmakers and Pacita Abad. During 1981–82, 1982–83, and 1983–84, the BUAG mounted several juried exhibitions that included Boston-area women artists. The BUAG began to acquire a new kind of reputation—one good for women in the community.[8]

To return to 1981: When Patricia Johnston came to BU in September, she was determined to organize a WCA Boston chapter. She had returned to graduate school for doctoral work after having been on the board of the Southeast WCA and having organized exhibitions of women's art work as a university art gallery director and museum curator and registrar. She was eager to launch a membership drive.

On October 4, 1981, within a month after her arrival, Johnston wrote to the San Francisco office of the national WCA asking for names of national WCA members then living in the Boston area and information on forming a chapter.[9] In February 1982, both Johnston and I attended the WCA Conference in New York and met with Muriel Magenta, the national WCA president, who taught studio courses at Arizona State University. Magenta followed up by writing to both of us in early May, urging us to move ahead:

We feel that it is extremely important the WCA be represented in your locale. The large number of women art professionals in the metropolitan Boston area will contribute significantly to the national status of our organization, which represents women in the visual arts throughout the United States.
We know from the networking experience of chapter members in the existing 23 affiliates, participation on the local level directly benefits the professional careers of each individual involved."[10]

Magenta and Beatrice Weinstein, the Business Administrator of the WCA, also sent us copies of the WCA By-Laws, a dues schedule, and guidelines for establishing a chapter.[11]

Meetings Get Started

In early June, Johnston placed an ad in several local newspapers, including the *Boston Globe*, *Equal Times*, and the *Boston Phoenix* to announce the June 22, 1982, organizing meeting.[12] The people at the first meeting included Anne Noble and artist Florrie Povirk, along with those of us from BU: Johnston, Melissa Dabakis (another doctoral student who had taught extensively in area colleges), and me.[13] Undeterred by the small attendance, we pushed ahead and planned a second meeting for that summer.

We were delighted when artist Susan Schwalb telephoned. I had heard from New York friends that we should be in touch with her. Schwalb had recently moved to Boston from New York, where throughout the 1970's she had been active in a number of women artists' organizations, including Women Artists News, Coalition of Women's Art Organizations (CWAO), and the New York WCA chapter. She had also been involved as Project Director for the U.S. Committee for the First International Festival of Women Artists, held in Copenhagen in July 1980. [14] She volunteered to help us organize in Boston.

Schwalb recalls the planning meeting that met in Johnston's apartment on September 19, that included not only Johnston, Schwalb, and me, but also art historians Alicia Faxon, who taught at Simmons College, and Liana Cheney, who taught at the University of Massachusetts Lowell, both of whom had doctoral degrees in art history from BU. The two others were artist Adria Arch and Diane Radycki, a published scholar and also a doctoral student at Harvard.[15] We all felt that in order for a Boston WCA chapter to grow we needed to conduct the business of the chapter as professionally as we could and to offer to members a variety of programming along with the regular monthly business meetings.

Magenta wrote from the national office asking how we were doing, so Johnston reported on October 2, 1982:

> Finally I can send you good news from Boston! After two meetings with disappointing attendance this summer, we have finally gathered an enthusiastic and growing crowd into an organized WCA chapter. . . . [W]e decided to go ahead and schedule monthly programs and to try to double our number (from 10 to 20) in the next month by each inviting another person. I felt there was a great deal of energy and enthusiasm in the room which will hold the chapter together.[16]

Events were planned for the whole year.

We now had an organization. It made sense to have co-chairs—one an artist and the other an art historian, so Schwalb and I filled those roles. Povirk became Treasurer and served as Membership coordinator, and Dabakis was elected Secretary. Cheney became Program Coordinator.[17] I recall that Faxon took on the job of getting together the necessary papers for our certification as a non-profit organization in the Commonwealth of Massachusetts. The chapter had a letterhead of sorts, and Dabakis mailed announcements of meetings to Boston area national members and to those who had attended previous meetings.

The October 18, 1982, meeting was held at the home of Schwalb's husband (composer Martin Boyken) in Newton Centre, Massachusetts, where Schwalb had showed her recent silverpoint and metalpoint drawings and mixed media works. I believe it was at the November meeting that Shirley Levy of the Boston Visual Artists Union and Patricia King, director of the Schlesinger Library of Radcliffe College, spoke to us about the past contributions of their organizations to women's careers and history, although Schwalb recalls their speaking at the October meeting.[18] It was always our plan that meetings should include not just organizing business but a talk on art or art matters by one of us or by a guest speaker.

In early November, Magenta sent a letter to Schwalb, Johnston, and me: "On behalf of the entire Women's Caucus for Art Organization, I welcome the Boston Chapter of the WCA. You are making a significant contribution to the feminist art movement by establishing a chapter in this important metropolitan center." She enclosed a check for $100 for "seed" money to get the chapter started. She then invited us to send a news article about the chapter to be published in *Huepoints: Women's Caucus for Art Newsmagazine*, along with a picture. [19]

The December meeting was held at the Cambridge, Massachusetts, home of Faxon, with a talk by Diane Radycki on the German artist Paula Modersohn-Becker.[20] In January, Elinor Gadon, a cultural historian affiliated with Harvard Divinity School, hosted the meeting at her Cambridge home, and spoke about the cultural context of women's images and symbols. Patricia Johnston talked about feminist art theory.[21] Artist Adria Arch hosted the February meeting at her Watertown, Massachusetts, home, where she showed WCA members her recent figurative works in acrylic.[22]

Not only were activities percolating in Boston, but we also felt ourselves as part of the national movement. In February, the WCA National Advisory Board met in Philadelphia, at the time that the CAA had its annual conference. Schwalb felt it important that we, as a new chapter, have a presence there.[23] I was unable to go, but Johnston and Schwalb attended, and reported back on the finances of the WCA, its fundraising efforts and membership rolls. Although Muriel Magenta was upbeat about the national WCA, during the academic year 1982-1983 the organization was in financial straits. She knew that new members in Boston meant new sources of revenue. Sometime during that period, Magenta and Bea Weinstein sent out notices to all Caucus members pleading for contributions and proposing a new dues structure. In bold letters they declared: "WE NEED SUBSTANTIAL CONTRIBUTIONS IMMEDIATELY; \$25.00, \$100.00, MORE—OR WHATEVER YOU CAN AFFORD—TO EXTRICATE THE WCA FROM THE PRESENT FINANCIAL *EMERGENCY*."[24]

In Boston, we were committed to helping the national cause while also building our own membership. We understood the importance of a national organization involved in advocacy and public education in all areas of the country. However, we resented the fact that the national office began to return checks from new members that did not meet their recent, hastily instituted dues structure. In April 1983, Povirk wrote an indignant letter to Weinstein: "As a fledging chapter, I feel your initial request is unacceptable. We are trying to generate support and recruit more members; we cannot afford to either alienate or penalize new members for inadequate information. Therefore, I feel that you have either the choice of accepting my initial payment or losing new members. We still intend to warmly accept these women as new local chapter members." Povirk ended with the firm but appeasing note: "The annual dues increase can be dealt with more effectively and efficiently next year."[25] The national office backed down.

Our big outreach event to attract new members that first year was the panel discussion, "Women Art Professionals: The Boston Scene," held at the BUAG on March 24, 1983. I persuaded a variety of women to participate: artist Marcia Lloyd; the former Director of the Fogg Art

Museum, Agnes Mongan; gallery owner Helen Shlien; the Curator of the Institute of Contemporary Art, Elizabeth Sussman; sculptor Marianna Pineda; and *Boston Globe* art critic Christine Temin. As the moderator of the panel, I asked each to discuss briefly their careers and address the current situation for women in the arts.[26] Over one hundred women and men attended the discussion in the spacious BUAG. The event succeeded in attracting both good publicity for the Boston WCA and new members. One of the new arrivals to join us was performance artist Faith Wilding, who had worked with Judy Chicago at the Feminist Art Program at California Institute for the Arts (CalArts) in 1971.[27] I personally felt that Wilding, a person who knew how to be outrageous if need be, added a savvy activist sophistication to the group of Boston area artists unfamiliar with a feminist/activist mind-set.

We continued to have our usual monthly meetings, with anywhere from 14 to 20 people attending. In April, we met at Simmons College, where Faxon taught. She spoke on Russian women artists in the early twentieth century.[28] The May meeting was held in a classroom at BU, where Johnston gave a talk on fashion and feminism.[29] For our final meeting on June 6, before the summer dispersal of artists and their families, we had a potluck supper at my home in Brookline, Massachusetts, where we congratulated ourselves for a good inaugural year. A nominating committee, consisting of Arch, Dabakis, Johnston, and Mary Goodwin (another BU student, then finishing her dissertation), proposed a slate of officers for election. There was never any contention or competition for the positions. We collectively felt grateful to anyone wanting to be involved. Hence, for the second year, 1983–84, Adria Arch and I were elected co-coordinators; Carole Borggren (a graduate from BU's art history MA program), recording secretary; Florrie Povrik, treasurer and membership coordinator. The program coordinators were Patricia Johnston, Susan Schwalb, Liana Cheney, and Diane Radycki. Jackie Becker, an MA student at BU, was the publicity coordinator. At that time, we could report to members that we had $300 in the bank and were exploring sources for grants.[30]

In the spring of 1983, we had already begun to plan events for the 1983–84 academic year. We tried to think creatively. Some of our ideas were for panels on women photographers, images of pregnancy, women and landscape, issues in feminist art and theory, women in the arts and crafts movement, art and politics, and women's performance art. We also wanted to have another outreach evening featuring art professionals, a festive December holiday party, and slide nights for artist-members. During the academic year 1983–1984, Johnston was the manager of the

BUAG, and I, the director. It made sense to have the majority of the meetings at the Gallery, with its large space, all the folding chairs we needed, plus screens and projectors for showing slides. Johnston and I had access to photocopying machines, telephones, and a long table for folding flyers. Moreover, many of the BWCA exhibitions provided a good backdrop for the ambitious panel discussions and talks we were planning for the WCA.

The Second Year

I kicked off the 1983–84 year with a lecture at the Gallery on September 28 on Alice Neel—a preview of my Neel book slated for publication that October. The second meeting, held on October 24, also at the BUAG, featured Radycki and Maureen Giovanni, of the Anthropology Department of BU, speaking on "Images and Reality of Pregnancy."[31] On November 22, the WCA had a panel discussion at the BUAG focused on Elements of Landscape, a juried exhibition then on view at the BUAG. The speakers included three women included in the exhibition: Constance Jacobson, Marion Miller, and Sarah Supplee.[32] In December, artist Prilla Brackett had the meeting and holiday party at her home in North Cambridge. On January 23, 1984, we held at "Artists Members' Night," advertised in *The Boston Phoenix,* with artists Sarah Sutro, Leslie Sills, Maria Müller, and Emma Luna Larsen showing slides of their work.[33]

The BUAG held two exhibitions that I curated in the spring of 1984 that were of interest to WCA members: Social Concern in the '80s: A New England Perspective, held during February, and May Stevens: Ordinary. Extraordinary. A Summation, 1977–1984, held in March. The BWCA newsletter announced all of the BUAG programming in connection with the two shows.[34] Social Concern had works by WCA members Suzanne Hodes and Sarah Sutro, and on February 16, the BUAG invited the nationally known critic Lucy Lippard to speak on political art in connection with the exhibition. Wearing my hat as co-chair of the WCA, I used the occasion to host a WCA potluck supper so members could meet Lippard before her talk, which filled the Concert Hall at BU. And on March 15, the BUAG presented an evening with May Stevens and critic Donald Kuspit in dialogue, which WCA members attended in numbers.

On April 18, Eleanor Munro, author of *Originals: American Women Artists* gave a lecture at the BUAG, co-sponsored by the BWCA and the Boston Visual Artists Union (BVAU). That was one of several occasions that the BVAU came in as a co-sponsor of WCA events. On April 30, artist Jo Ann Rothschild presented her research on the status of women art teachers at Boston area colleges and universities. She found that at the School of the Museum of Fine Arts, only 18 percent of the studio faculty were tenured women; at Massachusetts College of Art, only 14 percent, and at BU there were no tenured women in the studio program.[35] In June, we ended our year with the Annual Potluck Supper at my home in Brookline. It had been, we felt, a second successful year.

During the academic year 1984-1985, Leslie Sills and Liana Cheney became the co-chairs of the Boston Chapter. Artists Prilla Brackett and Sarah Sutro were in charge of programming. Although that year I was on sabbatical leave from BU, I still actively participated in the WCA, as did Johnston, then the Acting Director of the Art Gallery while still writing her dissertation.

Sills, an enthusiastic co-chair, wrote a letter to "Boston Women" published in *Sojourner: The Women's Forum* in October 1984. She spoke about her own experiences a few years before, when she had joined the national chapter and had gone to a WCA conference in Washington DC, only to discover she alone was from Massachusetts:

> Discouraged, I returned to Boston feeling totally isolated. . . . Stuck in my inertia, I did nothing until last year, when I heard about a panel discussion at Boston University Art Gallery on "women art professionals." It was a forum of critics, historians, gallery dealers, and artists talking about their roles and the effect being a woman has had on what they do. It was very provocative, very well-attended, and, to my surprise, sponsored by a newly formed chapter of the Boston WCA. . . . I decided to go to one meeting and see how I felt. . . . What I found as I gradually got to know these women is that I was more isolated than I realized. There was an enormous source of energy and support I had missed because I was looking to women only in my exact profession. Suddenly I saw a network and the possibilities connecting could produce.[36]

She liked the unique quality about the BWCA chapter—the range of artists and art historians. Sills continued in her letter by urging artists to join the WCA.

The fall 1984 program got off to a good start. Because WCA member Marsha Hewitt was having an exhibition, Rituals and Mysteries, at the Simmons College Trustman Art Gallery, we held our first meeting there, on September 17, with Cheney and Faxon speaking on aspects of Surrealism. The October 16 meeting was back at the BUAG and featured a major panel discussion, "Critics' Criteria" moderated by *Boston Herald* art critic Nancy Stapen. The other panelists were *Boston Globe* senior art critic Robert Taylor, *Boston Phoenix* critic Ken Baker, art historian Pam Allara, and artist Nan Freeman. The year passed with the usual array of panels, talks, and artists' nights. We were now firmly established and could count on meetings with about 25 to 30 women.

For 1985–86, Cheney and Hewitt stepped in as co-chairs of the BWCA, with Sills moving on to manage publicity. The highlights of that season of BWCA meetings were Edmund Barry Gaither's talk on the art of Lois Mailou Jones on February 19 at the Museum of the National Center of Afro-American Artists in Roxbury, and Joyce Kozloff's talk at the BUAG on March 12, 1986, in connection with the BUAG exhibition Joyce Kozloff: Visionary Ornament, curated by Patricia Johnston.[37] Later that spring sculptors Penelope Jencks, Marianna Pineda and Isabel MacIlvain spoke at the Gallery about their sculpture in the BUAG exhibition, The Human Presence in Sculpture, curated by BWCA member Arlette Klaric, then Associate Director of the BUAG.

The Boston WCA Hosts the National Conference

But the big challenge in 1985–86 was our ambitious planning for the WCA national conference scheduled to take place in Boston during February 1987. I'm not certain if I had any specific responsibility, other than to troubleshoot, make connections with the national officers, and introduce Agnes Mongan, one of the WCA Lifetime Achievement Award honorees, at the Honorees Ceremony. In September Annie Shaver-Crandell, the newly elected WCA national president, came to Boston to give us a pep talk about what needed to be done, and in what order, to ensure a successful conference. Shaver-Crandell asked Cheney to be in charge of the Boston Conference; Faxon helped Cheney put together the art history and studio sessions. Schwalb and Sills volunteered to be in charge of conference exhibitions.[38] By telephone, Ofelia Garcia, the outgoing WCA national president, later made explicit to me that they wanted three kinds of exhibitions. The first would be a national juried show inviting all WCA members across the country to submit slides of their work; but it should not be a show displaying all media. Instead, Garcia urged, there needed to be a theme or a topic, with the work preferably mounted in an academic setting, and with documentation (such as a catalogue).[39] The second would be a regional show or shows—in this case, an exhibition of New England women. And third, the national WCA needed to have an appropriate venue for the display of the art and books of the 1987 WCA honorees. The national WCA would pay the exhibition costs for the honorees' show, but we had to fundraise to pay for the other exhibitions.

All of us pitched in and worked hard on organizing tasks, even when strains began to show. Some members were persistently contrary and unwilling to come to a consensus. We had meetings and more late-night meetings to iron out our differences and suggest creative solutions—at Liana Cheney's, at X Bonnie Woods's, and at other places I can barely recall. But our plans all fell into place.

Three art schools—The Art Institute of Boston, the Massachusetts College of Art, and the two galleries at Northeastern University—were persuaded to mount the regional show New England Women Artists, which was coordinated by Boston WCA member Prilla Brackett, who spelled out the process in the "Exhibit Guide and Checklist." Three regional curators—Joy Gordon, Director of the Danforth Museum, and free-lance curators Amy Lighthill and Constance Brown—narrowed the selection down from 727 artists (each sent in five slides) to 110 artists. Then Lowery Stokes Sims, Associate Curator at the Metropolitan Museum of Art, who had been lined up a year in advance by Susan Schwalb, made the final selection of 53 artists.[40] In addition the gallery directors of the three institutions, Cathy Smith, Jeff Keogh, and Mira Cantor, "grouped the work into balanced shows for the three locations."[41]

BUAG Associate Director Arlette Klaric organized Contemporary Quilts, the national exhibition (that had to have a theme or a selected single media), and she asked Annie Shaver-Crandell, Nancy Halpern, and Faith Ringgold to serve with her on the jury panel. That exhibition was subsequently picked up by the Smithsonian Institution for their traveling exhibition program and circulated overseas, including a venue in Athens.

Cheney secured the auditorium and meeting rooms of the Boston Public Library (BPL) for the conference of 24 panels and performances held between February 10 and February 12 in the auditorium and meeting rooms of the BPL. The Massachusetts Council on Arts and Humanities provided $10,000 for the conference, which included feminist writer Marina Warner from England as the keynote speaker.[42] At the conference, Faxon proudly displayed the anthology *Pilgrims & Pioneers: New England Women in the Arts* that she had co-edited with Sylvia Moore and which had been recently published by Cynthia Navaretta's Midmarch Arts Press.[43]

I recall the panel organized by May Stevens, "The Politics of Identity, of Entering, Changing, and Being Changed." I will never forget hearing and seeing on stage at the BPL the Irish performance artist Alana O'Kelly keening as old Irish women do upon hearing the death of a villager or loved one. The memory of those mournful sounds still sends chills through me.

The WCA Honorees for 1987 included Boston women Agnes Mongan, whom I introduced, and Maud Morgan.[44] The coordinators Amy Lighthill and Leslie Sills negotiated with the Federal Reserve Bank Gallery in Boston to be the site for the awards ceremony and the display of the honorees' work. At the banquet, Thalia Gouma-Peterson and I were "Honored at Mid-Career" at a WCA ceremony. I felt that all of us were being honored, and I said so in my remarks.

But there was more that happened from BWCA efforts. We outdid probably any other WCA conference. Susan Schwalb persuaded 62 other university and college art galleries and commercial art galleries, from Boston to outlying Massachusetts towns and cities including Framingham and Northampton, and even Providence, Rhode Island, to show women artists during the month of February. She was helped by Ellen Banks, who taught at the School of the Museum of Fine Arts, and who put Schwalb in touch with African American organizations. Boston WCA committee members followed up on all the details including persuading fourteen of the galleries to hold receptions during the second week of February.[45] Although we were all collectively proud of the success we had achieved and saw our chapter's membership soar from 100 in 1986 to 229 by the end of 1987, we were exhausted.[46] The Boston Chapter of the WCA took a long time to recover. But I understand that such ambitious overreaching has also been the undoing of other chapters.

My Post-Conference Years

My last major effort for the BWCA came in the late spring of 1988. The Artists in Residence, Inc. (A.I.R.) Gallery, a women's cooperative gallery in New York, invited the Boston Chapter to exhibit there during the month of June. A jury consisting of Alicia Faxon, *Art New England* editor Carla Munsat, and me selected 30 works by 12 artists: Adria Arch, Ellen Banks, Prilla Brackett, Radka Donnell, Sally S. Fine, Marci Gintis, Joyce McDaniel, Francine Perlman, Marianna Pineda, Annee Spilleos Scott, Susan Schwalb, and X Bonnie Woods. (Munsat, as editor of *Art New England*, made certaisn that exhibitions by women were covered in her monthly publication.) I went down and installed the show, called Boston Women Artists: WCA Invitational, a day or so before the opening on Tuesday, June 7.[47] The show looked great in New York, and the Boston chapter now had national visibility for its artists.

In 1989, I left my job as Director of the BUAG, although I still continued, as before, to teach full-time in the Art History Department at BU. This meant that I could no longer use the BUAG to host WCA meetings in the evenings, nor was I in the business of scheduling exhibitions that would have had a relevant WCA slant. An exception was the Marianna Pineda exhibition that I curated and brought to the BUAG in 1998. Pineda, an excellent figurative sculptor who sometimes taught at BU, had been a regular participant at BWCA meetings in Boston.[48] Many of the BWCA meetings began to be held at the Bunting Institute, at 34 Concord Avenue in Cambridge.

Patricia Johnston stayed involved with the BWCA chapter for a few more years. She served as a co-chair with Carlota Duarte during 1988–89. They expanded the BWCA Newsletter, the flyers became better designed, and, in October 1988, Johnston organized an exhibition, Boston Women's Caucus for Art Members' Exhibition that was held at the Winfisky Gallery on the Salem State College campus.[49] In connection with this Johnston organized a star-studded two-day symposium, "Talking about Women's Art: History, Criticism, and Education," also held at Salem State College and funded in part by the Massachusetts Council on the Arts and Humanities. Speakers included BWCA members Johnston, Alicia Faxon, and Emma Luna, along with Christine Havice, Vivian E. Browne, Sandra L. Langer, Patricia Matthews, May Stevens, Patricia Gozemba, Harmony Hammond, and Ingrida Mangulis [Raudzens].

These are the bare bones of the first six years of the Boston Chapter of the WCA. Of course the organization continues today with new people, new ideas, and new energy.

An Assessment of the 1980s Moment

What kept us going, back in the years of 1982 to 1988? Why did we spend so much time, energy, and frantic organizing to come up with highly successful programs? It was a moment when feminists felt optimistic about changing the world. It was also a time when many art historians hoped to connect with practicing artists and to find a common ground. I made many friends among the artists, and although we have drifted apart, I warmly greet them when chance encounters occur. Johnston and I were always involved with programming for the BWCA during those years, whatever our position on the steering committee might be, and it was great fun also to organize exhibitions for the BUAG that would appeal to women and smart men. Those exhibitions provided occasions to bring in outside speakers: Alice Neel, Lucy Lippard, Donald

Kuspit, May Stevens, Lowery Stokes Sims, Cecilia Vicuña, Elizabeth Hess, Deborah Bright, and others.

At that time I also mounted political art exhibitions at the BUAG, with the hope of radicalizing some of the Boston area women artists, many of whom lived nonpolitical lives—even while experiencing inequities because of their gender. I don't think I ever succeeded in radicalizing artists who were not already radicalized, but I did contribute to the effort of getting them connected to something larger—to the collective knowledge and belief that what women did, mattered. And, in turn, the artists helped me to feel connected—to art, to the New York art world, to people in the world working for change. In a way, as Patricia Johnston reminded me recently, it was not about personalities but about a moment. But more than that, it was a moment when a movement flourished.

---

[1] During the dog days of August 2006, Patricia Johnston and I spent a couple of days trying to sort out the BWCA files from the years 1982 to 1988 stashed in her attic. These held press releases, drafts of agendas, lists of meeting attendees, BWCA newsletters, newspaper clippings, and other scraps of notes. Those files and the collective memories of early members testify to the dozens of women who were involved and are the sources for this history/memoir. Besides Pat, I also want to thank Liana Cheney, Alicia Faxon, Leslie Sills, and Susan Schwalb for reading an early draft of this essay and offering corrections, and Alicia and Susan for giving me the notes of their presentations at the WCA February 2006 conference in our session, "Reflections: Art and Feminism in Boston, the 80s and Today." The other panelists were early Boston WCA members Marsha Hewitt and Mela Lyman. I also want to thank Kevin Whitfield for his reading of various drafts of this manuscript.

[2] In 1982, many of the established women artists belonged to the Boston Visual Artists' Union, founded in 1972, which was dominated by men and had no art historians.

[3] For a history of the early years of the WCA and the context in which it grew and flourished, See Mary D. Garrard, "Feminist Politics: Networks and Organizations," in, *The Power of Feminist Art: The American Movement of the 1970s, History and Impact*, ed. Norma Broude and Mary D. Garrard, 88–101 (New York: Abrams, 1994).

[4] My first consciousness-raising group in New York was organized by a woman who had been active in the Berkeley Free Speech movement of the late 1960s. I left after a year to join a second group, a spin-off from a consciousness-raising group that Marcia Tucker belonged to. Her group had invited women to come to their session; so many attended that the new people were encouraged to form their own group, which we did. Our members included Barbara Zucker, Toba Tucker, Susan Williams, Margorie Kramer, and Hermine Fried. With the encouragement of the consciousness-raising group, Zucker and Williams founded A.I.R. Gallery, the

first women artists' collective in Manhattan. I recall that my name was on the A.I.R. Gallery masthead as advisor in the early years.

[5] At the Whitney, Helen Ferrulli, another staff member, and I launched a petition drive among the Whitney employees to protest the introduction of admission fees, which we felt discriminated against underemployed artists and students, and we met with staff members from other museums. From these beginnings, a Whitney staff union was eventually formed; but by then I had resigned from my full-time job in order to teach at York College (CUNY), although I remained a part-time Adjunct Curator through 1987. Hans Haacke videotaped one of the meetings of the Museum Workers' Association, held at a public school in downtown Manhattan.

[6] John Arthur, then the director, was in the process of being ousted by the upper administration, and the Art Gallery had been closed for several months.

[7] By September 1980, the terrific group of graduate students who worked in the BUAG included Amy Lighthill as gallery manager, with Robert Workman and Donna Cassidy as graduate assistants. With a full teaching load I had to draw on my old New York connections to organize some of the first shows.

[8] The BU studio artists (all male except for one woman who ran the Art Education program) generally ignored the shows my student staff and I organized. Whereas artist Jim Weeks invited Alice Neel to speak to his students, David Aronson advised people not to bother to see the Neel show. (Conversation with Mrs. David Aronson, mid-1980s.) Involvement with college art gallery exhibitions of contemporary artists count for nothing when art historians come up for tenure.

[9] The letter reads: "I have recently moved from the Southeast to Boston and was quite surprised to find that no WCA chapter was listed for the city. I have talked to several women here at Boston University (as well as Dr. Patricia Hills who is on the national advisory board) and there seems to be some interest in forming a local chapter. Could you please send me the names, addresses and phone numbers of women—in the Boston area who are WCA members? I plan to contact them & ask if they are interested in a local chapter. Also please send additional information on hand to start a chapter. Thank you." Carbon handwritten copy, October 4, 1981, Boston WCA Archives, Patricia Hills and Patricia Johnston files, hereafter called BWCAA. I was at that time on the national advisory board but was never able to attend meetings because of child care responsibilities.

[10] Identical letters dated May 3, 1982, were sent to both of us; BWCAA.

[11] Copies are in BWCAA. Johnston had also been handed a flyer addressed to Carl Chiarenza, Chair of BU's Art History Department, announcing an internship program sponsored by Women Art Professionals, Inc., of Somerville, Massachusetts. Interns would contribute to a project called "Women of Vision," an ambitious "multi-media presentation of the history of women's art in the greater Boston area." When Johnston reached the contact person, Gayle Vernon, she discovered that the group was no longer in existence. (Announcement and mission statement of Women Art Professionals, Inc., BWCAA.)

[12] Clipping reads: "Women's Caucus for Art meets to organize a Boston Chapter at 7 p.m. at George Sherman Union, room 320, Boston University. Free; call 491-6593." (BWCAA) There was also a flyer, "You Are Invited to an Organization

Meeting to Form a Boston Chapter of the Women's Caucus for Art," which listed eight solid accomplishments of the WCA, e.g., "WCA originated the study that proved the existence of discrimination in the hiring practices of college level art history and studio art departments;" see BWCAA.

13 Patricia Hills's meeting notes; BWCAA. I don't believe Anne Noble attended another meeting.

14 See flyer announcing "Next Meeting, October 18, 1982," BWCAA.

15 Susan Schwalb, "History on the Chapter and My Background," rough notes delivered at the session "Reflections: Art and Feminism in Boston, the 80s and Today," of the WCA Conference in February 2006. I thank Susan for e-mailing me these notes.

16 Carbon copy of handwritten letter from Patricia Johnston to Muriel Magenta, October 2, 1982, BWCAA. The remainder of the letter reviews the dues structure, i.e., how much goes to the national and how much to the chapter and to whom checks should be made. At the time a WCA member would contribute $10 to the national and $6 to the local chapter.

17 See copy of "Articles of Organization," The Commonwealth of Massachusetts, dated December 20, 1982, BWCAA.

18 The "1983 Newsletter," June 13, 1983, authored by "MD" [Melissa Dabakis] . BWCAA, reviews the names and topics of the speakers for the 1982–83 season, but not the specific dates.

19 Muriel Magenta to Susan Schwalb, Patricia Johnston, and Patricia Hills, November 8, 1982, BWCAA.

20 See flyer announcing "Next Meeting, December 13, 1982," BWCAA.

21 See flyer announcing "Next Meeting, January 31, 1983," BWCAA.

22 See flyer announcing "Next Meeting, February 28, 1983," BWCAA.

23 Letter from Susan Schwalb to Pat Johnston, January 13, [1983], BWCAA.

24 Muriel Magenta and Beatrice Weinstein letter to "Caucus Member," n.d., BWCAA.

25 Copy of letter from Florrie J. Povirk to Beatrice Weinstein, April 20, 1983, BWCAA.

26 See Patricia Hills, draft of Press Release, BWCAA.

27 See Faith Wilding, "The Feminist Art Programs at Fresno and CalArts, 1970–75," in *The Power of Feminist Art*, ed. Broude and Garrard.32-47.

28 See flyer announcing "Next Meeting, April 25, 1983," BWCAA.

29 See flyer announcing "Next Meeting, May 16, 1983," BWCAA.

30 Patricia Hills's notes of meeting, BWCAA. Soon we began speaking of "co-chairs" rather than "co-coordinators."

31 See flyer announcing "Images and Reality of Pregnancy, October 24, 1983," BWCAA. Beginning with September 1983 all flyers announcing meetings included a WCA Membership Form as a tear sheet at the bottom of the page.

32 See "WCA News Release," [November 1983] issued by Jacqueline Becker, BWCAA.

---

[33] See *The Boston Phoenix*, (January 25 1984), 26; BWCAA. Our goal was to advertise our meetings in the press, but that did not always happen. However, our mailing list was efficient.

[34] The Boston Chapter Newsletter also announced exhibitions, for example, the work of Prilla Brackett and Marianna Pineda in local venues, and announced a call for potential exhibitors for an exhibition that Amy Lighthill, the assistant curator of Contemporary Art at the Museum of Fine Arts, Boston, was planning for the summer.

[35] My notes of the April 30, 1984 meeting, BWCAA.

[36] Leslie Sills, "Boston Women," Sojourner Truth: The Woman's Forum (October 1984) clipping in the BWCAA.

[37] BWCA Newsletters, October 1985 and February 1986, BWCAA.

[38] E-mail from Liana Cheney to Patricia Hills, January 28, 2007.

[39] Patricia Hills, Notes of Telephone Conversation with Ofelia Garcia, October 9, 1985, BWCAA.

[40] Letter from Susan Schwalb to Lowery [Stokes] Sims, February 25, 1986; BWCAA. Some of the statistics come from Alicia Faxon, "The First WCA Conference in Boston in 1987 and Its Offspring," presented in the session, "Reflections: Art and Feminism in Boston, the 80s and Today," held in February 2006 at the WCA Conference.

[41] "New England Women Artists: 1987, Exhibit Guide and Checklist;" BWCAA.

[42] E-mail from Liana Cheney to Patricia Hills, January 28, 2007. Also see Faxon, "The First WCA Conference in Boston," 2.

[43] See Faxon, "The First WCA Conference in Boston," 2. Cynthia Navaretta had published books organized from the papers of previous WCA conferences. The authors included not only Faxon, but also local WCA members Sarah Sutro, Penny Redfield, Erica Hirshler, Diana Korzenick, Doris Cole, Helen Shlien, Pattie Chase, Bonnie Grad, Leslie Sills, Johanna [Branson] Gill, and X. Bonnie Woods.

[44] I wrote and read the tribute to Miss Mongan at the awards ceremony. The other awardees were painters Grace Hartigan and Honoré Sharrer, quiltmaker Elizabeth Talford Scott, and ceramist Beatrice Wood.

[45] The listings of all the exhibitions, venues, exhibition committee members, and curators, are spelled out in the poster used to advertise the WCA 1987 conference; see BWCAA. See also Faxon, "The First WCA Conference in Boston," who lists 75 galleries and acknowledges Schwalb's and Banks's work on this.

[46] Statistics courtesy Prilla Bracket; see Faxon, "The First WCA Conference in Boston," 1. In 1987–88 we broke with tradition and had two artists as co-chairs: Prilla Brackett and Mela Lyman. Many of the art historians had dropped away, but Patricia Johnston stayed on as membership chair, and Amy Lighthill and I served as co-chairs of the program committee; see "Officers—Boston WCA through June 1988"; BWCAA. For 1988–89, the co-chairs were Patricia Johnston and Carlotta Duarte, but by the summer of 1989, no one had stepped forward to be a co-chair or a treasurer. However, Karen Frostig was on the Program Committee; she provides a link with the current Boston WCA.

[47] Because A.I.R. was a non-profit gallery, each of our twelve Boston WCA members were asked to pay about $250 to $300 to help defray the costs of shipping, advertisement in the Gallery Guide, and postage costs for an A.I.R. mailing.

[48] Unfortunately she died before she could see her exhibition.

[49] Jurors for the show were Johnston, art historian Bonnie Grad, and critic Nancy Stapen; artists included Deborah Bright, Ikuko K. Burns, Deborah Friedman, Mela Lyman, A. E. Ryan, Leslie Sills, Sarah Sutro, Dawn Southworth, Catherine Tutter, and Olivia Bernard Wilson. Announcement and program in the BWCAA.

Works Cited

Faxon, Alicia. "The First WCA Conference in Boston in 1987 and Its Offspring," unpublished text delivered at the session, "Reflections: Art and Feminism in Boston, the 80s and Today," the WCA Conference, Boston, MA, February 18, 2006.

Faxon, Alicia and Sylvia Moore, eds. *Pilgrims and Pioneers: New England Women in the Arts*. New York: Midmarch Arts Press, 1987.

Garrard, Mary D. "Feminist Politics: Networks and Organizations." In *The Power of Feminist Art: The American Movement of the 1970s, History and Impact.* Edited by Norma Broude and Mary Garrard. New York: Harry N. Abrams, Inc., 1994.

Schwalb, Susan. "History on the Chapter and My Background," unpublished notes delivered at the session "Reflections: Art and Feminism in Boston, the 80s and Today," at the WCA Conference, Boston, MA, February, 2006.

Boston Chapter, Women's Caucus for Art Archives, Patricia Hills and Patricia Johnston files, Miriam Schapiro Archives for Women Artists, Rutgers University.

HONORING FEMINIST PATHS: THE LIFETIME ACHIEVEMENT AWARDS

SUSAN KING

Shaping the Ideal

For over 25 years, the Lifetime Achievement Awards for Women in the Arts have been the single most important annual event sponsored by the Women's Caucus for Art (WCA). Conceived in the late 1970's, at a time when women's outstanding achievements went largely unnoticed by the public, the awards were meant to fill a void. The organization's first president Ann Sutherland Harris, who also chaired the first selection committee, clearly stated their mission to the broader membership—they wanted "to publicly recognize exceptional women artists while they were still living."[1] There was no formal age restriction for the award; however, all of the first year's honorees were over seventy-five years of age. Their names—for example Georgia O'Keeffe and Louise Nevelson—now spill off the lips of just about any well-educated college freshman. Yet at the time, they were virtually unknown to many audiences. While women in the visual arts have gained numerous sources of public recognition over the years, the awards' parallel function—as an embodiment of the collective spirit of the WCA—continues to this day.

Since the awards' prestigious beginning at the Carter White House in 1979, every year (but two) a select group of eminent artists and scholars from within the WCA has chosen an equally select group of honorees.[2] In metaphorical terms, these new honorees join with those of the past to collectively form the ideal WCA membership. Usually each woman comes to the award with a national reputation for excellence in her field (at least among her women peers, if not her male counterparts or the larger public), and each honoree has built a career on feminist principles to the profound benefit of the broader community. The honorees' 150+ names line the backs of WCA membership forms and fill the WCA Web site as promotional propaganda. This is the case even though most of these women had lost touch with the organization or were unfamiliar with it, at least until they were swept up into the maelstrom of the awards ceremony, and WCA newsletters began arriving on their doorstep—a benefit of the free lifetime membership granted with each award. But this personal disconnection with the WCA holds little importance. Their legacies embody the collective aspirations of all WCA members, and their risk-taking and candor in the face of opposition and opprobrium inspire younger women. This is the case even though being a feminist in 2007 means something radically different from what it meant to women in the activist 1970s, or during the conservative backlash of the 1980s, or even for women making their way in the global 1990s.

Barometer of Political Trends

Over time, the ceremonies have served as both barometer and bellwether of political trends in the WCA. The venues chosen for the awards, the individuals and events associated with the ceremony, and the press surrounding it change each year, yet they necessarily combine to reflect the ambitions, energy, and focus of the WCA. The first ceremony—strategically staged at the White House in conjunction with the College Art Association (CAA) and WCA annual conferences held in Washington DC that year—was the most highly visible of all. The next year offered starkly different circumstances—the Caucus was in turmoil over whether to attend the CAA conference in New Orleans, Louisiana—a state flatly refusing to ratify the Equal Rights Amendment (ERA). A small but radicalized group of WCA members, committed both to making their feminist presence known at CAA and steadfastly protesting the ERA's demise in Louisiana, attended the New Orleans conference under the condition that no money be left in the state by a feminist. That year in New Orleans, the WCA presented awards to five artists: Bauhaus textile designer Anni Albers, sculptor Louise Bourgeois, social satirist Caroline Durieux (from Louisiana), and abstract expressionists Ida Kohlmeyer (from Louisiana) and Lee Krasner. Refusing to go to New Orleans altogether, another group of the WCA leadership organized an alternative awards ceremony, again in Washington, DC, and this time focusing on high profile feminists who did not necessarily have deep roots in the visual arts. This essay will briefly trace events during these two pivotal early years in the awards' history in an effort to uncover their larger implications for feminist interventions on the national front.

As Mary Garrard noted in her essay on the WCA in *The Power of Feminist Art* and Eleanor Dickinson has reiterated in her history of the WCA, the Caucus rapidly gained strength in the late 1970s, evolving from its tumultuous birth as a renegade CAA affiliate group of feminist art historians to an independent non-profit organization with local chapters throughout the nation. While the WCA founders were historians, their first awards were made exclusively to artists. Their concern that women of the past were not adequately represented in the annals of art history was to be rectified with women artists of the present. Today, local chapters consist primarily of artists, with a smattering of scholars, critics, and museum professionals among their ranks. While art historians cease to lead the WCA, the current leadership has honored their groundbreaking work, along with that of women critics and writers, through a steady stream of Lifetime Achievement Awards.[3] It is my hope that this essay, like their provocative accomplishments, will challenge assumptions about our feminist past and stimulate discussion about how best to honor future-wave feminists in an environment where the feminist project has gained iconic status, and as some would argue, has diluted power. Yet feminism's radical nature has surely helped transform the field of art history with its new focus on visual studies and cultural theory. The tactics first conceived by our older sisters in the 1970's have also been reshaped by a myriad of critics and artists—male and female—eager to assert their identity at the turn of the twentieth-first century.

1979: The White House Awards

Each of the first four WCA presidents—Harris (1972–1974), Garrard (1974–1976), Judith Brodsky (1976–1978), and Lee Anne Miller (1978–1980)—nurtured close alliances with women in government. With those connections, Miller was the first to establish the annual tradition of an exhibition and ceremony to honor senior women artists.[4] At that time, Joan Mondale was the nation's leading spokesperson for the arts and a vocal supporter of women artists. In 1978, Mondale had attended the convocation for the WCA conference in New York City under Brodsky's tenure,[5] and she was instrumental in presenting the first Lifetime Achievement Awards with Miller in the following year.[6] While a committee of highly visible scholars within WCA had selected the recipients long before the first ceremony,[7] the WCA leadership preferred that someone who might bring even more publicity to the Caucus actually present the awards.[8] Rosalynn Carter was glad to do it, but she felt that if she did, the story would appear on the women's page, whereas if Jimmy did it, the story would be front-page news.[9]

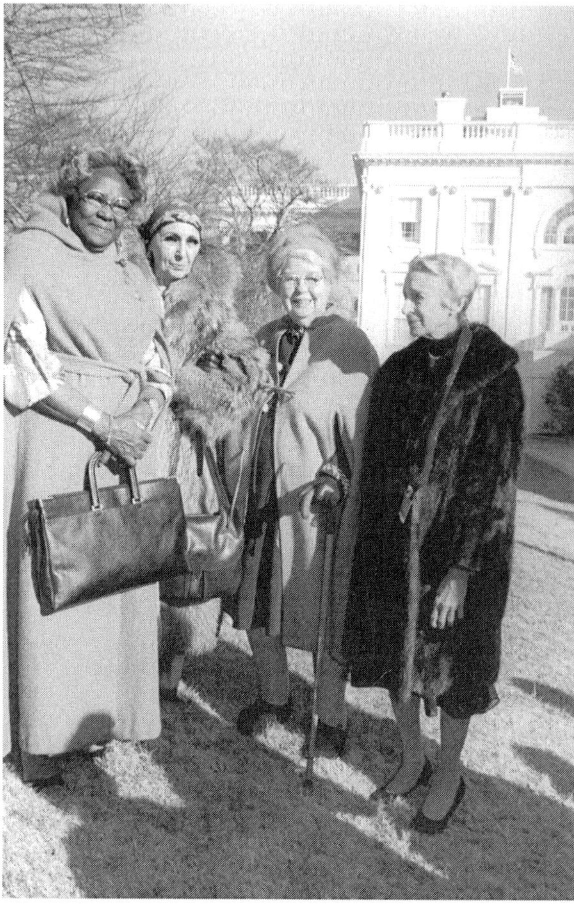

Fig. 1-1
1979 Lifetime Achievement Award Honorees on the White House lawn, Washington, DC. Left to Right: Selma Burke, Louise Nevelson, Alice Neel, and Isabel Bishop. Photograph courtesy of Lee Ann Miller. Photograph Copyright Martha Madigan, 1979.

After months of back-door negotiations with the Office of the Vice-President and the First Lady, President Jimmy Carter agreed to honor the five outstanding women artists selected the year before, but he could not commit to a definite date or time because of meetings with the Chinese. So everyone had to wait until the last minute to establish the precise day and time. When the WCA conference program director Charlotte Robinson finally received the green light, she notified the senior art critic for *The Washington Post* Paul Richard, as well as the honorees: social realist painter Isabel Bishop, African American painter and sculptor Selma Burke, painter Alice Neel, sculptor Louise Nevelson, and painter Georgia O'Keeffe (who was awarded in absentia). The ceremony took place in the Oval Office, and it was very impressive.[10] The White House staff was cordial, and photographers from *The Post* were there to cover the story. The President's staff had allotted 30 minutes in his schedule for the ceremony, but Carter kept them there for close to an hour, taking his time to give the awards. Miller had someone in her school hand print scrolls that President Carter presented to each honoree, after Joan Mondale read the award citation. The only members of the WCA present were Miller, Harris, and Robinson.[11] Immediately following that heady yet intimate ceremony, there was enough afternoon light for photographs bundled in coats on the White House lawn (Fig 1-1). Later that day, the WCA leadership staged a larger, more public ceremony at the Embassy Row Hotel where members of the selection committee read the honorees' citations for the crowd and younger women artists presented each honoree with an artwork.[12] The room was filled to capacity with "wildly enthusiastic Caucus members."[13] While the President was absent from the hotel, both Joan Mondale and Mary Ann Tighe, Deputy Chair of the National Endowment of the Arts (NEA) attended the public awards ceremony. Later that evening, the Middendorf/Lane Gallery on P Street threw a spectacular opening for an exhibition of the honorees' works.[14] On the following day, *The Washington Post* ran a feature-length article on the events surrounding the Coalition of Women's Art Organizations (CWAO) and WCA conferences held in conjunction with the White House awards ceremony.[15]

The highly visible and politicized awards of 1979 were the culmination of two years of intense national lobbying to build support for ratification of the ERA and to urge the NEA to include more women on their panels.[16] Members of the CWAO—a political entity cleverly designed by Brodsky to combine the collective forces of the WCA (its primary institutional member) with the full diversity of United States women's arts organizations—and the Washington Women's Art Center (WWAC) had grown savvy to Washington insider politics in their efforts to lobby Congress for the ERA.[17] As Ellouise Schoettler, Executive Director of the CWAO, put it to *The Post's* art critic in January 1979, "We've done Jimmy Carter a favor, and we know it. We allowed him to follow the firing of Bella Abzug—an insult to all women—with an action wholly safe.[18] A pat on the back for women artists, particularly elderly ones, lets him appear gracious, loving, sensitive—and a little patronizing too."[19] Robinson iterated that "Things work that way in Washington. He lends us the White House and national attention. Perhaps we help him, too."[20] As Garrard noted in *The Power of Feminist Art*, it is a mistake to assume that Carter bestowed the awards on these women—rather they were awards given to women by women.[21] Ultimate responsibility for the awards fell on the WCA selection committee: Harris and Linda Nochlin who co-curated the groundbreaking exhibition Women Artists 1550–1950 at the Los Angeles County Museum of Art in 1977, critic Lucy Lippard, and professors Athena Tacha, Eleanor Tufts, and Ruth Weisberg.

1980: Deep Divisions, Common Goals

The following year the WCA was pitted against itself. The Caucus had gained from 1977 to 1979 the clout to get into White House and wanted to keep that momentum going in New Orleans in 1980, but important members were steadfast in their refusal to visit an un-ratified ERA state. As Garrard who helped organize the alternative DC conference looked back on it, "I wish I could say that the spirit of complementarity and sisterhood prevailed; in reality, there was a great deal of anger, suspicion, and mistrust on both sides."[22] Since 1977, women's organizations including the powerful CWAO "had made an all-out effort to ratify the ERA through an economic strategy that almost worked: for over three years, they sustained a national boycott of un-ratified states."[23] As early as 1977, the WCA had petitioned the CAA to move the New Orleans conference to another city in an ERA ratified state, yet the CAA board chose to honor its contractual agreements over the strong objections of its female members. Without the same financial restraints, the WCA board was faced with a dilemma—follow the parent organization and mount a viable convention as the women of New Orleans, the Florida chapter, and the Southeast Women's Caucus for Art (SWCA) strongly urged them to do; or fully maintain the national boycott that the CWAO and WWAC had worked so hard to enforce. A majority of the WCA board voted with the CAA, despite many members' adamancy that the national boycott not be broken. That decision was reached with stipulations that 1) they sustain a modified boycott in solidarity with their southern sisters, and 2) that they vocally protest in favor of the ERA while in New Orleans. Ultimately, however, two competing WCA conferences and awards ceremonies were held in 1980.

In New Orleans in late January, the awards ceremony was staged rent-free in Gallier Hall, while the WCA conference panels took place in the Hyatt hotel booked by the CAA.[24] Miller presented awards to five older artists as part of a highly radicalized conference staged in association with a number of performance artists including Suzanne Lacy.[25] Performance art was chosen as a political vehicle in New Orleans for its immediacy, and because it fit with the indigenous traditions of Mardi Gras and jazz processions.[26] Participants created large banners to publicize their support of the ERA, decorated umbrellas to represent women artists of the past, and constructed two 13-foot street puppets to bob among the crowd of men and women who gathered at high noon for the awards ceremony. With agitprop in tow and local TV cameras trained on them, they marched with the New Orleans jazz band The Third Line from the CAA conference hotel to Gallier Hall.[27] Mildred Jeffrey, National Women's Political Caucus Advisory Board Chair, and Helen Miliken, National Co-chair of ERAmerica, positioned themselves front and center with WCA president Miller.[28] The marchers paused to circle and dance in front of Gallier Hall, and once inside, the music and dancing continued.

Instead of a convocation speech, Barbara Rowe offered a very moving portrayal of nineteenth-century civil rights leader and suffragette Susan B. Anthony—a delegate to a much earlier political convention—weeping that the male delegates would not even let her speak. The Mayor of New Orleans, Ernest N. Morial, welcomed the participants to the ceremony, and Milliken gave an address in which she made the point that "The combination of art, politics and the Equal Rights Amendment may seem, on the surface, to make strange bedfellows."[29] But the conference was timely, and she iterated, "As organizers, as artists, as professionals, as supporters of the ERA we need to look at the lessons of the past, to re-define the goals and our strategies and to move ahead with renewed energy."[30] Like in Washington, DC the year before, to celebrate passing the torch from one generation to the next, an admiring younger artist or student presented each honoree with an artwork.[31] The First Lady of New Orleans, Sybil Morial, who co-chaired the New Orleans Arts Policy Task Force, closed the ceremony. Similar to the year before, the Bette Clair McMurray Foundation sponsored an exhibition of honorees' work in conjunction with the conference.[32]

In the weeks prior, from January 30th to February 2nd, New Orleans conference, local women procured an empty house that was soon to be sold or redecorated and placed mattresses on the floor for their visiting sisters who refused to leave their money in the state. Swatting cockroaches in a vacant house was preferable to staying in hotels. A few restaurants graciously offered free meals to the women participants and agreed to donate the money that would have been paid to them to the ERA campaign. To draw more attention to their cause, some Caucus members also entered non-participating restaurants, plastering their menus with bright red stickers—"No Sale Until ERA Passes!" and "We're not eating here!!"[33] Shop storefronts were also easy targets for the bright red stickers, and the friction mounted. When their actions began to hurt business, local wealthy women contributors with a stake in the community threatened to pull their promised donations for the conference expenses.[34] The related CAA New Orleans conference was framed on feminist ground as well—as Garrard remembers it, Alessandra Comini delivered the CAA convocation address "with characteristic style and iconoclastic humor, sharply challeng[ing] the 'holy cows and pure bull' of the traditionally phallocentric profession of art history."[35]

The group that refused to break the national boycott of non-ratified ERA states organized a more solemn and dignified awards ceremony on Sunday, 13 January 1980 in the Corcoran Gallery of Art auditorium.[36] The Alternative Conference, *Social Change Takes Courage*, was dedicated to another set of honorees. In line with the broad-based movement to ratify the ERA, these "women of courage" were selected and hailed for their efforts in catalyzing profound change across the entire fabric of American society.[37] The Alternative Conference and related awards were held in the nation's capital—a city not known for marrying art and politics—yet on neutral ground, "where voices would be heard, in full and unequivocal support of the ERA effort."[38] The conference was co-sponsored by the CWAO, with the support of the Arizona chapter and the Marxist Caucus.[39] While the New Orleans conference was designed to make a local impact, the Washington conference was to draw attention to the national ERA campaign and the efficacy of a "total economic boycott as a tool to bring about its passage."[40] Norma Broude iterated the conceptual framework for the conference and awards with a public statement: "We as artists see a relationship between the social acts of these women of courage and feminist art performance. We are identifying an aesthetic component in their social and political acts."[41]

To maintain the CWAO's focus on ratification of the ERA, and to move beyond the usually insular goals of artists and art historians coming together in a professional organization, the honorees were chosen for their visibility in the larger feminist movement and in the fight for civil rights. Bella Abzug had served in the House of Representatives from 1971–77 and was the underdog whose firing as head of the President's Advisory Committee for Women perhaps stimulated Carter's participation in the awards ceremony the previous year. Lynn Campbell had founded Women Against Violence in Pornography and Media and helped organize the first "Take Back the Night" march in San Francisco. Sonia Johnson had been excommunicated from the Mormon Church for her efforts to nationally organize in support of the ERA. Sister Theresa Kane had aggressively advocated for women's ordination in the Catholic Church. Jewish writer Grace Paley was a prominent anti-Vietnam war activist and had staged an anti-nuclear demonstration at the White House the previous fall. Rosa Parks had indelibly marked the civil rights movement, and Gloria Steinem had founded *Ms.* magazine. Similar to the year before, a prominent and admiring woman artist gave each honoree an artwork in tribute to her accomplishments. Both Neel and Bishop who were honored by President Carter offered their works for the ceremony.[42] The public awards ceremony was followed with a speak-out on the ERA, led by Carol Bellamy who was then president of the City Council of New York.

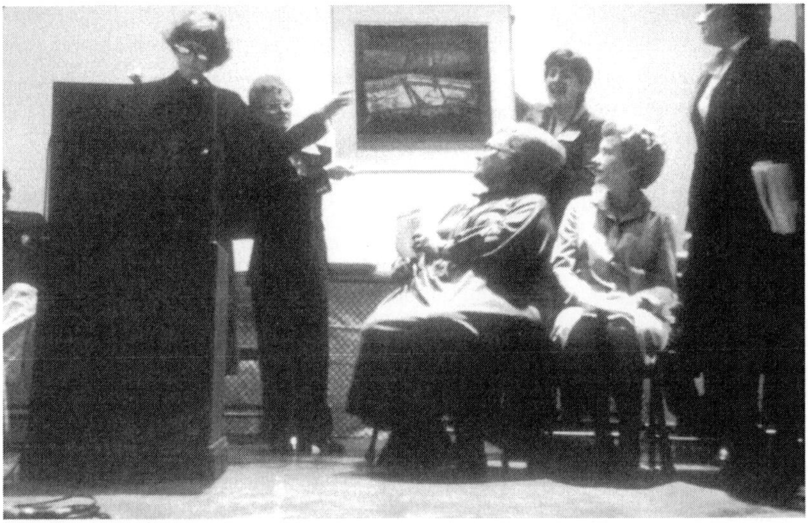

Fig. 1-2
1980 WCA Washington, DC, Alternative Conference Awards. Left to Right: Judith Brodsky at the podium, Mary Garrard and Norma Broude standing; front row seated, Susanne Steinem Patch (who accepted the award for her sister Gloria Steinem), and Sister Doris Gottemoeller, (accepting the award for Sister Mary Theresa Kane). Bella Abzug shown standing at the right. Photograph courtesy of Mary Garrard.

As Garrard has pointed out, the mood of the two conferences could not have been more different, despite their common goals (fig. 1-2). The DC conference and awards were held in a bastion of institutional power; while the New Orleans group hooked up with street musicians on the fly and slept on the floor with cockroaches.[43] Years later, Garrard was able to clearly distinguish the benefits of their polar opposites:

> But I cannot entirely condemn the controversy as wasteful, because it generated on each side a determination to prove itself right to the other, a desire to gain the other's respect. And out of that strange competitive tango came two feminist art performances that had value in themselves. Framed in self-consciously differing terms, each was addressed not only to its immediate audience, but also to the other, each speaking a different theme of feminism to those who would best understand.[44]

Garrard's ability to look beyond the political infighting that infected the protest in New Orleans and so quickly eroded established bonds between women in the DC and New Orleans groups is both remarkable and important for future feminists to consider.

Conclusions for the Future

Many of the circumstances of the late 1970s have irrevocably changed, and over the years, there have been ups and downs in the awards. When Native American artist Charlene Touchette served as chair of the selection committee, there was a concomitant rise in the number of Native American and Latino honorees. With the near collapse of the WCA in its financial crisis of the late 1990s, awards and annual conferences were foregone altogether for two years. In that void of national leadership, members of the Los Angeles chapter took it upon themselves in 1999 to host a conference and honor women with more ties on the west coast than in the east. Yet each of those honored had been instrumental in shaping feminist visions worldwide, and all expanded what we have come to know as the field of art.[45] In 2000 under Magi Ammi's tenure as the sixteenth president of the WCA, Eleanor Dickinson, as chair of the awards committee, established specific rules for selecting honorees to insure the awards' feminist integrity, to safeguard their diversity across disciplines in the visual arts, and to further breakdown of old racial divides.

The present Lifetime Achievement Awards selection committee consists primarily of past honorees, and most of the members of the early selection committees have since been awarded. The events of the late 1970's are also riddled with inconsistencies—for example, the most visible ceremony was the first, held shortly after the WCA membership had expanded nationally. Its visibility in large part was due to the concurrent highly politicized drive to ratify the ERA. Even so, if we are interested at all in basing future behavior on lessons learned in the past, the events and emotions of these two pivotal years in the history of the awards might offer some useful insights. Indeed, Garrard has spent time reconsidering the events of 1979 and 1980, and many of my conclusions here were prompted by her comments in a recent telephone interview.[46] Garrard's bridge to the past (through her lived experience that I as a younger historian cannot share) puts her in a unique position to see the larger implications for our current practice. Her comments from 1979 remind me that those of us in the arts "are in a unique position to dramatize the feminist issues of our time, through our artistic talents and our great numbers. We are also in a unique position to recognize the powerful role played by aesthetic rightness in courageous and influential social acts."[47] I think she would agree that vision is critical to our success. We must continually ask ourselves:

> What ideals do we want to embody?
> What purposes do our organizations fulfill?
> What change must be impacted?
> What tools would be most effective to impact that change?

In any age, social change takes courage. And in the arts we have honed the special skills to understand dramatic gestures—performative acts and political tactics—on aesthetic grounds. The aesthetic effectiveness of those acts contributes to their political effectiveness. And conversely, their political power increases their aesthetic significance.

In the late 1970s, the WCA was effective in spearheading the national drive for ratification of the ERA—the primary national political agenda of the late 1970s. To do it, the Caucus went directly to the seat of power. We might learn from them that the large caches of money that drive our late capitalist economy and are now sought by national non-profits were not a defining factor in their groundbreaking efforts—rather their power rested in their resistance to spend money. It also rested in harnessing the political strength that is gained with a popular movement, in effectively organizing volunteers into networks for communication and change, in building their connections to government officials, and in performing courageous acts far beyond the halls of power.

Money was again an issue when the WCA came back from the cliff of bankruptcy from overspending in the late 1990s. With renewed solvency, a new wave of feminists is now reconsidering how to consolidate their WCA efforts with those of other arts organizations to maximize the potential for broader social change.[48] These dynamics have clear parallels in the past. Perhaps the more diffuse feminist goals of the early twenty-first century (and the globalized marketplace in which we operate) cause us to suffer from nostalgia for the apparent clarity and singular mission of those earlier years. Yet in the turbulent moments of the late 1970s, did our older sisters feel as united in purpose as we would like to so fondly believe? Rather than feeling nostalgia for what has been lost to time, we might do better to gain from the shared aspects of our experience.

---

[1] Mary Fish, "WCA Announces Presentation of First Annual Awards to Five Distinguished Women Artists in Washington, DC," *Women's Caucus for Art Newsletter* 8, no. 1 (1978): 1. See Appendix for complete list.

[2] Awards were not given in 1998 and 2000, a period when the WCA was reconsolidating its focus. Because of the financial insolvency of the national WCA, awards would not have been given in 1999 if the Los Angeles conference organizers had not stepped in to do so. Usually five to six women are honored each year. However, in 1984 only one woman was honored—Barbara Morgan, famous for her photographs of Martha Graham and other dancers.

[3] Alessandra Comini received the award in 1995; followed by Elsa Honig Fine in 1996; Moira Roth in 1997; Linda Frye Burnham and Arlene Raven in 1999; Thalia Gouma-Peterson in 2001; Linda Nochlin and Marilyn Stokstad in 2002; Suzi Gablik, Grace Glueck, and Eleanor Munro in 2003; Garrard and Harris in 2005; Elinor Gadon in 2006; and Wanda Corn and Lucy Lippard in 2007.

[4] Judith Brodsky, "Exhibitions, Galleries, and Alternative Spaces," In *The Power of Feminist Art: The American Movement of the 1970s, History and Impact*, eds. Norma Broude and Mary Garrard (New York: Harry N. Abrams, 1994), 116. While Brodsky gives Miller credit for initiating the awards, Brodsky, Norma Broude, Cynthia Navaretta, and Ellouise Schoettler have all been credited with forming the idea for such a tradition.

[5] Ibid., 119.

[6] Fish, "First Annual Awards," 1. Carter had recently appointed the wife of the Vice President as honorary chair of the Federal Council on the Arts and Humanities.

[7] Harris, then Chair for Academic Affairs at The Metropolitan Museum of Art, headed the first selection committee. Other members of the committee included art critic Lippard; Nochlin, then Mary Connover Mellon professor of the history of art at Vassar College; Athena Tacha, then associate professor of sculpture, Oberlin College; Eleanor Tufts, then professor of art history, Southern Methodist University; and Ruth Weisberg, who remains professor of art, University of Southern California and serves as a member of the 2007 selection committee.

[8] Charlotte Robinson, telephone conversation with author, September 2006. I also thank Ellouise Schoettler for her insights given in a telephone conversation, September 2006.

[9] Robinson, telephone conversation.
[10] My account of the White House ceremony is from Robinson.
[11] According to Robinson's personal notes regarding the 1979 awards, "Joan Mondale, the Vice President's wife took each of the scrolls from me and then handed them to President Carter. He, in turn, gave them to each of the women along with a few words of compliment about their work and their distinguished career. Each of the women (Bishop, Burke, Neel, and Nevelson) responded with a joke or a few words. We were worried that Alice Neel would say something off color or anti-establishment, as that is her usual behavior, but she refrained."
[12] Tufts read Bishop's citation, and Ora Lerman presented her with an artwork. Tritobia Benjamin read Burke's citation, and L. Thomas presented her with an artwork. Harris read Neel's citation, and Pat Mainardi presented her with an artwork. Tacha read Nevelson's citation and presented her with an artwork. Weisberg read O'Keeffe's citation and presented her with an artwork.
[13] Robinson, personal notes
[14] Palmer Lane, a young woman who co-owned the new Middendorf/Lane Gallery with her husband Cris Middendorf, instigated the exhibition. While she had not been involved in the women's movement, Lane recognized the political significance of mounting the exhibition. Lane and Middendorf underwrote the costs associated with producing the catalogue and the gallery opening, as well as shipping and insurance for the works shown.
[15] Paul Richard, "Women in the Arts," *The Washington Post*, January 31, 1979. While Brodsky and Navaretta conceived and formed the CWAO as a vehicle for the political lobbying not allowed to the WCA or other women's arts organizations as non-profit groups, the organization remained necessarily distinct from the WCA. CWAO officers included: Joyce Aiken, President; Schoettler, Executive Director; Weisberg, Vice President for Programs and Goals; Linda Cunningham, Vice President for Membership and Nominating; Muriel Magenta, Vice President for Publicity and Communications; E. Dickinson, Vice President for Finance; Susan Chaires, Treasurer.
[16] Mary Garrard, "Feminist Politics: Networks and Organizations," In *The Power of Feminist Art*, 98.
[17] Richard, "Women in the Arts." Highly visible, the CWAO was said by Richard to represent 60,000 American women among its institutional members. Richard numbered the membership of the WWAC at 700. WCA/CWAO promotional materials from the 1980 Alternative Conference indicate that the CWAO represented 75,000 individuals from 85 national women's arts organizations, and that the WCA had 4,000 members. (Documents related to the 1980 Alternative Conference were provided to me by Garrard and Broude.)
[18] Because of her outspoken stance, Carter was forced to fire Abzug as head of the President's Advisory Committee for Women. Lynda Johnson Robb replaced her.
[19] Richard, "Women in the Arts."
[20] Ibid.
[21] Garrard, "Feminist Politics," 98.
[22] Ibid., 99.

---

[23] Ibid. 98.
[24] Gallier Hall was located at 545 St. Charles Ave.
[25] According to the conference program, the concept and design of the conference were the responsibility of Miller as WCA President and Lacy as Conference Performance Designer. To live out a celebration of Judy Chicago's *The Dinner Party* on local terms, Lacy organized an enormous potluck and communal performance, *River Meeting: Lives of Women in the Delta,* to open the four-day conference. Mary Beth Edelson led a performance ritual during the *River Meeting* dinner. Eleanor Antin performed *Battle of the Bluffs* at the Contemporary Arts Center. The Feminist Art Workers—Nancy Angelo, Cheri Gaulke, Vanalyne Green, Laurel Klick, and Sue Mayberry—performed *Bill of Rights,* the first in a series of 15 staged in non-ratified states. Betsy Damon and Marsha Grubb performed *The Blind Beggar Woman and the Virgin Mary* for three days at a busy New Orleans intersection. Leslie Labowitz, Barbara Smith, and Faith Wilding performed *The Hunger Strike* at the CAA hotel site. In the CAA registration area, Poppy Johnson performed *This Work is this Work.* Katy Dickinson (who served as the first WCA national administrator under fifth president Susan DeRenne Coerr and was present in New Orleans) provided insights on the New Orleans conference in a telephone conversation with me, January 8, 2007.
[26] Ruth Iskin, *Artweek*, March 22, 1980.
[27] A vivid description of the march and subsequent awards ceremony is provided by Suzaan Boettger, "Art, Politics, Equal Rights," *Women's Caucus for Art Newsletter* 9, nos. 3–4 (1980): 10.
[28] E. Dickinson donated an edited videotape of the New Orleans conference to the Smithsonian Archives of American Art. On another occasion with video camera in hand, she spontaneously followed a marching band through the French Quarter as they played funeral dirges in the wake of a hearse carrying the casket of a local jazz great.
[29] Boettger, "Art, Politics, Equal Rights," 11.
[30] Ibid.
[31] Ibid. Mary Jane Jacob read Albers's citation, and Harris presented her with an artwork by Judith Shahn. Weisberg read Bourgeois's citation written by Lippard, and Barbara Zucker presented her with an artwork. Marilyn Symmes read Durieux's citation, and Sue Hirtzel presented her with an artwork. Harris read Kohlmeyer's citation written by Luba Glade, and Ellen Lanyon presented her with an artwork. Audrey Flack read Krasner's citation and presented her with an artwork by Fay Lansner. Three of the honorees were not present due to illness. Katherine Weber of the Albers Foundation accepted the award on behalf of Annie Albers. Susan Witig, Dean, Sophie Newcomb College, accepted the award for Caroline Durieux. Gail Levin of the Whitney Museum accepted the award for Lee Krasner.
[32] Ibid. The exhibition was held at the E. Lorenz Borenstein Gallery on Royal Street from January 31 to February 16, 1980. The WCA published an awards catalogue.
[33] Eleanor Dickinson, telephone conversation with author, September 2, 2006.

[34] Ibid.
[35] Garrard, "Feminist Politics," 99.
[36] Garrard and Broude provided me with documents related to the January 11–13, 1980. Alternative Conference. Conference events also took place at the WWAC offices at 1821 Q St. NW, lower level and DC Space at 443 7th St. NW.
[37] Panel topics at the conference included: "How artists change the community;" "The great women artists' issue: A reappraisal, eight years later;" "The old and new past: Perspectives on teaching and art history;" "The new future: Feminist art education;" and "Feminist performance and social change."
[38] WCA/CWAO, "Details of the Conference," January 11–13, 1980.
[39] Garrard, "Feminist Politics," 99.
[40] WCA/CWAO, "Details of the Conference."
[41] From documents related to the Alternative Conference.
[42] Bishop, Brodsky, Vivian Brown, Neel, Miriam Schapiro, May Stevens, and June Wayne offered their works to the honorees.
[43] Garrard, "Feminist Politics," 99.
[44] Ibid.
[45] In keeping with the Los Angeles conference, a number of the 1999 honorees were selected to focus attention on Southern California as a nucleus for the early Feminist Movement. They included muralist Judy Baca for her groundbreaking work with the Social and Public Art Resource Center (SPARC) in Venice, CA; artist Judy Chicago for her contributions in establishing the feminist art movement on the West Coast; Los Angeles performance artist Linda Frye Burnham for founding the critically acclaimed High Performance Magazine; African American artist Evangeline Montgomery for fostering cultural diversity in arts diplomacy abroad; writer Arlene Raven for bringing a critical voice to the Feminist Movement; and Los Angeles-based performance artist Barbara T. Smith for her innovative and collaborative works.
[46] Garrard, telephone conversation with author, October 6, 2006.
[47] Garrard, "Conceptual Ideas about the 1980 Women's Caucus for Art (WCA) and the Coalition of Women's Arts Organizations (WCAO) Alternative Conference, Washington, DC, January 11–13," (personal papers, photocopy).
[48] Discussion centered on this topic at the WCA annual board meeting held at the Graymoor Spiritual Center, Garrison, New York, July 23–25 2004 under the direction of WCA president Dena Muller.

Works Cited

Boettger, Suzaan. "Art, Politics, Equal Rights." *Women's Caucus for Art Newsletter* 9, nos. 3-4 (1980).

Broude, Norma and Mary Garrard, eds. *The Power of Feminist Art: The American Movement of the 1970s, History and Impact*, New York: Harry N. Abrams, 1994.

Mary Fish. "WCA Announces Presentation of First Annual Awards to Five Distinguished Women Artists in Washington, DC," *Women's Caucus for Art Newsletter* 8, no. 1 (1978).

REPORT ON THE HISTORY OF THE WOMEN'S CAUCUS FOR ART

ELEANOR DICKINSON

The Women's Caucus for Art (WCA) was born in anger, and nurtured by challenge and innovation for many years thereafter. Following a series of major upheavals in Europe and the United States, never-ending wars, "police actions," and war protests left widespread feelings of dissatisfaction with the conditions of life that previous generations had been willing to fight for. The civil rights movement, begun to end racial discrimination in America, had raised awareness of many other kinds of discrimination in the educational system, employment, and housing, and in the military forces where racial segregation both of the African Americans and the Japanese Americans had forced them into concentration camps on doubts of their patriotism. These movements raised questions of many other forms of discrimination, such as when women were forced to give up their wartime jobs as men returned from the battlefields.

After a century of turmoil, women had finally gotten the right to vote in 1920, but this did not greatly change their conditions of living. As signs warning "Whites Only" vanished, women realized there were just as many unwritten signs repressing them. Jobs were listed separately for "men" or "women" in ads in the papers. A married woman could not get a credit card without her husband's permission. Unmarried working women could not get bank loans or mortgages without a co-signer. In 1953, in Tennessee, I could not have willed my own property without the permission of my father or husband. Women earned 59 cents for every dollar a man earned. Abortions were illegal, and birth control might not be legal or available. These conditions changed slowly as women began to realize that what was normal was completely wrong; the women in art and in academic fields realized that they too were oppressed.

Only recently had the most prestigious Ivy League universities admitted women as students or employed women as faculty. Ann Sutherland Harris noted,

> Distinguished women scholars retired with the rank of Associate Professor; few were even awarded tenure at the most famous universities until women at Colombia, Chicago, Harvard and elsewhere started to ask questions in the late 1960's and early 1970's and documented the impressive numbers of women who had earned the necessary degrees to teach at serious universities. In the UK, women had to found their own colleges at Oxford and Cambridge in order to hold fellowships and be able to work, and women only got proper degrees at both places after WW II. . . my husband got a job at Columbia, we both moved to New York City, where I was lucky enough to get an appointment at Barnard and Columbia in 1966. That's where I discovered the glass ceiling for women faculty there—Assistant Professor OK but tenure—hardly ever. Later I testified before Edith Green's Subcommittee on Higher Education in Washington about this widespread pattern of discrimination against women in higher education.[1]

One woman made a major change in this pattern. Bernice Sandler, in Washington, had realized that two Executive Orders of President Johnson that forbade discrimination by race or sex by federal contractors meant that millions of dollars in federal grants could be denied to academic institutions that received federal funds that discriminated against women. Our statistics proved that Columbia University (and others) did and had for years, and she sued them and succeeded in holding up millions in funding! That really opened the floodgates and made many women and men begin to realize how unconsciously yet pervasively women were seen as lower class citizens not entitled to the benefits, status, salaries, pay, and so forth, of men.[2]

Disregarded

By the mid twentieth century, there were 105,000 artists and art teachers in the United States. However, although by any standard—numbers, training, skills, quality—about 35 percent of trained U.S. artists were female and 44 percent of trained art historians, but less than 11 percent were art teachers, only 12 percent were invited to exhibit their art, 7 percent got fellowships and grants, and less than 4 percent were included in the important art textbooks.[3] Especially problematic to women art historians was Professor H. W. Janson, whose authoritative textbook *The History of Art* of 1962 proclaimed his belief that an artist's work must "have changed the history of art"[4] to be worthy of inclusion in his tome. His compilation of "3,000 artists from the Old Stone Age to the present" included no women artists—and no black or Latino artists either.[5] Surprisingly, he was highly regarded in the major organization for professionals in the visual arts, the College Art Association (CAA), and served on its board of directors. After its appearance, his book was the required textbook for most introductory art history classes in the United States, and had a discouraging effect on the young female artists and art historians who were trained by it.

Women art historians had dual concerns: reexamining the accepted importance and power of individual inventiveness and competition of the artists and the accompanying progression of the "right" artistic ideas over past errors. Norma Broude commented that:

> [u]nderlying both of these influential ideas—the mystique of the innovative avant garde and the paradigm of art history as a sequence of styles that vanquish and supersede each other—is the psychosexual model of heroic patricide, the competitive revolt of the sons against the fathers.[6]

In many and varied ways, women historians saw art as a tool for change and hungered for the opportunity to change the "litany" of art from the "universal value" espoused by Kenneth Clark. Brice Marden, quoting Cezanne, said, "The subject matter became irrelevant—what he was really doing was making the paint."[7] The women felt that there was always an intent and philosophy behind the artist's work, and that the meaning and content were of much greater importance than the unique style or individual technique. At the CAA Conference in New Orleans in 1980, Alessandra Comini said, "Art can deny reality, it can transform, it can almost move reality. Art can deal with private or metaphysical problems or—it can go public and comment on society."[8] The women's movement in art was the force that abolished the tyranny of technique in American painting that had reigned in the 1950s and 1960s.

In northern and middle California, the female visual artists were feeling challenges of a different nature. Interactions and experimentations began among them that would spread across the nation and completely change the way women related to one another. Where once it was grudgingly accepted that if one woman was asked to be in an exhibition, no others would be—tokenism was unnamed and tolerated—a change came. Joyce Aiken had taught art at the California State College Fresno since 1961, bringing her creative talents into the classroom. Judy Chicago arrived in 1970 as a sabbatical replacement to teach outdoor site sculpture, but changed the course (during which she identified strong female students) to an investigation into feminist art. Held off-campus, this was the first course like this in the country and it started a fire. As Nancy Youdelman said, "We felt a special sense of risk and importance and a freedom from history."[9] When Chicago left a year later, first Rita Yokoi and then Joyce Aiken continued the class with innovative teaching methods until Aiken retired in 1992. Students from these classes, such as Suzanne Lacy, Nancy Youdelman, Cay Lang, Laurel Glick, and others carried their enthusiasm throughout the community starting performances and exhibits.

Something New

In the spring of 1971, Judy Chicago and Miriam Schapiro held a new type of class for women artists featuring panels and skits. Rita Yokoi, Patricia Tavenner, and Jeannie O'Conner attended this class then returned to Oakland and Berkeley where they organized a picket of the University of California at Berkeley's Museum, and formed many consciousness-raising groups with the help of West-East Bag (W.E.B.).[10] Credit for the structure of these groups must go to Joyce Kozloff, who came from New York, and had joined the first San Francisco Bay Area group, bringing all her skills of organizing and sense of unity and sisterhood to the subsequent groups.[11]

At this time in New York, many groups had developed to support civil rights and to protest political events, the anti-war movement, and the lack of women in museum shows. In 1970, Dorothy Gillespie was instrumental in founding the Women's InterArt Center, "the first alternative feminist space."[12] The groups included—Women Artists in Revolution (WAR) (against the Whitney Museum's lack of women in their Annual Exhibition), the Art Workers Coalition (protesting the invasion of Cambodia, the Kent State killings, and violence in Mississippi), Women, Students and Artists for Black Art Liberation (WSABL) demanding quotas in art, the Ad Hoc Group (against discrimination in the Whitney Museum Annual Exhibitions), Women in the Arts (WIA) for an exhibition of 500 women, and many others.[13] These groups surprisingly did not join together in common cause but often formed even more protest groups against yet another perceived evil.

Chicago, taking many of her Fresno students with her, then worked with Schapiro at California Institute of the Arts in Valencia, developing the Feminist Art Program there (skeptical faculty at that time included Nam June Paik, John Baldessari, Allan Kaprow, and Herb Blau). This program dramatically showed the difference between the training of male and female art students from mentorship to myth: "[t]he myths of (male) genius and mastery deemed as necessary to the making of art."[14] A three-day Women in Art Conference was organized in 1972 at Womanhouse, a 17-room abandoned house on Mariposa Avenue in Hollywood, lent by the

City of Los Angeles, which became a famous landmark for the unprecedented performance art of subjects dealing with women's roles. Performances were of mopping, ironing, birthing, waiting, and rape. In one piece, women stood in the doorway of a small room, "Leah's Room," watching with tear-streaked cheeks as the woman seated inside at the mirror laboriously put on careful makeup, then removed it, then put it on again, then removed it again, then . . . Faith Wilding performed an intense "*Waiting:* 'waiting to get pretty—waiting to get married—waiting for my baby to be born—waiting for my children to grow up—waiting to get ugly—waiting for a visit from my children——."[15]

What began in Fresno was echoed across the country with an exuberance that transcended time and place. For the next 35 years—and counting—women in art stepped forward and changed the art world: not counting the credit but gladly working with each other again and again, changing roles, learning new skills, calling each other "sister" with an almost religious fervor.

Changes

Personal art became political, as women's experiences became the stuff of performances around the world. Moreover, the question asked changed from "Who am I?" to "Who are we?" according to Norma Broude and Mary Garrard.[16] Womanhouse of 1972 inspired the Los Angeles Woman's Building, "the public center for women's culture," founded in 1973 by Arlene Raven, Judy Chicago, and Sheila de Bretteville, based on Paula Harper's idea.[17] This housed many women's organizations, galleries, workshops, and a bookstore. Two national conferences there brought together such artists as Yvonne Rainier, Martha Rosler, Eleanor Antin, and Pauline Oliveros, who joined with Los Angeles artists Barbara Smith, Nancy Buchanan, and Rachel Rosenthal and catalyzed the work of Suzanne Lacy and Leslie Lebowitz. A new approach was the feminist use of media to reach mass audiences, often with subjects such as woman as victim. One of Chicago's pieces, *Ablutions*, used images of bondage, abuse, rape, fertility, cleansing, and healing. One of her prints, *Red Flag*, featured a hand pulling a bloody Tampax from a vagina. This emphasis on insistently female imagery shocked New York male artists, and triggered debates for years thereafter as to whether there was—*or ought to be*—feminist subject matter.

Recruitment

In 1971, Chicago and Schapiro had made lecture trips to New York, connecting with Lucy Lippard, Marcia Tucker, and Ellen Lanyon. W.E.B. emerged as an international network, and spread to 20 states and other countries: "our second class citizen ratings were all too clear."[18] Linda Nochlin had just published her famous essay in *Art News*, "Why Have There Been No Great Women Artists?,"[19] which shocked and galvanized all women artists. Nochlin followed this by "organizing a session the following year at the annual CAA conference titled 'Eroticism and the Image of Woman in Nineteenth-Century Art,' which addressed the issue of sexism in art."[20] W.E.B. groups were an effective tool in response. It was apparent that often-isolated women artists and writers had a great deal in common with each other; consciousness-raising groups exploded throughout New York and the San Francisco Bay Area. Some W.E.B. meeting topics were: each woman must speak, don't give advice or therapy, pick topics such as "How was your education affected by your sex?" "How have you been encouraged to be an artist/creative? Discouraged? By whom?" "Are you competitive with other women? With men?"[21] The trust that was developed by these groups was of enormous importance in solidifying unity, certainty, and freedom for radical experimentation; unifying all was the surprising similarity of the problems encountered. The continuation of these weekly groups was difficult and took daring in the face of angry husbands' objections.

Tools for Change

Hunger for more knowledge of women artists of the past required art history slide registries that developed in 1971 by Lucy Lippard, proliferated through W.E.B. groups. Jo Hanson photographed the work of many Mexican women artists; Kate Delos and Eleanor Dickinson, photographed women's art on view in European museums (there wasn't much); and Tavenner's friend at the Walters Museum gave her slides of art by women. Even poor slides were copied and recopied to feed the hunger for images by their ancestors.

In Los Angeles in 1960, June Wayne founded the Tamarind Workshop, revitalizing printmaking in the United States as well as abroad. To accomplish this, she had to create a "print ecology" that reached from artists and the training of master printers into the art market at large: the manufacture of paper, presses, inks—everything needed for the creation of graphics. Along with this, she urged colleges and universities to include arts management in their curricula and published business studies of art galleries, magazines, and the economics of printmaking. In 1971, she organized a ten-week seminar in her studio called "Business and Professional Problems of the Visual Artist," nick-named "Joan of Art," teaching women artists how to cope with their professional problems. This was a "seminal movement to break away from behaving like mommies working on the dining room table to being professionals," according to Wayne. After this training, each artist had to give the seminar to others, thus creating a whole business infrastructure in the arts and greatly assisting artists (men as well) to handle their precarious relations with dealers, curators, and collectors as well as in the art education job market. "Artists should never forget that theirs is niche ecology and is subject to distortions and pressures that gravely deviate from the norm of most societies."[22]

The 1971 Corcoran Biennial in Washington, DC, aroused fury and resolve when Washington artists learned that no women had been included in this prestigious exhibition. They organized a major forum, the Conference of Women in the Visual Arts in 1972 at the Corcoran, which featured feminists from California and New York such as June Wayne, Miriam Schapiro, Linda Nochlin, Judy Chicago, and Adelyn Breeskin. Mary Garrard said, "Many of the women who came together in Washington were radicalized on the spot."[23] One was Washington artist Charlotte Robinson who, with Dorothy Gillespie and Alice Baber, "decided to ask women artists to design quilts as a way of celebrating the year 1975, designated as the International Year of the Woman by the United Nations,"[24] as Judith Stein declares "subverting the myth of isolated genius" in an early merging of the fine and decorative arts. In New York, following political actions such as Women's International Terrorist Conspiracy from Hell (W.I.T.C.H.) in 1968, and Redstockings (Sisterhood) in 1969, Dorothy Gillespie and Alice Baber developed a somewhat more formal course at the New School of Social Research called "Functioning in the Art World." Baber and Gillespie organized the first women's show in New York at the InterArt Center. Artist Sylvia Sleigh and art writer Lawrence Alloway were very supportive, assisting both with the art and with critical writing.

Revolution

This simmering cauldron of awareness and frustration came to a head in 1972 when the largest professional art organization, the CAA, held its 61st conference for the first time in San Francisco. Founded in 1911, the

Association is composed of scholars, artists, art historians, teachers, critics, museum curators, and so forth—that is, all practitioners, interpreters, and conservators of visual art and culture. The CAA's aim is the "understanding of art as a fundamental form of human expression."[25] Given the expanding enthusiasms of the women's movement all over the country, it was frustrating to view the predominantly male board of directors (one woman among 24 directors) and to listen to the papers and presentations chosen by mainly male chairs of male-dominated panels.

On January 28, 1972, "Several women on both coasts contacted CAA Executive Director Rose Weil about holding a meeting for women members concerned about these issues; it was publicized by posting some signs at the conference Hotel"[26] (the Hilton). "Thanks to ground work laid by art historian Ann Sutherland Harris, the San Francisco meeting drew an overflow crowd."[27] When the meeting room proved too small, the number of angry women grew larger and larger, and they opened the doors to double the space: all who had experienced gender discrimination in art told and retold their stories. Ann Harris said, "…discrimination against women artists, past and present, must have made it difficult, if not impossible, for their gifts to be discovered, supported and written about … why not twice as many Rembrandts, Vermeers, Michelangelos?"[28] The art historians met the studio artists, the writers met their subjects, curators met the craftswomen, and all found common ground in understanding their unjust obliteration. Ann Harris, who had testified in Congress regarding the negation of professional women, was very impressive to women who had not ever had female art teachers other than Sister Mary Corita.[29] Harris said, "…at least 300 women came with stories of gender discrimination and the energy and willingness to set up a Women's Caucus of the CAA."[30] Thus the Women's Caucus of the College Art Association was born, possibly to the great surprise of the CAA.

A formal organization was decided upon; it was felt that the women in art must organize very well—and quickly. Ann Sutherland Harris was chosen as the first Chair/President from 1972 to 1974: "We passed the hat and I went home with 300 names and addresses and maybe a couple of hundred dollars to get things going." At first, as Harris says, she ran the fledgling organization from one drawer in her desk with help from Linda Bantel sorting out the financial records as the first de facto WCA Treasurer.[31] She set up an organization and planned dues, a newsletter, referrals, and publication of various books and articles such as "The Second Sex in Academe," compiled by Harris and Barbara White, listing the lowered status of women art historians. Nancy Spero and Joyce Kozloff created the "Rip-Off File" of horror stories. Norma Broude and

Meredith Johnson set up the WCA Job Roster.[32] Broude became the first Affirmative Action Officer and worked hard identifying affirmative action concepts, contacting major universities, advising them of their statistics, and pointing out that they were in "violation of national affirmative action mandates." When they were put on notice that they were being watched, a lot of defensive responses arose. That gave momentum to the WCA's ongoing effort to monitor and publicize delinquent schools"[33] based on various surveys and statistics from June Wayne, Eleanor Dickinson, the WCA, and a new CAA Committee on the Status of Women constituted by the CAA in 1972. This Committee was first chaired by Linda Nochlin in 1972, and again in 1974 to 1978, and by Ann Sutherland Harris in 1973. "The Committee has acted in part as liaison between the WCA and the CAA, which has often given its moral support and financial assistance to Caucus projects. Its primary concern has been the gathering of statistical information."[34]

Growth

With the initial enthusiasm growing, new groups began to be formed as women from the CAA Conference spread out all over the country. Following extensive picketing of New York museums by Women in the Arts (WIA) for showing so few women, an important and first exhibition "Women Choose Women" was held in New York in 1973 at the New York Cultural Center.[35] By 1974, women's studies courses were in 1,000 U.S. colleges and universities across the country. At that time, Ann Harris asked Mary Garrard to continue the Caucus and Garrard became its second president (1974–76).[36] Garrard set up a national advisory board and "gave structure and stability to a rapidly expanding organization."[37] Mary Garrard requested that the CAA provide regular meeting times and spaces for meetings and workshops during the annual CAA meetings. Ellouise Schoettler provided vital organizing skills as the Secretary.

As enthusiasm for the Caucus spread, the executive board of the CAA seemed more and more uncomfortable with the size and energy of this new association. This came to a head when the CAA Attorney Gil Edelson became worried about liability for the legal activities of Caucus supporters all across the country and suggested setting it up as an affiliate organization.[38] Therefore, on July 23, 1974, Mary Garrard saw to the organization incorporating legally as the Women's Caucus for Art while maintaining its relationship with the CAA.[39]

Under Garrard's leadership, Lee Ann Miller set up the first official regional WCA chapter in 1974 in Kansas City.[40] Other early chapters—

each has claimed to be the first—were New York (1972), Northern California (1972), and the Miami chapter "WAIT" (in 1971), which changed its name to WCA in 1973. The Northern California Chapter was organized from the earlier W.E.B. groups by Patricia Tavenner, Susan Perkins, and Theresa Heyman, Oakland Museum curator. At the first Bay Area meeting, art historian Wanda Corn reported on the National College Association. There was little support for women or the Caucus from museums other than Oakland.[41] Performance groups developed using autobiographical work by Bonnie Sherk, Linda Montano, and Lynn Hershman. In 1977, Hershman created the Floating Museum, which presented shows using the facilities of other institutions in unusual locations such as inside San Quentin Prison. One such exhibition was H'ERRATA, her correction of an (H)error, with Jo Hanson as curator.[42]

Women's Groups

The WCA differed in almost every respect from the previous miscellaneous organizations of women artists across the country. Most of these were composed of groups whose primary purpose was to organize and present exhibitions for the members. They spoke of promoting art, were often started by friendship groups, and their primary benefit was the support and networking offered to isolated artists.

The advent of the WCA was like a violent wind that devastated the ordered landscape. The shocking art and artists of the 1970s demolished all previous definitions of "women's art," and, with its emphasis on content and social commentary, helped to end the domination of Modernism and Abstract Expressionism. The new emphasis was on group actions, and on using personal experience to critique political agendas asserting, "The personal IS the political!"[43]

Education

Urged on by the many historians within the new Women's Caucus, research on women artists was promoted, as was the inclusion of feminist perspectives in art; many women's studies courses were developed. The WCA published *Women's Studies in the Arts* by Athena Tacha Spear; this was later edited and reissued by Lola Gellman, Elsa Honig Fine, and Judy Loeb as *Women's Studies in Art and Art History. Slides of Works by Women Artists: A Sourcebook* (1974), and was published by Mary D. Garrard. The year 1976 saw the production not only of the book *Women Artists: Recognition and Reappraisal from the Early Middle Ages to the*

Twentieth Century by Karen Petersen and J. J. Wilson but also four sets of slides of the works featured in it. In 1978, Elsa Honig Fine published *Women and Art: Women Painters and Sculptors from the Renaissance to the Twentieth Century*, and in 1980 she began a magazine of art history, the *Woman's Art Journal,* featuring often unknown women artists; it is still published maintaining the highest standards of scholarship. In 1979, Eleanor Munro published *Originals: American Women Artists.* Garrard and Broude's 1994 *The Power of Feminist Art* is an essential reference for any study of the history of women in the visual arts."[44] Eleanor Tufts published the first important listing of *American Women Artists, Past and Present.* The *Heresies* journal with inventive group editors had a different theme for each issue; it was published 1977–96 by Lucy Lippard and May Stevens, Harmony Hammond, Joyce Kozloff, Mary Beth Edelson, and others. *Chrysalis*, a quarterly journal, began in Los Angeles in 1977 and only survived until 1980; it had exceptionally high editorial standards. *Women Artists News* and other excellent publications were produced by Cynthia Navaretta at her Midmarch Art Press. Cindy Nemser, as editor with Pat Mainardi and Irene Moss, brought out the *Feminist Art Journal* 1972–77. *Womenart* was published from 1976–78 and *Helicon Nine* was published from 1979 to 1989.

The Caucus urged members to conduct education and discrimination surveys in its new role as gadfly to the CAA. Especially important was a study of MFA programs; this was done by the WCA's Janice Koenig Ross, and published by the CAA. Following the lead of June Wayne's research in "Sex Differentials in Art Exhibition Reviews"[45] published at Tamarind, Eleanor Dickinson compiled, and in 1973, published "Statistics: Discrimination in the Art Field," which is still updated yearly.[46] One target of the WCA was the CAA Board of Directors: of 24 directors only one was female (five years later there were 11 women). The CAA board soon had three female presidents: Ruth Weisberg, Judy Brodsky, and Anne Coffin Hanson (1972–74). Fortunately Norma Broude, as WCA correspondent to the CAA's *Art Journal* and the *CAA Newsletter,* could check on the CAA position listings.

The WCA's third president and the first artist was Judith K. Brodsky (1976–78.) She published the discrimination guide, "Anger to Action."[47] Brodsky also added 15 more WCA chapters during her term of office. She was particularly interested in mounting exhibitions of contemporary women artists in each city where the CAA Conference would be held. In Los Angeles in 1977 came the first of many such shows, the WCA's first national exhibition at the first annual conference. The important historical exhibition Women Artists: 1550–1950, (with the book of the same name), curated by Linda Nochlin and Ann Sutherland Harris, was held at that same time at the Los Angeles County Museum of Art. The exhibition drew women from around the country for this first major documentation of the hitherto forgotten, hidden, or successful-but-ignored Old Mistresses of Art, thus providing ancestors for women artists.[48]

Other Organizations

In 1977, the Coalition of Women's Art Organizations (CWAO) was formed as a political arm of the WCA. The CWAO president and executive director served on the WCA Board as ex-officio members. It was proposed by Judy Brodsky, co-founded by Cynthia Navaretta, and the first chairperson was Ellouise Schoettler. Susan Schwalb and Charlotte Robinson joined in urging women all over the country to go to Houston as part of the (continuing) International Year of the Woman (IWY). The State Department gave them space to organize at this first National Women's conference. Joyce Aiken was named CWAO president and Ellouise Schoettler was named director: Joyce lived at Ellouise's for a year to get it organized. Linda Cunningham designed the structure and wrote the by-laws before the first national meeting in New York in January, 1978. The Women's Caucus was a 501(c)(3) non-profit organization, and as such was legally limited to 20 percent spent on any political activities both in time and cost. The Coalition, however, was set up as a 501(c)(6) organization, which allowed unlimited political activities. One such activity was a national boycott of Dr. Janson's book in 1979; in that same year, the CAA awarded Dr. Janson a top honor, "Distinguished Teaching of Art History Award,"[49] to the frustration of CWAO members. Other political actions included lobbying Congress and testifying on arts legislation and the publication of statistics on sex differentials in employment and in exhibition opportunities.[50] Later in 1984, Dorothy Provis became CWAO president and Kyra Belan became director: Eleanor Dickinson often served as vice president. A great many women's organizations throughout the country became CWAO members for a $25 yearly fee and received constant notifications of political actions that they should support. This feisty group also became an affiliate organization of the CAA and as such received free space for meeting and a regular panel that was used to describe all the political issues of importance to women. Frequently these subjects covered the business of art and were useful in educating women artists in the practical problems of an art career.[51]

Growth and Honors

Lee Anne Miller was the WCA's fourth president (1978–80). She continued the efforts to gain more awareness of the WCA through both public speaking and issues such as the ERA and artists' rights. Norma Broude and Ellouise Schoettler proposed giving national achievement awards to various important women in the arts, building on extensive activity of the Washington, DC-area women artists; efforts to hold an annual Honor Awards Ceremony for Lifetime Achievement in the Arts was begun. The first awardees were chosen by Ann Sutherland Harris, Lucy Lippard, Linda Nochlin, Athena Tacha, Eleanor Tufts, Mary Mellon, Arthur Kittredge, and Ruth Weisberg. In June, the Caucus sent a delegation to the White House to propose a national honoring of women in the arts; approval was finally given.[52] Charlotte Robinson and Joan Mister had contacted Joan Mondale, an artist and wife of Vice President Walter Mondale, who also became involved.

In 1980, the first WCA award ceremony was held in the Oval Office in the White House. The Caucus and President Jimmy Carter recognized Isabel Bishop, Selma Burke, Alice Neel, Louise Nevelson (in absentia), and Georgia O'Keeffe (all over 75 years old), to great public acclaim and publicity. President Carter "acknowledged and expressed understanding of the lack of opportunities that women artists have faced and the difficulties they have experienced in achieving recognition."[53] Charlotte Robinson's notes read:

> Joan Mondale, the Vice-President's wife, took each of the scrolls from me (read them aloud) and then handed them to President Carter. He, in turn, gave them to each of the women along with a few words of compliment about their work and distinguished career. Each of the women responded with a joke or a few words. We were worried that Alice Neel would say something off color or anti-establishment as that is her usual behavior—but she refrained. It was a beautiful ceremony. Afterwards we went to the Embassy Row Hotel (site of the WCA Conference) where we had another ceremony so that all the Caucus members could see the distinguished women.[54]

WCA President Lee Anne Miller introduced Joan Mondale, as an artist, wife of the Vice President and also as Honorary Chair of the Federal Council of Arts and Humanities at the public ceremony. The honorees were presented works of art as gifts from other women artists, and the citations on the scrolls were read. Louise Nevelson (who was ill) sent a message: "Today is a very important day for women not only in America, but all over the world—and I don't say it lightly."[55]

Charlotte Robinson had arranged for an eager and new gallery, the Middendorf Lane Gallery, to give an elaborate exhibition of the work of the awardees. Ms. Lane even paid for the catalog for the honor ceremony. The Washington Women's Art Center produced a huge number of volunteers to run the conference and did so much fundraising they were able to give a profit to the National WCA afterwards.[56]

Testing

Lee Anne Miller also presided over two national conferences in 1980. Despite great pressures on the CAA to change the site of their yearly conference away from New Orleans in Louisiana, a state that had not ratified the Equal Rights Amendment (ERA), the CAA could not change due to legal and financial commitments. The WCA then voted to go to the official Conference "under protest conditions." Eleanor Dickinson was Affirmative Action Officer at that time and made extensive plans to "leave no money in Louisiana. We succeeded in this with a great deal of effort, sleeping in the homes of WCA members and eating only at restaurants that promised to send our money to the ERA as a donation. We left a strengthened and enlivened local WCA chapter behind us, particularly happy over the awards given to Ida Kohlmeyer, Louise Bourgeois, Anni Albers, Carolyn Durieux, and Lee Krasner". Several caucuses in the South had banded together as South East WCA (SEWCA) and presented an impressive large regional exhibition in the French Quarter. Suzanne Lacy staged an "expanded performance . . . The conference opened with a potluck meal that brought together five hundred ethnically diverse women to celebrate their southern heroines."[57] Other WCA Board members chose to set up a second, alternative conference in Washington, DC, for members wishing to honor the boycott of non-ratified ERA states. They gave alternate honorary awards to Bella Abzug, Rosa Parks, Sonia Johnson, Sister Theresa Kane, Grace Paley, and Gloria Steinem; non-artists but great contributors to the dignity of women.

In the late 1970s, many WCA members around the country wished to hold regional events and meetings between the annual conferences to network, train members, share information, hold exhibitions, develop slide registries, hold studio visits, and pursue the aims of WCA through events on a smaller scale that more members could attend. This helped to form many early WCA chapters—often in cities, but many times within a region or state, allowing for better relationships and joint projects. These efforts reached many arts professionals who worked outside academic or institutional settings, and accounted for a rapid growth of WCA membership across the country, expanding the WCA network in both breadth and depth.[58]

The WCA began to sponsor or mount regional exhibitions. The first was Women Artists '77 in Kansas City, organized by Lee Anne Miller; the second was Women Artists '78 of work from New York, New Jersey, and Connecticut chapters held in New York City at the City University of New York. Other organizations and galleries developed at this time, such as the Washington Women's Art Center in 1976. Working with these groups, Washington artist Nancy Cusick spurred the participation of women artists around the world in various United Nations Women's Conferences such as the "Mid-Decade Conference" in Copenhagen, "The Decade of the Woman" in Nairobi, the "1985 An American Album," Focus International, American Women in Art, United Nations World Conference, Kenya (and touring), and, in 1995, "'Global Focus', UN World Conference, Women," Beijing, China, Moscow, Russia, which was co-sponsored by the National Museum of Women in the Arts.[59]

Organization and Expansion

The WCA's fifth president, S. DeRenne Coerr (1980–1982), registrar of the Fine Arts Museums of San Francisco and the first museum professional to head the organization, tackled the hard job of accommodating the increasing demands of a growing national association, which expanded from 18 to 23 chapters during her term. As the Caucus grew larger and more ambitious, its records grew more and more voluminous, and were shipped from president to president every two years. The resulting confusion made it obvious that a national office of some kind was badly needed. Coerr's main contribution was to regularize and organize the internal procedures of the WCA. Chapters had been founded with no controls, no national standards (example: for usage of the WCA name), and no agreement to send a share of dues collected to the central organization. The worst habits of small local arts groups had sometimes been adopted, and the image of an important women's movement was in danger of being forgotten.

President Coerr said:

> As a volunteer I was responsible for two national conferences, two annual Honors Ceremonies and exhibitions, 16 to 20 page newsletters three or four times a year, and ongoing chapter relationships, in a time with no personal computers, no email, no word processing, nor internet sites, etc. Cash flow was variable following receipt of the newsletters.[60]

Coerr received help from newsletter editor Suzaan Boettger and other officers and the Board, but only limited support from her museum, highlighting the need for institutional backup for the WCA presidents.[61] Membership lists were being kept by a paid mailing house; addresses came in paper labels to be put on by hand and at least one-third were erroneous. Coerr hired the first operations officers of the WCA, Katy Dickinson and later Denise Schultz. They regularized the membership roster and prompt forwarding of chapters' lists, set standards for dues collections (ending the practice of allowing local members to join only a chapter and not also the National WCA), handled accounts payable, and did their best to correspond with members.[62] Coerr worked with an attorney to rewrite the bylaws for Board consideration.

With the growth of chapters continuing, most WCA members were studio artists with local or regional interests who needed the focus of a national Board with a continuing business manager. The assistance of the local chapters in each conference city was invaluable; conferences could not always be led nationally. Ann Sutherland Harris presented the goals of the WCA Five Year Planning Committee, set up in 1981 by the National Advisory Board, which included establishment of a permanent office for a National WCA headquarters, along with plans for a $1,000,000 Endowment Fund.

Awareness of this need for centralization continued with artist Muriel Magenta, the sixth WCA President, (1982–1984) who hired the WCA's next business manager and treasurer, Beatrice Weinstein. In 1983, Magenta obtained a permanent inexpensive office space at Philadelphia's Moore College of Art. Under Magenta's leadership, the WCA also published the first of its biennial membership directories, increased its fundraising, and revised its newsletter to a magazine format, renaming it *Huepoints.*[63] A national exhibition was held at Lehigh University. As a skilled media artist, Magenta established the World Wide Web of Women in cyberspace and presented the first international showcase of the work of women entitled, "The World's Women On-Line."[64]

Broadening the Membership

Under the seventh WCA President Ofelia Garcia (1984–1986), a Cuban-American artist and administrator as president of the Atlanta College of Art, the programs of the WCA were broadened, encouraging the membership of women of color. The position of vice president for minority affairs was set up, first held by artist Faith Ringgold, and conference publicity was extensively promoted to artists of all backgrounds. During this time a "president's assistant" was hired to assist with all the office work; this became a regular item in the WCA budget. The annual recognition of important Mid-Career Women in the Arts was also begun at this time as the "President's Award"; the first honorees were Ann Sutherland Harris and Linda Nochlin.[65]

During the administration of historian and eighth WCA President Annie Shaver-Crandell (1986–1988), WCA membership benefits were increased to include optional hospitalization insurance. As an art historian, she also worked to secure the historical record of contributions by women to the arts by setting up the WCA Archives at Douglass College, Rutgers University, under WCA archivist Janet Miller, National Administrator (1984–1986). Shaver-Crandell and Assistant Carol Grape created a national celebration of women's contributions to the visual arts in September 1986, with WAVE II: Now You See Us, observed from coast to coast with 16 chapters participating and aimed at museum practices that discriminate against women.[66] Her special thrust was to insist on affirmative action within the Caucus for implementation of positive inclusiveness. In 1987, Mary Hopkins became national administrator, with Essie Karp as assistant administrator.

These efforts were continued under art historian and educator Christine Havice (1988–1990), the organization's ninth president, who attempted to reach out to other women's professional organizations to improve national communication and inter-chapter collaboration. Working with other national organizations such as Artists' Equity Association, the WCA organized national lobbying efforts in support of artists' tax rights and freedom of expression. By 1990, there were 37 chapters; the WCA was a founding member of the National Network of Women's Caucuses and Organizations. More exotic groups had developed that kept the fires alight for social change: the witty Guerrilla Girls, the satirical Sister Serpents, the Women of Color Caucus (WoCA), and Vistas Latinas, the later two both demanding racial as well as gender parity. In 1990, Flo Oy Wong and Betty Kano co-founded the Asian American Women Artists Association (AAWAA) in Northern California, which eventually to led to the founding of another fiery group called Godzilla in both New York and San Francisco.

After the unfortunate death of tenth WCA President Carol Neiman in March 1990, artist Iona Deering of Dallas (1990–1992) became the organization's eleventh president. She worked with Board member Helen Solomons to develop and strengthen the WCA Board of Directors and the internal structure with aims of inclusivity and a better financial base. The important development of a "Board Manual" standardized procedures for all chapters. She implemented organized lobbying against censorship and promoted support for the National Endowment for the Arts. Many young women were now refusing to call themselves "feminists," especially in the art schools. The feeling that all the problems had been solved was now linked with a backlash; often the young women felt they would not be shown in the mainstream art galleries if they proclaimed their feminist sympathies.

Expansion

With the twentieth anniversary of the WCA in 1992, the twelfth president artist Jean Towgood (1992–1994) urged a recommitment to the feminist ideals that marked the organization's founding. Other groups such as the dynamic Women's Action Coalition and NOW tackled the non-art social problems of women with increasing fervor. Jo Hockenhull, national vice president, said, "I recall the 90s as an exciting and experimental time. The presidents and Boards were very ambitious for the Caucus. We took risks that in the long run enriched many lives and brought to light amazing artworks."[67] Muriel Magenta called on teachers in art schools to start WCA Student Chapters on their campuses. Several were formed; many members were enthusiastic, especially as the student members moved into the regular chapters. As student members paid lesser dues, however, the WCA Board felt they were not paying their way, and in 2001 cancelled all student chapters.

Towgood's leadership goals included greater visibility as an organization and a membership whose diversity reflected national demographics. She increased the number of women of color in leadership positions. Imna Arroyo assumed the position of Vice-President of Women of Color in 1993.[68] The Women of Color in the Arts (WoCA) slide series, curated by prominent arts professionals, was realized after years of effort by Flo Oy Wong and Eleanor Merritt.[69] This was a very expensive project published (paid for) by the Universal Color Slide Company in 1997 with the WCA paying $3,000 for the services of eight curators as jurors. This was intended for sale to teachers, museums, and artist slide companies; few purchased the series initially but sales continue each year.[70] Wong noted that a primary result of WoCA was the formation of many groups of women of color such as the AAWAA, and the empowerment of various communities such as Mexican Americans and Latinas. She said, "The dialogue began. We had to help each other before we joined the larger group. WCA was very instrumental in bringing women artists to the consciousness of the art public."[71] The Board worked hard to attract more working class women and women of color to its leadership; they brought with them diverse views and perspectives.

Foreign travel became an exciting way to increase international activism in the WCA with a trip to the 1995 International Conference on Women and NGO Forum of the United Nations in China, the Fourth World Conference on Women. Chaired by Jo Hockenhull and led by artist and educator Helen Klebesadel, the thirteenth president (1994–1996), this trip of 99 women and one man (from the United States, Canada, and Mexico), traveled across China, meeting with Chinese women artists, and visiting art colleges and universities. The Chinese government gave permits for the Chinese women to attend the conference and participate, but the women did not come. Flo Oy Wong was invaluable in advising on cultural issues and language; she moderated one panel "Asian-American Women Artists" and co-curated the WCA exhibition there with Joyce Koskenmaki.[72] All 100 members of the Caucus on this trip came together for the NGO forum, joining 35,000 other women and men from across the globe dedicated to recognizing women's rights as human rights. Many presented papers, workshops, performances, shows, and events on human rights issues.[73] Jaiyi Ling, WCA student member, was invaluable in keeping communications flowing. This was an exciting and important moment for the Caucus! The outcome of the global connections can be documented in the amazing number of regional conferences, exhibits, lectures and other events held in the U.S. after the UN/NGO Conference in China.[74]

Noreen Dean Dresser noted that "[t]he volunteer WCA Board spanned the country and only met twice a year. While new ideas and energy were evident in the fresh vision, the careful follow through of advanced fundraising, hiring of experienced staff and financial prudence was not."[75] Margaret Lutze elaborates that "[t]here were 3,300 members at that time; the budget was $130,000."[76] Inflated figures showed that $175,525 was budgeted but losses were $27,000 and budgets were over run, especially the annual conference. A new computer system was installed in the office to deal with an increased membership. The chapters now numbered 30 (plus three remaining Student Chapters) and the membership hovered between 3,000 and 6,000. The annual budget averaged $100,000.[77] President Arroyo cautioned, however:

> There was a problem with inefficiency with the accounting system in the national office…There was also a problem getting accurate membership numbers because of the way the national office functioned. The reports were never accurate because of the way we collected the dues. National did the bookkeeping by hand and sent the information to the company. So we

> never had accurate accounting of the money or the membership. Moreover, an outside accountant had not audited the WCA for over 15 years...The first order of business I did was to hire a bookkeeper to begin to create categories and in-put the expenses and generate the reports.[78]

The long-term treasurer, Sandy Knell Tamny (1989–1995), resigned.

Troubles and Challenges

A very difficult period almost ended the existence of the Women's Caucus. National officers felt strongly about, and worked hard to increase the demographic and socio-economic diversity of women on the Board of the WCA, even some with no experience in the WCA or any similar boards, but who had credibility with under-represented constituencies. Dresser commented that "[f]eminist ideals fueled inclusion and prompted solidarity, but Board members failed to track expenses against income in their idealism."[79] Some members that would experience financial hardship were paid to attend Board meetings and WCA national conferences; many expenses and phone bills were reimbursed; committees had large budgets. One of the major ongoing expenses of the organization was its annual National Honor Awards given out at the annual conferences. As the only organization recognizing outstanding women in the arts, the WCA was committed to honoring senior United States women artists and art historians with a major exhibition, an extensive catalog and an awards ceremony. The national honorees (usually six) and their companions were honored and their expenses paid including air travel and hotels.[80] This was a major financial burden for WCA, which was not always offset by the income from the conference. This Annual Conference in 1995 was budgeted at $46,015, and overran that by a third.[81]

This period was a coming of age for the WCA, and a major test of a women's organization to face extreme problems and overcome them. A national Board with little experience in management of money or organization, but with strong desires to help others, can cause havoc in a short time. The national administrator said that "it was frightening to see how fast the money went!"[82]

Artist Imna Arroyo was elected the fourteenth president (1996–1998). She said:

> When I became President, I inherited an organization that was spending beyond its means, living very much hand to mouth in that all the revenue that came in was used to pay bills and other obligations which the previous administration's policies had instituted (such as Honoree expenses, Board

> reimbursements etc.) The organization had become bloated with expenses, and was teetering on the edge of insolvency well before I took over …Because I d[id] not have financial expertise, I recruited Matilde Bingemer to join the Board. She was a senior executive at Chase Bank, an experienced financial analyst and volunteer. Her main job was to look at the organization's finances and plan for the short and long term financial security of the WCA. She recommended that the WCA get a financial audit from a CPA firm…she prepared standard financial reports such as Profit and Loss Reports, Account Balance sheets, etc. Further, Matilde was the first person to sound the alarm about the financial state of the WCA at the Boston Conference. She told the entire Board…I went to work on moving the office, standardizing the WCA accounting practices and planning the conferences.[83]

An Endowment Fund of $10,000 was established as proposed by Susan Grabel, president of the New York Caucus, and chair of the 1994 national conference in New York. "We sold art at the conference to fund it."[84]

The 1997 National WCA Conference was held in Philadelphia with no local chapter in charge. The two conference coordinators had little prior experience on how to organize it, and worked with Essie Karp as the new director of special events (fundraising.) Plans had been made in 1995 to hold a shorter conference celebrating the twenty-fifth birthday of the WCA, since the annual CAA Conference would be held in New York that year; this made it difficult for academic members to attend both events.[85] As a result of trouble with the Philadelphia printer, no fall conference announcements, labels, or membership applications were sent out to the membership; when they were mailed just before the February conference, it was too late: few came. It was a disaster. The WCA had signed contracts with the hotel, the caterer, and the printer, and had all the costs of a conference but few attendees to pay the bills. The long-time WCA administrator, Essie Karp, said she felt forced out.[86] Matilde Bingemer, the financial specialist and a volunteer, was chosen to replace her.[87] Susan Grabel, a Board member, and also as a volunteer, then became the treasurer to replace Sandy Tamny. The Board insisted on proceeding with the Toronto conference, with Susan Platt as the chair, and tried to raise money in various ways to cover a minimal conference.[88]

The chapters felt overlooked and neglected as the National WCA now looked to New York believing "the action was there."[89] President Arroyo proposed and the Board agreed to give up the national office ($250 month) at Philadelphia's Moore College of Art; the College wanted this space back for renovation. The choice for WCA was elsewhere on the campus: Philadelphia, New York, or where? Arroyo described, "The CAA Conference was taking place every other year in New York, so it made sense to have the organization close by to support the annual meeting."[90] Increasing the prestige of being a national organization, the Board had announced to the membership their future access to a gallery in New York. The Board voted to move to a New York space at 625 Broadway, Suite 810 (at $750 month).[91] The announced "gallery" was an unsupervised long hallway outside the office. The Board did have two exhibitions there of small works for sale by members as a donation to help the WCA, as there was now substantial rent to be paid monthly. Fortunately, there were many sales.

A great deal of "stuff" was trucked to New York, especially old catalogues. Many were packaged together and mailed out to the membership. After this move, almost all of the library, the archives, files, and records of the WCA were at first dumped temporarily in a storage room, with Essie Karp commenting that "the office looked ransacked."[92] Among these records were three boxes containing the research of the Lifetime Achievement Awards Committee.[93] In the midst of the chaos of moving, organizing a new office, and setting up the new computer, the Board and President needed to hire a new national administrator, and turned to one highly recommended by a New York Agency. This person was careless at best and had unfortunate associations at the worst;[94] under her supervision, a large number of things was stolen. All the computers were taken from WCA, and other businesses in the suite, along with two discs of the entire database of the WCA, assorted software, records of credit card information, keys, access codes, about $5,000, and 30 checks from members—everything of value.[95] Reluctant to follow the recommendations of the bank, landlord, and Board, Treasurer Bingemer first confirmed the facts with the administrator, then informed her that she was fired, took her keys and searched a folder from her bag as she was leaving; she discovered therein a large amount of WCA mail, forms, and other valuables! The police were called and given a long list of the missing items.[96] To compound this tragedy, when her final check was withheld, the administrator sued the WCA for her pay.

Retrenching

A new national administrator was needed.[97] Grabel said:

> Isis (Mattei) was hired after the disastrous experience with the previous administrator, when WCA needed someone they could trust in a hurry. (Mattei had worked as President's Assistant to Arroyo [her mother] so was trustworthy and familiar with the WCA.) We spent a lot of time and effort

reconstructing the chapter lists and inputting the 1997 and 1996 financial records.[98]

Denise Mumm was hired on a part time basis.

With almost all of the treasury spent, little left of the office, business and membership records gone with the computer, most bills unpaid, insurance unpaid (so there was no coverage for the thefts), no money to pay the rent, and lots of debt owed to creditors, the national office was closed.[99] A crisis meeting of the executive committee of the Board (Imna Arroyo, C.J. Lori, Sharon Vatsky, and Isis Mattei) was held on March 28, 1997, to decide what to do next. After meeting with an accountant and restructuring the accounts, they were urged to contact the creditors and call the Volunteer Lawyers of America (VLA) to arrange a consultation.[100] The June Board meeting had to decide now whether to shut down the WCA, declare bankruptcy, or rescue the organization. A decision was made at first to choose to go bankrupt. Arroyo called past presidents for their advice: some said "Let it go: it's fulfilled the mission." The next day after careful discussion of the benefits and difficulties—and what would be lost if the WCA collapsed—this was reversed. They decided to try to rescue WCA. Gail Tremblay proposed an auction and was given six months to do it working with Bernice Steinbaum. President Arroyo said:

> All the decisions that were made during my time as President were made in good faith. They were transparent, information was communicated to the Board . . . There was nothing done that was not done with the WCA's well being at heart and at mind. We operated with integrity and dignity at one of the most difficult times in our professional histories because we believed in the WCA; we were devoted to its missions and because we were determined to keep it alive.[101]

Susan Grabel obtained an attorney through the Volunteer Lawyers for the Arts, Giorgio Bovenzi of Skadden, Arps, Slate, Meagher, and Flom, LLP (a major restructuring law firm), who negotiated with all the creditors and worked out a repayment schedule. Susan Platt changed the Toronto Conference to a new model of working with Canadian groups (such as Women's Art Resource Center in Toronto) that had support from the Ministry of Culture in Canada. Contributions also helped in avoiding the usual costs of a conference.[102] "The Executive Committee did an enormous amount of work paying the bills, the lawyer and moving. Imna Arroyo, C.J. Lori, Sharon Vatsky and Susan Grabel worked for months on day-to-day stuff. I was on the phone every day to the attorney," said Grabel. She added, "He had a lot of experience; he was able to calm down the creditors. He got an 80 percent reduction from the printer and 30 percent from the others; and we were able to pay back salaries to Karp and Mattei."[103] Imna Arroya elaborates, "Then a transitional group was created to empower the membership to change from a centralized organization to decentralized chapters; a Web site was set up for communication instead of newsletters."[104] Essie Karps adds, "Gail Tremblay and others (Klebesadel and Amy Bethel) sent out desperate letters to the membership to help![105] Arroyo led a trip to Mexico, and Tremblay led one to China, as fundraisers, but they only broke even. At that time, the organization was $40,000 in debt. Grabel said:

> Denise Mumm, the new National Administrator, and I worked together to finish entering the 1996 books toward the goal of getting audited books (a necessity for getting grants). We spent hours and hours culling the ledgers…the books were as good as was possible under the difficult circumstances. Many members helped."[106]

In October 1997, Gail Tremblay organized an auction at the Fiddlehead Restaurant in Portland, Oregon, which raised $6,483. Many chapters held fund-raising events to help National. The WCA Board held an auction November 7, 1997, at the Bernice Steinbaum Krauss Gallery in New York, organized by Gail Tremblay[107] and thereby raised $19,000. Many artists who donated works to the auction were famous women such as Jaune Quick-To-See Smith, and Elizabeth Catlett, showing their thanks to the WCA for all that was done toward making women artists of color better known in the art world. Another $16,000 was raised through direct contributions. "The Endowment was used also," to pay expenses and creditors in the last months of the crisis."[108]

This period of financial crisis for the Caucus was a dark moment of the soul, even for the great numbers of members across the country who were unaware of the problems faced by a volunteer national Board. Certainly they were tested by fire—and the consequences were not play money. Few boards, even with experience, could have overcome the triple threat of a financially disastrous national conference, a sudden and expensive move of the national office, and theft of all of the organization's business records, membership records, archives, checks, and computer equipment, leaving the whole organization deeply in debt. In debt financially, yes, and yet this volunteer Board chose to deal with the problems, to acknowledge the debts, and to save the honor of the organization.

Recovery

Upset and uncomprehending, nevertheless the WCA members rallied to the organization's defense and sent in money and offers of help. Board members Magi (Bollock) Amma, Catherine Carilli, and Amy Bethel initially, along with Gail Tremblay and new member Margaret Lutze, formed a Transitional Leadership Committee. The last creditor would be paid off on February 15, 1998.[109] Amma was the first president-elect, and she and Tremblay worked as transitional leaders. Then, artist Gail Tremblay was appointed by the Board as the fifteenth president (1999); her job was to try to resuscitate the WCA. The membership demanded answers, and many refused to renew their memberships; however, under Tremblay's leadership slowly things began to turn around. There was a great reservoir of trust in the membership, which sensed the importance and integrity of the WCA.

In 1999, the Annual Conference was scheduled to be held in Los Angeles concurrent with the CAA Annual Conference. With the national office in disarray Jean Towgood flew to New York and told the Board that the Los Angeles Chapter under Pres. Ada Brown would take on the responsibility of mounting the next National Conference in Los Angeles. The burden of this was enormous: the whole chapter worked hard at raising money and planning all aspects of an elaborate conference in a very short time. To establish credit (with the hotels, the printers, the restaurants…) Jean Towgood even mortgaged her house! The Chapter decided to nominate Lifetime Achievement Awardees of their own choosing as there was no longer a National Committee (or records) in place to do this. They mounted such an elaborate conference that they even made a profit on it and sent a donation of $3,000 to National WCA to help them out financially.

In 2000–2002, artist Magi Amma became the sixteenth president for a complete two-year term and embarked on a massive effort to rebuild the Caucus, especially reinstating the Lifetime Achievement Awards. This involved an enormous amount of work on her part with the help of an invigorated dynamic Board, and the scrupulous financial control by this Board that reviewed all financial reports. A Web site was continued with online news notification, and the newsletter was restarted.[110] The lifetime achievement awards were reinstituted after a gap of a few years, with a large complete list of potential honorees over 70 years old. A new National Office was set up temporarily in Santa Cruz, California, and a new National Administrator, Dana Spanierman, was hired to develop computer databases.[111] The WCA maintained its NGO status with the

United Nations. Eighteen members paid for and went on an exciting (and fundraising) trip to Nepal and Northern India managed by Helen Newman.

Restructuring

After these two strenuous years of Amma's presidency, she left the office with the Caucus in the black, having—amazingly—a treasury of $30,000. In 2002, artist and administrator Noreen Dean Dresser became the seventeenth president (2002–2004). It was decided by Dresser, with Board approval, to move the national office back to New York. Space was rented there, and a new national administrator, Karin Luner, brought professional computer organization to the office. It took some time to get, and update, the files from the California office.[112]

President Dresser set up, with the Board's approval, many internal controls so that no national officer would receive compensation of any kind: travel and Board costs were an individual's responsibility. Matching funds for multi-chapter and regional projects were doubled. Fundraising for the national awards and special projects was made a group responsibility, both for chapters and the Board. Dresser said she "pushed for involvement and recognition of younger women both in her Board appointments and committee assignments. Dr. Laurie E. T. Hall was appointed to the NGO and international committee of the United Nations." Visiting every region at her own expense, Dresser promoted changes "bringing credibility to the national office. The planned Matrix Project was an especial focus, using the unique quality of the chapters to encourage members to understand the business of art."[113]

The work and talents of the WCA National Administrators have been an essential and valuable force in the constant reorganization of the WCA. Chosen for her skills and moral trust, Karin Luner in 2002 commented "there were 750 paying members . . . it was sheer mayhem." She pushed to "have the organization function again in its infrastructure, reestablishing trust between the chapters and national, establishing new lines of communication, creating a file system that worked." She "made the databases, got health insurance, made the '*Artlines* Newsletter' and 'Catalogue' and saved the organization thousands of dollars." As with other National Administrators, she "sat on the pulse of what was needed to move the WCA forward."[114]

Dena Muller, a young professional arts manager, was chosen to become the eighteenth President (2004–2006). She brought special skills to this office as Director of the A.I.R. Gallery in New York, well known as the first artist-run, not-for-profit gallery for women artists in the United

States. Muller and Luner concentrated on reforming the structure of the WCA, expanding membership benefits, and improving the content of the *Artlines* newsletter and the national Web site. The Endowment continued its growth and potential for Caucus stability. Muller established a formal collaboration with Rutgers University, including the WCA national office on their campus. Once again placed solidly within the current feminist agenda, Muller made bold moves into the future such as developing an alliance with the CAA Committee for Women in the Arts to co-host the annual awards ceremonies of both in 2007. At this time, there were 30 active chapters with 90 percent of the 1,430 members within a chapter.

The present leader of the WCA is the nineteenth President, educator Jennifer Colby, (2006–2008). She has a PhD in humanities, a master's degree in art, and a master's degree in theology. Jennifer was director of the Bade Museum, and is lecturer at California State University, artist, gallery owner and co-founder of the Monterey Bay Chapter. The focus of her presidency is to bring the WCA and all the chapters up to date in non-profit management practices. [115] The twentieth president (2008–2010) will be Marilyn J. Hayes, artist and manager. Trained in the social sciences, she put her skills to work for many years managing programs and staff at the Equal Employment Opportunity Commission. A special need and skill was "empowering people to successfully embrace change." She served as an effective president of the Washington, DC, WCA chapter and will focus her future efforts as National President of the Caucus on developing additional sources of income and effective partnerships with other organizations. The Caucus is once again in unusually talented hands.

The chapters of the WCA had discovered that mounting exhibitions was a useful way to build up membership, especially among younger artists hungry for recognition. WCA exhibitions continue to differ greatly from the exhibitions of the genteel ladies' groups in the 1950s and 1960s. They tend to have a political point, or moral, such as a recent one proposed by Rusty Cantor and toured by NCWCA called Violence Against Women—Women Against Violence, saying, "We are concerned deeply with the violence that permeates all aspects of our lives."[116] The chapters also had stringent rules against censorship, and presented work that more timid galleries and museums avoided.

The Leaders

The Presidents of the WCA have been a very interesting group: professional, passionate feminists at a high level of achievement in their profession, whether studio art, art history, teaching, or writing. Their enthusiastic leadership and their enormous passion for justice and parity in the arts have made the difference in the longevity of this unusual organization, sustaining it for over 35 years.

The Future

Looking back at 35 years since the WCA began in the anger and frustration of an ignored, yet important—even majority—group within the art world, we can say that it has achieved and surpassed its goals of that time. As it tackled its major aim—to monitor and change the patterns of gender discrimination in the field of art and especially art history—it also found it urgent to present and reassess the achievements of women artists of the past and to determine if their contributions differed in some fundamental way from the achievements of male artists of their period. And as these goals were being met by art historians and artists working together, the organization found another more fundamental reason for being. Its purpose now was to gather together to train, foster, and develop professionalism, pride, and respectful collaboration in all women artists and art historians so that our past may be prologue to the new challenges of our chaotic world and nation.[117]

---

[1] Ann Sutherland Harris, e-mail to author, October 26, 2006.

[2] Rosalind Rosenberg, "The Woman Question," in *The Colombia History of the Twentieth Century*, Richard W. Bulliet ed., (Colombia University Press, 1998).

[3] Eleanor Dickinson, "U. S. Census," Paper presented at *Statistics: Discrimination in the Art Field,* State of California Commission on the Status of Women, Los Angeles, California, February 24, 1987; and CWAO Panel, College Art Association, February 15, 1990.

[4] Eleanor Dickinson, "Interview with H. W. Janson, February 1, 1979," College Art Association, *Women Artists News,* September/October 1979, 12.

[5] Ibid.

[6] Norma Broude, *Feminism and Art History: Questioning the Litany*, (New York: Harper and Row, 1982), 15.

[7] Brice Marden, Wall comments, San Francisco Museum of Modern Art, 2007.

[8] Alessandra Comini, WCA Conference Address. Los Angeles, California, February 13, 1985.

[9] Fresno Art Museum, "A Personal Perspective: the First Feminist Art Class," Fresno State College, 1970–1971, (*Eighteen Profiles,* 2006.)

[10] "W.E.B—west east bag." (Newsletter, New York, June 1972).

[11] Patricia Tavenner and Jo Hanson, "The Early Years: History and Performance," (University of California, Berkeley, The University Museum, March 23, 2000).

[12] Judith Brodsky, "Exhibitions, Galleries, and Alternative Spaces" in *The Power of Feminist Art*, Norma Broude and Mary D. Garrard eds., (New York: Harry N. Abrams, Inc. 1994), 106.
[13] Faith Wilding, "The Feminist Art Program" in *The Power of Feminist Art*, Norma Broude and Mary D. Garrard eds., (New York: Harry N. Abrams, Inc. 1994), 39. Judith Brodsky, *In Passionate Pursuit*, (Douglass Library, Rutgers University, New Brunswick, New Jersey, September 12, 2006).
[14]Arlene Raven, "Womanhouse," in *The Power of Feminist Art,* Norma Broude and Mary D. Garrard eds., (Harry N. Abrams, Inc. 1994), 58.
[15] Ibid.
[16] Norma Broude and Mary D. Garrard, "Introduction," in *The Power of Feminist Art*, Norma Broude and Mary D. Garrard eds., (New York: Harry N. Abrams, Inc., Publishers. 1994), 22.
[17] Arlene Raven. "Womanhouse," in *The Power of Feminist Art*, Norma Broude and Mary D. Garrard eds., (New York: Harry N. Abrams, Inc., Publishers. 1994), 48.
[18] "W.E.B." June, 1972, 1.
[19] *ARTNews* 9, (1969).
[20] Linda Nochlin. "Starting from Scratch: the Beginnings of Feminist Art History," *The Power of Feminist Art* in *The Power of Feminist Art*, Norma Broude and Mary D. Garrard eds., (New York: Harry N. Abrams, Inc., Publishers. 1994), 135. Marilyn Stokstad, *Art History, Revised Edition*, vol. 2. Prentice Hall, (New York: Harry N. Abrams, 1999), 1146.
[21] "W.E.B." June, 1972, 1.
[22] June Wayne, interview December 3, 2006; e-mail to author, December 5, 2006.
[23] Mary D. Garrard, "Feminists Politics," in *The Power of Feminist Art*, Norma Broude and Mary D. Garrard eds., (New York: Harry N. Abrams, Inc., Publishers. 1994), 93.
[24] Judith E. Stein, quoted in "Collaboration," in *The Power of Feminist Art*, Norma Broude and Mary D. Garrard eds., (New York: Harry N. Abrams, Inc., Publishers. 1994), 245.
[25] Mission Statement, College Art Association, 2006.
[26] Ann Sutherland Harris, e-mail to author, October 26, 2006.
[27] Broude and Garrard, *The Power of Feminist Art*, 94.
[28] Ann Sutherland Harris, e-mail to author, October 24, 2006.
[29] Patricia Tavenner, telephone interview with author, July 23, 2006.
[30] Ann Sutherland Harris, e-mail to author, October 26, 2006.
[31] Ibid.
[32] Broude and Garrard, *The Power of Feminist Art*, 94.
[33] Mary Garrard, e-mail to author, October 9, 2006.
[34] Sheila McNally, "CAA Committee on the Status of Women," *WCA Newsletter* 8 (1978), 17.
[35] Dorothy Gillespie, telephone interview with author, September 29, 2006.
[36] Broude and Garrard, *Power of Feminist Art*, 94.
[37] Mary Garrard, e-mail to author. October 9, 2006.

[38] Gil Edelson, Legal Counsel to the CAA, telephone interview with author, April 29, 2006.
[39] Letters of Incorporation, National Office, WCA, New York.
[40] Lee Ann Miller, telephone interview with author, December 3, 2006.
[41] Patricia Tavenner, telephone interview with author, July 23, 2006.
[42] Jo Hanson, *The Early Years: Origins of the WCA*, University Museum, University of California, Berkeley, March 23, 2000, 12.
[43] Broude and Garrard, "Introduction," *Power of Feminist Art,* 29.
[44] Judith Brodsky, *In Passionate Pursuit*, 49.
[45] June Wayne, "Sex Differentials in Art Exhibition Reviews," and "Tamarind Issues Bias Report," *Feminist Art Journal*, (April 1, 1972).
[46] Eleanor Dickinson, "Statistics: Discrimination in the Art Field," 1972–2007, to present.
[47] "The Woman's Caucus for Art: Purpose and History," (National Women's Caucus for Art, New York, 1992). 1–2.
[48] Ibid.
[49] Emmanuel Lemakis, College Art Association, e-mail to author, December 1, 2006.
[50] Eleanor Dickinson, *Statistics,* (1978) and *CWAO NEWS*, August 1985.
[51] The Coalition of Women's Art Organizations, Material furnished to officers, 1977. "Papers of Eleanor Dickinson," Archives of American Art, Smithsonian Institution. www.aaa.si.edu/collections/oralhistories/transcripts/dickin00.htm#top. Access date June 10, 2007. See also essay by Susan King and the appendix for a complete listing of WCA Lifetime Achievement Award recipients.
[52] Lee Anne Miller, e-mail to author. December 3, 2006. See Appendix for complete list of WCA Lifetime Achievement Award Honorees.
[53] *WCA Newsletter* 8, no. 2–3 (Spring 1979), 1-2.
[54] Charlotte Robinson, letter describing the ceremony, January 1979.
[55] Ibid.
[56] Charlotte Robinson, telephone interview with author, September 29, 2006.
[57] Judith E. Stein, "Collaboration," in *The Power of Feminist Art*, ed. Norma Broude and Mary D. Garrard, 226-245, (New York: Harry N. Abrams, Inc., Publishers. 1994), 235.
[58] The Woman's Caucus for Art: Purpose and History," National WCA, New York, 1992.
[59] Nancy Cusick, telephone interview with author, September 29, 2006.
[60] DeRenne Coerr, e-mail to author, December 6, 2006.
[61] Ibid.
[62] Katy Dickinson, telephone interview with author, October 1, 2006.
[63] "The Woman's Caucus for Art: Purpose and History," National WCA, New York, 1992. 1–2
[64] Muriel Magenta, e-mail to author, October 25, 2006.
[65] "The Woman's Caucus for Art: Purpose and History," National WCA, New York, 1992. 1–2.
[66] Ibid.

[67] Jo Hockenhull, e-mail to author, May 31, 2007.
[68] Susan Platt,.e-mail to author, May 30, 2007.
[69] "The Woman's Caucus for Art: Purpose and History", 1–2.
[70] Essie Karp, National Administrator (1987–97), telephone interview with author, November 19, 2006.
[71] Flo Oy Wong, Interview with author, January 3, 2007.
[72] Ibid.
[73] Susan Platt, e-mail to author, June 3, 2007.
[74] Jo Hockenhull, e-mail to author, May 29, 2007.
[75] Noreen Dean Dresser,.e-mail to author, May 29, 2007.
[76] Margaret Lutze, WCA Treasurer 2000–2007, interview with author, July 28, 2006.
[77] WCA Balance sheets, 1994–95.
[78] Ibid.
[79] Dresser,.e-mail to author, May 29, 2007.
[80] WCA 1994–95 Budget, July 20, 1995.
[81] Essie Karp, National Administrator, telephone interview with author, October 24, 2006.
[82] Ibid.
[83] Arroyo, e-mail to author, May 30, 2007.
[84] Susan Grabel, telephone interview with author, January 1, 2007.
[85] WCA Officers. "Summaries of Mid-Year Board Reports," July 1995, 17.
[86] Essie Karp, telephone interview with author, October 24, 2006.
[87] Karin Luner, Margaret Lutze, and Ruth Waters, interview with author, July 28, 2006.
[88] Susan Grabel, telephone interview with author, January 1, 2007.
[89] Ibid.
[90] Imna Arroyo, e-mail to author sent by Susan Platt, May 30, 2007.
[91] Essie Karp, telephone interview with author, October 24, 2006.
[92]Karp, telephone interview with author, November 19, 2006; Luner, Waters, and Lutze, interview with author, July 28, 2006.
[93] Charleen Touchette, telephone interview with author, 2001.
[94] Sarah Caruth Agreement with WCA, New York Department of Labor Authorization, August, 22, 1997.
[95] Matilde Bingemer, Letter to State of New Jersey, November 25, 1996, and letter to Department of Labor, New York, February 24, 1997.
[96] Matilde L. Bingemer, "National Office situation," WCA Memorandum, November 14, 1996.
[97] Susan Grabel, telephone interview with author, January 1, 2007.
[98] Grabel, e-mail to author, January 17, 2007.
[99] WCA balance sheets, statement of the WCA Treasurer, 1998.
[100] Grabel, e-mail to author, January 18, 2007.
[101] Arroyo, e-mail to author, May 30, 2007.
[102] Arroyo, e-mail to author. June 3, 2007.
[103] Grabel, telephone interview with author, January 1, 2007.

[104] Arroyo, telephone interview with author, June 1, 2007.
[105] Essie Karp, telephone interview with author, October 24, 2006.
[106] Grabel, telephone interview with author, January 1, 2007.
[107] Grabel, "1997 WCA Fiscal Crisis Summary," WCA National Office, 1997.
[108] Grabel, e-mail to author, January 4, 2007.
[109] Grabel, "1997 WCA Fiscal Crisis Summary," National Office, 1997.
[110] Magi Amma, e-mail to author, November 27, 2006.
[111] Waters, Lutze, and Luner, interview with author, July 28, 2006.
[112] Lutze, telephone interview with author, July 28, 2006.
[113] Dresser, e-mail to author, November 16, 2006.
[114] Luner, e-mails to author, October 30, 2006 to November 2, 2006.
[115] Jennifer Colby, telephone interview with author, November 10, 2006.
[116] Northern California WCA publicity card, Louie Meager Art Gallery, Ohlone College, 2006.
[117] Additional copy-edit assistance of this report provided by Barbara Benziger.

Works Cited

Norma Broude and Mary D. Garrard, eds. *The Power of Feminist Art*, (New York: Harry N. Abrams, Inc. 1994).

Norma Broude, *Feminism and Art History: Questioning the Litany* (New York: Harper and Row, 1982).

Eleanor Dickinson, "Interview with H. W. Janson, February 1, 1979," College Art Association, *Women Artists News,* September/October 1979.

Fresno Art Museum, "A Personal Perspective: the First Feminist Art Class," Fresno State College, 1970–1971, *Eighteen Profiles* (Fresno State College, 2006.)

Rosalind Rosenberg, "The Woman Question," in *The Columbia History of the Twentieth Century*, Richard W. Bulliet ed. (Columbia University Press, 1998).

Patricia Tavenner and Jo Hanson, "The Early Years: History and Performance," (The University Museum, University of California, Berkeley, March 23, 2000).

June Wayne, "Sex Differentials in Art Exhibition Reviews," *Feminist Art Journal*, (April 1, 1972).

THE COLOR IS GREEN: ART, WOMEN, AND THE ART MARKET

NOREEN DEAN DRESSER
AND LAURIE ELIZABETH TALBOT HALL

Setting the Direction—Noreen Dean Dresser

At the time of the founding of the Women's Caucus for Art (WCA) in 1972, the initial feminist goals were identifying and increasing female opportunities in studio art and art history for students and professors in the College Art Association (CAA). Feminist art historians expanded the pedagogical discussion of the accepted canon that had excluded women artists. The feminist perspective transformed the discussion and opened the art canon revealing the social constructs that defined art objects. Feminism further delineated the hierarchical ordering of society's cultural assets and viewpoints. The interfacing of issues of color and ethnicity with the role of gender redefined the discourse and reshaped the visual arts.

As this wave of cultural revision washed over the twentieth century's final decades, the number and variety of galleries, publications, and museums exploded. Comparing 1990 to 2003 provides an indication of the successes the feminist-directed effort achieved.[1] Gender discrimination reports by Eleanor Dickinson cite an increase in art degrees awarded to women from 53.1 percent to 63.3 percent.[2] The percentage of United States Art Grants and Fellowships awarded to women increased from 27 percent to 37 percent. The proportion of faculty positions held by women increased from 20 percent to 27.8 percent. Women represented 58.7 percent of artists exhibiting in Juried Exhibitions (open call) as opposed to 47 percent in 1990. In art textbooks in 2003, work by women made up 12 percent of the illustrations rather than the 3.3 percent seen in 1990. Advances in the achievement of women as art professionals reflect changes for women in general in the U. S. workforce. The changes are in the desired direction but are minimal when we consider the magnitude of inequity that must be eliminated. The textbook illustrations of art by women, for example, did improve from 3.3 percent to 12.0 percent. This change does not accurately reflect, however, the relative number of women artists. The same gap emerges in invitational exhibitions versus open calls, where women received 19 percent of exhibition opportunities and men 81 percent in 2003.[3] If we want women to move from model and object to the creator and shaper of the cultural discourse, significantly greater numbers of women artists will need to be reflected in corporate and private collections, museum exhibitions, and published commentary.

Women's roles as wives and mothers viewed through cultural lenses, at the micro level of family, have monumental consequences in political, social, and economic alliances. The cultural debate on women's roles in family is rippling across and redrawing boundaries through both regional wars and economic development. Women artists and art professionals have a significant international opportunity and responsibility to influence and to critique culture. A requirement for women's achievement of power in the field of art is for women to know the map of the art market and to have opportunities to enter and influence it.

During my presidency of the National WCA, cognizant of the vitality of local markets, I initiated the Matrix Project. This project is a strategy for building an ongoing network for accessing and increasing women's cultural assets in the visual arts. We asked members in our then 30 plus chapters spanning the United States to interview curators, gallery directors, collectors, foundations, and publishers with the intent of mapping their local markets. The Matrix Web site, created by information supplied by individual artists and art historians regarding regional opportunities, feeds current information into a national/international grid. This web-grid updates regional source material and produces articles for the *Artlines* publication of the WCA. *Artlines* then distributes timely pertinent art market information across the United States in print and on the web.

This essay is meant to be an indispensible forum for linking the feminist discourse on the making of art, to women's actual access to the art market. In order for feminist art to have access to exhibition venues and to influence the cultural dialogue, such art must interact with contemporary perspectives on exhibition opportunities, raise questions about approaching collections, and consider the role collections and exhibitions play in validating cultural viewpoints. In addition, we must consider the psychological factors influencing women's relationship to achievement.

The economics of art and how art is valued within the art world are critical components to understanding one's place in our postmodern world of cultural globalization and media markets. We had the opportunity to hear from Joyce Cohen, PhD, an art historian at Simmons College in Boston, Massachusetts, and former art advisor to corporate and private collectors. On our Boston panel, Dr. Cohen discussed the importance of corporate collections as opportunities for sales and visibility. Dr. Cohen recommends that artists establish a relationship with an advisor/consultant. She advocates choosing a consultant who bills for his or her time rather than one who charges a percentage of the sale. In this way, the consultant does not sell art or profit from a mark up but acts as an intermediary between artist and buyer. The "gate keepers" for corporate collections include art advisors in the Association of Corporate Art Advisors, the Association of Corporate Art Managers, and those recommended by local galleries and museums. Dr. Cohen also emphasized the importance of artists establishing a presence for their art in online galleries and the need for intelligent, coherent written statements about the work.

Gallery director Randi Hopkins also participated, sharing her keen perceptions on the art market. She is the co-director of Allston Skirt Gallery, a contemporary art gallery in Boston that she founded in 1999 with Beth Kantrowitz. Randi Hopkins also writes a weekly column previewing upcoming exhibitions for *The Boston Phoenix*. Hopkins emphasizes that every gallery develops a particular viewpoint or aesthetic, and that this is an ongoing, evolutionary process, one that is critical to the gallery's success. Hopkins' focus is emerging national and international artists. Being that her artists did not appeal to the more traditional Boston art collector, Hopkins sought to build a new collector base for her artists. Through outreach, education and the establishment of personal relationships, she succeeded. Hopkins offered insights into the changing face of art collecting in an art world that is now truly global. The current commercial art world involves art fairs and biennials from Johannesburg to Dubai, and peripatetic, nomadic independent curators. On-line galleries and blogs increase the opportunities for exposure. Hopkins articulated that artists must represent themselves, bringing quality work to the market, and actively promoting their own interests.

Response: Self-Efficacy and the Business of Art —Laurie Elizabeth Talbot Hall

Real differences in the achievement levels of women and men in art professions are well documented. The most obvious include these examples: women with equal education and experience are less likely than men to be hired or promoted; women earn less than their male counterparts when they are performing at the same career level; and men's artwork is more likely to be exhibited and collected and, when sold, to obtain higher prices.[4] What prevents women from closing these gaps? Are women responsible for maintaining them? Art and artistic talent are often romanticized. The truth is that an art career involves knowledge, skill, and ambition to the same extent that achievement in any field demands these assets. This essay considers psychological factors involved in maintaining the observed discrepancies in the achievement between men and women in the arts. The psychological factors are considered to result from lack of knowledge or insufficient experience; persisting prejudice; realistic expectancies; and personal intrapsychic processes.

Power dynamics are present in all socio-cultural contexts. The less powerful are well advised to attend most closely to the power differentials. As women, we need to understand how our position and relative power affect our own behavior as well as that of others.[5] Attempting to achieve in a patriarchal society can feel like a competition or a battle for limited resources.[6] Developing alternative models of power and status distribution would be to our advantage. Jean Baker Miller and her colleagues at the Stone Center described women's tendency to view events within a relational context and to see all action as occurring in a relational mode.[7] Women are inherently intersubjective and typically do not view increasing interpersonal distance and separation as desirable. Women tend to see power in being together and acting together.[8] This explains why women tend to use collaboration as a leadership style more often than men.[9]

Women's experience in the field of art must be considered in the broader context of the history of women's participation in public life. In the United States, it has been less than 100 years since women were legally allowed to own property in their own names.[10] Positions of power for women in managing financial and material resources have come only recently. The first woman to serve on the Interstate Commerce Commission, Virginia Mae Brown, was appointed by President Lyndon Johnson in 1964. The first association of women business owners was not founded until 1972. Juanita Morris Kreps became the first female director of the New York Stock Exchange Board of Directors in 1972, and then became the first woman Secretary of Commerce, appointed by President Jimmy Carter in 1977.[11] Nancy Pelosi became the first female Speaker of the House of Representatives in the United States in 2007. Women must strive for this level of visibility and influence, and we need to mentor young women and girls so that they perceive this level of achievement as attainable.[12]

The fact that we need to educate ourselves and obtain experience does not nullify the persistence of real prejudice in an often hostile environment. Former Harvard University President Larry Summers explained gender inequity in top positions by saying that women are inherently less gifted in mathematics.[13] Although rarely as blatant as Summers's statement, unfounded biases against women exist. Attribution research in the field of psychology demonstrates ways in which the interpersonal environment remains inhospitable. People expect men to be more competent. More demanding criteria define competence for women than for men. Observers attribute a woman's success at a task to luck; they attribute a man's success at the same task to ability. Because luck is an external, unstable characteristic, when a woman succeeds, she is not expected to continue to be successful. Because ability is an internal stable factor, the man is judged as being more likely to succeed in the future. Thus, even when behavior is identical, the woman's performance is not rated as highly as the man's, and she is less likely to be rewarded.[14]

Exclusion from education and commerce, and the persistence of prejudice, produce the development of disadvantageous yet realistic expectancies. On one hand, there are realistic expectancies that one is less likely to succeed and that one would have to work much harder to achieve the same level of success as one's male counterpart. Is it worth it to try? On the other hand is the knowledge that there are negative consequences for achieving. Women are judged harshly for displaying the same behaviors for which men are rewarded. Women are punished for using aggressive or domineering leadership styles. Women at times constrain their own efforts out of fear of rejection, fear of abandonment, or fear of loss of perceived femininity. Whereas the most professionally successful men are more likely to be married than single, the most professionally successful women are more likely to be single than married.[15] Stereotypes about women interact on the dimensions of sociability and competence in ways that form false dichotomies. "Person perception research" in psychology demonstrates that the descriptors "career woman" and "feminist," for example, are considered to be compatible, and that both categories are judged to be "competent." They are also both judged to be "not nice" and "not feminine."[16] Carol Gilligan has written extensively on the way in which adolescent girls begin to doubt themselves and their own perceptions as they interact with the patriarchal world and its biased rules.[17]

Having been so different on the outside, women's experience is most certainly different on the inside as well. Intrapsychic processes, the internal personal reasons for failing to achieve one's potential, may be the factor over which one can exert the most direct control. Whereas the preceding factors represent an account of averages, this factor is strictly individual and must be considered on a case-by-case basis. Every person has a unique set of values, beliefs, and experiences. Personal growth involves seeing the value and the shortcomings in each of them. The earliest determinants of personality sometimes play a role in preventing action in adulthood. The internal factors impinging on the psyche must be identified, incorporated, and reconciled if one is to live in a fully conscious way.

As stated earlier, "competent" in a woman is "not nice." What is the cost of appearing nice? Some women refrain from acting on their own behalf because they want to appear good. Julia Cameron wrote of this tendency as the "virtue trap."[18] The price of appearing good rather than of being authentic is paid in the differences in achievement we are currently struggling to overcome.[19] Some women are controlled by shame. In childhood, they were made to feel shame for their curiosity or their exploration. Some women are controlled by deeply held self-doubt. They feel fraudulent. They feel less capable than they have somehow managed to convince other people that they are. They fear that if they put themselves forward, they will be exposed as incompetent.[20] Some women have a problem with unacknowledged either/or reasoning, as in: I can be romantically happy, or I can be an artist; I can be financially successful or an artist. Sometimes perfectionism can be behind one's refusal to move ahead. If I were not so old, if I were not so busy, if I were not so neurotic I could…Sometimes failure is blamed on a lack of money. It is more likely due to a sense of powerlessness. Obsessing about financial concerns can be a way to avoid action.

Inaction is the result of many self-sabotaging intrapsychic processes. It may be seen as a failure to educate oneself to the limits of one's ability, as a failure to achieve at a level commensurate with one's training, or as a failure to strive in the face of rejection or set back.[21] The internal psychological reasons for inaction have a far-reaching and powerful influence. In its most innocent version, inaction is waiting—waiting to be discovered; waiting to be admired; waiting to be encouraged, funded, or promoted. It is the subject of fairy tales and myths that describe but also shape our culture, such as Snow White, Rapunzel, and Sleeping Beauty. Marion Woodman and Madonna Kolbenschlag have both written perceptively about this phenomenon.[22] Waiting at its most severe is a form of paralysis in which one is not free to use the talents and abilities one actually has. Inaction is a response to internalized negative beliefs. Intentional, productive introspection is necessary to identify those beliefs and then to transform or discard them.

In *Art and Artist*, Otto Rank described the process of managing the intrapsychic factors in this way: The artist appoints herself an artist and then must justify this assertion. The individual abstracts herself. So, creativity begins with the individual and the self-making of the personality into the artist. The personality is thus the first work of the artist and remains the chief work, since all other works are partly the repeated expression of this creation.[23]

In every case, internal introspection is necessary to identify the beliefs that run uncensored in the interior monologue. What is the payoff for inaction? What is gained by not making the phone call, not visiting the gallery, not showing the portfolio? Prejudice exists. Biases in attribution exist. After acknowledging these facts, growth requires taking responsibility for what can be done. Consistently resisting prejudice in our own behavior, refraining from using stereotypic behaviors in an effort to enlist protection, using intentionality in the exorcism of our own negative beliefs, we can free the energy that has been bound. Individual psychotherapy or a therapeutic process group will deepen and facilitate this journey. A trained therapist can be of great benefit in providing support, reflection, and clarification as one attempts to confront aspects of oneself that have gone unacknowledged and that are typically not easy to face. In choosing a guide, it is essential that one locate a person who is engaged, empathic, and empowering.

From this perspective, power is not a scarce resource. We need not think of power as control, dominion, or winning. In the patriarchal hierarchical sense, power is limited. If someone gets it, someone else loses it. If someone gains more, someone has less. If we recognize that women have a great capacity for investment in relationships, we can adapt this knowledge to employ our own strengths. Preferring to act within relationship is not a weakness. Strength lies in establishing relational contexts that facilitate psychological growth and mutual empowerment.

We are active agents of both coping with, and of changing, our environments.

Collaboration is an effective and desirable strategy for changing organizations. When a critical mass of women leaders is reached in an organization, change can occur.[24] If we understand our own blind spots and eradicate our own paralyses, we can then use our natural collaborative and facilitative communication styles to work our way into leadership roles. We will then be in position to use our leadership to create mutually empathic relationships that facilitate growth and empowerment. In this way, we will build socially responsible, equitable institutions that value art and the women who make it.

The Path Forward—Noreen Dean Dresser

The ideas presented here plant the seed for a needed conversation on the changing opportunities that shape the art market for women. Dresser's vision seeks to expand the conversation to women's influence and values within the varying professional roles contributing to cultural assets in museums, collections, and media venues. The pace of change is dramatic. Major shifts in our perceptions, caused by the global market's economic engines, have transformed questions of race, ethnicity, regional wars, ideological religion, and modernity. Identity itself attempts to span old cultures and new media. Art and its discussion promise insight into women's status and conditions. Because the professional ranks of women in the arts - artists, museum curators, art advisors, gallery directors, curators and critics - have grown, we can now embrace the expanded opportunities. To accomplish this we must know each other and ourselves. Hall's paper discusses the psychological factors that influence underachievement and encourages a fearless examination of our own process and how we may be limiting our own advancement. By making an agenda, we can shape the cultural landscape so that our ideas of image, beauty, truth, the psychology of relations, power, climate, spirituality, materiality, and traditions are made manifest.

---

[1] Eleanor Dickinson, personal interview, July 9, 2005.

[2] Eleanor Dickinson, "U. S. Census," in *Statistics: Discrimination in the Art Field*, State of California Commission on the Status of Women, Los Angeles, California, February 24, 1987; and CWAO Panel, College Art Association, February 15, 1990.

[3] Ibid.

[4] Eleanor Dickinson, interview by the author, July 9, 2005; Mathiason, *What Went Wrong with the Women's Movement*, (Paris: UNESCO, 2005), 1–10.

[5] M. Helweg-Larsen, S.J. Cunningham, A. Carrico, and A.M. Pergram, "To Nod or Not to Nod: An Observational Study of Nonverbal Communication and Status in Female and Male College Students," *Psychology of Women Quarterly* 28, no. 4 (2004): 358–61.

[6] R.W. Connell, M. Kimmel, and J. Hearn, *Handbook of Studies on Men and Masculinities* (Thousand Oaks, California: Sage Publications, 2005), 35–46.

[7] Judith Jordan, A. Kaplan, Jean Baker Miller, Irene Stiver, and Janet Surrey, *Women's Growth in Connection* (New York: Guilford Press, 1991), 146–75.

[8] Ibid, 197–205.
[9] J.L. Chin, "Feminist Leadership: Feminist Visions and Diverse Voices," *Psychology of Women Quarterly* 28, no. 1 (2004): 1–8.
[10] L. Noun, *The Emergence of the Woman-Suffrage Movement in Iowa* (Ames, Iowa: Iowas State University Press, 1969), 124–57.
[11] P. Read and B. Witlieb, *The Book of Women's Firsts* (New York: Random House, 1992), 17–244.
[12] R.A. Downing, F.J. Crosby, and S. Blake-Beard, "The Perceived Importance of Developmental Relationships on Women Undergraduates Pursuit of Science," *Psychology of Women Quarterly* 29, no. 4 (2005): 419–26; and P. Lockwood, "Someone Like Me Can Be Successful: Do College Students Need Same-Gender Role Models?," *Psychology of Women Quarterly* 30, no. 1 (2006): 36–46.
[13] Larry Summers, in a presentation to the National Bureau of Economic Research, January 17, 2005.
[14] C.N. Dewell, T.W. Altermatt, and H. Thompson, "Understanding the Structure of Stereotypes of Women: Virtue and Agency as Dimensions Distinguishing Female Subgroups," in *Psychology of Women Quarterly* 29, no. 4 (2005): 396–405.
[15] J.S. Bohan. "Sex Differences and/in the Self: Classic Themes, Feminist Variations, Postmodern Challenges," *Psychology of Women Quarterly* 27, no. 2 (2002): 74–88; and M. Agars, "Reconsidering the Impact of Gender Stereotypes on the Advancement of Women in Organizations," *Psychology of Women Quarterly* 28, no. 2: 103–11.
[16] Dewell, Altermatt, and Thompson, "Understanding the Structure of Stereotypes of Women: Virtue and Agency as Dimensions Distinguishing Female Subgroups."
[17] Carol Gilligan, *In a Different Voice: Psychological Theory and Women's Development* (Cambridge, Massachusetts: Harvard University Press, 1982): 38–89.
[18] Julia Cameron, *The Artist's Way* (New York: Putnam, 1992), 96–104.
[19] Jordan, Kaplan, Baker-Miller, Stiver, and Surrey, *Women's Growth in Connection*, 223–36.
[20] J. Kolligian and R.J. Sternberg, *Competence Considered* (New Haven: Yale University Press, 1990), 107–38.
[21] Irene Stiver, "Work Inhibitions in Women," in *Women's Growth in Connection*, Jordan, Kaplan, Miller, Stiver, and Surrey eds. (New York: Guilford Press, 1991).
[22] Marion Woodman, *The Pregnant Virgin* (Toronto: John Deyell, 1985), 33–49; Marion Woodman and R. Bly, *The Maiden King* (New York: Henry Holt and Company, 1998), 88–114; and M. Kolbenschlag, *Kiss Sleeping Beauty Good-Bye* (New York: Harper & Row, 1979), 7–216.
[23] Otto Rank, *Art and Artist* (New York: W.W. Norton, 1932/1968), 26–30.
[24] J.S. Bohan, "Sex Difference in the Self: Classic Themes, Feminist Variations, Postmodern Challenges," *Psychology of Women Quarterly* 26, no. 1: 74–88; and Agars, *Reconsidering the Impact of Gender Stereotypes on the Advancement of Women in Organizations*, 103–11.

Works Cited

Agars, M. "Reconsidering the Impact of Gender Stereotypes on the Advancement of Women in Organizations." *Psychology of Women Quarterly* 28, no. 2 (2004): 103–111.

Baker Miller, Jean. "Women and Power." In *Women's Growth in Connection*, edited by J. V. Jordan, A. G. Kaplan, Jean Baker Miller, I. P. Stiver, and J. L. Surrey, eds. New York: Guilford Press, 1991.

Belle, D. and J. Ducet. "Poverty, Inequity, and Discrimination as Sources of Depression among U.S. Women," *Psychology of Women Quarterly,* 27, no.2 (2003): 101–13.

Bohan, J.S. 2002. "Sex Differences and/in the Self: Classic Themes, Feminist Variations, Postmodern Challenges," *Psychology of Women Quarterly,* 26, no. 1 (2002): 74–88.

Cameron, Julia. *The Artist's Way.* New York: Putnam, 1992.

Chin, J.L. "Feminist Leadership: Feminist Visions and Diverse Voices," *Psychology of Women Quarterly,* 28, no. 1(2004): 1–8.

Connell, R.W., M. Kimmel, and J. Hearn. *Handbook of Studies on Men and Masculinities.* Thousand Oaks, California: Sage Publications, 2005.

Dewall, C.N., T.W. Altermatt, and H. Thompson. "Understanding the Structure of Stereotypes of Women: Virtue and Agency as Dimensions Distinguishing Female Subgroups," *Psychology of Women Quarterly* 29, no. 4 (2005): 396–405.

Downing, R.A., F.J. Crosby, and S. Blake-Beard. "The Perceived Importance of Developmental Relationships on Women Undergraduates' Pursuit of Science," *Psychology of Women Quarterly* 29, no. 4 (2005): 419–26.

Gilligan, Carol. *In a Different Voice: Psychological Theory and Women's Development.* Cambridge, Massachusetts: Harvard University Press, 1992.

Greenfield, S. "Women and Research: Tangible progress?" Second International Colloquium on Research and Higher Education Policy. UNESCO Headquarters, Paris, January 1, 2006.

Helweg-Larsen, M., S.J. Cunningham, A. Carrico, and A.M. Pergram. "To Nod or Not to Nod: An Observational Study of Nonverbal Communication and Status in Female and Male College Students," *Psychology of Women Quarterly* 28, no. 4 (2004): 358–61.

Jordan, Judith, Alexandra Kaplan, Jean Baker Miller, Irene Stiver, and Janet Surrey. *Women's Growth in Connection.* New York: Guilford Press, 1991.

Kimmel, M. "Men and gender equality: Resistance or support?," Section for Women and Gender Equality of the Bureau of Strategic Planning Seminar, Paris, May 5, 2006.

Kolbenschlag, M. *Kiss Sleeping Beauty Good-bye.* New York: Harper & Row, 1979.

Kolligian, J. and R.J. Sternberg. *Competence Considered.* New Haven: Yale University Press, 1990.

Lockwood, P. "Someone Like Me Can Be Successful": Do College Students Need Same-Gender Role Models? *Psychology of Women Quarterly* 30, no. 1, (2006): 36–46.

Macrae, C.N. and G.V. Bodenhausen. "Social cognition: Thinking categorically about others," *Annual Review of Psychology* 51 (2000): 93–120.

Mathiason, J. *What Went Wrong with the Women's Revolution?* Paris: UNESCO, 2005.

Noun, L. *The Emergence of the Woman Suffrage Movement in Iowa.* Ames, Iowa: Iowa State University Press, 1969.

Rank, Otto. *Art and Artist.* New York: W. W. Norton, 1932/1968.

Read, P. and B. Witlieb. *The Book of Women's Firsts.* New York: Random House, 1992.

Stiver, Irene. "Work Inhibitions in Women." In *Women's Growth in Connection*, Judith Jordan, Alexandra Kaplan, Jean Baker Miller, Irene Stiver, and Janet Surrey eds. New York: Guilford Press, 1991.

Summers, Larry. Presentation to the National Bureau of Economic Research, January 14, 2005.
http://www.president.harvard.edu/speeches/2005/nber.html.

Woodman, Marion. *The Pregnant Virgin.* Toronto: John Deyell, 1985.

Woodman, Marion and R. Bly. *The Maiden King.* New York: Henry Holt and Company, 1998.

GROWING AN ART MUSEUM

RUTH VON JAHNKE WATERS

Art museums are founded by major collectors and/or philanthropists, mostly men. They function as monuments to their taste and a legacy to their communities. The Peninsula Museum of Art was founded by a working artist, a woman, me. I have an interesting collection of art from fellow artists and travels, an art center (a complex of working studios for twenty-seven visual artists, small gallery, since 1977), and an enduring dream—but no money to speak of.

The dream emerged when we (husband, three children) returned to Northern California from the Washington, DC, area. For 20 years I dropped the need for an art museum into art community conversations with no noticeable effect. Everyone assumed that San Francisco's art scene was and would always be sufficient.

Then our world shook with the 1989 Loma Prieta earthquake on the notorious San Andreas Fault, and everything changed. Transportation issues, especially, have encouraged residents of the San Francisco Peninsula to look around their neighborhoods for their cultural amenities. Biotechnology industries had already developed in the northern part of the county, and high-tech had expanded from the south. The expansion of the corporate world altered all the patterns, and we were no longer just a collection of bedroom communities. By 1997, a public forum hosted by ARTshare of San Mateo County, California, a regional non-profit, identified an art museum and a performing arts center as the two major holes in our cultural fabric. That day the Working Committee for an Art Museum organized, scheduled monthly meetings, and started brainstorming ways and means, goals and strategies, and names.

We decided the art museum should be centrally located in an urban area, preferably within walking distance of public transit. We searched for a suitable existing building and found one—a large Depression-era Works Progress Administration (WPA) building in Redwood City, the county seat, that the County was vacating in favor of a new modern office building. By this time we had named ourselves San Mateo County Art Museum (SAMCAM).

This first iteration of the dream crashed on the shoals of bureaucracy. The building we wanted had been glued onto the façade of the historic County Courthouse (stained-glass dome, stained-glass ceiling in Courtroom A—remember the movie "Mrs. Doubtfire?), and the powers that be, official and otherwise, were determined to destroy the WPA building in order to restore the Courthouse. They had all the marbles, so we bowed out after two years of hard work.

Our next step took us to the Internet. After all, the San Francisco Peninsula is the northern sector of San Francisco's Silicon Valley. We had just welcomed a new member to the core group, a retired professor of corporate strategy and consultant to high-tech startups, and so it evolved: we renamed ourselves Silicon Valley Art Museum (SVAM) and proceeded to create our museum (with exhibitions and an excellent art education program for children) in cyberspace. SVAM launched in August of 2000.

We added a few more corporate-type Board members who brought potentially useful experience and resources, heeding the standard advice to extend the Board into the business world, and continued to dream of a real, physical, bricks-and-mortar art museum where everyone could experience the power and magic of wonderful art.

Then a local non-profit organization collapsed from fiscal malnutrition and the City of Belmont offered the lease on their historic building to the Museum (my art center had leased an old elementary school from the City for many years, so we had a relationship and credibility).

The good news was that now we had a "starter home" with formal gallery, museum store, and art reference library. We share the building with two other arts nonprofits and a flock of studio artists (upstairs). The bad news was that we had to face an unbridgeable schism in our Board. Half of the Board (basically the corporate types) was only interested in the Internet museum, and the other half still had a firm grasp on the dream of a real physical museum serving the community.

The first indication of a serious problem came with the lease offered by the City. The "others" insisted that they would approve the lease only with the assurance that none of the corporate budget would be spent on the physical museum.

Two pertinent bits of information are needed here: first, our primary source of operating funds since 2000 has been the O.P. Decker Foundation (Arabella Decker, an artist, is a core member of the Museum Board and one of the three Decker Foundation trustees). Second, the studio artists rent the upstairs rooms and their cash pays the City lease (services are provided by the three non-profits in lieu of cash).

We tried strategic planning, we endured a Board Retreat, and the split merely widened. With the acquisition of Board members from the corporate community, we found ourselves evenly split. We couldn't risk a substantive vote, and the "others" were increasingly free with comments that made it quite clear that they intended to take over the corporation. In late summer of 2003, then, Arabella Decker was planning her annual trip to Chicago for the annual Decker Foundation trustees meeting and the dispensing of grants. She was upset by the prospect of handing over the check to Board members who were obviously planning a corporate coup, so we talked. I reminded her that most foundation grants came with a letter specifying restrictions on the spending of the money. With that hint, she cheered up and went off to Chicago. She came back with a check and a letter stating that the funds could be spent only on the development and operation of the physical museum. She returned with the check in November, just after our Board meeting. Several members of the Board had plans to travel during December and suggested canceling the December meeting. We did.

It wasn't until the January Board meeting, then, that the letter was presented and the financial impact realized. They were not pleased. On the other hand, how dumb did they think we artists were, not to catch on to their obvious plans? And do something about it? So—we did a corporate divorce.

We split the assets. The "others" took all the virtual assets, the Web site, the name (SVAM), and the "501(c) 3" corporation non-profit status. (The name had become an albatross anyway; the "locals" hated it.) We kept all the physical assets, the lease, and the money. We immediately took the name Peninsula Museum of Art (PMA), incorporated, and applied for (and received) our own 501(c) 3 tax-exempt status.

PMA has settled into a workable schedule of four exhibitions a year, each opening followed by a newsletter with pictures from the reception and articles about what's coming next. Periodically we present a Sunday Seminar on art ("Fine Art Prints: What Is and What Isn't," "Originals vs. Reproductions," etc.).

We're still operating on about $25,000 a year ($20,000 from the O.P. Decker Foundation plus Board contributions and memberships). We have no paid staff, just one independent contractor who maintains our Web site, www.peninsulamuseum.org. Our Board is small (seven), tight, and hard working. Board meetings are now a pleasure.

With something resembling normality established, we dusted off our dream: a site where we can build a medium-sized fine art museum, in the 50,000-square-feet range, to serve the communities of the San Francisco

Peninsula. The dream gained credibility in November of 2005 when a life-long artist and Museum supporter introduced me to her friend who was interested in using his money to make a difference in the community he grew up in. Bottom line: he wrote us a check for $1 million to launch our Building Fund. The million has been placed with a major investment firm to "grow" our funds.

This is just the beginning. As soon as we have a commitment on a site, the fundraising will begin, and it is never easy. We know that we have to raise around $25 million to build, and another $25 million for an endowment to ensure the income to operate the museum.

And what about the site? As I write, we are in serious discussions about a wonderful piece of undeveloped land, centrally located, aesthetically exciting, and close enough to other cultural facilities to constitute a county cultural center—when everything gets built.

The time seems to be right. Meanwhile, there is so much art to see, and so many exhibitions to plan and install, newsletters to write, elected officials to schmooze, potential donors to meet—and now and then I play hooky and work on my own art. Now and then.

Epilogue

What have I learned on this journey?

1. Look every gift horse in the mouth and check references, informally if possible. It's much easier to not need, or to divert, an eager volunteer, than to get rid of an albatross or shark.

2. Assume everyone, and I do mean everyone, has a private agenda. The good news is that at least part of that private agenda probably overlaps with yours. Find out and plan accordingly.

3. Don't be shy but learn to recognize the body language of boredom and know when to shut up and listen.

4. Pester your elected officials. It isn't really pestering, and I don't do nearly enough of it. They need to be "insiders," and they need constant reminders of how important they are in the community.

5. Look for your natural allies and develop creative partnerships (the new term for collaborations). The goal? To make new friends and get your mission and message out.

6. Leaders wear the white hat, but you are likely to need a "black hat" from time to time (preferably a board member who is

willing to ask the tough questions and point out the elephant in the room).

7. Timing. A concept or project may be wonderful, but it may need to ferment until the timing is right. Of course, when the time *is* right, you need to be ready to run through the door that has opened.

8. Ah yes, fundraising. I don't have money and I don't move in those socio-economic circles (and neither do my wonderful board members), but we will have to somehow raise a *lot* of money. The answer, we hope, will be to recruit ever-higher circles of connection and gradually move our campaign up the food chain. Cold calls and knocking on doors don't work, connections do. Research is vital—who in the community loves art *and* has disposable income or assets? Who do we know who knows someone who knows them? Patience and perseverance are required. . .

9. An attractive package is essential. The support you need will only respond to a project that your potential supporters will find socially irresistible, so go ahead and dream well out of your range knowing that you may have to scale back.

10. Know that nothing wonderful like this will happen quickly. Believe in your heart and soul that the goal is worth years of your life, or don't start.

11. Fun and laughter are essential to the creative life, in this as in all else.

And what did I bring to the table?

Good question. To begin with, a degree in Journalism (now called Communications) from Stanford University, followed by a number of years working as a tech writer/editor in the corporate world and as a community college instructor. On the other hand, I have been a sculptor for 50 years (first solo exhibition in 1962) and a painter for five or six years.

Third, I opened my art center (working studios for 27 visual artists and gallery) in 1977 and am active in several community arts organizations (co-founder of Peninsula Sculptors Guild and co-founder and board member of ARTshare of San Mateo County, which has morphed into the Peninsula Arts Council, as well as two stints on the WCA National Board and founder / past president of the WCA Peninsula Chapter).

As for endurance and tenacity, I've been a long-distance runner for 35 years, including 16 marathons trained for, run, and mostly won (in my age group, thank you very much). I took up tennis at 63, and am playing on several USTA teams.

Answer: if the concept or project is worthy, and you are the right person, then everything you have done and been and everyone you have worked with will become who and what you need.

PIONEER CHICANA/LATINA ARTISTS: CREATING INSTITUTIONAL INCLUSION

PATRICIA RODRIGUEZ

I was born in Marfa, Texas. I came of age when racism—and its "dream crushing limitations"[1]—extended throughout the Southwestern United States, touching the lives of people like me. My family migrated with the seasons, until we eventually settled down in Ventura County, California.

I saw my first college on a church trip to the University of California at Irvine, an educational trip for the migrant children.[2] I knew in an instant, I wanted to go to college. To speak openly of my dream defied all logic; I knew Mexican women did not go to college, let alone become artists. My parents and elders saw my dream as an act of defiance. The Civil Rights/Chicano Movement[3] gave me my first hope—and the courage, to speak my dream aloud.

I submitted my portfolio for a scholarship to the San Francisco Art Institute. I was stunned to be accepted. I could see through that window a career path as an artist and arts educator. I have fulfilled my dream, and continue working as an artist and educator to this very day. I submitted this article to offer my experience with institutional inclusion for Chicana/Latina artists, and to make recommendations for the future.

I interviewed several pioneering women whose work forms part of the foundation of the 1970s Chicana art movement, as part of a larger documentary project, and to better inform my suggestions for institutional inclusion. I draw on my interviews with Juana Alicia and Yolanda Lopez. Both artists have been successful Chicana artists for more than 20 years, recognized and exhibited nationally and internationally. Their art and murals are often cited and published in art history journals and books. All three of us share institutional experiences as professors and lecturers at various California universities. Combined, our experience is offered to better understand how we can develop institutional relationships and collaborations.

The Chicano Art Movement and Chicana Artists

I attended the San Francisco Art Institute in the days of the early seventies, when San Francisco and University of California at Berkeley were important spokes in the wheels set in motion by the social movement that rolled first through the southern United States in the sixties. The first murals in San Francisco's now famous Balmy Alley were painted in 1971. The Chicano/Latino art movement was transforming individuals and gaining momentum in San Francisco, as well as in Los Angeles communities struggling with the death of journalist Ruben Salazar,[4] sharing common frustrations over the Vietnam War, and growing resistance to long standing discrimination. It was in this historical context that I began to define myself as Chicana. I was certainly not alone. The murals and poster art of the time reflected the struggles of the Chicano movement for equality.

I learned the art of painting at the San Francisco Art Institute, yet my experiences outside the school walls afforded me the chance to serve as a working artist. At school, male colleagues and professors did not believe I would ever be an artist. Beyond self-created opportunities to exhibit our work, graduating students found few options. Finally, I had arrived as a member of a new generation of Chicana/Latina artists with the opportunity to study art, only to graduate with few chances for exhibits, grants, or fellowships. Many artists survived working as art professors. Their full-time, tenured positions provided opportunities for greater exposure, which made applying for art grants and awards less a game of chance for funding organizations, the game continued to be more of who you know. For Chicana/Latina artists, these teaching positions were mostly off-limits.

In contrast to the institutional status quo, the art movement surging through the community felt inclusive. The Chicano art movement in San Francisco was lively, offering a means for expressing reaction to the politics of the country at that turbulent moment. It was a transforming time that inspired many feminist Chicana/Latina artists to break free.

Creating Institutions

California is a land of transformation, shifting with the impact of its history, people, and cultures. The Chicano art movement served as an important catalyst, its imprint felt most on the landscape of the state's cultural, social, and political life. Yet, despite a rising popular interest in Chicano art during the seventies, the doors to the country's art institutions remained closed. In 1972, the Los Angeles-based, Chicano performance art collective Asco[5] ("nausea" in Spanish) protested the Los Angeles Contemporary Museum of Art's refusal to show their artwork. The performance artists spray-painted their names on the front wall of the museum, declaring their work deserved to hang alongside the art of their contemporaries.

The Chicano art community of San Francisco also struggled in the late seventies to break through the institutional walls. Rene Yañez, a pioneer Chicano artist and founding member of the Galería de la Raza in San Francisco, proposed co-producing together with the San Francisco Museum of Modern Art (SFMOMA) a traveling Frida Kahlo[6] exhibit, to be curated by Judith Kirshner[7] and Hayden Herrera. The proposal went unanswered, until Mr. Yañez finally received this reply: "Please have Frida call the museum for an appointment." Many years later, SFMOMA would learn of Kahlo's work, and play a crucial role in her almost universal recognition as the most celebrated Mexican female artist of our times.

The lack of institutional inclusion spawned ingenuity and independent strategies for sharing and distributing work, propelling the creation of spaces such as Galería de la Raza, Mission Cultural Center, and many other landmark Chicano art institutions established in the Bay Area, including the Mexican Museum, Royal Chicano Air Force artist collective's Centro de Artistas Chicanos, and El Teatro Camposino.

Frustrated by the museum's rejection, in 1977, Yañez redirected his energy into an exhibit at the Galería de la Raza in honor of Frida Kahlo, the first of its kind in San Francisco. The call for artists invigorated the community, and the Galería received an overwhelming response from local Chicano artists. Amalia Mesa-Bains and Maria Pinedo[8] sorted through the submissions and selected work. The exhibit was a success, and the Galería firmly established as a resource for the community, a Chicano art space offering exhibits and performances at the vanguard of Chicano and American art. Today, the Galería de la Raza continues to bring emerging artists to the stage, and serves as a respected and recognized force in the Chicano Art Movement for more than three decades.

I learned the art of a being a curator at the Galería de la Raza. Always pushing forward, the Galería inaugurated the first Chicana/Latina exhibit in San Francisco in 1970. The exhibit featured the work of young Chicana artists from California, many of who are now considered icons of the Chicana art movement.[9] Graciela Carrillo and I crafted the groundbreaking exhibit of approximately 25 Latina artists working in tapestries, installations, paintings, and printmaking. I saw the diversity and artistic treasures of so many Latina artists, and recognized their desire to share their work with each other and the community. Before that exhibit, there had been doubt, even at the Galería, whether we would find enough Latina artists to fill the show. Instead, the exhibit brought out every Latina artist in San Francisco! The opening reception was a great celebration.

Mujeres Muralistas of San Francisco

In 1972, I founded Mujeres Muralistas with Irene Perez, Consuelo Méndez, and Graciela Carrillo while we were students at the Art Institute.[10] The Mujeres Muralistas dared to change the course of muralism by wrenching itself free from its male-dominated base, and working collectively as women. The Mujeres Muralistas were greatly influenced by the early Mexican muralists of the 1920s and sympathized with the obstacles faced by the women muralists working in Mexico City in the early 1900s. María Izquierda and Fanny Rabel, both acclaimed artists, nevertheless were constantly harassed when painting murals on public walls by their fellow male muralists, including Diego Rivera and David Alfaro Siquieros. The two men, like many others, believed women should not paint public murals.[11] The Mujeres Muralistas joined alongside Latina women such as Judith Baca[12] in Los Angeles to be the first women artists since that era to freely paint public murals without being obstructed. The Mujeres collaborative influenced the Chicano art movement, as well as the evolution of American art, and its impact reverberates even today.

The members of the Mujeres Muralistas collective, which eventually grew to a collaborative of nine women artists, still today break barriers in their creative work and professional lives. Susan Kelk Cervantes continues to paint murals and educates youth through her Precita Eyes Mural Center in San Francisco. Irene Perez, whose images have traveled around the world, continues to create art and now also works with music. Consuelo Méndez is a performance artist and a professor/dean of the University of Caracas in Venezuela. Ester Hernandez is a visual artist whose images are iconic in the Chicano movement. Ruth Rodriguez is now a dentist in Puerto Rico, Miriam Olivo lives in Caracas, Venezuela, and Fran Velasco lives in the Bay Area. She is currently an instructor of art for San Francisco State University and the San Francisco Art Institute.

I was the first Chicana artist to teach a university-level Chicano art class, and I created the Chicano Art History class curriculum and reader.[13] I taught as a full-time professor at UC Berkeley in the Chicano Studies department for five years.[14] As an artist, my work has evolved. After years of working as a muralist, I began making and exhibiting small box art constructions that eventually traveled around the nation in exhibitions at galleries and community spaces. Currently, I produce mono-prints, a medium that affords the chance to create images with a painterly quality in a fairly rapid fashion and that is easily exhibited in galleries. Printmaking is more conducive to my heavy work schedule as curator and gallery coordinator at the Mission Cultural Center. I believe life is short, and I don't want to loose any time so I make use of the materials available to me. Economically, printmaking is feasible, as I juggle the usual demands of an artist trying to survive while still creating art.

Today, I share my experience as a working artist and curator with emerging artists as gallery director and arts administrator for the Mission Cultural Arts Center (MCCLA). MCCLA is a well-respected national alternative exhibition space for the Latino community, showing the work of artists from as far away as Europe, Latin America, Miami, New York, and the Southwest, as well as of California-based artists. It is here that I am able to offer emerging artists their opportunity to reflect on the experiences of their lives today.

Still More Inclusion Needed Today

The artists of the Mujeres Muralistas are invited to participate in many international exhibits, journals, and books.[15] Our images have traveled the world. Yet, the Mujeres Muralistas do not find the same inclusion in our own backyard. The Mujeres Muralistas were interviewed and asked to consider participating in WACK! Art and the Feminist Revolution, an exhibit inaugurated at the Los Angeles Museum of Contemporary Art (MOCA) in 2007. The exhibit's curators originally showed enthusiasm for the work of the Mujeres, as well as the work of other Chicana artists they interviewed, which definitely sparked a feeling of inclusion. There was excitement, dare I even say, happiness in finally being acknowledged as important feminist artists, the invitation a symbol for some well-deserved and long overdue acknowledgment of Chicana/Latina artists' contribution to the Feminist Movement.

Yet, at the last minute, Mujeres Muralistas and other well-known Chicana artists and muralists in San Francisco and Los Angeles were completely left out.[16] The sense of exclusion that followed causes me to question the premise of the Feminist Movement of liberating and reversing oppression against women. In what ways haven't Chicana/Latina artists fought the very same patriarchal powers as the feminist artists included in WACK!? In what ways did we not meet the same challenges, such that our work is so unexpectedly excluded from such an important forum on feminist art? Once again, I felt like a young girl with only her dream to attend college. Why is it we can still only dream of inclusion in 2007? As a group, we have asked (then) MOCA curator Connie Butler and other feminists we know to explain why we were wiped off the slate. The experience left a distinct sense of exclusion, and highlighted the institutional lack of interest in the feminist evolution of such key Chicana artists. Most significantly, the exclusion fosters a sense that the struggles we faced against cultural machismo and challenges we have overcome to maintain our artistic identity are now institutionalized.

Despite sustaining public interest for Chicano art, U.S. art institutions have largely dismissed the movement's impact on American art as a whole and ignored the national influence of Chicano/Latino art trends initiated in California. Overall, we find that Chicano art and artists are an unknown entity in the American art world and in discussions of American art history. Chicano/Latino artists are rarely recognized with institutional and academic positions, and with even fewer awards and fellowships. My research revealed very few Latino/Chicano curators, museum directors, or art administrators.[17] Often, it's the same artists who receive any available support or positions, despite a vast pool of talent. Iconic images often become reminders of the presence of Chicana/Latina artists, yet speak very little to the breadth, depth, and diversity of Chicana/Latina art. As we reach the mature phase of our careers, we can offer insights into the future of Chicano art and institutional inclusion that we hope will inspire change. We fully embrace the Chicano art movement as a significant, transforming movement within the trajectory of American art.

Recommendations for Inclusive American Art Institutions

During the late seventies, U.S. universities established academic programs dedicated to the study of Chicano art, culture, and philosophy. These programs responded to the growing number of Latino and Chicano students within the university system and the social/political situation outside. However, by the late eighties and during the nineties, many programs were cut back and academic inclusion became less common. This lack of institutional consistency, and the negative impact on inter-generational teaching and sharing, is detrimental to our university system and our national culture, which is increasingly multicultural. If art truly is to have its place in society, American art must broaden its embrace of the arts that reflect the diversity in its universities and art study programs.

As the Chicano art movement gained momentum, the artwork of Chicanos was being made more widely known with the pioneering work of Shifra Goldman, University of California at Los Angles professor and author of many books/articles. Her seminal work *Dimensions of the Americas: Art and Social Change in Latin America and the United States*[18] is credited with introducing Chicano art to the general public. Today, Peter Selz's recently completed book *Art of Engagement: Visual Politics in California and Beyond*[19] is encouraging for its focus on the historical impact and influence of Chicano artists in the American art world and culture. Yet, sadly, there are too few scholarly works written about the Chicana/Latina movement and its impact.

The young Chicano/Latino artists of today know the proverbial door has been opened. They walk through with confidence in their ability to succeed, far more confident than we had been when Juana Alicia, Yolanda Lopez, and I set out on our journey. Yet, it is the generational lack of inclusion that can thwart the dreams of entire generations of artists.

If we are admitted into universities as students, why are we not as professors? If we are awarded scholarships for education, why not fellowships allowing us to create in a dedicated way? How can we offer American art education that fails to acknowledge and teach one of our nation's most influential art movements? Lastly, does it make any sense not to make available to art students our collective wisdom gained through experience as practicing artists and administrators?

According to Yolanda Lopez, our generation served as the "shock troops." We were the first in line, so it fell to us to break the barriers. Perhaps, today, this is our role once again, to bring attention to the lack of institutional acceptance and support for Chicano art. Despite sustaining artistic careers and broad public appeal, our pioneer artists and movement shapers have not been included institutionally beyond lecture requests and citations in papers, articles, and books.

To honor the progress of the past, we must take another step forward. Institutional support for emerging and established artists with recommendations for inclusion in arts funding, tenure positions, and art institution management positions is the next step to ensure institutional collaboration. Partnerships can flourish in a meaningful way when the Chicano/Latino art movement is recognized, embraced, and accepted as a significant contribution to American art.

The answer to the riddle of inclusion requires a frank and honest dialogue between the art and institutional communities. To ignore this problem any longer represents a blindness that threatens to overwhelm the entire movement of American art. By ignoring the art of our multicultural population, we fail to accurately reflect who we are as a people, as Americans. We need Chicano/Latino curators, art professors, scholars, and artists in America's art institutions. Today, we can inspire the dreams of the next generation of Chicana/Latina artists by example, so they may see a brighter future.[20]

---

[1] Pat McCarran, "The Denaturalization aspect of the Immigration and Nationality Act of 1952, Titles I and II," in,*Occupied America, the Chicano's Struggle Toward Liberation*, ed.Rodolfo Acuña (San Francisco: Canfield Press, 1972), 214. Pat McCarran was a senator from Nevada.

[2] Mexican and Chicano migrant children from Mexico and Texas living in Oxnard, California in 1954.

[3] F. Arturo Rosales, *Chicano! The History of the Mexican American Civil Rights Movement* (Houston: Arte Publico Press, 1996).

[4] Ruben Salazar (March 3, 1928–August 29, 1970) was a Mexican American news reporter killed by the police during the National Chicano Moratorium March against the Vietnam War on August 29, 1970 in Los Angeles, California. Wikipedia entry at http://en.wikipedia.org/wiki/Ruben_Salazar.

[5] Asco ("nausea") was a Chicano performance group in Los Angeles. The group created many public conceptual and experimental performances, as well as murals, phototgraphy, super-8 films, costumes, street theater, and tableaux. For more information, see http://cemaweb.library.ucsb.edu/chicanoArt.html

[6] Frida Kahlo, b. July 6, 1907, d. July 13, 1954.

[7] Judith Russi Kirshner has been Dean of the College of Architecture and the Arts at the University of Illinois at Chicago since 1997. She has also served as director of the School of Art and Design and professor of Art History. Judith Russi Kirshner was educated at Barnard and Bryn Mawr Colleges. Kirshner previously served as curator at the Museum of Contemporary Art in Chicago from 1976 to 1980, and at the Terra Museum of American Art from 1985 to 1987.

Hayden Herrera is a biographer and historian. Hayden Herrera has lectured widely, served as curator for several art exhibits, and as professor of Latin American Art at New York University. Hayden was awarded a Guggenheim Fellowship. She is the author of numerous articles and reviews for such publications as *Art in America, Artforum, Connoisseur,* and *The New York Times*, among others. Her books include *Frida: A Biography of Frida Kahlo*, *Frida Kahlo: The Paintings*, *Mary Frank* and *Matisse: A Portrait*. She lives in New York City.

[8] Amalia Mesa-Bains and Maria Pinedo were the co-curators for the Frida Kahlo art exhibition at Galeria de la Raza, with director Rene Yañez, held in 1978. See http://www.galeriadelaraza.org/eng/exhibits/timeline.html

[9] Graciela Carrillo, a visual artist, and I met at the San Francisco Art Institute when we were students in 1970. We were the first Latinas to attend the San Francisco Art Institute on full scholarships. We continued to work together throughout school and later, when Graciela became one of the founding members of the collective Mujeres Muralistas.

[10] The Mujeres Muralistas collective was the first all-women muralist collaborative in San Francisco. We came to the collaboration in the spirit of muralism, and in response to the exclusion of Chicana women in leadership and content decisions within the larger Chicano mural movement. As Amalia Mesa-Bains states, the

Mujeres Muralistas represented an "intercultural struggle for equality and respect"; see the paper "Memory, Cultural Identity and the Social Imaginary: Art of the Chicano/a Community," presented at the Tenth Annual Ernesto Galarza Commemorative Lecture, 1995, Stanford Center for Chicano Research, Stanford University. See also, Teresita Roma. "A Collective History: Las Mujeres Muralistas," *in Art/Women/California, and Parallels and Intersections 1950–2000*, edited by Diana Burgess Fuller and Daniela Salvioni, 177–186 (Los Angeles: San Jose Museum of Art and University of California Press, 2000). Teresita Romo (author of article) appears in *Art/Women/California, and Parallels and Intersections 1950–2000*, edited by Diana Burgess Fuller and Daniela Salvioni, published in association with the San Jose Museum of art, University of California Press Berkeley/Los Angeles/London 2000.

[11] Elena Poniatowska, *Las Siete Cabritas* (Mexico, D.F.: Ediciones Era, S.A. de C.V., 2000), 79–100. Elena Poniatowska writes in this section about the difficulties Mexican women muralists faced. Poniatowska focuses on seven woman in particular who bravely faced opposition to their activities as artists, and made a mark on Mexican art history for their courage to face even aggressive attempts to limit their possibilities. As an example, Elena cites Maria Izquierda, the first Mexican woman to have a solo exhibit in the United States when her work was shown in New York in 1930. Yet, by 1945, Maria met with soul crushing resistance from her trusted instructor, Diego Rivera, who, despite claiming she was the best of his students, worked together with David Alfaro Siqueiros to ensure Maria did not work again as a muralist. Maria had prepared a proposal to paint a mural for the Mexico City government. Maria's project was chosen and a contact for the work was signed. Maria later found out that her two colleagues had insisted as members of the project evaluation committee that she not be awarded the project. They told Javier Rojo Gómez that she was not capable of painting the mural because her painting was very elemental. Maria was told to abandon the project and tear up the contract. The explanation for the change was that "in Mexico, there are no Mexican women muralists. Elena Poniatowska "Maria Izquierdo al derecho y al revé" in *Las Siete Cabritas, 79-100.*. (Mexico, D.F.: Ediciones Era, S.A. de C.V., 2000).

At the time, only two North American women were accepted as muralists, Grace and Marion Greenwood, sisters who painted murals in the Mercado Abelardo Rodriquez. Maria was blocked from painting murals, which destroyed her emotionally and impacted her health. Of course, she recovered and became an important painter whose work is valued even today.

[12] Judith F. Baca, artist, educator, and activist. Judith F. Baca is one of the leading muralists in Los Angeles, and serves as director of SPARC (Social Political Art Resource Center) in Venice, California. See http://latino.si.edu/virtualgallery/OJOS/bios/bios_Baca.htm.

[13] I taught Chicano Studies 130 at U.C. Berkeley 1975–1980. I developed a course "Chicano Art History" and discovered there were no text books available on the subject. I spent that summer doing research in the UC Berkeley, and the UC Santa Barbara Libraries. I compiled a 556 page reader for my students, incorporating

written publications, magazines, articles, and small pamphlets that spoke to the art activities at Chicano cultural centers across the US. Shifra M.Goldman complimented the work in saying "This unpublished compilation remains the most comprehensive reader available on Chicano Art. *Arte Chicano, A Comprehensive Annotated Bibliography of Chicano Art*, 1965–1981, Shira M. Goldman and Tomás Ybarra-Fraustos, 6, (Chicano Studies Library Publications Unit 3404 Dwinelle Hall, University of California, Berkeley, CA. 94720), 1985. My reader has been assigned reading at many colleges and universities that teach Chicano Art History.

[14] I was hired to teach at U.C. Berkeley so that I could share my experience as a local Chicana artist/muralist, at a time when universities were establishing Chicano Studies courses and the doors were opening for Chicano artists. These changes occurred at the height of the Chicano art movement, a time when murals were going up around the country, standing next to political posters reflecting the frustrations and hopes of the community. I was invited to participate as an instructor because of my role as a founding member of Mujeres Muralistas and as a result of the recognition within the mural movement itself.

[15] Maria Ochoa, *Creative Collectives: Chicano Painters Working in Community* (Albuquerque: University of New Mexico Press, 2003), 27, 33–36, 38–39, 41–42, 46–47, 54–55, 91, 95, 96; Peter Selz, *Art of Engagement, Visual Politics in California and Beyond*, (San Jose: University of California Press, San Jose Museum of Modern Art, 2006). More book listings can be found at http://www.patriciarodriguezarts.com.

[16] Exhibition catalogue *WACK! Art and The Feminist Revolution, March 4–July 16, 2007*, curated by Connie Butler, (Los Angeles: The Geffen Contemporary at MOCA, Los Angeles, 2007). *WACK! Art and the Feminist Revolution,* Organized by Cornelia H. Butler and Lisa Gabrielle Mark. Essays by Cornelia H. Butler, Judith Russi Kirshner, Catherine Lord, Marsha Meskimmon, Richard Meyer, Helen Molesworth, Peggy Phelan, Nelly Richard, Valerie Smith, Abigail Solomon-Godeau and Jenni Sorkin .

[17] Rita González, "Archiving the Latin Arts Before It Is Too Late," *Latino Policy & Issues Brief* 6 (April 2003), published by the UCLA Chicano Studies Research Center; Pedro A. Malavet, Afterword: *Outsider Citizenships and Multidimensional Borders: The Power and Danger of Not Belonging*, 52 Cleveland State L. Rev. 321–338 (2004). Four museums stand out as the first American museums to showcase, collect, promote, and display works reflecting Chicano, Mexican, and Puerto Rican art and culture. El Museo del Barrio, founded in New York in 1969 by artist and teacher Rafael Montanez Ortiz, become a leader among institutions devoted to interpreting Puerto Rican and Latino culture. The Mexican Museum in San Francisco, founded by artist Peter Rodriguez in 1975, developed and promoted artists in the primacy of Latino self-definition and interpretation. The Mexican Fine Arts Center, founded in 1982 in Chicago by high-school history teacher Carlos Tortolero and a group of educators, addresses critical contemporary topics such as cultural diversity and community development. Finally, the Mexico-Arte Museum in Austin, Texas, started in 1983 by artists and activists Sylvia Orozco,

Pio Pulido, and Sam Coronado, is dedicated to cultural enrichment and education through the display and promotion of traditional and contemporary Mexican, Latino, and Latin American art and culture.

[18] Shifra M. Goldmanm, *Dimensions of The Americas: Art and Social Change in Latin America and the United States* (Chicago, IL: University of Chicago Press, 1994) 209–210, 212–213.

[19] Selz, *Art of Engagement, Visual Politics in California and Beyond* . 171–175.

[20] The author thanks Catherine Herrera for her additional editorial assistance.

Works Cited

Acuña, Rodolfo. *Occupied America, The Chicano's Struggle Toward Liberation*. San Francisco: Canfield Press, 1972.

Acuña, Rodolfo ed., I*n Occupied America, The Chicano's Struggle Toward Liberation*, California State University at Northridge, Canfield Press San Francisco, 1972.

Butler, Cornelia, and Lisa Gabrielle Mark ed. *WACK! Art and The Feminist Revolution, March 4–July 16, 2007*, Cambridge, MA: MIT Press

California Ethnic and Multicultural Archives. http://cemaweb.library.ucsb.edu/chicanoArt.html

Chadwick, Whitney. *Women, Art and Society (World of Art).* London: Thames & Hudson, 1990.

Cockcroft, Eva Sperling and Holly Barnet-Sanchez, eds. *Signs from the Heart: California Chicano Murals.* Albuquerque: University of New Mexico Press, 1993.

Del Castillo, Richard Griswold. Teresa McKenna, Yvonne Yarbro-Bejarano eds., *El Mundo Femenino: Chicana Artists of the Movement- A Commentary On Development and Production*. Place? CARA: Chicano Art Resistance and Affirmation, Wight Art Gallery. University of California, Los Angeles: Regents of the University of California, 1991.

Fuller, Diana Burgess and Daniela Salvioni eds. *Art/Women/California, Parallels and Intersections 1950–2000*. Los Angeles: San Jose Museum of Art, University of California Press, 2000.

Galarza, Ernesto. "Memory, Cultural Identity and the Social Imaginary: Art of the Chicano/a Community" Tenth Annual Commemorative Lecture. Stanford Center for Chicano Research, Stanford University, 1995.

Goldman, Shifra M. *Dimensions of the Americas: Art and Social Change in Latin America and the United States,* Chicago: University of Chicago Press, 1994.

Goldman, Shifra M., and Tomás Ybarra-Frausto. *Arte Chicano: A Comprehensive Biography of Chicano Art, 1965–1981.* Berkeley: Chicano Studies Library Publications Unit, University of California, 1985.

Herrera, Hayden. *Frida: A Biography of Frida Kahlo*. New York: Harper & Row, Publishers, 1983.

Kirshner, Judith Russi. "Judith Russi Kirshner, Dean of the College of Architecture and the Arts at the University of Illinois at Chicago since 1997." http://www.ia.umich.edu/tt-bio.kirshner.html.

La Raz de Aztlan. http://www.aztlan.net/default3.htm. Access date June 10, 2007.

Lippard, Lucy R. *Mixed Blessings: New Art in a Multicultural America.* New York: Pantheon Books, 1990.

McCarran, Pat. "The Denaturalization aspect of the Immigration and Nationality Act of 1952, Titles I and II." http://www.galeriadelaraza.org/eng/exhibits/timeline.html. Access date June 10, 2007.

Mesa-Bains, Amalia. "Memory, Cultural Identity and the Social Imaginary: Art of the Chicano/a Community." Tenth Annual Ernesto Galarza Commemorative Lecture. Stanford Center for Chicano Research, Stanford University, 1995.

Ochoa, Maria. *Creative Collectives: Chicano Painters Working in Community.* Albuquerque: University of New Mexico Press, 2003.

"Our Journeys/Our Stories: Portraits of Latino Achievement." http://latino.si.edu/virtualgallery/OJOS/bios/bios_Baca.htm

Poniatowska, Elena, *Las Siete Cabritas.* Mexico, D.F.: Ediciones Era, S.A. de C.V. 2000.

Rodriguez, Patricia. *Chicano Art History, reader for Chicano Studies 130 at U.C. Berkeley 1975–1980.* Self-published, 1977

Rosales, F. Arturo, *Chicano! The History of the Mexican American Civil Rights Movement*. Houston: Arte Publico Press, 1996.

Selz, Peter. *Art of Engagement, Visual Politics in California and Beyond*, San Jose: University California Press, San Jose Museum of Modern Art, 2006.

THE BURDEN OF INCLUSIVITY: SECOND-WAVE FEMINISM AND THE THIRD-WAVE ERA

DENA MULLER

In the fall of 2003, the Veteran Feminists of America (VFA)[1] celebrated "Feminist Artists Who Changed the World, 1966–1980" by organizing an exhibition, a reception, and a panel discussion in New York City under that title. The events were star-studded, with many of the most accomplished women artists of the feminist art movement of the 1970s in attendance. The day before the panel discussion, organizer Gloria Orenstein[2] visited A.I.R. Gallery[3] where I was then director. After listening to me describe A.I.R.'s Fellowship Program for Emerging and Mid-career Artists, and my hope that the program would not only encourage the participation of younger women in the gallery's programs but also facilitate intergenerational feminist dialogue, she invited me to attend the panel the following day. I did so, looking forward to hearing more about the visionary women whose actions and art I had studied in my women's studies classes at University of Wisconsin at Madison and New York University.

The panel consisted of several presentations by women artists whose work and activism had characterized the feminist art movement. After these presentations, the discussion opened to questions from the floor. As one of only a few women under the age of forty in the room, I listened disappointedly, as the first comments raised concern for the future of feminism based on the lack of interest, involvement, knowledge, and respect on the part of younger women. A few audience members, particularly those who taught, said that they did find their students to be informed and interested, but the overall tone of the conversation was to identify a new site for activism by "second-wave" feminists[4]: the education of younger women. This new site for activism is in accordance with the mission of the VFA as articulated on its Web site:

> The VFA is a nonprofit organization for veterans of the Second Wave of the Feminist Movement. The goals are to enjoy the camaraderie forged during those years of intense commitment, to honor ourselves and our heroes, to document our history, to rekindle the spark and spirit of the feminist revolution and act as keeper of the flame so that the ideals of feminism continue to reverberate and influence others.[5]

My disappointment in the panel's focus on the seeming failure of younger women to be the right kind of feminists, or feminists at all, turned to relative horror, as moderator Gloria Orenstein leaned into the microphone and asked "Is Dena Muller in the room? If she is, maybe she could speak to the concerns of younger women . . ."[6]

Not being a natural or easy public speaker, I reluctantly took to the front of the room and accepted the microphone. I began by speaking of the concept of the greatest American generation recently articulated through Tom Brokaw's book, *The Greatest Generation*,[7] on the generation that fought World War II and built American society in the years that followed. I explained that my greatest American generation was instead the generation that radicalized society by framing and carrying out the movements for social justice—anti-war, civil rights, and the women's movement—of the 1960s and 1970s. I went on to say that I was interested in the VFA's use of the word "veteran" to define its members' relationship with the women's movement. The use of the word interested me, especially in light of our collective re-evaluation of the term as we grappled to understand our country's return to war in Iraq through the "Shock and Awe"[8] campaign that began earlier that spring. I asked them to consider the relationship between the soldier-soon-to-be-veteran and the citizen's of the "liberated" territories in which they fight. Is it well considered to resent those who are exercising freedoms fought for and secured on their behalf?

And so began my participation in an ongoing dialogue about intergenerational feminism, centered on efforts to define "third-wave feminism"[9] in a way that opens up the feminist conversation to multiple perspectives. The most important aspect of this dialogue is the challenge of inclusion—of younger people, of people of color, of feminist men, of gender justice ideologies, and of activist strategies articulated outside the context of second-wave, American feminism—facing established women's organizations if they intend to continue their work beyond the span of the generation that founded them. The ability of established women's organizations to continue to have an impact seems uncertain, as younger feminists develop new initiatives and organizations, sidestepping the strategies and organizations put in place in the 1960s and 1970s.

Recent postings on the VFA Web site show that while the intergenerational questions within the feminist dialogue have become much more nuanced, they have not been satisfactorily resolved. VFA President Jacqui Ceballos writes in an invitation to younger feminists:

> Dear Young Women—pioneer feminists, who worked around the clock from the 1960s to the 1980s are now enjoying the comraderie and deep friendship that soldiers in bloody wars feel for one another—all the result of years fighting together in the trenches. In our old age (from 60s to 90s) those of us still in good health are very active—but in different ways. The very young feminists we've met at NOW conferences[8] and our own VFA events seem to appreciate us, but there are younger feminists in the 30 and 40 age group who think we're concentrating too much on the past instead of working for the future . . . Please join our dialogue . . . Give us YOUR COMMENTS. Let us know if there is any way we can inspire you.[10]

And in a later post, she reassures VFA members,

> One of our goals is to inspire younger generations and pass the torch . . . The July NOW conference in Albany showed that we're doing it. Where a few years ago younger feminists didn't pay [attention] to us, now they are hanging on every word we say—. And they're organizing in different ways. The next newsletter will have comments from the young women who attended. We want to help you to continue to work for feminism—not just in this country, but around the globe.[11]

In the nearly ten years I have worked for women's organizations established during the second wave of American feminism, and having been born in the early 1970s myself, I have often been in this position of needing to explain my peers. We hear that we are not feminists, not feminist enough, not the right kind of feminist, and so on. The dialogue has changed in the five years since the VFA event, and these days I am more often one of several people in the room, or on the panel, who know from experience that our generational peers *are* feminists, and *active* in promoting feminists concerns. I take any opportunity that I can, to show in a positive light, the sophisticated and varied ways that women in the earlier stages of developing their careers in the art world today are addressing a complex range of feminist issues. While I generally try to stay away from the second-wave versus third-wave polemic in discussions I organize, or am included in, it is often necessary to define our terms.

An important concept was articulated by panelist Maria Elena Buszek, assistant professor of Art History at the Kansas City Art Institute, during the Women's Caucus for Art National Conference in Boston in 2006.

Maria offered an important distinction in defining third-wave feminism that helps to break down the intergenerational polemic. Maria's position is that third-wave feminism—and not a specific generation of people—characterizes this moment in time. I add that anyone interested in feminist inquiry today is a feminist, working in the third-wave era, and the use of exclusively second wave analysis and practice to address the conditions of today is not contemporary. Just as the "personal is political" guided feminism 35 years ago, it should guide feminism today. The world that younger women and men are entering to be educated, to begin careers, social lives, and family lives, and to create a meaningful sense of self as a citizen of the world is greatly altered by the social justice movements of the preceding generation and the contemporary conditions of global society. While many of the concerns included in third-wave feminism were first raised in the second-wave, they are more fully realized and are inclusive of broader social justice concerns. Third-wave feminism supports inquiries into transnationalism, including issues of globalization, immigration, and postcolonialism. Third-wave feminism supports inquiries into gender justice, including transgender identity and queer culture. Third-wave feminism supports inquiries into race and class by considering how they interrelate to create socio-economic injustices. Third-wave feminism supports inquiries into sexuality defined by consensual, subject-driven use of the body and open to a discussion of eroticism and pleasure.

While my experience with VFA is limited to participation in events, such as the celebration of veteran feminist artists held in 2003, and collaboration with many of its members on other projects over the years, I also have direct experience with two established organizations of the Feminist Art Movement: A.I.R. Gallery as the director from 1998 to 2006, and the Women's Caucus for Art (WCA) as a board member from 2001 to today, serving as president from 2004 to 2006.

Initiated by a group of women artists in 1972, A.I.R.'s artist-run, not-for-profit, feminist framing, was a sign of the times. Beginning with the Jane Street Gallery founded in 1944, artists' collectives were common in the decades preceding the founding of A.I.R. Generally well respected as an artist-based alternative to traditional commercial representation, coops were experiencing a revival on the scale of a movement by the early 1970s. While the cooperative structure of the gallery was not a new model in 1972, the feminism at the gallery's source was revolutionary. All of the coops founded previously were, by nature of the gender imbalance in the art world, predominantly or exclusively male. A.I.R. insisted on an all-woman membership. The original founding artists, Dotty Attie, Mary

Grigoriadis, Susan Williams, and Barbara Zucker used resources provided by the burgeoning women's movement to identify other artists they would invite to form the first full membership of the coop. Writing about the founding of the gallery, in the February 1973 issue of *Ms. Magazine*, Marcia Tucker said:

> Regardless of the internal challenges and external judgments, the twenty-two women of A.I.R. believe in their gallery as a genuine option. For those of us in the art world who are not affiliated with A.I.R., it also provides options. Rather than griping about weaknesses and exclusivity of the existing system, we can look to A.I.R. as an alternate model that can function successfully.[12]

Billed as the first, artist-run gallery for women in the United States, the short-lived Womanspace Gallery[13] in California is sometimes said to be an earlier project: A.I.R. brought to a head the feminist consciousness-raising occurring amongst artists and art world professionals and gave it a distinctly New York focus. It confronted the gender discrimination prevalent in the New York art market by providing a venue for women artists that removed the pressure to respond to commercial trends; and, the primary trend in 1972 was the marketing of work made exclusively by male artists. The earliest articulation of A.I.R.'s philosophy included a description of the pressure the members felt, prior to the founding of gallery, to make artwork that was derivative of the work of successful, marketable male artists at the time. By insisting on an alternative gallery model based on feminist critique of the situation for women artists, A.I.R. was part of the counterculture groundswell that initiated and carried out postmodernism's multifaceted but precise process of dismantling establishment, institution, and canon alike.[14]

The Women's Caucus for Art was also founded in 1972, as the feminist sub-caucus of the College Art Association. Its history is fully elaborated in this volume, but for my purposes here, it's important to highlight certain aspects in its founding and growth. In 1972, at the annual CAA conference, there were only a small number of women who were members of CAA. An even smaller number of feminists among them convened to raise feminist challenges to the sexist structures and practices of the academy. The group radicalized the way studio art and art history are made, researched, taught, and exhibited; the way women are treated in academic institutions—in both the classroom and the faculty; and the way women artists are supported within academia and the broader art world. It grew quickly, establishing its own 501(c)(3) non-profit status[15] separate from CAA, and today encompasses a large national membership of predominantly studio artists. WCA began as a cornerstone organization of the second wave of feminist activity in the art world, and exists now as a resource for women in the arts throughout the country.

Both of these organizations, vital to the second-wave of feminism, and its particular manifestation in the art world, today struggle to transcend the generational framework in which they were founded, and reorient themselves to a future that promises the continuing realization of their missions: A.I.R. to provide an alternative venue for women artists, and WCA to provide opportunities and recognition for women in the arts. My involvement with all these organizations, and with the Feminist Art Movement more broadly, informs my position on the need for a redefined, contemporary feminism that includes multiple viewpoints and sees the early work of American feminists in 1960s in continuity with contemporary feminism and all its manifestations. The challenge is for established women's organizations to develop strategies and programs that not only invite all feminists and gender justice activists to participate, but actually welcome and support this participation when it arrives.

While my own formative years have been the same as the years that inform the third-wave era, during the ten years I served in a leadership role in these historic, second-wave organizations, I was charged with taking their missions forward and communicating their histories, structures, and goals to the public. My work led me to attempt a resolution to the inter-generational disconnect within established second-wave organizations, even as their constituencies, actual and desired, collectively experience the third-wave era. I look forward to a time when we dispense with the constant rehashing of the second-wave/third-wave failure to communicate, but in the meantime, it is the crux of these organizations' struggle to move forward, and to carry their missions through another generation into the future.

While our culture has absorbed and left generally unquestioned a maligning of upper case "F" feminism from the second wave as rigid, angry, dogmatic, and something to be avoided, it has also absorbed a notion that younger women are not feminists, are unaware of feminist contributions to history, and that lower case "f" feminism as a value system that underpins the social justice work of progressive young people is non-existent.

If people with a third-wave orientation—all people including men, women, and the transgender and queer communities—do not find their experiences validated, their own voices understood, and their projects resourced within established women's organizations, they will circumvent them as a new establishment that functions as a barrier to their progress. It is of critical importance to find ways to invite people with a third-wave orientation to come through established women's organizations into their professional lives. The resolution to this intergenerational disconnect is in improving communication through more empathetic, mutual understanding between the feminists who worked to establish women's organizations during the height of the women's movement and feminists beginning their careers today. Today's feminists not only reap the benefits of that earlier hard work, but also add to it their own interpretations of the sources of discrimination, the continuing need for gender justice and the strategies for achieving it.

---

[1] VFA is a non-profit organization for veterans of the second wave of the Feminist Movement. The goals are to enjoy the camaraderie forged during those years of intense commitment, to honor ourselves and our heroes, to document our history, to rekindle the spark and spirit of the feminist revolution and act as keeper of the flame so that the ideals of feminism continue to reverberate and influence others" The Veteran Feminists of America, http://www.vfa.us/mainsection.htm. Access date June 1, 2007.

[2] Professor Orenstein researches women's studies in contemporary art, literature, and culture; ecofeminism in the arts; surrealism; women and surrealism; shamanism and Jewish women artists. Her first book, *The Theater of the Marvelous: Surrealism and The Contemporary Stage*, paved the way for her pioneering work on the women of surrealism. She has recently written *The Reflowering of the Goddess*, a feminist analysis of the movement in the contemporary arts that reclaims the Goddess as a symbol of a paradigm shift and a change in our mythos and ethos. More recently, she has become a contributing editor to FEMSPEC, an interdisciplinary feminist journal dedicated to critical and creative works in the realms of science fiction, fantasy, magical realism, surrealism, myth, folklore, and other supernatural genres. She is currently at work on pieces about other women in the surrealist movement in Mexico whose work has, as yet, been unrecognized. She hopes to extend the article on Jewish women artists into a book.
University of Southern California, Faculty, Department of Comparative Literature, http://www.usc.edu/schools/college/faculty/faculty1003588.html. Access date June 1, 2007.

[3] A.I.R. Gallery was founded in 1972 as the first artist-run, not-for-profit gallery for contemporary women artists. It is described in depth in paragraphs nine and ten of this essay. A.I.R. Gallery's mission is to advance the status of women artists by exhibiting quality work by a diverse group of women artists and to provide leadership and community to women artists. "The History of A.I.R.," A.I.R. Gallery. http://www.airgallery.org. Access date June 1, 2007.

[4] Second-wave feminism refers to the women's movement of the 1960s and 1970s in America and is characterized by grassroots social activism, and is framed by an inquiry into the role of patriarchy in discrimination against women.

[5] Veteran Feminists of America. http://www.vfa.us. Access date June 1, 2007.

[6] Gloria Orenstein, VFA Panel November 2003.

[7] Tom Brokaw, *The Greatest Generation* (New York: Random House, 2005).
[8] The U.S.-led "Shock and Awe" campaign began on March 22, 2003 by launching a massive aerial assault against Iraq in the cities of Baghdad, Mosul and Kirkuk. "Shock and Awe Campaign Underway in Iraq," CNN Student News, http://www.cnn.com/2003/fyi/news/03/22/iraq.war/. Access date June 6, 2007.
[9] Third-wave feminism refers to the current era feminism beginning in the early 1990s in America and throughout the world. It is characterized by both grassroots social activism and change effected from within institutional contexts, and is framed by an inquiry into gender injustice that includes issues of race, class, globalization, immigration, sexuality, transgender identity, and queer culture.
[10] Veteran Feminists of America, http://www.vfa.org. Access date May 25, 2007.
[11] Ibid.

The National Organization for Women (NOW) is the largest organization of feminist activists in the United States. NOW has 500,000 contributing members and 550 chapters in all 50 states and the District of Columbia. Since its founding in 1966, NOW's goal has been to take action to bring about equality for all women. NOW works to eliminate discrimination and harassment in the workplace, schools, the justice system, and all other sectors of society; secure abortion, birth control, and reproductive rights for all women; end all forms of violence against women; eradicate racism, sexism, and homophobia; and promote equality and justice in our society. Offered at the National NOW Conference, the NOW Young Feminist Leadership Institute is a set of workshops, roundtables, and activities designed to help younger feminist leaders develop the grassroots and political organizing skills necessary to effect change in their communities. "About NOW", National Organization for Women. http://www.now.org. Access date June 6, 2007
[12] When *Ms*. was launched as a "one-shot" sample insert in *New York Magazine* in December 1971, few realized it would become the landmark institution in both women's rights and American journalism that it is today. The first regular issue hit the newsstands in July 1972. Its 300,000 "one-shot" test copies sold out nationwide in eight days. It generated an astonishing 26,000 subscription orders and over 20,000 reader letters within weeks. *Ms.* was the first U.S. magazine to feature prominent American women demanding the repeal of laws that criminalized abortion, the first to explain and advocate for the ERA, to rate presidential candidates on women's issues, to put domestic violence and sexual harassment on the cover of a women's magazine, to feature feminist protest of pornography, to commission and feature a national study on date rape, and to blow the whistle on the undue influence of advertising on magazine journalism. *Ms.* was the first national magazine to make feminist voices audible, feminist journalism tenable, and a feminist worldview available to the public. Today, the magazine remains an interactive enterprise in which an unusually diverse readership is simultaneously engaged with each other and the world. The modern *Ms.* boasts the most extensive coverage of international women's issues of any magazine available in the United States. "HerStory: 1971–Present," about *Ms. Magazine*. http://www.msmagazine.com/about.asp. Access date June 6, 2007.
[13] The founding of the Woman's Building in Los Angeles in 1973 was the

culmination of several years of activity by women artists who were energized by the Feminist Movement in this country. When the Woman's Building first opened in, it occupied the site of the old Chouinard Art Institute near MacArthur Park. The facility was also home to Womanspace Gallery, Sisterhood Bookstore, Womantours Travel Agency, a coffeehouse, and the offices of the National Organization for Women. "Brief History," The Women's Building. http://www.womansbuilding.org/history.htm. Access date June 6, 2007.

[14] The information on A.I.R. Gallery is quoted from "One True Thing—A.I.R. Gallery," the introductory essay of the catalogue written by curator Dena Muller for the exhibition One True Thing, A.I.R. Gallery, 2007.

[15] Public charities constitute the majority of 501(c)(3) organizations, with private foundations also falling under this category. To be recognized as a public charity, a nonprofit must be organized and operated for purposes that are beneficial to the public interest. These purposes include: relief of the poor, distressed, or underprivileged; advancement of religion; advancement of education and science; creation or maintenance of public buildings or monuments; lessening the burden of government; elimination of prejudice and discrimination; defense of human and civil rights; and, combating community deterioration and juvenile delinquency. The organization must not operate for the benefit of a private person. *Q&As: What is a 501(c)(3) organization?* BoardSource: Building Effective Nonprofit Boards. http://www.boardsource.org/Knowledge.asp?ID=3.172. Access date June 6, 2007.

Works Cited

BoardSource: Building Effective Nonprofit Boards. *Q&As: What is a 501(c)(3) organization?* http://www.boardsource.org/Knowledge.asp?ID=3.172.

Tom Brokaw. *The Greatest Generation*. New York, NY: Random House, 2005.

Ms. Magazine. "HerStory: 1971–Present," http://www.msmagazine.com/about.asp

The Women's Building. "Brief History," The Women's Building, http://www.womansbuilding.org/history.htm

University of Southern California, Faculty, Department of Comparative Literature, http://www.usc.edu/schools/college/faculty/faculty1003588.html.

The Veteran Feminists of America, http://www.vfa.us/mainsection.htm.

NEW PARADIGMS FOR NEW MEDIA

JEANNE PHILIPP

Within continuously shifting cultural paradigms, contemporary media addresses issues of marginal voices, fragmented identities, and cultural hybridization. Feminist media-makers link community engagement with cultural practices, meaning, and social response. At the same time, fluctuating geopolitical boundaries frequently alter the face of community. Cultural goods serve as capital and resource within local, regional, and even national economies. A Rand Corporation study has shown that products and services supporting cultural production increase economic development and stability within community.[1] Nevertheless, women's independent media production still lacks sufficient visibility and economic parity. The New Media Committee in the Women's Caucus for Art (WCA) supports professional opportunities for women in media through ongoing programming that includes video screenings, conferences, and archival preservation.

Feminist media of the sixties and seventies marked an important historical period when women redefined and reclaimed social agency through identity/body politics. With the invention of the consumer portable video equipment, experimental film and theater coalesced in video art. Women artists directed this new medium toward performance art. Video's unique qualities of mimicry in mirror/screen of viewer/subject position provided artists a new visual language with which to question identity politics. The "personal is political"[2] became an underlying theme of speaking the personal as participation in a shared, collective voice. As a time-based medium, video afforded immediate feedback to examine personal issues in daily life. Through video, feminists enacted Lacan's "mirror gaze"[3] as self-reflexive concept of the "Other" or, alternately image/imagemaker, to question shared social assumptions. Critic and art historian Rosalind Krauss, denounced this psychoanalytic approach as narcissistic, because the time-based analog signal never produces a true double or fully constituted object as "Other." Krauss states:

> … video's real medium is a psychological situation, the very terms of which are to withdraw attention from an external object—an Other—and invest it in the Self. Therefore, it is not just any psychological condition one is speaking of. Rather, it is the condition of someone who has, in Freud's words, "abandoned the investment of objects with libido and transformed object-libido into ego-libido." And that is the specific condition of narcissism.[4]

The elusive video image is in a constant state of emergence and decay. For many avant-garde artists this state of continuous renewal served as metaphor for consciousness. The Dalai Lama has stated:

> The Buddhist doctrine of consciousness, from one point of view, is a subjective agent that has the potential to arise correspondent to an object that appears to it. Through the force of the stimulus of the object, consciousness has the ability to arise in an aspect corresponding to the object. [5]

Incorporating the video apparatus as meaning and metaphor for questioning the construction of identity, feminist video artists of the seventies applied the new technology to reclaim power through performed subjectivity, behind and in front of the camera.

The influence of feminist critique of subject/viewer position is most visible within the field of documentary and ethnographic film. The theory and praxis of filmmakers such as Trinh T. Minh-Ha and David and Judith MacDougall, has produced a new sense of audience as well as increased responsibility toward subjectivism. With increased access to technology, indigenous communities are documenting and preserving their histories and cultural traditions in First Voice.[6]

In the twenty-first century, exploration of identity is located within interpersonal social issues relating to class and power relations. Emerging global feminists use and manipulate media to illuminate cultural difference and "place" as loci of stories and hidden histories. These feminists expose the corporate role in the construction of complex cultural identifications, perpetuated through mass media markets that create class barriers to social and economic equality. Dr. Judith Huacuja, a Chicana scholar researching Chicano, Latino, and Latin American art activism in the Americas, calls for research into new pedagogies that would engross students in a critical dialogue where complex cultural identifications and social practices are explored, with the intention of promoting new ways of relating to social and material relations.

> Chicana artists, at the forefront of interdisciplinary cultural analysis, bring

> to their art praxis a number of interventions including an emphasis on language, history and power, as well as an examination of how the construction of knowledge participates within relations of power. Their pedagogies include research, documentation, and performance of previously marginalized histories, as well as student and community based dialogue, analysis, and interpretation that assert a consciousness-raising function. They create art that challenges viewers to understand their subject position within the social fabric and to seek change within the larger social reality.[7]

The Reagan-Thatcher years of privatization of cultural funding limited cultural production within communities. We now face reduced funding of media resources such as Corporation for Public Broadcasting (as of June 2006, a 28 percent reduction in combined funding to $380 million was recorded on the Corporation for Public Broadcasting Web site[8]. National Public Radio and Public Broadcasting Service have a long history as community-based resources for interaction and exchange within all segments of community. In 2007, several states are also passing legislation to eliminate all funding to local community access stations. Nonprofit community media play a critical role in producing and sustaining cultural practice in music, theatre, dance, and visual art. Targeted populations are lost when funding for community-based media is reduced or eliminated. Many women in the media field are leaders in community organizations that provide advocacy and support for minorities. These organizations, such as the Community Film Workshop of Chicago, provide training and equipment access.[9] Control of Internet access would establish further class barriers to information exchange. Contemporary media journals, such as Felix, n.paradoxa, Women and Performance, and Camera Obscura offer online articles, providing accessibility and dialogue with an audience beyond academia.

Feminist media artists continue to offer innovative alternatives to a prepackaged, consumer driven media market. Home markets have provided alternative distribution possibilities. In the seventies, filmmaker Julia Reichert co-founded the highly successful feminist distribution company New Day Films, demonstrating a commitment to a "socialist feminism that values cooperative, nonhierarchical institutions that seek to redress the systematic inequities of gender, class, and racial oppression."[10] Women Make Movies is another leading resource and distributor for women in media. Women Make Movies was founded more than 30 years ago to address the under-representation and misrepresentation of women in media.[11] In the nineties, Miranda July, a rising young filmmaker/videographer, initiated a distribution network in which artists sent her tapes along with five dollars, and she reciprocated with nine short tapes of other artists' works. Her process, based on Internet communication, was a low-cost, open-ended distribution system.

Women pioneering media in the seventies lacked mentors, experimented with low-end equipment, and worked together as activists to find alternative, cooperative solutions to reaching diverse audiences. In the late seventies, many of these filmmakers/videographers touched the lives of young women in film through artist residencies in colleges and universities.[12] During the eighties, more women entered academia and integrated theory and praxis in their teaching, writing and media work.[13] Increased academic access provided equipment for new work as well as economic support to further theoretical research and writing. Published feminist writings on media theory give students access to historical precedence through secondary sources.[14] Nevertheless, primary archived media materials remain relatively inaccessible to most media programs due to lack of proper conservation of flexible media material and the high cost of purchase or rental. The range of women's contributions to the media field will be virtually invisible without access to properly archived works that can be re-screened in public venues.

Today women still make powerful art with low-end equipment, create new global distribution markets, and question the litany of the Feminist Movement. Feminist critic, Lucy Lippard, argued in 1980 that feminist art was "a value system, a revolutionary strategy, a way of life."[15] The legacy of the feminist "movement" has been transformed, through global networks, into multiple languages of resistance and activism, producing new models for social interactions.[16] JPparalelos (Juan-Si Gonzalez and Paloma Dallas) and the multimedia performance collective Los Dialoguistas (Bertha Cohen, Fernando Calderon, and Graciela Bustos) create works that pull from a wide variety of media—photography, digital media, sound, text painting, and sculpture—to make commentary about their local and distant communities, including Dayton, Detroit, Antigua, Buenos Aires, and Sao Paolo. These artists create installation art as a means to explore trans-border dialects, multiracial identities and the use of language, or the confusion of language as it becomes reinvented by the artists' in their efforts to create a renewed sense of place and home between cultures.

The Women's Caucus for Art (WCA) connects international communities of media artists. In 2003, Noreen Dean Dresser, WCA president, initiated a New Media Committee to address the use of new technologies as artistic medium and information platform. Dresser proposed to strengthen and provide new points of connection within

WCA's diverse age groups and communities with advocacy and support of new media practices. She appointed Liz Dodson, video artist, social activist, and co-president of the Minnesota WCA Chapter, and Jeanne Philipp, WCA Midwest regional vice president, media artist and educator, to serve as co-chairs of the New Media Committee. Liz Dodson brought ten years of WCA Board experience and WCA midwest regional leadership and development as well as media work with Women's International League for Peace and Freedom (WILPF) to the Committee. The mission of this Committee is to develop relational approaches to programming, audience development and archiving of information and media works by women. To accomplish these goals, the Committee initiated screening opportunities to view seldom seen work that spanned over 40 years of intergenerational media production.

In 2004, Dodson and Philipp co-chaired a College Art Association Conference session, "Negotiating Collaboration in Aesthetics and Social Change" in Seattle. Papers presented historical and contemporary perspectives on collaboration as a feminist strategy for negotiating social change through media arts. The panel session focused on how artist centered cultural practices interface with cultural policy decisions. Panelists included: Marilyn Cuneo, professor emeritus at the University of Minnesota and founding member of the Women's International League for Peace and Freedom (*Sharing Stories, Creating Hope Artists, Activists & Immigrants Working Jointly for Social Change*); Vivien Green Fryd, professor of Art History from Vanderbilt University (*Suzanne Lacy's and Leslie Labowitz's In Mourning and in Rage: Erasing the Silence About Rape);* Ruth Miller, professor of Art History from University of California, Santa Barbara (*Commitment to Community: Recent Projects of Feminist Artist-Educators, Judy Chicago and Amelie Mesa-Bains*); and Anna Sigridur Arnar, professor of Art History at Minnesota State University Moorhead (*The Art of Seduction: The Collaborative Performances of the Icelandic Love Corporation*).

In tandem with this panel, a retrospective of early works merging computers, film, and dance by seminal filmmaker/videographer Doris Chase was held at the Seattle Art Museum. Chase, internationally known for innovative works in videodance and video theater, created works for television probing critical issues facing women today, in collaboration with Thulani Davis, Jessica Hagedorn, June Plowright, and many others, Filmmaker Yvonne Rainer, a central figure in postmodern dance and film, received a WCA Life Time Achievement Award in 2004 for her contributions to the field. Rainer is a recipient of numerous awards and fellowships for her work, including Guggenheim Fellowships (1988, 1990), a MacArthur Fellowship (1990–95), and a Wexner Prize (1996).

In 2005, the WCA International Video Shorts Festival, held at Georgetown University in Atlanta, Georgia, provided yet another opportunity for bringing together and spotlighting works by well-known and emerging filmmakers, including the American Premiere of *Ultima Llamda / Last Call* and *Atisbos y Estellos / Glimpses and Flashes,* two haunting and evocative works by Julia Barco, an independent filmmaker and media activist from Mexico City and recipient of the Rockefeller and MacArthur Film/Video/Multimedia Fellowship. Works by Doris Chase included powerful, video theatre performances from her Concept series, including *Thulani,* a riveting performance by Thulani Davis, writer and Village Voice senior editor, with complex video textures, giving added meaning to the poetry. This year offered a special screening of Eleanor Dickinson's *Stigmata,* a sensitive documentary on Cloretta Robertson, who at age ten became the first Black to receive the "Stigmata" (bearing on her body the wounds of Christ). Dickinson, media artist, activist, curator, author, and professor emeritus at the California College of Arts and Crafts, was recipient of the WCA Honor Award for Outstanding Achievement in the Visual Arts 2003. Mahyar Nili, an emerging Iranian-American videographer, questioned time and space as well as social constructions in the lyrical and visually striking *on becoming human.* This work subtly alluded to aleph, the descent of light as creative ray that initiates existence, reflecting the inner world and the figure emerging in glimpses from a metaphoric veil. *American Carwash* by Krista Steinke, professor at Moravian College, offered an experimental short film, intended as visual metaphor for the whitewashing of Corporate America's sins in the news media.

The Third Annual WCA International Video Festival program was held in Boston, Massachusetts, at Brandeis University in 2006. Katherine Turczan, Chair of Media Arts at Minneapolis College of Art and Design, curated this program to "showcase the diverse, intelligent, unpredictable and challenging ways contemporary women of all ages and ethnicities express themselves through time-based media."[17] *Digging Deeper to Build New Paradigms: Women Behind and In Front of the Camera* comprised a program of film/video pieces from 11 American female artists. Dr. Turczan writes in her program descriptions:

- Liz Nofziger's video *Bubblegum* begins with a woman's mouth innocently chewing gum, but slowly but surely turns into a dark, sexual and humorous vision. In contrast,

- Margaret Lazzari's sobering autobiographical *Chemo Sequences* cleverly challenges us to redefine beauty in the face of ravaging illness.
- Priscilla Briggs *True Confessions* breaks from traditional narrative forms by mixing a story in sound with an impeccably edited visual collage from television. The result is a powerful story of sexual abuse.
- Cultural, social and psychological implications haunt Sejal Patel's Trilogy: *Red Purple Blue.* Patel confronts herself and the traditional expectations of Indian pre-arranged marriage through vignettes imagined as self-portraits and transformed by color.
- Japanese-American Emily Hanako Momohara explores heritage through her family's incarceration in the Idaho detainee camps during World War II. She uses a former internee's song voice to emphasize the agony of her family's past.[18]

Further descriptions are included in the program notes of works by Mary Oesterreicher Hamill, Brooke White, Dawn Nye, Anne Stoddard, Deborah Wing-Sprout, and Krista Steinke.[19] FemLink, an international media collective of women artists from 32 countries, premiered their video collage *Fragility* at the 2006 WCA screening in Boston.[20]

Sheryl Mousley, curator of Film at Walker Art Center in Minneapolis, juried the WCA Video Shorts Festival 2007 held at Barnard College, New York City. Mousley writes in the program notes to *Place, Identity, Children, and Memory:*

> This program represents the work of twenty-two artists, grouped thematically, but unified by the clarity of their vision. Using moving images, whether video, film or digital formats, these women explore ideas of place, identity, children, and memory.
>
> - The six films that make up Place each take a specific site or group of sites and then give us, the viewer, a way to connect—whether to its history, its markings in the world, its blurred imprints from television images, its beauty, or the fear that it provokes. It is the sense of place that anchors the position from which the filmmaker sets out on her journey of creating this work.

The next six films are layered treatments of Identity. The first layer can be most recognized by geographic origin—Poland, Turkey, Korea, Italy, or America. The second layer is, in some cases, more subtle as it reveals the relationships between men and women, the feeling of alienation as a foreigner, or what makes up the complex American identity.

- Children are fascinating subjects, whether watching them learn, hearing them report on their day, or contemplating the underlying fear of having them.

- To visualize the repeated return to an ordinary place like a bed, to diaristically create a work of art to help remember each day, to record and contextualize the graffiti of an abandoned prison, or explore the relationship of fifteenth century icons with today's questions about religion, all these works are concerned with Memory.[21]

The New Media Committee provides arts advocacy to promote a greater understanding of social structures that inform our multiethnic communities and to connect these structures through the arts to a larger political-economic structure. In 1994, noted cultural theorist B. Ruby Rich, in *Dissed and Disconnected: Notes on Present Ills and Future Dreams*, called for "development of new aesthetic strategies based in practices of hybridity, crossover and syncretism without assimilation."[22] The face of media and "feminisms" are continuously changing with the advance of new global technologies and the rise of transnational media artists, producers, and theorists.[23] As cultural workers, we stand on the shoulders of our ancestors. In these critical times, we have a responsibility to honor and remember their voice while supporting emerging multivocal feminisms.

---

[1] Kevin F. McCarthy, Elizabeth H. Ondaatje, Laura Zkaras, and Arthur Brooks, *Gifts of the Muse: Reframing the Debate About the Benefits of the Arts* (Santa Monica, California: Rand Corporation, 2004). A seminal research report providing the means for evaluating public contributions to the arts and setting a research agenda for testing claims about the importance of art to the wider society.

[2] David Ross, "The Personal Attitude," in *Video Art: an Anthology*, ed. Ira Schneider and Beryl Korot (New York: Harcourt Brace Jovanovich, 1976).

[3] Jacques Lacan, *Écrits: A Selection*, trans. Alan Sheridan (New York: Norton, 1977).

[4] John G. Hanhardt, "Video: The Aesthetics of Narcissism, in *Video Culture: Critical Investigation*. (Layton, Utah: G.M. Smith Books, in association with Visual Studies Workshop Press. 1986), 185.

[5] Jacques Derrida, "Signs and the Blink of an Eye," in *Speech and Phenomena and Other Essays on Husserl's Theory of Signs,* trans. David B. Allison (Evanston: Northwestern University Press, 1973), 60.

[6] Aboriginal Film Video Art Alliance, Women's Video Workshop of Igloolick.

[7] J.P. Huacuja, "Chicana Critical Pedagogies: Chicana Art as Critique and Intervention" in *Proceedings on the Interpretation and Representation of Latino Cultures: Research and Museums* (Washington, DC: Smithsonian Institution Press, 2003). A conference convened for scholars in Latino studies, archivists, and museum professionals. The purpose was to examine the current status of research and educational literature on the interpretation, representation, and documentation

of Latino cultures in museums and academic programs within the United States and Puerto Rico.

[8] The Public Broadcasting Service (PBS) http://www.pbs.org/aboutpbs/news/20060607_publicbroadcastersstatement.html accesed June 7, 2007.

[9] Boston Film and Video Foundation, Bay Area Video Coalition, Downtown Community Television in New York City, and Media Alliance.

[10] A. Juhasz, ed., *Women of Vision: Histories in Feminist Film and Video*. Minneapolis: University of Minnesota Press, 2001).

[11] Online at Women Make Movies, http://www.wmm.com/ acessed June 10, 2007.

[12] Carolee Schneemann, Joan Jonas, Steina Vasulka, Jeni Engel, Beverly Grant, and Storm DeHirsch.

[13] Although it is not possible to cite all outstanding women media artists who have influenced the field through academia, seminal artists include Adrian Piper (Wellesley College), Suzanne Lacy (California College of the Arts), Martha Rosler (Rutgers University), Amalie Mesa-Bains (California State University, Monterey Bay), Moira Roth (Mills College), Dara Birnbaum (Nova Scotia College of Art and Design), Lynn Hershman (University of California, Davis, and Cornell University); Coco Fusco (Columbia University). Eve Oishi (California State University, Long Beach), Chris Hill (Antioch College), and Constance Penley (University of California, Santa Barbara).

[14] Seminal contemporary women author/theorists include but are by no means limited to Trinh T. Minh-Ha, Donna Harraway, Kathy High, Suzanne Lacy, Barbara London, Peggy Gale, Laura Mulvey, Catherine Elwes, Lauren Rabinowitz, Sara Diamond, and Alexandra Juhasz.

[15] Lucy R. Lippard, "Sweeping Exchanges: The Contribution of Feminism to the Art of the 70's," *Art Journal* Vol. 40, No. ½ (Fall/Winter 1980): 362.

[16] Peggy Diggs (Domestic Violence Milk Carton Project); Judith Baca (ongoing murals with SPARC); L.A. Coyotes, Mujeres de Maiz, and Las Comadres Artistas; Margaret Caples (Community Film Workshop, Chicago).

[17] Katherine Turczan, Exhibition Program, WCA 2006 International Video Festival, 2006.

[18] Ibid.

[19] Ibid.

[20] Online at Femlink http://www.femlink.org/. Access date June 10, 2007. The video collage project builds a link throughout the world between women video artists and their work. The structure is simple: one artist from each country will create a one to two minute video around a common theme. As videos are collected for the project they are added to the collage sequentially without regard to content. The video-collage values each artist's creative response and respects the many diverse interpretations of its first theme: Fragility.

[21] Sheryl Mousley, Exhibition Program, WCA 2007 International Video Festival, 2007.

[22] B.R. Rich, “Dissed and Disconnected: Notes on Present Ills and Future Dreams, in “*The Subversive Imagination : Artists, Society, and Responsibility*, ed.Carol Becker (New York: Routledge, 1994), 243.

[23] Los Dialoguistas (Graciela Bustos, Fernando Calderon, and Bertha Cohen); JPparalelos (Juan Si Gonzalez and Paloma Dallas). Yvonne Welbon (Our Film Works); Frances Negron Muntaner (Polymorphous Pictures); Shirin Neshat; Yolanda Lopez, Barbara Hammer; Natalie Bookchin; Pipilotti Rist; Tracey Moffatt; and Magdalena Campos Pons.

[23] Los Dialoguistas (Graciela Bustos, Fernando Calderon, and Bertha Cohen); JPparalelos (Juan Si Gonzalez and Paloma Dallas). Yvonne Welbon (Our Film Works); Frances Negron Muntaner (Polymorphous Pictures); Shirin Neshat; Yolanda Lopez, Barbara Hammer; Natalie Bookchin; Pipilotti Rist; Tracey Moffatt; and Magdalena Campos Pons.

Works Cited

Derrida, Jacques. "Signs and the Blink of an Eye." *Speech and Phenomena and Other Essays on Husserl's Theory of Signs.* Trans. David B. Allison. Evanston: Northwestern University Press, 1973.

Hanhardt, John G. *Video Culture: Critical Investigation.* New York: Visual Studies Workshop, 1986.

Huacuja, J. P. "Chicana Critical Pedagogies: Chicana Art as Critique and Intervention." In *Proceedings on the Interpretation and Representation of Latino Cultures: Research and Museums*. Washington, DC: Smithsonian Institution Press, 2003.

Juhasz, A., ed. *Women of Vision: Histories in Feminist Film and Video.* Minneapolis: University of Minnesota Press, 2001.

Lacan, Jacques. *Écrits: a Selection.* Trans. Alan Sheridan. New York: Norton, 1977.

Lippard, Lucy R. Sweeping Exchanges: The Contribution of Feminism to the Art of the 70's." *Art Journal, Vol. 40, No. ½* (Fall/Winter, 1980).

McCarthy, Kevin F. Elizabeth H. Ondaatje, Laura Zkaras, and Arthur Brooks. *Gifts of the muse: reframing the debate about the benefits of the arts.* Santa Monica, California: Rand Corporation, 2004.

Mousley, Sheryl. Exhibition Program. WCA 2007 International Video Festival, 2007.

Rich, B. R. "Dissed and Disconnected: Notes on Present Ills and Future Dreams." In *The Subversive Imagination: Artists, Society, and Responsibility*. Edited by Carol Becker. New York: Routledge, 1994.

Ross, David. "The Personal Attitude." In *Video Art: An Anthology*, edited by Ira Schneider and Beryl Korot. New York: Harcourt Brace Jovanovich, 1976.

Katherine Turczan, exhibition program, WCA 2006 International Video Festival, 2006.

CRITICAL WRITINGS ON FEMINIST TOPICS

JOAN M. MARTER

The year 2007 augurs well for women in the United States. Although they waited two hundred years for this moment in American history, recent events suggest that women have broken through the "marble ceiling," as the new Speaker of the House Nancy Pelosi proudly proclaimed. In January 2007, Senator Hillary Rodham Clinton became the first serious woman contender to declare her intentions to run for president of the United States. This year women are represented in both the House of Representatives and the Senate, but they are far from achieving parity with their male counterparts.

Have comparable changes improved the situation for women artists? Although more women appear in gallery exhibitions, the situation in museums has not changed appreciably. Most galleries exhibiting the permanent collections of museums seldom reflect the well-acknowledged contribution of women artists throughout the ages. Even in galleries of contemporary art, male artists dominate.

When Elizabeth Murray is featured in a solo exhibition at the Museum of Modern Art, as she was in 2006, attention is drawn to women artists. Likewise, in March of 2007, Wack! Women Artists and the Feminist Revolution opened at the Los Angeles Museum of Contemporary Art, and traveled to the National Museum of Women in the Arts. The Elizabeth Sackler Center for Feminist Art opened in March 2007 at The Brooklyn Museum of Art, providing a permanent venue for Judy Chicago's *Dinner Party*, and presenting an exhibition devoted to Global Feminisms, curated by Linda Nochlin and Maura Reilly.

With all the attention generated by feminists for women artists in 2007, is it possible that women artists and historians no longer have a need for publications devoted exclusively to feminist issues? Have women artists been recognized so forcefully in mainstream art publications that journals devoted to feminist topics and the exclusive presentation of women's art are no longer necessary? A survey of recent issues of *Art in America, Flash Art,* and *Artforum* would suggest otherwise.

Beginning in the early 1970s, feminist literature responded to a growing awareness of gender issues, but each publication had specific agendas. Carrie Rickey noted in "Writing (and Righting) Wrongs: Feminist Art Publications" that during the 1970s critics and historians created a cultural network: "It is not an overstatement to say that one of the best predictors of American art during the 1980s was the feminist art press of the 1970s, which fired upon the dominant modernist canon well before the mainstream periodicals dared, and suggested other aesthetic and political alternatives."[1]

It is true that articles and reviews by women critics, historians, and artists presaged the direction of postmodernism, providing the discourse that anticipated major art world movements such as Pattern and Decoration, Body Art, and Performance. The challenge to mainstream art world practice was initiated in 1971 with Linda Nochlin's ground-breaking essay, "Why Have There Been No Great Women Artists?," which appeared first in *ARTNews* in January 1971.[2] If Nochlin explained that women's problems in securing art instruction and lack of access to life classes accounted for the dearth of women artists through the ages, younger art historians took up the challenge. They explored historical periods and discovered the remarkable achievements of many neglected women artists, such as Artemisia Gentileschi, Judith Leyster, and Elisabeth-Louise Vigée-Lebrun. In the contemporary realm, the answer to Nochlin's challenge was found in the efforts of women artists and critics who rushed to provide full coverage for the plight of younger women artists.[3] Judy Chicago joined feminist art historian Arlene Raven and artist Sheila de Bretteville in publishing an article about her efforts to educate young women titled "The Feminist Studio Workshop," in *Womanspace Journal* (February/March 1973). Although this journal was short-lived, Judy Chicago used this publication and previously *Everywoman* to espouse her "central core imagery."[4]

Other journals were initiated in these years, including the *Feminist Art Journal*, which first appeared in a tabloid format, but four years later changed to a more formal design. The first editors, including art historian Patricia Mainardi, art critic Cindy Nemser, and artist Irene Moss, pledged to be the voice of women artists in the art world, and to improve the status of all women artists.[5] The same issue included many responses to the plight of women, including serious attacks on major museums such as the Metropolitan Museum of Art for their employment policies, and charges of sexism by male reviewers and male chauvinism among curators. In addition to this policing of the art world, there were articles on the "feminine sensibility" and others written mostly by East Coast artists.[6]

Wisely, *Feminist Art Journal* began to limit the number of exposés of offending curators, museums, critics, and publishers, and to focus more attention on living women artists. Reviewers covered gallery and museum exhibitions and women's conferences, and many articles were devoted to individual artists. Cindy Nemser, who became sole editor in 1973, featured her interviews with women artists, which resulted in a useful book titled *ArtTalk, Conversations with Women Artists.*[7] But Nemser was criticized for choosing to emphasize the personal lives of the artists, and for trying to push her renowned female interview subjects (Sonia Delaunay and Barbara Hepworth, among others) into a feminist argument. Some of these women refused to be identified with the feminist struggle. In addition, Nemser cut off any discourse concerning central core imagery. Her articles on women artists were largely informational, with little analysis of individual works of art. Following an attempt to expand its readership, the journal ceased publication in 1977.

Other journals were short-lived, an exception being *Women Artists News,* which began as *Women Artists Newsletter.* Published by Cynthia Navaretta (now the proprietor of Midmarch Press), the newsletter began in 1975 and continued until 1991. Primarily informational in focus and using the format of a tabloid, *Women Artists News* included short articles, reports on exhibitions, political commentaries, and reviews. *Womanart,* founded in 1976 by writer and critic Ellen Lubell, lasted only two years but left its mark. Splashed across the cover of its 1977 issue was the question, "What Ever Happened to the Women Artists' Movement?" In her answer, Pat Mainardi declared that the movement had transformed the art world for contemporary women artists by providing a revision of art history and bringing to light the great women of the past. Indeed the few issues of this journal introduced some of the major themes that women artists addressed. *Chrysalis,* published in Los Angeles, began its three-year run in 1977, the same year that the first issue of *Heresies: A Feminist Publication on Art and Politics,* appeared in New York. Both journals targeted a feminist audience, with a growing presence of lesbian artists. *Heresies* featured thematic issues with teams of artists and writers contributing essays, poems, or works of art. When the first issue appeared in January 1977, it included a critique of the Women Artists' Movement, and Adrienne Rich's "Notes on Lying." Issue #3 (Fall 1977) was devoted to Lesbian Art and Artists, and included an essay by Louise Fishman entitled, "Cautionary Advice from a Lesbian Painter." In Issue #4, Joyce Kozloff and Valerie Jaudon gave attention to the Pattern and Decoration Movement, of which they were a part. In 1978, a special issue was devoted to "The Great Goddess." Until 1989, energetic artists and writers joined together to expand feminist discourse through this journal.

The sole surviving journal from the first decade of the women artists' movement is *Woman's Art Journal.* Begun by art historian Elsa Honig Fine, the journal remained a steady, reliable presence, presenting almost 300 well-documented articles that have contributed enormously to the steady progress of women artists and scholars in academic and commercial publishing. In 2005, Rutgers University undertook the sponsorship of *Woman's Art Journal,* and for the last year I have co-edited the journal with Margaret Barlow. To address the question of what *Woman's Art Journal* continues to offer feminist readers in the twenty-first century, we remain open to all points of view, to voices different from our own approach to feminist writing. We will continue to integrate the remarkable achievements of women artists within the mainstream of art history while incorporating feminist theory and methodologies. Through our interest in "representations of women" throughout the history of art, we will offer a feminist reading of the art of both male and female artists. Finally, we recognize that issues of gender, race, and ethnicity are essential aspects of the contemporary discourse on works of art, and the search for identity often leads to a new awareness of artists of diverse ethnic and racial backgrounds. While these topics might find occasional coverage in the mainstream press, *Woman's Art Journal* will continue to offer a lively discourse on a range of feminist topics. Undoubtedly, feminist art and scholarship on feminism have demonstrated that postmodernism owes an enormous debt to the Women Artists' Movement.

N. Paradoxa, International Feminist Art Journal began publication in London in 1998, and continues to thrive under the editorship of Katy Deepwell. Issues have focused on such subjects as "Body, Space & Memory" and "Women and New Media," and a 2006 issue was devoted to "Curatorial Strategies." Issues typically include artists' pages, book reviews, exhibition reviews, and important discussion of feminist theory and practice. This journal must continue its international coverage of women's issues.

Suddenly, there seems to be a burgeoning interest in feminist art by mainstream media and institutions. Are feminists in positions of power in the mainstream? The debate about what is feminist art seems to have been recycled. Feminist periodicals and other publications should be documenting women artists of achievement who have produced significant work despite gender restrictions. Diversity needs to be encouraged, and articles and essays should attempt to foreground identity within the global community of the twenty-first century.

[1] Carrie Rickey, "Writing (And Righting) Wrongs: Feminist Art Publications," in *The Power of Feminist Art, The American Movement of the 1970s, History and Impact*, ed. Norma Broude and Mary D. Garrard (New York: Abrams, 1994), 120.
[2] Linda Nochlin, "Why Have There Been No Great Women Artists?" *Art News*? (January 1971): 22–39.
[3] See, for example, Cindy Nemser, "The Women Artists Movement," *The Feminist Art Journal* (Winter 1973/1974), 8–10.
[4] Judy Chicago and Miriam Schapiro, "Female Imagery," *Womanspace Journal* I (Summer 1973):13.
[5] Editorial, *Feminist Art Journal* (April 1972).
[6] Patricia Mainardi, "Feminine Sensibility?—Two Views," *Feminist Art Journal* I (April 1972): 4.
[7] Cindy Nemser, *Art Talk: Conversations with Twelve Women Artists* (New York: Scribner's, 1975).

Works Cited

Chicago, Judy and Miriam Schapiro. "Female Imagery," *Womanspace Journal* I (Summer 1973):13.

Editorial, *Feminist Art Journal* (April 1972).

Mainardi, Patricia. "Feminine Sensibility?—Two Views," *Feminist Art Journal* I (April 1972): 4.

Nemser, Cindy. *Art Talk: Conversations with Twelve Women Artists.* New York: Scribner's, 1975.

——. "The Women Artists' Movement," *The Feminist Art Journal* (Winter 1973/74): 8–10.

Nochlin, Linda, "Why Have There Been No Great Women Artists?" *Art News* (January 1971): 22–39.

Rickey, Carrie. "Writing (And Righting) Wrongs: Feminist Art Publications," in Norma Broude and Mary D. Garrard, editors, *The Power of Feminist Art, The American Movement of the 1970s, History and Impact.* New York: Abrams, 1994.

PART II: CRITICISM

PERMA-WAVE: BRIDGING FEMINISM'S GENERATION GAP

MARIA ELENA BUSZEK

For the young feminist artists, critics, and writers who joined their professional colleagues in the annual tradition of flooding the respective, back-to-back conferences of the National Women's Caucus for Art (WCA) and College Art Association (CAA), 2006 was something of a banner year. Not only did each conference dedicate panels to the subject of "third-wave" feminism in contemporary art—in which emerging feminists in their respective field represented themselves in presentations about the generation gap that plagues the Feminist Movement as a whole—each panel was marked by lively intergenerational dialogues and praise that followed. At the WCA panel, efforts to effectively name and further movement-wide the goodwill that these discussions brought about led to panelist and artist S.A. Bachman declaring, to the delight of all, that perhaps we have finally reached the era of "Perma-wave," where feminists of different generations might finally work together to further the cause of women's rights even as they acknowledge and debate one another's differences.

To those at the WCA's panel at the CAA annual conference just four years earlier, the possibility of this kind of intergenerational love-in seemed a far-distant, if not impossible prospect. At this New York conference, the National WCA had assembled speakers to pay well-deserved tribute to the New York Feminist Art Institute (NYFAI). The fruit of the dynamic "women's liberation" movement begun in the late 1960s, NYFAI's successes in giving women a voice for their self-expression, using art as a vehicle for consciousness-raising and activism, and encouraging women to take all these tools into broader gallery and academic systems reflect the larger successes of this generation of activists. However, discussion of the institute's closing in 1990 led to inevitable questions of feminism's future in the panel's subsequent question-and-answer session, as one audience member after another each essentially rephrased a single question: "Where are the young feminists?"

As a young feminist in attendance, my first instinct was to slink down in my seat and look around me with the same question on my mind. However, a cursory glance at the rows to my left and right revealed something: I was hardly the only younger woman in attendance. Indeed, with each rephrasing of the question, my neck craned around a few more degrees to gradually take in the entire crowd. Easily a third of the audience appeared to be comprised of women under the age of 40. By the time the woman seated directly to my right stood up to angrily ask the question once again—"Where *are* the young feminists?"—I raised my hand in frustration: "We are right here. *Right next to you.*"

The situation, as I pointed out then, felt familiar as well as symbolic of a much larger problem of the women's movement—ironically, perhaps best summarized here with a football metaphor. A group of feminists who came of age during the second-wave stand in a huddle over the movement's game-plan, exhausted and battered at half-time and—looking searchingly at one another—ask themselves, "who do we put on the field?" Meantime, there sits a group of sprightly rookies warming the bench, waving frantically at the all-star huddle, but who—programmed by the unspoken hierarchies that always emerge even in the most team-oriented of activities—have been made to feel too outranked, too insignificant to dare break the concentration of the huddled captains with so much as a shout or a tap on the shoulder. So, there they sit: ready, willing. . .unnoticed. The applause that my comments at drew from the audience made it appear as if the open recognition of this situation bought about a sense of relief to *all* the women in attendance. The focus of questions from that point shifted from the panel to the audience; beginning a contentious but thrillingly necessary dialogue about this unfortunate reality of contemporary feminism's intergenerational tension—although *tension* would perhaps be an inappropriate word for it. Intergenerational *blindness* might be a better way of stating our present situation, because it really is a matter of not seeing, and of subsequently not understanding.

Tension, however, certainly does come into the picture, particularly when it comes to the day-to-day realities of feminist activism, because few young women are content to warm the bench for long. Indeed, it seems as if the cultural blindness to a third-wave of feminism in the United States has resulted not in the mass rejection of feminism that many—including older feminists—assume has happened since the 1980's, but instead in either a storming of the field or, rather, a change of venue altogether as young women create their own work and conduct their own research in a parallel feminist universe that the women who *would* be coaching them are either unaware is happening or, worse, have little interest in either supporting or acknowledging. (To underscore this problem, it bears noting that at this same conference where young women's alleged rejection of feminist bonds and ideals was so casually discussed as fact, there were nine panels specifically dedicated to women's art and feminist art history, in which easily half, if not the majority of participants were early-career artists and scholars; and the White Columns exhibition Regarding Gloria, dedicated to young feminists whose work paid homage to that of their predecessors, had just closed after a much-publicized and successful run.[1]) My intention, however, is not to scold established, older feminists for hogging the ball—especially not when their example and nurturance led younger feminists such as myself to the women's movement in the first place. Instead, I am interested in exploring the utility of acknowledging feminism's evolution based on the experiences and interactions of each different generation that affects it.

My interest in identifying a "third-wave" of feminism stems not just from my age—born in 1971, by all accounts I grew up smack-dab in the middle of the splintering postmodern feminist world that arguably led to the emergence of a third-wave of the women's movement—but also from my research, which focuses upon the ways in which the evolution of feminist thought has affected visual culture since the nineteenth century. Most recently and extensively I explored this evolution in my book *Pin-up Grrrls: Feminism, Sexuality, and Popular Culture,* where I use the pin-up as a "case study" toward a broader investigation of feminism's complicated relationship to both women's sexual expression and its representation in pop culture. Because of my interest in focusing on this historical sweep rather than zeroing in on a single period or movement, I also inevitably explain the evolution of feminist activism and theory alongside feminist imagery—an evolution I have followed historians of the modern women's movement in addressing as three "waves" of feminist expression and organizing that have emerged since the late eighteenth century.

The first-wave of feminism is by far the most nebulous, in large part because for nearly 150 years its myriad participants were almost uniformly involved in the one battle that tended to connect them: enfranchisement in democratic societies. As such, feminism's first-wave encompasses individuals and movements as separated by time and approach as Mary Wollstonecraft—whose 1792 *A Vindication of the Rights of Woman* was published in the wake of the American and French revolutions to contrast women's universal powerlessness against the self-congratulatory, democratic zeal of revolutionary philosophers—and Simone de

Beauvoir—whose groundbreaking 1949 book *The Second Sex* was begun shortly after French women first gained the vote in 1945.

However, the first-wave period between roughly 1920 and 1960 is marked by feminist activity ebbing as women in Europe and North America sorted out the limits of enfranchisement that they had won and applied throughout these years. In this period, feminism was also actively fought within these same cultures, a backlash against both women's gains to date and the world-upside-down that they threatened to many: a period that Shulamith Firestone would in 1970 call history's "first counteroffensive" against the women's movement.[2] Firestone, however, would be among the firebrands of feminism's second-wave, born largely of the labor and civil rights movements of the post-WWII era, which in the 1960s sought to take inventory of and fight against ongoing sexism that voting rights alone had been clearly incapable of undoing. Generally referred to, then as now, as the women's liberation movement, feminism's second-wave used strategies of the progressive movements from which its leaders sprung, similarly initiating and passing equal-rights legislation—concerning everything from reproductive rights to gender-specific classified ads—as well as producing feminist memoirs, theory, and collectives that raised consciousness concerning more insidious examples of sexism ingrained and normalized in everyday life. While this era is often discussed as not just popularizing but institutionalizing feminism—both *as* an "institution" with certain common goals and practices, and *within* institutions ranging from national governments to organized religion—the fact is that the second-wave was far more diverse and contentious than it is (or was) generally acknowledged to be, leading to visible fissures from the start of this era's feminist resurgence. Feminists of color and working-class women called attention to the middle-to-upper-class eurocentrism of second-wave leaders, straight and lesbian feminists debated the "proper" sexual positioning of the movement's members, and sex-radical and anti-censorship feminists declared their right to sexual self-expression in the midst of anti-pornography activism.

This expanding discourse—and the heated debates that it inspired—resulted not only in a diverse but an increasingly individualistic feminism that, as the evolving movement both shaped and responded to postmodern theory, would by the 1980s give way to what many have begun to both recognize and theorize as a third-wave of feminism in our present day. As reflected in the feminist practices of Generations X and Y—who, for better or for worse, are generally the most reported-upon and self-identifying members of our contemporary third-wave—our era is currently defined less by a single-minded focus on organization and activism (which, it is frequently argued, excluded as much as served women who did not meet certain leaders' "standards" for the same) than on the study of identity-formation, leading women to theorize and practice an individual feminist politics expressed more subtly in everyday-life actions.

I appreciate the feminist "wave" model because, as literary scholar Judith Roof puts it, it allows one to address feminism's evolution without resorting to the tempting mother/daughter framework in which age-based generations are pitted against one another. This inevitably privileges "a kind of family history that organizes generations where they don't exist, ignores intragenerational differences and intergenerational commonalities, and thrives on a paradigm of oppositional change."[3] As such, literary scholar Astrid Henry argues in her book *Not My Mother's Sister: Generational Conflict and Third-Wave Feminism,* "the metaphor of the wave seems to offer an alternative model for describing feminist generations."[4] The wave structure also allows for feminist scholarship to "flow," as it were, toward individuals, movements, and practices that may not in their own day have been recognized by—indeed, may even have been fought by—the period's dominant feminist culture, and recuperate them as preexisting models for subsequent generations.

However, like Henry, I also recognize a crucial problem in applying this seemingly fluid structure in our present moment of feminist history in that the

> emergence of feminism's third wave seems to profoundly alter our use of the metaphor of the wave. Given the early mapping of 'mother' and 'daughter' onto 'second wave' and third wave,' the wave metaphor and the mother-daughter relationship increasingly have become synonymous within feminist discourse. While initially offering a generational model located outside the family, then, the wave metaphor has [since] come to resemble the familial structure with its understanding of generations based on the human life cycle.[5]

As such, this binary construction of recent feminist history often lends itself to the polarization of women who identify by age or experience with one "wave" (read: side) or another. Moreover, it forces women who came to the movement in the late 1970s and early 1980s to choose either one side or the other in this illusory divide—or worse: "As they can be understood as neither 'mothers' nor 'daughters' within feminism's imagined family structure, such feminists [find themselves] frequently absent from recent discourse on feminism's (seemingly two) generations."[6] In other words, as literary scholar Diane Elam has put it: while most debates on the issue posit "senior," second-wave feminists against their "juniors" in the third-wave, in reality "most feminists find themselves to be both a senior and a junior at the same time."[7]

However, I remain among those advocates of "naming and claiming" a wave structure for feminist history because I maintain that, in addition to presenting one with the most straightforward chronology of dominant issues and ideas in the long history of the movement, a discussion of feminism's various waves provides one with the best available metaphor for precisely the paradoxes that have sustained the movement itself. Addressing feminist history as evolving in waves respects the fluidity and resiliency of the women's movement, but also respects the significance of difference and even conflict therein—which I believe many feminists who reject the wave metaphor wish to sweep under the rug in favor of a unity not only as illusory as a generation-based feminism but, ultimately, one that threatens to prove fatal. Sociologist Nancy Whittier has compellingly argued that "the presence and strength of conflicts over what it means to be a feminist and over appropriate feminist behavior and goals signify the continued vitality of the movement. A movement remains alive as long as there is struggle over its collective identity, or as long as calling oneself or one's organization 'feminist' means something."[8] This struggle has historically forced the question succinctly articulated by Elam: "Is feminism a *tradition* handed down by powerful ancestors, or is it a *progress* in which the latecomers, however dwarf-like, are always standing on the shoulders of those who came before, seeing farther, knowing more?"[9] And while efforts to pose this question have perhaps inevitably resulted in polarization within the movement, nuanced efforts to answer it have resulted in a productive paradox: the reality of feminism, of course, is that both answers are correct—a fact that instigates tension but also understanding across generations as a balance is necessarily struck between tradition and progress.

Thankfully, many contemporary feminist thinkers see in this problem a challenge that has led to their own attempts to represent the very contradiction of feminist evolution in their work and writing. Indeed, the paradoxical nature of the issue has forced feminist thinkers to approach feminism itself as a political paradox: not as a singular *feminism* but as multiple *feminisms*, which are simultaneously individual and (like the "communities" they produce), inevitably somehow common. As theorized by Donna Haraway, this organizational strategy for feminism does not deify movement-killing individualism above women's mobilization. Indeed, art historian Katy Deepwell has appropriated Haraway's use of the parasite *mixotricha paradoxa* as a creative metaphor for feminism's *growth* through diversity.[10] Deepwell argues, via Haraway's research, that this creature, like feminism itself, "has paradoxical and unexpected habits of survival and reproduction. . . . [I]t survives by attracting others to live on it [and] it reproduces by division."[11] In other words, each of these contemporary scholars promotes the logic to be found in both paradox and division in ways that feminist thinkers have been exploring, if perhaps not acknowledging, since its first wave.

Art historian Amelia Jones—in her contribution to the nine views on contemporary art and feminism recently published in the October 2003 issue of *Artforum*—weighed in on the relevance of recognizing how this balancing act applies not only to feminism's future, but feminism's past when she argued that "we are in danger of getting very confused about the complexity of past decades' feminist debates."[12] Contributing to this same *Artforum* discussion, Linda Nochlin voiced her own frustrations over this very "confusion" when she reminded her readers that, although second-wave activists were all "for justice, equity, and a fair shake for women artists, critics, and academics, our views were extremely varied, and we were often at odds with one another," and like Jones lamented the tendency for recent histories to pin down a unified trajectory for the second-wave in such a way that a culture "that seemed open and dynamic [is] now pinned down and displayed like butterflies in a case."[13] By way of conclusion to these *Artforum* perspectives, art historian Peggy Phelan spoke to both the openness of which Nochlin wrote and its legacy for subsequent generations of feminists. Her piece articulates the ways in which our contemporary art world was shaped not only by second-wave challenges to patriarchal, heterosexist accounts of history, but also by the anxiety of documenting its own history as postmodern artists and art historians simultaneously came to acknowledge the limits of doing just that. Phelan reiterates the degree to which the resulting ambivalence—as she puts it, "in the fullest sense of that term"—was the product of the increasingly self-critical, multicultural, and relativist postmodern culture ushered in by second-wave inquiry. Indeed, as Phelan asserts, the ambivalence that marks feminism's third-wave is not just a logical progression of second-wave thought, but today a necessary worldview: "In these days of hideous fundamentalism, the capacity to acknowledge ambivalence is revolutionary."[14]

Yet, while all these scholars fight for the recognition of emerging feminist voices by their more established elders as a strategy for unity within the movement, it is important to remember that the lack of recognition that plagues feminism works both ways. Faith Wilding—a creative pioneer at the start of feminism's second-wave whose recent work on "cyber-feminism" finds her continuously contributing new theory in our contemporary third-wave—rightfully criticizes the ways in which young women's "repudiation of historical feminism is problematic" because it tends to throw out "the baby with the bathwater and aligns itself uneasily with popular fears, stereotypes, and misconceptions about feminism."[15] One cannot forget that many younger women's embrace of the term "third-wave" is rooted not in a drive toward feminist continuity, but an antagonism born of the desire to build their own feminist identity far from the institution constructed by their mothers. (As put in an exasperated tone by the painter Cecily Brown: "My generation was born feminists. We don't have to keep proving it."[16]) And this stance is itself another consistent one in feminist history. As no less an iconic second-wave figure as Gloria Steinem recently said of her own feminist beginnings to young interviewer (and leader of feminist punk bands Bikini Kill and Le Tigre) Kathleen Hanna in the glossy feminist magazine *Bust:*

> I knew less about the suffragists than you know about the second wave, [and] I did the same thing of positioning myself in opposition to them, because I had heard that they were these puritanical, sexless bluestocking folks. . . . I'm sure I made feminists older than I feel uneasy as I wandered around in the '70s in miniskirts and boots with a button that said "Cunt Power."[17]

With this in mind, I would like to return to Katy Deepwell's appropriation of Donna Haraway's pesky *mixotricha paradoxa* parasite as a hopeful model for feminism's future. When first approaching the subject of the various "waves" of feminist art history in my own work, I felt certain that the contemporary artists whose work led me to the topic would in turn lead me toward the theme of rebellion in the Feminist Movement, and that their art would provide me with a useful icon symbolic of the third-wave's difference from previous eras in the women's movement. I found instead that the truth of feminism's history is far more complex, as this drive to survive and reproduce has consistently led the movement to evolve according to each moment in which it has found itself, with participants striking a necessary balance between tradition and progress. But, I also feel that the influence and lived familiarity of postmodern philosophy presents early twenty-first-century feminism with a unique opportunity in relation to this fact. Postmodernism's idealization of plurality has provided the contemporary Women's movement with a manner of embracing its own multifaceted history without abandoning its activist nature—provided, however, that feminists are willing to both refute the popular stereotypes of generations not their own, and engage respectfully with these generations' ideas so that feminism's "reproduction by division" does not simply prove divisive.

As beautifully put by emerging feminist historian Ednie Kaeh Garrison, we must come to accept that "the simultaneous confidence and uncertainty about what constitutes feminism doesn't have to be conceptualized as a 'problem.' Rather, it is a consequence of the proliferation of feminisms."[18] Were this approach to the movement and each other to happen more frequently, I believe that we might begin to not only recognize one another, but also perhaps finally reach a place where we might reevaluate the utility of identifying each other in terms of feminist "waves" at all. Though it may be helpful for us to identify ourselves according to the shared experiences of the generation in which we were born, I believe that it is equally instructive for us to understand that we live through certain waves together, and waves are, literally, fluid. Beside their nebulous beginning and end, they also flow into one another. No matter one's date of birth, as I write we are all living through and defining the third-wave—an evolving *present,* not just a generational *label*—and, as such, are all invested in contributing to and vigilantly looking out for what is made of it as the tide continues to roll.

---

[1] See *College Art Association, 91st Annual Conference Program* (February 19–22, 2003); and Catherine Morris and Ingrid Schaffner (eds.), *Gloria: Another Look at Feminist Art of the 1970s* (New York: White Columns, 2002).

[2] Shulamith Firestone, *The Dialectic of Sex: The Case for Feminist Revolution* (New York: Bantam Books, 1970), 24.

[3] Judith Roof, "Generational Difficulties; or, The Fear of a Barren History," in *Generations: Academic Feminists in Dialogue*, ed.Devoney Looser and E. Ann Kaplan (Minneapolis and London: University of Minneapolis Press, 1997), 72.

[4] Astrid Henry, *Not My Mother's Sister: Generational Conflict and Third-Wave Feminism*, Bloomington and Indianapolis: Indiana University Press, 2004), 4.

[5] Ibid.

[6] Ibid.

[7] Diane Elam, "Sisters Are Doing It for Themselves," in *Generations: Academic Feminists in Dialogue*, 63.

[8] Nancy Whittier, *Feminist Generations: The Persistence of the Radical Women's Movement* (Philadelphia: Temple University Press, 1995), 18.

[9] Diane Elam, "Sisters Are Doing It For Themselves," 56.

[10] See Donna Haraway, "Otherworldly Conversations; Terran Topics; Local Terms," *Science As Culture* 3, no. 1: 64–98.

[11] Katy Deepwell, editorial statement, *n.paradoxa: international feminist art journal.*

[12] Amelia Jones, "Feminism and Art: Nine Views," *Artforum* 42, no.2 (October 2003), 143.

[13] Linda Nochlin, "Feminism and Art: Nine Views," 141.

[14] Peggy Phelan, Feminism and Art: Nine Views," 148–49.
[15] Faith Wilding, "Where is the Feminism in Cyberfeminism?" in *Feminism-Art-Theory: An Anthology*, ed. Hilary Robinson (Oxford: Blackwell Publishers, 2001), 397. Originally published in *n.paradoxa* 2 (1998).
[16] Quoted in Elizabeth Hayt, "The Artist is a Glamour Puss," *New York Times* April 19, 1999, B7.
[17] Quoted in Celina Hex, "Fierce, Funny, Feminists," *Bust Magazine* (Winter 2000): 56.
[18] Ednie Kaeh Garrison, "U.S. Feminism—Grrrl Style! Youth (Sub)Cultures and the Technologies of the Third Wave," *Feminist Studies* 26, no. 1 (Spring 2000): 149.

Works Cited

College Art Association, 91st Annual Conference Program (19–22 February 2003).

Deepwell, Katy. 1999. "Editorial Policy," *n.paradoxa: international online feminist art journal* 11 (October 1999). http://web.ukonline.co.uk/n.paradoxa/edit.htm

Elam, Devoney. 1997. "Sisters Are Doing It For Themselves," in *Generations: Academic Feminists in Dialogue*. Edited by Devoney Looser and E. Ann Kaplan, 55–68. Minneapolis and London: University of Minneapolis Press, 1997.

Firestone, Shulamith. *The Dialectic of Sex: The Case for Feminist Revolution.* New York: Bantam Books, 1970.

Garrison, Ednie Kaeh. "U.S. Feminism—Grrrl Style! Youth (Sub)Cultures and the Technologies of the Third Wave," *Feminist Studies* 26, no. 1, (Spring 2000): 141–70.

Haraway, Donna. "Otherworldly Conversations; Terran Topics; Local Terms," *Science As Culture* 3, no. 1 (1992): 64–98.

Hayt, Elizabeth. "The Artist is a Glamour Puss." *New York Times,* April 19, 1999, B7.

Henry, Astrid. *Not My Mother's Sister: Generational Conflict and Third-Wave Feminism,* Bloomington and Indianapolis: Indiana University Press, 2004.

Hex, Celina. "Fierce, Funny, Feminists," *Bust Magazine* (2000): 56.

Jones, Amelia. 2003 "Feminism and Art: Nine Views," *Artforum* 42, no.2, (October 2003): 143.

Morris, Catherine and Ingrid Schaffner (eds.). *Gloria: Another Look at Feminist Art of the 1970s*. New York: White Columns, 2002.

Nochlin, L. "Feminism and Art: Nine Views," *Artforum* 42, no.2, (October 2003): 141.

Phelan, Peggy. 2003. "Feminism and Art: Nine Views," *Artforum* 42, no.2, (October 2003): 148–149.

Roof, Judith. "Generational Difficulties; or, The Fear of a Barren History." In *Generations: Academic Feminists in Dialogue*. Edited by Devoney Looser and E. Ann Kaplan, 69–87. Minneapolis and London: University of Minneapolis Press, 1997.

Whittier, Nancy. *Feminist Generations: The Persistence of the Radical Women's Movement.* Philadelphia: Temple University Press, 1995.

Wilding, Faith. "Where is the Feminism in Cyberfeminism?" In *Feminism-Art-Theory: An Anthology*. Edited by Hilary Robinson, 396–404. Oxford: Blackwell Publishers, 1998/2001. Originally published in *n.paradoxa* 2, 6–12.

EXPECTED? CURIOUS? THE PLACE OF FEMINISM IN THE PUBLIC ART CLASSROOM

CHER KRAUSE KNIGHT

In an interview with Tom Finkelpearl, Maya Lin was asked how she felt being a woman might affect her work. In response to this query, Lin acknowledged that there are "gender and cultural issues" to consider, but she would rather have "someone else" decipher these.[1] I find her answer both expected and curious. I, too, acknowledge the aspects of gender that crop up in my teaching and research, but at the same time, do not always choose to focus on these. This essay provides an opportunity to explore the junctures of feminism and pedagogy in public art, while interrogating my own teaching practices. Although tracing feminism's entry into art history and its classrooms is beyond my scope here, it is instructive to revisit briefly a few events in that trajectory. By 1971, Linda Nochlin had already acknowledged the elephant in the room when she first published "Why Have There Been No Great Women Artists?" in *Art News.* Female artists, she observed, had been around a long time, and yet few seemed able to gain much notice or sustain greatness. Although her arguments were met with a firestorm of criticism, their implications could not be ignored, especially as it was a woman who was taking these artists to task. But Nochlin's achievement came not only in asking the question out loud (and committing it to paper), but also in underscoring the roles our social and educational institutions played in discouraging women to study the arts and practice them professionally. Yet Nochlin would not permit us to wallow in these circumstances: "What is important is that women face up to the reality of their history and of their present situation, without making excuses or puffing mediocrity. Disadvantage may indeed be an excuse; it is not, however, an intellectual position."[2]

In contrast to Nochlin's outspokenness was the dismissive tone of Horst Woldemar Janson's *History of Art*, a massive tome still among the staples in many college survey classes. Here the issues of feminism were entirely skirted (pun intended) until after H.W.'s death in 1982, when son, Anthony F., took over the *History of Art* enterprise. As inferred from

H.W.'s account, women had made no substantive contributions to the history of art. His complete omission of women implied more than simple disregard; the unwillingness to spill any ink on their behalf attested to their inferiority in his eyes. Female artists did not fare much better under Anthony. As described by Paula Modersohn-Becker (a pseudonym, of course), member of the legendary artists' group the Guerrilla Girls: "*Janson's History of Art,* the most widely-used textbook, didn't mention a single woman artist until Janson died. Then, his son revised it, including a big 19 out of 2,300."[3] For many art historians, especially those sympathetic to feminist concerns, the value in *Janson's* was that it had become "something to teach against."[4] (Future generations of scholars shall have to ascertain if the severely overhauled 2006 edition will usher in any lasting pedagogical changes.) Yet a flurry of feminist-specific studies was on the way to counter Janson and his compatriots. Perhaps the best known of these is a series of anthologies co-edited by Norma Broude and Mary D. Garrard, beginning in 1982 with *Feminism and Art History*, to their most recent offering, *Reclaiming Female Agency* of 2005 (for other titles see the works cited). Although critics such as Lilly Wei complained these were perhaps too "evenhanded" and could stand a "grittier approach,"[5] the books were widely acclaimed for their insightful and informative treatment of feminist art and its history not as topics du jour, but as subjects worthy of purposeful documentation and careful scrutiny. Through such scholarship feminism earned credence, proved longevity, and became an ever-more common feature in art's pedagogical terrain. In short, gender's impact on the arts could no longer be denied.

As an art historian, an educator, and a woman, I continually face the question of how feminism should, and should not, affect my teaching. I see my classes as collaborative ventures between my students and myself; my job is not to proselytize, but to help sharpen their analytical faculties through meaningful exchanges that move beyond reactionary opinion to well-founded critique. Discussing issues and art about which I am passionate enables me to share my enthusiasm with students; I, too, have been outraged by the oversight of women in the art historical canon and have made efforts to integrate feminist issues into several courses, ranging from the introductory to the advanced. In my post-World War II class, for example, I added a brief section on feminism (it is a survey course) as our primary textbook includes many women artists, but does not accentuate the rise of feminist discourse and the artwork it subsequently spurred. In a course such as my seminar on art of the 1970s and 1980s, which is organized around thematic issues rather than chronologically, an entire topic is devoted to the investigation of "Gender and Feminism," with in-depth discussions of writings by scholars and critics such as Nochlin and Lucy Lippard, and the work of artists like the Guerrilla Girls. Yet in my seminar, *Urban Public Art: Theory and Practice*, there is no gender-based or specifically feminist content. This I find, as stated above, curious. Why might the issues of feminism seem organic to some modes of inquiry, and not to others? Why have I not emphasized feminism when teaching about public art? And should I reconsider that choice?

As currently structured, my public art seminar covers the following subjects: practical concerns; funding and patronage; activism and collaboration; monuments and memorials; public response; permanent versus temporary work; and the friction between notions of the public and the private. These topics correlate with the semester's field trips, assignments, readings, and projects, and evolved after teaching the course several times and discerning which topics were the most useful, relevant, and held the greatest student interest. Certainly, we consider feminist concerns if an artist or artwork we are studying, such as the *Boston Women's Memorial* by Meredith Bergmann (2003), has been clearly informed by these. But such issues are examined as pertinent to the material at hand, and I have never isolated them for treatment as a subject on their own in the public art course.

Lately, as I am revising my syllabus and preparing to teach the class again, I have been thinking more about that decision, and why I am likely to stick by it. If my course were intended to provide an expansive account of public art, I would be more likely to integrate the plight of women artists throughout history as part of the story. In the other courses I mentioned above, feminism is discussed as a social, historical, and aesthetic movement within the wider framework of a specific era. I do not perceive feminism as a moment frozen in amber, which has no current influence on the arts. But to delineate it as a discrete subject of study makes more pedagogical sense when it is placed alongside other movements such as Conceptualism and Performance Art in the post-World War II class, or Postmodernism and Neo-Expressionism in the 1970s and 1980s course. The public art seminar focuses on urbanism (I teach it in Boston, a city rich with examples) with an emphasis on contemporary American works, but no particular movement or specific time period is highlighted. To do so for feminism in this context would ghettoize and weaken it, implying that its presence can only be felt when it is singled out. It may well still be a "man's world," but that is unlikely to change unless we stop acting like it is. Here it might be wise to take the lead of Nancy Holt and Jeanne-Claude, neither of whom was intimidated by her (more) famous artist-husband. After Robert Smithson's tragic death, Holt completed his unfinished *Amarillo Ramp* (1973), and then went on to produce works of ecological sensitivity and cosmological complexity such as *Sun Tunnels* (1973–1976) and *Dark Star Park* (1979–1984). Jeanne-Claude and husband Christo, functioning as a unified collaborative entity, have created some of the most renowned and sublime works in the history of public art, most recently in New York, with *The Gates* at Central Park (1979–2005). When I consider the quality and substance of work by artists such as Holt, Jeanne-Claude, Lin, Suzanne Lacy, Mary Miss, and Athena Tacha (to name just a handful), and their achievements (winning competitions, landing major commissions, and placing important artworks), I think they probably do not need too much help from me.

I shall continue to talk about issues of gender, as they relate to public art, and encourage my students' interest in such, but I will not feel obligated to shoehorn feminism into the public art seminar as an independent topic, or have it dictate the terms of the course. Like Nochlin, I am aware of and informed by feminism's history, but I do not want to take it out of context, or to be enslaved by it. At its pedagogical best, feminism questions the status quo and bolsters confidence in our own critical abilities. To be a good feminist does not mean that I must force a feminist agenda on every class I teach; rather it means that I take advantage of my own training and knowledge to forge rich educational experiences for my students. These are sure to morph over time, and so might my sentiments on feminism and public art as well. But for now I am committed to the notion that the essence of what makes something "public" seems to have less to do with matters of gender, and more with a broader sense of humanity. This, I realize, is a somewhat generic statement, but it fits. In our culture, there are certainly activities, events and places that skew either more "male" or "female," but in the most conventionally public spaces (such as parks, city streets, and transit stations), and even at privately maintained ones (shopping malls, business lobbies, restaurants, and so forth), we rarely encounter any kind of gender identifications or restrictions beyond the restroom. While I am not naïve enough to believe that gender-based stereotypes and segregation are things of the past, the law, political correctness, and our personal value systems do not usually permit the open toleration of such. Perhaps it is in the raw and tense slippage between social acceptability and subtler forms of discrimination that feminism and public art might have their most fruitful meetings. For example, in 1985 the Guerrilla Girls launched a poster campaign that revealed latent sexism in the art world. Taking to the streets of New York City's then-trendy art districts, the Guerrilla Girls exposed the inequities of life for female artists that existed under a veneer of patronizing niceties. By providing statistical data and naming specific culprits, the Guerrilla Girls sought to shame fellow artists, gallery dealers, and art institutions into better behavior. In the introduction to her *Vision and Difference*, Griselda Pollock posited that the production of a "new" feminist art history was an inherently flawed project; she maintained that we could not go back and retroactively insert female artists into the canon, and queried whether it were even very desirable to do so. Instead, Pollock asserted that the most potent tactic would be to stake our own ground by making feminist *interventions* into the history of art,[6] which is precisely what the Guerrilla Girls had done with their posters.

At the beginning of this essay, I cited an interview between Tom Finkelpearl and Maya Lin that bares further investigation here. Finkelpearl's question was actually quite specific, and Lin's response, intriguing:

> TF: The history of public art is full of overpowering monuments which [sic] are so authoritarian—vertical, phallic. Do you think that being a woman contributes to the less authoritarian nature of your work?
>
> ML: Of course there are gender and cultural issues. Though I have a sense, I would rather have someone else decipher that. In a hundred years, when more women have designed buildings, I'd like a psychiatrist to study the way we build, and see how it has changed.[7]

To my mind, this exchange provides some vital cues as to how we might integrate feminism more meaningfully into the discourse and study of art in general, and public art more particularly. First, it would be wise to avoid some of the most stereotypical preconceptions about the intersections of gender, art, and the built environment. Finkelpearl was surely well intended in his attempt to introduce feminist concerns into the discussion, but by resorting to cliché, he has given them short shrift. It is not only males who design soaring structures, although when such is conceived by a woman, it is rarely described as "phallic." Likewise, females are not relegated to a collection of earthbound, organic forms, and can be as "authoritarian" in their designs as men. Curiously, works rendered by artists such as Georgia O'Keeffe or Judy Chicago are frequently labeled as "vaginal," yet this term is unlikely to be applied to architecture or a monument. Apparently, media such as painting, ceramics, and fiber are comfortably perceived as "feminine," while architecture and monuments are decidedly not. These assumptions, and Finkelpearl's question, reveal how deeply embedded essentialism has become in the terrain of art and architectural history, and the problems this situation brings. It is, indeed, *essential* to acknowledge how the differences between men and women might affect the choices they make as artists. But it is equally important that we take stock of the full range of those differences, encompassing cultural, socio-economic, and historical dimensions as well as biological ones. Likewise, similarities between the sexes must be interrogated with the same zeal; to gloss over these only further promotes an inaccurate understanding of how the issues of gender impact art.

Second, while Lin responded that she was certainly aware of the issues of gender and culture afoot in her work, she calls upon others to divine their meaning. She does this not because she has no thoughts on the matters (in fact she lets us know she has "a sense" of these), but to broaden the conversation about them. This is significant as it indicates two things: reverence for her audience, whom she trusts enough not to graft her own interpretations onto theirs; and her respect for other professionals outside of her field, who can offer new insights. When bringing feminism into the classroom, it would be apt to follow Lin's lead here too. A more interdisciplinary perspective will be useful, and we should call upon the work of our colleagues not only in women's and gender studies, but in sociology, cultural studies and anthropology, history, urban planning, engineering, and so on. We also need to believe that our students are capable of digesting the complexities of gender issues, and give them the analytical tools to open that dialogue.

As part of her *Full Circle* project for Sculpture Chicago's "Culture in Action" program (1993), Suzanne Lacy invited an international group of prominent women to have dinner together at the Hull House (home of Jane Addams, an activist from the early twentieth century). She encouraged other women throughout the city to host their own meals, and consider women's challenges in and contributions to our society.[8] In this case, conversation was both a vehicle and medium for the art. A lot can be gained from sitting around a table or in a classroom together discussing such ideas; we ought to think about how men, as our colleagues, students, and friends, can be brought more frequently into that dialogue. To do so would help build what Nochlin characterized as "institutions in which clear thought—and true greatness—are challenges open to anyone, man or woman, courageous enough to take the necessary risk, the leap into the unknown."[9] As Lin had noted when her ethnicity and the role it might play in the *Vietnam Veterans Memorial* commission were discussed, critics were quick to simplify these in "a narrow and specific way."[10] We must be careful to shirk off reductive formulas when speaking of gender or ethnicity, or any other multifaceted aspect of our humanity. Not only does this best serve the causes of feminism, but to do otherwise would be rash, unthinking, and probably quite un-ladylike.

---

[1] Tom Finkelpearl, "Interview: Maya Lin: Landscapes and Memorials," in *Dialogues in Public Art* (Cambridge: MIT Press, 2001), 117.
[2] Linda Nochlin, "Why Have There Been No Great Women Artists?" *Art News* 69, no. 9 (1971): 70.
[3] Guerrilla Girls, *Confessions of the Guerilla Girls* (New York: Harper Perennial, 1995), 26.
[4] Randy Kennedy, "Revising Art History's Big Book: Who's In and Who Comes Out?" *New York Times* Mar. 7, 2006, Late Edition, National Desk. http://www.lexis-nexis.com. Access Date June 10, 2007.
[5] Lilly Wei, "Feminists in the Art World. Review of *The Power of Feminist Art*, ed. by Norma Broude and Mary D. Garrard." *Art in America* 83, no. 1 (1995): 37.
[6] Griselda Pollock, *Vision and Difference: Femininity, Feminism and Histories of Art* (London: Routledge, 1988), 17.
[7] Finkelpearl, "Interview: Maya Lin: Landscapes and Memorials," 117.
[8] Allison Gamble, "Reframing a Movement: Sculpture Chicago's Culture in Action," *New Art Examiner* 21, no.5 (1994): 21.
[9] Nochlin, "Why Have There Been No Great Women Artists?," 70.
[10] Finkelpearl "Interview: Maya Lin: Landscapes and Memorials," 118.

Works Cited

Broude, Norma, and Mary D. Garrard, eds. *The Expanding Discourse: Feminism and Art History.* New York: Icon Editions, 1992.

——. *Feminism and Art History: Questioning the Litany.* New York: Harper and Row, 1982.

——. *The Power of Feminist Art: The American Movement of the 1970s, History and Impact.* New York: Abrams, 1994.

——. *Reclaiming Female Agency: Feminist Art History After Postmodernism.* Berkeley: University of California Press, 2005.

Finkelpearl, Tom. "Interview: Maya Lin: Landscapes and Memorials." In *Dialogues in Public Art*, 111–125. Cambridge: MIT Press, 2001.

Gamble, Allison. "Reframing a Movement: Sculpture Chicago's Culture in Action." *New Art Examiner* 21, no.5 (1994): 18–23.

Guerrilla Girls. *Confessions of the Guerilla Girls.* New York: Harper Perennial, 1995.

Kennedy, Randy."Revising Art History's Big Book: Who's In and Who Comes Out?" *New York Times* Mar. 7, 2006 Late Edition, National Desk. http://www.lexis-nexis.com.

Nochlin, Linda. "Why Have There Been No Great Women Artists?" *Art News* 69, no.9 (1971): 22–39, 67–71.

Pollock, Griselda. *Vision and Difference: Femininity, Feminism and Histories of Art.* London: Routledge, 1988.

Wei, Lilly. "Feminists in the Art World. Review of *The Power of Feminist Art,* ed. by Norma Broude and Mary D. Garrard." *Art in America* 83, no.1 (1995): 35–37.

GENDERED IN STONE: WOMEN IN NEW YORK CITY'S PUBLIC ART

HARRIET F. SENIE

> Monuments….stand for common ideas, memories, and hopes. They mark the men and events chosen by a society as part of its image…Monuments are a way men transmit communal emotions, a medium of continuity and interaction between generations, not only in space but across time, for to be monumental is to be permanent.
>
> Marvin Trachtenberg, *Statue of Liberty*[1]

As recently as the United States' Bicentennial, the noted and respected art historian, Marvin Trachtenberg, in the introduction of his book about New York's most famous public sculpture, the Statue of Liberty, wrote of monuments in totally masculine terms. A contemporary (2006) look at the women represented in New York City's public art reveals that they are few in number, the largest category by far representing symbolic virtues or goddesses, with a few merry maidens, fictional characters, and abstracted fragments, and only two full scale depictions of actual women.[2] In the 1990s, two women created temporary public installations from a feminist perspective: one raised issues of childbearing and its attendant responsibilities; the other highlighted traditional women's work. Briefly, they called attention to the pervasive invisibility of women in public art.

Marina Warner began her groundbreaking study, *Monuments & Maidens: The Allegory of the Female Form* (1985), with a discussion of the Statue of Liberty, "identified from the start with an American ideal of democracy,"[3] and arguably the single sculpture most closely associated with national identity. In 1903, Emma Lazarus's famous poem was inscribed on the base of the Statue of Liberty, defining it as an archetypal image of maternal welcome.[4] Warner describes the typical immigrant journey to the United States: "Departure, sailing across an ocean, docking at a small leafy haven, gazing up at the colossus who is benign and approachable, and then, to enter her, to find that she is enfolding, even pregnable: these are the phases of a common dream of bliss."[5] The childlike hope for maternal succor is pervasive, recognizable; the sexual implications disturbing, perverse, at first glance inexplicable. Frederic-Auguste Bartholdi (1834–1904), sculptor of the Statue of Liberty, was raised by his mother; his father died when he was two. He imposed his mother's visage on Liberty even his wife served as his model.[6] Since Liberty's appearance was based on the conflation of two women, mother and wife, the maternal and sexual implications of the statue are understandable, but hardly comforting or even comfortable.

Although none is so grand or famous as the colossal Statue of Liberty in New York's harbor, the city displays many statues of women as allegorical figures or goddesses atop significant buildings or structures. These include *Charity* with two children on the Union Square Drinking Fountain (1881); *Justice* over the cupola of City Hall (1887); *Hebe* above the Temperance Fountain (1888) in Tomkins Square; *Civic Fame* on the tower of the Municipal Building (1913–1914); *Memory* reclining above the Straus Memorial (1913–1914) on the upper west side (Broadway and 106th Street); and *Pomona* atop the Pulitzer Fountain (1913–1916) in Grand Army Plaza at 59th Street and Fifth Avenue. Others are depicted in association with a specific man: *Discovery* stands at the base of *Giovanni da Verrazzano* (1909) in Battery Park; and *Victory* on foot is part of *William Tecumseh Sherman* (1892–1903) at Grand Army Plaza, between the Pulitzer Fountain and the entrance to Central Park.[7] A work of Augustus Saint-Gaudens, the Sherman monument is the most famous and centrally located of the above examples.[8] Although the figure of *Victory* is an integral part of the composition and clearly leads the general on horseback, her wings define her other worldly status. The role of actual women in war has yet to be commemorated in New York. The prevalent historical practice of using the female body to express ideas and ideals is completely removed from the earthly reality of women; these women in stone stand for values actual women didn't enjoy at the time they were created.[9]

Two sculptures of fictional women depict a legendary author of children's poems and an equally famous imaginative girl. *Mother Goose* (1938) and *Alice in Wonderland* (1958) are both located in Central Park within a few blocks of one another. Frederick George Richard Roth represents the typical image of Mother Goose, an old woman wearing a pointed hat and riding a goose; occasionally she is portrayed as an actual goose.[10] Either way, she bears no resemblance to an actual woman. José de Creeft presents Alice seated on a mushroom throne with open welcoming arms. This pose allows children to climb onto her lap, implicitly imposing a maternal, nurturing role on a young girl.

Occasionally, women are depicted generically as mothers or merry maidens. Chaim Gross's *Mother Playing* (1961) was for many years located on the campus of Fordham University at Lincoln Center, clearly visible from the street.[11] Apparently nude but without defining sexual characteristics except long hair pulled back from her face, the mother uses her body as a seesaw for the young girl seated just below her knee. The title of the sculpture notwithstanding, it is the child who is playing, or at least being amused, while the mother's body serves as both playground and support. By contrast, in Walter Schott's *Untermeyer Fountain* (before 1910) in the Conservatory Garden in Central Park, three young women dance around a central water element.[12] Also called the *Fountain of the Three Dancing Maidens*, the sculpture reveals lithe female bodies in apparently wet garb, laughing and cavorting with joy. Their similarity emphasizes the use of their bodies to express an ideal of youthful gendered abandon. Although realistically depicted, they are no more specific than Matisse's abstracted figures in his roughly contemporaneous painting, *The Dance* (1909) in the collection of the Museum of Modern Art.

With the adoption of abstract styles in the twentieth century for public art as well as private, women fared no better. Henry Moore's *Reclining Figure* (1963–65) in a shallow pool at Lincoln Center consists of two forms.[13] Like much of Moore's sculpture, it conflates a woman's body with landscape elements, prompting the general equation of women with "mother nature," a source of nourishment and sustenance. Despite the sculpture's abstract style, audience response appears decidedly positive; even among those who claimed indifference some apparently went out of their way to sit as close to the sculpture as possible.[14] Its somatic appeal prompts a desire to touch, to experience the work viscerally. The implicit intimacy of Moore's public art is both seductive and comforting, reflecting all too well the dual role imposed on women in life and art.

By contrast, Picasso's 35-foot-high *Head of Sylvette* (1968) is an abstracted form that remains intellectualized. Enlarged in concrete from a much smaller model, the head was selected by I.M. Pei, the architect of the complex of three New York University-owned apartment buildings just north of Soho where the sculpture is sited.[15] Although based on an actual woman, Sylvette David, the giant head serves more as a vehicle for cubist experimentation than portrait. Indeed, the most significant aspect of the sculpture is the artist; first and foremost this is a Picasso. *Head of Sylvette* thus reflects the typical anonymity of artist models.

Astonishingly (or perhaps not), there are only two full figure statues of actual women in Manhattan, both in somewhat marginalized locations on the Upper West Side. Like the Statue of Liberty, *Joan of Arc* (1915) was intended to cement French-American relations, this time during World War I. Anna Vaughn Hyatt Huntington who had studied in France exhibited a plaster version of the equestrian monument at the French Salon of 1910 where it was seen by Americans planning to commemorate the 500th anniversary of Joan's birth.[16] The artist used actual models for both the figure (her niece) and the horse (borrowed from the local fire department). Today the statue, at Riverside Drive and 93rd Street, is almost totally obscured by trees, so that its elaborate base becomes the visual focal point. If you enter Joan of Arc Island from 93rd Street, you stare first at the horse's hindquarters. With her body encased in armor, her sword raised towards the heaven, the statue of the "peasant maiden" (as she is described), who died when she was 20, is identifiable only by the plaque and recently added signage nearby. In any event, neither her image nor her history define her as a woman; part of her story is that she had to hide her gender. Then, too, since *Joan of Arc* was commissioned to solidify French-American friendship, her image was used symbolically, to represent something other than herself.

Not until 1996, could Manhattan boast of a full-scale public sculpture of an American heroine; to date, it remains the only one. *Eleanor Roosevelt*, installed at the southern end of Riverside Park at 72nd Street, is all but hidden in a copse of trees and plantings. Casually leaning against a rock, her chin supported by one hand, in a decidedly unheroic pose, Penelope Jencks' statue is part of a redesigned entrance to the park. The plaque that identifies Anna Eleanor Roosevelt (1884–1962), notes her contributions: expanding the role of First Lady; championing labor, minorities, the poor, women and young people; her appointment as U.S. delegate to the United Nations in 1946 and her chairmanship of the U.N. Commission on Human Rights, and ends with "She is remembered as First Lacy of the World." This small bronze label too is all but invisible among the green ground cover that surrounds it. Two quotations, one by her and one by Adlai S. Stevenson, inscribed on the pavement below are only slightly more apparent.[17]

In the spring of 2005, a graduate student observing audience response to the work, found that quite a few individuals were totally unaware of the memorial. Some did not recognize the subject, or know who she was.[18] One young woman thought the statue looked like "a sweet old lady." Quite a few individuals commented on its androgynous appearance, one actually mistaking it for a man. A substantial number of people, usually over 35, were enthusiastic about Eleanor Roosevelt and really pleased to have her commemorated. However, the observer noted that the site was often empty on weekdays and because the statue "is set apart from the surrounding rotunda by not only a planted area but also a wire fence, many people seem to walk by oblivious to, or unconcerned by its existence." In this way, *Eleanor Roosevelt,* the only statue in New York City of a woman active in American public life, has been rendered all but invisible by its placement.[19]

The relative obscurity of two other images of women in New York is further insured by their scale. *Golda Meir* (1980) by Beatrice Goldfine is located on what is identified as Golda Meir Square on a mid-block sign on a lamp post, adjacent to 1411 Broadway at 39th Street.[20] This somewhat larger than life bust of the former Israeli prime minister is placed on a raised platform at slightly higher than eye level, but a bust on a relatively short plinth is all there is. Looking old and sad, the image is neither monumental nor heroic, and was covered with bird excrement when I last viewed it in June of 2006. Dedicated in 1981, a plaque identifies the donors as the City of New York, the Jewish Community Relations Council, and Swig Weiner and Arnow.

In 1992, an image of seated Gertrude Stein by Jo Davidson was installed in Bryant Park behind the New York Public Library's central branch, at 42nd Street and Fifth Avenue.[21] All but obscured by the surrounding trees, and dwarfed by the much larger statues of men nearby, the smaller than life-size seated figure on a pedestal at least twice her height, reduces her typically monumental presence, suggesting a kind of referent rather than a representation.

So in 2006, the number of actual women represented in New York's public art is four. Only two of them were born in the United States, although one woman lived mostly in Europe. Only one is a full-size statue of an actual American heroine. At the time of this writing, a representation of Harriet Tubman, by Alison Saar, is scheduled to be installed in 2007 near Frederick Douglas Circle adjacent to the northwest corner of Central Park. This commission of the city's Percent-for-Art program will bring the total number to two heroines.

Earlier in the decade, two temporary installations sponsored by the Public Art Fund, a not-for-profit organization founded by Doris C. Freedman in 1977, challenged traditional gender inequalities and depictions of women in New York's public realm. In 1991, in various bus shelters, Barbara Kruger displayed three different photographic images of men, calling into question the impact of childbirth and child rearing on personal careers. In each, the man (variously a middle class white, a black teenager and a white construction worker) worried about the effect of pregnancy on their career. All featured a prominent call for HELP! across their chests in white letters on a red ground; an accompanying texts delineated their plight. The youthful white male in a cable knit sweater with his arm around a young boy, states: "I've got a great job. My wife just got a promotion. We're beginning to make a dent in the mortgage but it's tough in this economy. I just found out I'm pregnant. What should I do?" With these installations, Kruger hoped to "focus attention on our dreams and who can dare to dream them, and our bodies and who controls them."[22]

Rhonda Roland Shearer's *Women's Work* (1993) consisted of eight bronze sculptures depicting women in nine-foot-high outlines in various domestic chores: shopping for groceries, cleaning a toilet, vacuuming, ironing, and the like. Installed at ground level at the base of Henry Kirk Brown's *George Washington* (1853–1855) in Union Square, these wavy outlines suggested invisible bodies doing generally unacknowledged work. It was hard to hold their ethereal transparent forms in memory; when they were removed six months later, it was as if they had never been there. And this, in a sense, encapsulates the cumulative effect of the absence of honorific images of women in the public sphere.

While I was writing this article, I began asking people, "Which actual or fictional women would you like to see depicted in permanent public art?" With few exceptions, their response was a blank stare.[23]

---

[1] Marvin Trachtenberg, *The Statue of Liberty* (New York: Penguin Books, 1975), 15. My thoughts on this topic began with a brief talk presented in a panel titled "Missing in Action: Women and Public Art," sponsored by the Public Art Fund on March 23, 1993. For the purposes of this essay, I am considering only life-size or larger free-standing depictions of women at ground level, not relief sculptures that are easily absorbed by their architectural settings or figures so high up that they are not routinely seen by pedestrians. This is not to suggest that these depictions have no public impact but rather that those figures that stand in our midst have a greater and more pervasive one, given their size and visibility. I am confining my observations to works in Manhattan, which is what is typically meant by New York City.

[2] In addition to full figure representations of Joan of Arc and Eleanor Roosevelt, there is a bust of Golda Meir and a small seated Gertrude Stein. These are discussed further below.

[3] Marina Warner, *Monuments & Maidens: The Allegory of the Female Form* (New York: Atheneum, 1985), 7, 12. Warner observes, "She identifies the city and by extension the nation..."

[4] Emma Lazarus, "The New Colossus," was originally written in 1883 in response to Russian immigration to the US during the time of Tsarist pogroms. The following lines are indelibly associated with the Statue of Liberty and, arguably, the basis for our general understanding of the image:

> Give me your tired, your poor;
> Your huddled masses yearning to breathe free,

The wretched refuse of your teeming shore.
Send these, the homeless, tempest-tos't to me,
I lift my lamp beside the golden door!

Warner, states that Lazarus's "famous flight of rhetoric dissolves the harshness of Liberty's countenance, and she becomes a mother of mercy," more precisely the "Mother of Exiles" Ibid,10–11.

[5] Ibid, 3.

[6] Marvin Trachtenberg, *The Statue of Liberty* (New York: Penguin Books, 1975), 59.

[7] For discussion of these allegorical figures, see Margot Gayle and Michele Cohen, *Guide to Manhattan's Outdoor Sculpture* (New York: Prentice Hall, 1988), *Charity,* 94; *Justice*, 43–44; *Hebe*, 85; *Civic Fame*, 58–59; *Memory,* 287; *Pomona,* 192–93); *Discovery*, 7; *Victory*, 190–91. As Marina Warner observed, "The female form tends to be perceived as generic and universal, with symbolic overtones; the male as individual, even when it's being used to express a generalized idea," *Monuments & Maidens: The Allegory of the Female Form*, 12.

[8] For a discussion of the creation of Grand Army Plaza, the site of both the Sherman Monument and the Pulitzer Fountain, see Michele H. Bogart, *Public Sculpture and the Civic Ideal in New York City, 1890-1930* (Chicago and London, University of Chicago Press, 1989), 205–17.

[9] For example, in the United States women were granted the vote only in 1920, after the creation of all the allegorical images cited above, including, of course, the Statue of Liberty.

[10] See, for example, "Just Who Was Mother Goose?" online at http://www.librarysupport.net/mothergoosesociety/who.html, Access date June 8, 2006.

[11] Gayle and Cohen, *Guide to Manhattan's Outdoor Sculpture*, 266.

[12] Ibid, 234.

[13] For details of this commission see Harriet F. Senie, *Contemporary Public Sculpture: Tradition, Transformation, and Controversy* (New York: Oxford University Press, 1992), 106–10. See also Gayle and Cohen, 272.

[14] For a further discussion of audience response, see Harriet F. Senie, "Implicit Intimacy: The Persistent Appeal of Henry Moore's Public Art," in *Henry Moore: Sculpting the 20th Century*, ed. Dorothy Kosinski, 282–84 (Dallas and New Haven: Dallas Museum of Art and Yale University Press, 2001).

[15] For a discussion of the sculpture, see Gayle and Cohen, *Guide to Manhattan's Outdoor Sculpture.* 79–80 and Senie, *Contemporary Public Sculpture*, 100. On the changing role of sculpture and modern architecture, see Senie, 61–92.

[16] For details of the commission, see Gayle and Cohen, *Guide to Manhattan's Outdoor Sculpture,* 283–84. The New York City Department of Parks and Recreation Web site calls it "one of the finest works of art in the Parks' collection." http://www.nycgovparks.org/sub_your_park/historical_signs.html. Access date June 10, 2007. For a discussion of Joan of Arc see Marina Warner, *Joan of Arc—The Image of Female Heroism* (London: Vintage, 1981).

[17] Roosevelt's quote of 1958 inscribed on the pavement in front of the statue reads: "Where after all do universal rights begin? In small places, close to home. Such are the places where every man, woman and child seeks equal opportunity, equal dignity." Adlai Stevenson's 1962 quote inscribed on the pavement behind the statue reads: "She would rather light a candle than cure the darkness and that glow has warmed the world."

[18] Helen (Lilly) Tuttle observed the statue during the spring 2005 semester for a course on contemporary memorials that I taught at the City University of New York Graduate Center.

[19] Arguably, many if not most memorials become invisible over time, especially after the death of the generations directly associated with their subjects. The invisibility of the women in New York's public art, however, is insured by their placement.

[20] See Gayle and Cohen, *Guide to Manhattan's Outdoor Sculpture*, 148.

[21] See "Doubling the Number of Women Etched in Stone," *New York Times*, November 6, 1992, B1.

[22] See Senie, *Contemporary Public Sculpture*, 201–202. Kruger's quote is from a Public Art Fund news release dated February 7, 1991.

[23] One notable exception was Wendy Feuer, public art consultant and former director of the Art for Transit program of the Metropolitan Transit Authority. For years she has been trying to interest people in creating a memorial for Margaret Sanger.

Works Cited

Bogart, Michele H. *Public Sculpture and the Civic Ideal in New York City, 1890–1930.* Chicago and London, University of Chicago Press, 1989.

Gloria T. Delamar, 1987, "Just Who Was Mother Goose?" The Official Home of the Mother Goose Society, http://www.librarysupport.net/mothergoosesociety/who.html

Gayle, Margot and Michele Cohen, *Guide to Manhattan's Outdoor Sculpture.* New York, Prentice Hall, 1988.

New York City Department of Parks and Recreation, "Historical Signs", New York City Department of Parks and Recreation, http://www.nycgovparks.org/sub_your_park/historical_signs.html.

Senie, Harriet F., *Contemporary Public Sculpture: Tradition, Transformation, and Controversy*. New York: Oxford University Press, 1992.

——. "Implicit Intimacy: The Persistent Appeal of Henry Moore's Public Art," in *Henry Moore: Sculpting the 20th Century*, ed. Dorothy Kosinski. Dallas and New Haven: Dallas Museum of Art and Yale University Press, 2001.

"Doubling the Number of Women Etched in Stone," *New York Times,* November 6, 1992, B1.

Trachtenberg, Marvin. *The Statue of Liberty.* New York: Penguin Books, 1975.

Warner, Marina. Joan of Arc—The Image of Female Heroism. London: Vintage, 1981.

——. Monuments & Maidens: The Allegory of the Female Form. New York: Atheneum, 1985.

REPRESENTATIONS OF THE FEMALE NUDE

CYNTHIA FOWLER

In 1999, the Aldrich Museum of Contemporary Art organized the exhibition The Nude in Contemporary Art, marking the renewed focus on the nude body by both artists and art museums that has emerged in the 1990s. Artist Karen Finley is credited with inspiring the exhibition based on her frustration surrounding the constricted treatment of the nude female body in the art world. Harry Philbrick, the curator of the show, cites Finley's choice to pose nude for *Playboy* magazine as evidence that the female nude had become prisoner to poststructuralist theory so oppressive that Finley was "more comfortable having a conversation with an executive of *Playboy* magazine than with an art world insider."[1] His goal as curator was to provide a venue for an examination of the nude outside of the constraints of poststructuralist discourse. Although titled "Digging Deeper to Find New Paradigms," the 2006 WCA conference did not directly address this new paradigm of the female nude. But in spite of this omission, the new paradigm was not completely absent. Indeed, it was reflected by the video *Sheraton* (2006), a taped performance by artist Catherine McGregor (b. 1971), which was included in the conference panel "Ritual and Contemporary Art Practice." It was also reflected in the discussion after the screening of McGregor's work, by audience members like myself, which has led me to write this reflection on the new discourse of the female nude in art.

Before I begin an examination of McGregor's video, I would like to remind the reader of the perspective of many second-wave feminists on the subject of the female nude, followed by a discussion of some works by other women artists of McGregor's generation who have also engaged this subject in their art. In the 1970s and 1980s, artists incorporating nudity and erotica into their work were often castigated by second-wave feminists for perpetuating exploitative imagery of women, even in cases in which the work was a provocative exploration of women's sexuality. Art critic Lucy Lippard derisively commented, "I must admit to a personal lack of sympathy with women who have themselves photographed in black stockings, garter belts, boots, with bare breasts, bananas, and coy, come-hither glances. . . . The artist rarely seems to get the last laugh."[2] Art historian Griselda Pollock argued against the direct representation of the female body because she believed that these representations simply could not adequately disrupt "the 'dance of ideology' which engages us on behalf of oppressive regimes of class, sexist, heterosexist and racist classifications and placements."[3] But by the late 1980s and early 1990s, the tides were turning in feminist discourse about the body. As Amelia Jones describes, "A new generation of feminist writers and image-makers returned with a vengeance to the body, sometimes in explicit reaction against the 'anti-body' argument of previous dominant feminist discourse."[4] Not surprisingly, the return of the female nude has yielded further debate within the feminist community regarding the extent to which the female nude might operate transgressively in a heterosexist world.[5] My intention here is not so much to directly engage in this debate as to consider the representations of the female nude by women artists born in the 1960s and 1970s (Generation X) that had been included in some of the most discussed exhibitions of the last decade.

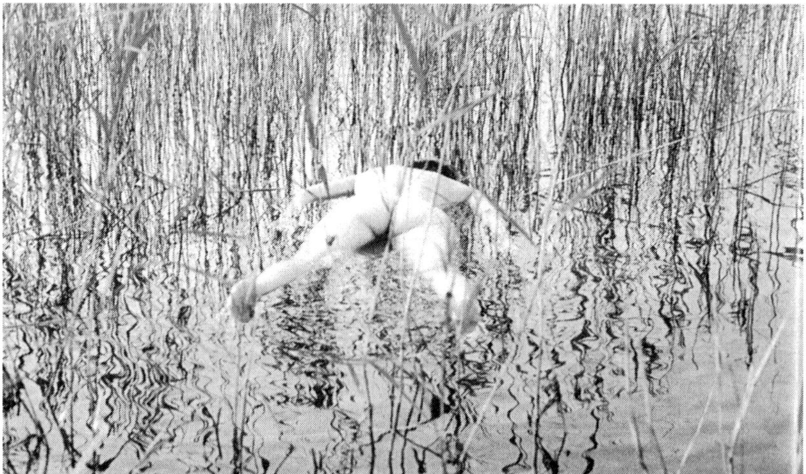

Fig. 2-1
Back to Nature. Photograph courtesy of Casey Kaplan Gallery, New York, NY. Photograph copyright Annika von Hausswolff 1993.

Annika von Hausswolff's (b.1967) *Back to Nature* (1993) (fig. 2-1), included in the 1999 exhibition Another Girl, Another Planet, clearly represents this new trend of repositioning the female nude in contemporary discourse on art. *Back to Nature* is characterized by the ambiguous way in which the female nude is now being depicted. The artist has staged a photograph of a naked woman lying face down in a marsh. Our view of the woman's body is feet first, so the spectator is forced to look directly between her spread legs. The position of the subject—with spread legs and face down in the water—suggests an unspecified narrative of sexual violence that has ultimately led to her death. Art critic Lucy Soutter considers the symbolic content of von Hausswolff's photograph: "The fact that the image has been made by a woman might seem to point away from the idea that it is contrived to create voyeuristic sexual pleasure or horror."[6] But Soutter concludes something quite the contrary because she fails to see any transgressive quality in the photograph, which relegates it in the realm of voyeurism. Indeed, Soutter concludes, "I do not feel that the image, even when framed by the rest of von Hausswolff's work, is clearly parody or an embodiment of feminist theory."[7] If not parody or feminist, what then is the work but a perpetuation of voyeurism and the exploitation of the female form? Indeed, Soutter's analysis of von Hausswolff's photograph positions the image outside of the 1980s feminist assertion that representations of the nude female must resist eroticization by politicizing the body.

While Soutter's analysis is indeed quite convincing, other critics have interpreted the photograph from a very different and equally convincing point of view. For curator Bill Arning, *Back to Nature* raises "unanswerable," questions, such as "Why, if women's bodies are seen as an earthly manifestation of creation, are they treated with disrespect?"[8] From this perspective, the photograph might be read as a direct critique of the essentialism for which the works of 1970s feminist artists, from Judy Chicago to Ana Mendieta, has been attacked. Arning explains:

> The lush greenery indicates that we are meant to be thinking of a world of health, in which running naked through the fields is a non-licentious celebration of the interconnectedness of all things natural. But, point of fact, bodies get dumped in the woods, and the most grisly murders most often occur surrounded by at least some picturesque shrubbery. The titular pun becomes grotesquely conspicuous when we realize that a decomposed body returns 'back to nature' more completely than we can ever hope to do on a three-day camping expedition.[9]

In direct opposition to Soutter, Arning positions von Hausswolff's photograph within feminist discourse in that it "documents" the disturbing ways in which a woman's body is abusively treated, a stark contrast to notions of women's "natural" connection to nature.

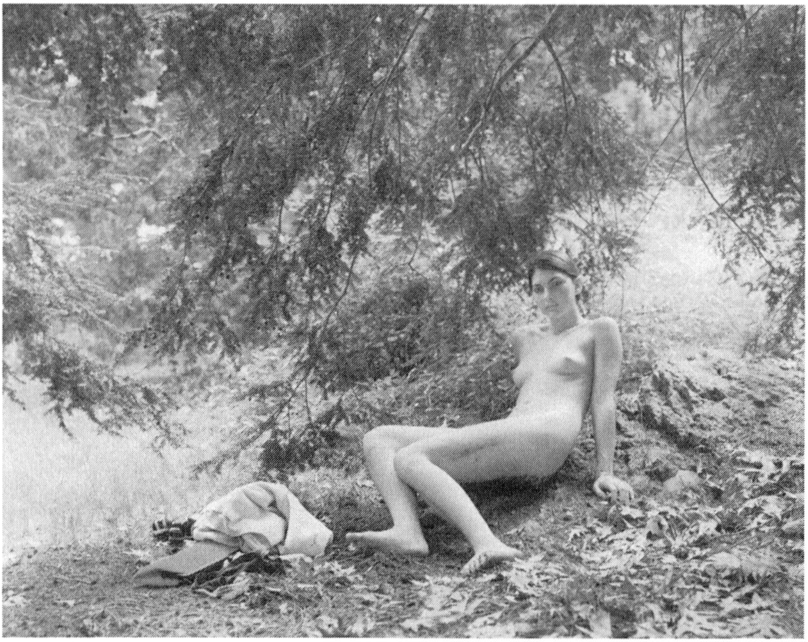

Fig.2.2
Carla, Arnold Arboretum, Jamaica Plain, MA. Photograph courtesy of Greenberg Van Doren Gallery. Photograph copyright Katy Grannan 2002.

These dramatically different interpretations of the same photograph by Arning and Soutter point to the ambiguity that has come to characterize art by women artists of the 1990s. Indeed, these artists often raise questions about the position of women without providing the clear social critique evident in 1980s works such as those by photographer Cindy Sherman. This resulting ambiguity is even more evident in Katy Grannan's (b.1969) photograph *Carla, Arnold Arboretum, Jamaica Plain, MA* (2002) (fig. 2.2), included in the 2003 exhibition Girls' Night Out. Here, a thin, young woman with dark eyes reclines a bit awkwardly on what looks like somewhat uncomfortable terrain. The subject is secluded from the more public spaces of this park by the tree behind her, and her colorful belongings can be seen by her feet. Unlike von Hausswolff's nude, this figure has not been dumped in this secluded area, although she does appear a bit tentative about her surroundings. Her reclining pose and thin, accessible, and traditionally beautiful body clearly position her within the discourse of the reclining female nude that has its roots in Renaissance painting. One clear disruption to this ideal is the dirt streaked along the outside of her left thigh and on the back of her legs and buttocks. In the exhibition catalogue, Irene Hofmann argues that the photograph "conveys a sense of haste and a heightened awareness of the model's nakedness."[10] She continues, "Carla's tentative posture and her rumpled pile of clothing make us acutely aware of the exposed, public, and perhaps even dangerous nature of the space, with the photographer and model having seemingly ducked under a tree for just a moment to shoot this image."[11] Hofmann's interpretation of Grannan's photograph suggests a reconsideration of the woman/nature connection as one grounded in discomfort and even fear. Also in the exhibition catalogue, Taru Elfving argues that Grannan's photographs of women "reveal the subtle failures of her subjects to become the desired images," and that this failure "carries with it a grain of resistance, a power to rupture."[12] But as in von Hausswolff's photograph, one could also persuasively argue the contrary, that the subject's awkward pose, the dirt on her body, and her pile of clothing are inadequate signifiers of resistance to the classical female nude presented for the voyeuristic pleasure of the viewer.

Elina Brotherus's (b.1972) *Femme a sa toilette* (2001), a self-portrait of the artist, was also included in the Girls' Night Out exhibition. This photograph, however, is the antithesis of *Carla* in the way that the female nude is displayed. While Carla's reclining pose provides the viewer with almost full access to her body, Brotherus's *Femme* recoils away from the camera and the viewer is only allowed access to her side and her back. Like Grannan, Brotherus engages art history, as her *Femme* recalls nineteenth-century paintings of bathers, which were extremely popular at that time. Brotherus transforms this nineteenth-century image, going much further than Grannan in challenging constructs of women's sexuality embedded in earlier works. Brotherus clutches her body tightly and her down-turned head suggests pain and alienation rather than eroticism. Indeed, this work specifically exemplifies personal pain. Much of Brotherus's work is autobiographical in content, but her nude, although a self-portrait, departs from autobiography in its direct engagement with art history. *Femme a sa toilette* provides an alternative narrative to this familiar 19th-century subject, replacing a traditional representation of the eroticized female body with an expression of the artist's subjectivity.

Examining the role of race in relation to the body, Carla Williams (b. 1965) addresses issues concerning the representation of the black female nude in her photographic projects. Williams is very much aware of the historical conditions that problematize representations of the black female nude. In their recent book titled *The Black Female Body*, Williams and Deborah Willis examine the ways in which colonialism, slavery, and more insidious forms of racism have historically defined the black female body.[13] In spite of this history of racism, Williams does not reject the black female nude as a legitimate subject for black women artists, but instead argues that they should "incorporate visual legacies with contemporary realities in order to present images of real black women who are no longer acted upon, but who possess, in one body, both active voice

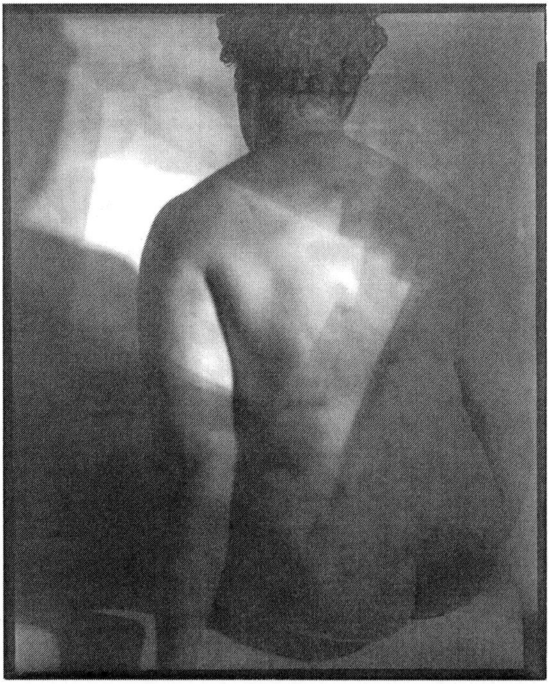

Fig. 2-3
Untitled (Bath). Photograph courtesy of Greenberg Van Doren Gallery. Photograph copyright Carla Williams 1994.

and visual self-presentation."[14] *How to Read Character* (1990–1991) is a series of paired images that juxtapose parts of her own body with photocopy transfers of nineteenth-century images and texts. In one example from the series, a large 5 × 4′ photograph of Williams's buttocks is displayed next to a smaller nineteenth-century drawing that includes multiple perspectives of Sarah Baartman, the so-called "Hottentot Venus." This juxtaposition forces a consideration of the extent to which Williams as an individual is able to escape the racist imagery and ideologies that permeates history. From 1992–1997, Williams also worked on a series of nude self-portraits. She describes them: "I make pictures of myself, and occasionally I will make one which looks as though I've been glimpsed, been glanced at by someone else, and it is these which are most personal to me. You cannot glimpse yourself by accident, I suppose, not even with a snapshot photograph. But I intend to try anyway."[15] In *Untitled (Bath)* (1994) (fig. 2-3), the artist is posed sitting on the edge of a tub with her back to the viewer, which, like Brotherus's *Femme a sa toilette*, connects her photograph to nineteenth-century artists depicting eroticized and exoticized women in baths. Similar to Brotherus, Williams also challenges these nineteenth-century images, in her case by choosing a very sparse room that is free from the exotic objects that characterize nineteenth-century works. Strong sunlight permeates a portion of the photograph, falling on her back, her left shoulder, and the wall. This sunlight more closely reveals the "real" body in the photograph, symbolically shedding light on more superficial representations of the nude. Commenting on the work of artist Zoe Leonard, Susan Kandel observes, "There are those who choose to dissolve the fetishized surface of the female body in order to reveal the traces of its interior."[16] Kandel's words are a compelling description of both Brotherus's and Williams's self-portraits. In both cases, the artists have revealed their own subjectivity through the voyeuristic and sexist lens of nineteenth-century imagery.

I will now return to McGregor's video as the final work for consideration in this essay. As for Brotherus and Williams, subjectivity is one of the McGregor's central concerns. In *Sheraton*, McGregor videotapes herself during her stay at Boston's Sheraton Hotel a few days before the WCA conference in which she would show her completed work (see fig. 2-4). As explained by the artist, the purpose of this performance and other performances she has created in hotel rooms is "to imagine the history of the room and reflect on emotional and physical memories that I have of similar rooms."[17] The emotions evoked in *Sheraton* range from loneliness to boredom. Indeed, McGregor films herself using a tube of lipstick to write on her nude body these and other words describing her emotional state. The hotel room becomes a site of sexual desire mixed with emotional pain. In the film, McGregor recounts the sexual encounters she has had in hotel rooms at different times in her life with partners with whom she was having unfulfilling relationships. Before she begins to describe these encounters, she lies naked on her bed, in which her hand moves toward her genitalia in an action that suggests she is about to masturbate. But the video shifts abruptly to her description of the emotional pain associated with her sexual encounters, again, emphasizing isolation and loneliness rather than sexual pleasure. In witnessing this private act, we are also reminded of the convergence of private and public space in the hotel room itself. In a recent telephone conversation with McGregor, the artist described her desire "to assert my body on my own terms."[18] In *Sheraton*, this is precisely her project, as her nude body becomes a map of her very personal emotional responses to the very impersonal hotel setting.

This very brief essay is not meant to be a comprehensive analysis of the return of the female nude in recent art, but a general reflection on the repositioning of the female nude in contemporary art discourse. Length limitations to the essay prevented me from discussing works by Jenny Saville (b.1970) and Melanie Manchot (b.1966) that were exhibited as part of The Nude in Contemporary Art. Their works would lead to a very different reading of the position of the female nude than those by the artists included in this essay. Clearly, there are many absences in this essay, just as this topic was absent at the WCA conference, including that of the lesbian and queer body. This absence reflects the exclusion of this body from the exhibitions I considered for this paper, The Nude in Contemporary Art, Girls' Night Out, and Another Girl, Another Planet, as well as my selection of works by Generation X women artists. Regrettably, my selection criteria led me only to the subject of the white female body and its assumed heterosexuality. Recognizing this limitation, I chose to include the work of Carla Williams, as I found it to be most relevant in addressing the concerns of this paper from the perspective of an African-American woman artist. Thus, the conclusion that follows is simply an effort to bring closure to this paper, with the hope that it will add to—and continue—the conversation I began with other participants at the WCA conference.

---

[1] Harry Philbrick, "The Nude in Our Time: A Brief Rumination of the Nude in Contemporary Art," in *The Nude in Contemporary Art* (Ridgefield, CT: Aldrich Museum of Contemporary Art, 1999), 9.

[2] Lucy Lippard, "The Pains and Pleasures of Rebirth: European and American Women's Body Art," in *From the Center: Feminist Essays on Women's Art* (New York: E.P. Dutton, 1976), 124.
[3] Griselda Pollock, *Vision and Difference: Femininity, Feminism and the Histories of Art* (London: Routledge, 1988), 158.
[4] Amelia Jones, ed., *The Feminism and Visual Culture Reader* (London: Routledge, 2003), 370.
[5] See, for example, Janet Wolff, "Reinstating Corporeality: Feminism and Body Politics," in *The Feminism and Visual Culture Reader*, 415. Taking an affirmative position, Janet Wolff argues that "a feminist cultural politics of the body *is* a possibility," even though it does run the risk of colluding with heterosexist ideology. Wolff, 415.
[6] Lucy Soutter, "Dial 'P' for Panties: Narrative Photography in the 1990s," *Afterimage* 27 (Jan./Feb. 2000): 3.
[7] Ibid, 3–4.
[8] Bill Arning, "Three Swedes: Jens Fänge, Annika von Hausswolff, Martin Gustavasson," *New Art Examiner* 25 (July/Aug. 1998): 2.
[9] Ibid, 2.
[10] Iren Hofmann, "The Artists," *Girls' Night Out*, 86.
[11] Ibid, 86.
[12] Taru Elfving, "Girl, Unmarked," *Girls' Night Out*, 44.
[13] Deborah Willis and Carla Williams, *The Black Female Body: A Photographic History* (Philadelphia: Temple University Press), ix.
[14] Carla Williams, "Naked, Neutered, or Noble."
[15] Carla Williams, "Untitled Self-Portraits, 1992–1997," http://carlagirl.net/images/art/1997/9297.html. Access date on June 10. 2007.
[16] Susan Kandel, "Beneath the Green Veil: The Body in/of New Feminist Art," in *Sexual Politics: Judy Chicago's Dinner Party in Feminist History*, edited by Amelia Jones (Berkeley, University of California Press, 1996), 196.
[17] Catherine McGregor, http://www.lucacurci.com/artexpo/home/events/video/lithuania/artists.html.
[18] Telephone conversation with artist, February 8, 2007.

Works Cited

Armstrong, Elizabeth, Irene Hofmann and Taru Elfving. Girls' Night Out. Newport Beach, CA: Orange County Museum of Art, 2003.

Arning, Bill. "Three Swedes: Jens Fänge, Annika von Hausswolff, Martin Gustavasson." *New Art Examiner* 25 (July/Aug. 1998): 24–29.

Buszek, Maria Elena. *Pin-up Grrls: Feminism, Sexuality, Popular Culture*. Durham: Duke University Press, 2006.

Farrington, Lisa. "Reinventing Herself: The Black Female Nude." *Woman's Art Journal* (Fall 2003/Winter 2004): 15–23.

Honigman, Ana Finel. "Artist/Photographer (female) Seeks People for Portraits." *Modern Painters* (Spring 2004): 80–83.

Jones, Amelia, ed. *The Feminism and Visual Culture Reader*. London: Routledge, 2003.

Kandel, Susan. "Beneath the Green Veil: The Body in/of New Feminist Art." In *Sexual Politics: Judy Chicago's Dinner Party in Feminist History*, Amelia Jones, ed. Berkeley: University of California Press, 1996.

Lippard, Lucy. "The Pains and Pleasures of Rebirth: European and American

Women's Body Art." In *From the Center: Feminist Essays on Women's Art*, Lucy Lippard ed.. New York: E.P. Dutton, 1976.

Meagher, Michelle. "Jenny Saville and a Feminist Aesthetics of Disgust." *Hypatia* 18 (Fall 2003): 23–41.

Nochlin, Linda. "Offbeat and Naked." *Artnet* 5 Nov. 1999 http://www.artnet.com/magazine/features/nochlin/nochlin11–5–99.asp

Philbrick, Harry et al. *The Nude in Contemporary Art*. Ridgefield, CT: Aldrich Museum of Contemporary Art, 1999.

Pollock, Griselda. *Vision and Difference: Femininity, Feminism and the Histories of Art*. London: Routledge, 1988.

Rohatyn, Jeanne Greenberg. *Another Girl, Another Planet*. New York: Lawrence Ruben Greenberg Van Doren Fine Art, 1999.

Soutter, Lucy. "Dial 'P' for Panties: Narrative Photography in the 1990s." *Afterimage* 27 (Jan/Feb 2000): 9–12.

Townsend, Chris. *Vile Bodies: Photography and the Crisis of Looking*. Munich: Prestel-Verlag, 1998.

Williams, Carla. "Naked, Neutered, or Noble: Extremes of the Black Female Body and the Problem of Photographic History." In *Skin Deep,Spirit Strong:*

The Black Female Body in American Culture, edited by Kimberly Wallace Sanders (Ann Arbor: University of Michigan Press, 2002). http://carlagirl.net/writing/nnn.html.

——. "Untitled Self-Portraits, 1992–1997." http://carlagirl.net/images/art/1997/9297.html

Willis, Deborah and Carla Williams. *The Black Female Body: A Photographic History*. Philadelphia: Temple University Press, 2002.

Wolff, Janet. "Reinstating Corporeality: Feminism and Body Politics." In *The Feminism and Visual Culture Reader*, edited by Amelia Jones. London: Routledge, 2003.

RITUAL AND PERFORMANCE: A COLLECTIVE INQUIRY

ANNA WEXLER, MARI NOVOTNY-JONES, JANET GILLESPIE, L'MERCHIE FRAZIER, CATHERINE MCGREGOR

Introduction—Anna Wexler

Recent critical discussions[1] locate inceptions of performance art[2] within three distinct historical narratives: avant-garde European theater, Jackson Pollock's "action painting," and a third matrix characterized as a "rejection of Modernism and western civilization" through "a revival of ancient ritual practices.[3] The latter, often involving disciplines of the body, has been loosely linked with shamanic and related traditions through physical ordeal/duration, trance, and mutually transformative dynamics between performer and audience, among other ritualized expressive modes. By the early 1970s, a significant stream of feminist performance art emerged, involving appropriation of non-Western ceremonial practices and myths that often foregrounded goddess imagery and themes.[4] Such intercultural work, though distinctive in its attempts to unify and empower women through envisioned female archetypes, may be situated within the turn toward ritual that characterizes the third matrix of performance art as outlined above.

Unlike the first two narratives, rooted in specific, primarily Euro-American, histories of avant-garde formations, the third matrix claims broad cultural sources and radical healing potentials emerging from neo-primitive re-workings of communal and spiritually charged ritual practices. In her essay, "The Other History of Intercultural Performance,"[5] Coco Fusco effectively exposes a violent subtext of this alternative narrative. Contesting its historical erasure, she situates the origins of intercultural performance art in the enforced, ethnographic exhibit of "specimens" of nonwhite, conquered peoples in museums, circuses, and theaters, World's Fairs, and so on, from 1493 to the present.[6] These individuals, clothed in exotic dress, often engaged in repeated, ostensibly ritual acts for the pseudoscientific edification, entertainment, and aesthetic inspiration of Europeans and Euro-Americans. As such, they provided sources for Dadaists and other European avant-gardes constructing oppositional symbols, gestures, and practices from the primitive displays of colonized peoples and their artifacts.

According to Fusco, this cannibalization continues unabated among contemporary white artists:

> ...This practice of appropriating and fetish-izing the primitive and simultaneously erasing the original sources continues into contemporary 'avant-garde' performance art. In his 1977 essay 'New Models, New Visions: Some Notes Toward a Poetics of Performance,' Jerome Rothenberg envisioned this phenomenon in an entirely celebratory manner, noting correlations between Happenings and rituals, meditative works and mantric models, Earthworks and Native American sculptures, dreamworks and notions of trance and ecstasy, bodyworks and self-mutilation, and performance based on several other variations of the shamanistic premise attributed to non-Western cultures.[7]

Feminist performance art engaged with these neo-primitive modes, whatever its transformational intent, is also deeply implicated in the colonialist legacies referred to here.[8] As a white female artist and scholar involved with the ritual traditions of Haitian *Vodou*, I take Fusco's critique as a major axis of interrogation of my own work and that of other performers engaged with intercultural dynamics and sources, whether or not they are explicitly tied to feminist issues. When I was invited to chair a panel for the 2006 Women's Caucus for the Arts Conference in Boston, and also learned that Fusco was to be the keynote speaker, I decided to focus the panel on ritual and performance as a means to stimulate inquiry into the difficult issues she raises.

My discussions with performance artist Mari Novotny-Jones were also a major shaping impetus for this project. I recently had the opportunity to work closely with her in the development of her master's thesis, *The Nature of Transformation in Ritual and Performance: A Study of the Relationship between Performer and Audience.* At the heart of this investigation is Novotny-Jones's commitment to ritually based performance as revelatory, as opening conduits for political, emotional, and spiritual states of awareness that can be transmitted between performer and audience members in non-hierarchical and unprogrammed moments of authentic contact. She examines this issue through grounded discussions of her Polish Catholic heritage and her extensive performance work in Eastern Europe—Poland, Macedonia and the Czech Republic—based on residencies in which she researched local ritual traditions within contexts of intense cultural and political upheaval. Her example has continued to inspire me to pursue the path, however perilous, of intercultural performance as a continuous expressive inquiry. In addition to Novotny-Jones, I invited other women artists—L'Merchie Frazier, Janet Gillespie, Catherine McGregor, and Kera Washington—involved with diverse media, whose performance work demonstrates connection to specific ritual practices shaped by critical awareness of themselves as agents of cultural translation, appropriation, and remembrance/revival within living legacies[9] of domination.

Rituals of Domesticity—Mari Novotny-Jones

> When women use their own bodies in their art work, they are using their selves; a significant psychological factor converts these bodies from object to subject.
>
> Jayne Wark, 2006[10]

The tenet of feminist ideals as expressed in this powerful statement embraces the over turning of the male gaze (object) to the knowledge and the power of the female gaze as she stares back (subject). This notion of subject as the essence of performance, especially that of early feminist performance work, galvanized two decades of work that sought to separate what was essentially female art from the dominant patriarchy. In the 1960s and 1970s, feminist art investigated our qualities that made us distinctly women. This "sameness" drew women together as a significant political force, a force that would advocate for equality in the art world and the business world. [11]

In performance, artists such as Mary Beth Edelson incorporated rituals that were devised and referenced from Eastern, folkloric, and indigenous cultures in an attempt to reclaim the past, through a connection to nature and spirituality.[12] In present poststructuralist theory, we now see these ritualized performances as naive and products of feminist "essentialism."[13] I am reminded of the use of the catchword "Her-story" as the quintessential metaphor of that homogenized revisionism.[14] Feminist discourse of the 1980s and 1990s was one of pluralisms and building constituencies among all our differences as women. Therefore, how does one define ritual performance practices that are authentic to each particular artist, and at the same time does not co-opt from particular cultural bases?

This essay investigates the domestic rituals already inherent in hotel as sites. The theme of domestic chores often intersects with extraordinary intentions. "The Exact Location of the Soul" was a piece that I performed nationally for over ten years. An investigation of the drudgery of ironing (my mother spent hours ironing everything from clothes to bed sheets) and its effects on the well-being of the spirit became the fodder of this performance. I wondered in particular, about the fantasies that may have swirled within the mind of my bedraggled mother as she took the cold clothing from the refrigerator, already soaked in starch, and speckled warm water on the freezing stiff shirts from a sprinkle-topped coke bottle. The ordinary became extraordinary in my performance, as I took up the task of ironing liver and later blending it with milk into a whipped concoction. I believed the concoction would enlarge my soul, give me courage, and be a symbolic release for my mother from all those years of domestic toil. This performance paints what my mother was dreaming as she blended into the iron landscape of the 1950s and the impossible model of the perfect home that was the mantra of many women in the United States at that time.

I naturally gravitated to the role of the maid in the conference hotel. My roots stem from working-class immigrant parents from Poland and Wales, both domestics and coal miners. Since we were in the Sheraton Boston, I decided to assume the persona of a maid. My performance focus was on the women who go about the chores of cleaning, clearing, and creating order or tidiness—the invisible cleaning lady, who works long hours on her feet and still is not left a tip by many guests staying in rooms of homogeneous coziness.

As both a performance artist and teacher of performance, I am attracted to contemporary art practices of durational actions, personae, and interventions. My strongest interest is in the diverse personae. I particularly admire the work of U.S. performance artists in 1970s, in particular, installation artist Suzanne Lacy, performance artist Linda Montano, and conceptual artist Adrian Piper. In her article, "The 1970's and 'Situation' and Recent Installation…," Amelia Jones writes eloquently about the notion of the body/self as both object and subject.[15] A performance artist (who is also the subject of the scene unfolding) can be read by an audience as a "real" self, but is in fact, a constructed "self." This constructed "self" communicates meaning not from the scene unfolding, but from the psychological effect of what the audience perceives. Their perception becomes the content.

Jones cites the "Catalysis"[16] series by Adrian Piper as an example of this particular paradigm. During the years 1970 and 1971, Adrian Piper explored her "otherness" on the streets of New York City by engaging in actions that bordered on everything from odd to disturbing and disgusting.

She rode public buses while asking for change for ketchup-covered money. She employed a rag stuffed into her mouth, sometimes trying to speak, other times sitting on the bus in close proximity to others. She was interested in providing a catalyst for audience engagement and provoking them to question their definitions of race and gender in a public setting (she, herself, is of mixed race). Piper not only was an object that people stared at, but in fact, a subject in which discourse could arise in the minds of the viewers as they encountered her on the streets of the city. Her actions demanded a reassessment of what is feminine and what is black. Piper figuratively sliced at the core of what the white world might actually fear: a deranged black woman. I also think of these actions as ritualized forms of oppression. Adrian Piper, by using the routines of street life (requiring change for the bus, wearing clothes with strange smells, and stuffing her mouth so as not to be understood), communicated through extraordinary measures in ordinary settings the fractured perceptions of race and class.

In considering the "maid" character for the panel, I immediately needed to recognize my own culpability in the fact that most of the maids in hotels are of races different from my own. As a middle-aged white woman with white hair from working class background, I have the privileges of education, artistic pursuits and of the dominant Anglo structure. I developed an artistic intervention with women who were like me, but remained on the outside of this circle. A larger inquiry came to mind, in terms of feminist discourse: who is considered part of the discourse and who is excluded? Therefore, I investigated the role of class in current feminist practices, contrasting that of educated women with the role of working class women. I began to ask myself: what would happen if I brought the "maid" somewhere that crosses thresholds of membership? What if the "maid" did her job with the same passion as those who attended the panel, the women who came to share and rejuvenate their mutual interests in the arts? What is the art of the "maid"? Will she be recognized for her contribution? What would it mean to slowly intervene in this audience to the point of taking focus because she must complete her job? How does she convey that she is really trying to help and that she is really concerned for safety issues?

I secured a maid's uniform from another hotel. My uniform did not replicate the Sheraton Boston uniform at all, but was perceived by everyone as a maid's uniform (the universal costume/mask). My performance began with my trying to bus the cups and detritus from the room (a typical maid's activity). The small conference room filled up with women very quickly, and my "maid" was trapped against the food counter, having a difficult time gathering, tidying, and leaving. One woman asked if I needed help, and I replied that it was very kind of her to offer but I could do my job. I did ask her to help clear a path for me and she did so with great aplomb. I wondered if she felt sorry for me. I wondered if she thought it odd that an Anglo middle-aged woman was doing this job. I had found the kitchen area earlier and was able to return the cups and plates to the correct place to be washed. So here is the first level of complexity. I was posing as a maid, but actually trying to fulfill the real duties of that position. When I walked into the kitchen, I smiled and placed my tray in the correct spot. I seemed to be accepted by the kitchen staff, even though my uniform was not correct. The manager said, "thank you" and I returned to find other duties. As the conference progressed, I filled water pitchers, brought clean glasses, and bused more dishes.

At one point, an older woman was having difficulty with coughing. I brought her a glass of water, and she was grateful. She asked me to help her out of the room and back to the registration table. I gladly obliged. As I took her there, I wondered if she asked me because I was the maid? In the interim, I left my tray of dishes on the floor near the door. Upon returning, a manager asked me whose tray it was. I replied that it was mine. He tersely told me to get it to the kitchen; it did not belong on the floor. I obeyed his orders.

I then stationed myself outside the door and asked women to move in away from the door because it was an exit. I chose to address each woman as "ma'am," a salutation of respect. Most attendees found the request oppressive as there was very little space left in the room. Still, I implored them to move inside. One woman came toward the end of the panel table and stood right in front of me, blocking the door. I proceeded to ask her in an official but soft voice, "Could you please move inside, ma'am. We need to kept the exit clear." The woman turned to me, and being surprised by the identification of "ma'am," said as if to teach me the correct manner in which to address her, "Ma'am, ma'am! It's Ms." I apologetically offered, "I'm sorry ma'am." She left, I believe, very confused.

For me, the question then becomes, "who is in need of emancipation?" If we are to embrace a neo-Feminist Movement for the twenty-first century that reflects inclinations toward our alliances as women, but at the same time recognizes our diversities, then how do we break through the barriers of class? Unconscious or direct expression of privilege inevitably sustains a hierarchical order, much like the oppression of patriarchy, so prevalent in early feminist discourse. Assuming the role of "Teacher" or "Emancipator" only continues to propagate another schism amongst us.

A performance artist, using ritualized actions, will first respond to the context of a particular situation. These actions can be employed to intervene or infiltrate particular sites. The audience, through a set of repetitive interactions, becomes familiar with the routines of the interloper. At the moment this groundwork is interpreted as "normal," the extraordinary devices of the performer can be put into play. By blurring the lines between art and life's roles, I create a state of confusion using the power of resistance to provoke discomfort. "Rituals of Domesticity" was meant as a small prod into the complex discourse of identity, work, and class: to loosen deeply held assumptions about the place of working class women, in opposition to the position of liberal, educated, and artistic women. As noted, Adrian Piper confronted us decades ago with her "Catalysis," and Coco Fusco[17] cross-examines, exposes, and unearths those soundless fears as we gaze at the object of otherness.

The Ostrich and the Swan—Janet Gillespie

Coco Fusco's work articulates for me the processes of assimilation, invisibility, and oppression that I have observed in my long career as a white dancer/choreographer and teacher. For many years, I trained and performed within the dominant, Europeanist traditions of ballet and modern dance. Fusco has pointed out that the African sources of highly influential white artists have been simultaneously appropriated and erased. Ballet, in particular, has reproduced this white, Western, patriarchal, and hierarchical structure.

Ballet has idealized a particular body type of white women: thin, long legs, separated from her "natural" woman's body. Years of rigorous, highly specialized physical training has elevated her, "en pointe,"[18] into an artificial, man-made realm of gravity-defying and nature-denying beauty. In contrast, African dance celebrates the human connection with the earth through its barefooted acknowledgement of gravity. Neoclassic ballet of the twentieth century has assimilated some of the physical effects of African dance, creating a fusion dance of stunning beauty and originality In so doing, it has erased, or made masculine, the cultural values originally embodied by those physical effects, "cannibalizing them," to use Coco Fusco's words.[19]

I invited the audience to sample the European and African dance basics. They enthusiastically participated in the brief movement based performance I designed to allow them to feel the patriarchal, body-denying aesthetic of ballet. Together we "pulled up" and stretched into that refined, rarified and superior realm beyond the "natural" body. This body, in Susan Bordo's words, is constructed according to the standards of the "panoptical male connoisseur."[20] We compared two videos of these contrasting world views embodied in two very different dances, both inspired by and referencing birds: the swan queen's variation from Act II of the classical ballet *Swan Lake*, where undulating arms, flexible upper back, brilliant leaps trace vague allusions to a bird in flight on the body of an idealized, aristocratic, enchanted woman; and the *Ostrich Dance,* a traditional West African dance performed in 1934 by Asadata Dafora for large, enthusiastic audiences in the United States.[21]

We then shared our reflections on how the physical aesthetic of ballet embodies European cultural values of a "man-made" art superior to nature. We concluded by sampling the joyously physical aesthetic of African movement: with loose knees, pliant spine, articulate torso, and low center of gravity valuing and celebrating the body's weight. In contrast to the rigid single unit torso of classical ballet, we felt how the pulsing pelvic movements of African dance affirm the generous creativity of the natural world. This performance explored, by contrast, how slender and powerful dancers, idealized by the intense training of the classical ballet, display the elite, patriarchal, body-denying aesthetic of ballet. This illustrated a "whiting out" of African earth centered/affirming values, and indeed from a traditional western patriarchal perspective, the "female" worldview.

Windows to the Soul: The Circle Unbroken—L'Merchie Frazier

Maude Southwell Wahlman, in her book *Signs and Symbols: African Images in African-American Quilts*, traces religious symbols of the Kongo, Ejagham, Fon, Mande, Yoruba, and other groups highlighting their vocabulary and presence in African textiles. She describes several ideological systems that have made their journey via the trans-Atlantic slave route through the African Diaspora into the Americas. These systems found in Cuba, Haiti, and Brazil present the Cosmogram of the Kongo people in Zaire. She explains:

> The Kongo cosmogram, displayed as a circle intersecting with a cross, represents birth, life, death, and rebirth in the underwater world of the ancestors . . . Also referred to as the four moments of the sun, it symbolizes the four stations in the cycle of life.[22]

Archaeological studies have uncovered stories of early African American communities that can be traced through the artifact of clay bowls called Colono Ware. While Colono Ware is concentrated in certain areas of the southeast United States, these objects have been found in riverbeds and other bodies of water in Haiti, Florida, South Carolina, and Virginia, and chards were even found in New England. Leland Ferguson, in *Uncommon Ground: Archaeology and Early African America 1650–1800*, links these bowls enscribed with "x" to cosmograms designed by the Bakongo people in present day Kongo and Angola.[23] His evidence highlights these artifacts, roughly shaped into circles, as important in the spiritual lives of enslaved Africans living in North America in the making of medicine, serving food, and ritual. As medicine carriers, they have become *minkisi*, classical healing containers of the Bakongo. He cites numerous examples of these "magic bowls" that mark the circle and have a connection with water. This circularity of form in the cosmogram and the exigencies of birth, life, death, and rebirth became a central focus of my exploration of memory, African cosmology, and retentions, and their application to universal human experience in my recent multimedia, one-woman performance installation, "Windows to the Soul: The Circle Unbroken."

These bowls position artifact to provide a portal into the practice of medicine-making, serving food, and rites of New World African women that have maintained Old World traditions, technology, and methodology to engage their domesticity in the healing arts. As a New World African woman, my continuous research is for the authentic voice of Africanisms through the device of archaeology that reveals eighteenth and nineteenth Century African American historical story. I have come to see artifact as no longer a term of historical distance but also a carrier of the immediate past. Through the power of the circle, I am reminded how much the past is a part of the present and extends into the future. "Windows to the Soul: The Circle Unbroken" is a part of my continuous work to participate in the dialogue of memory reclamation that documents the collective and individual human journey of women.

The performance poetry offers a portal through which we can examine the nature of memory itself. If each memory can be said to occupy its own moment fixed in time, then we can begin to crystallize these memories, and hold them, eternalized as artifacts. Each memory is a moment. When each moment passes, the moment then becomes artifact. The performer seated in a circle provides an opportunity for the viewer to evaluate one's own personal experience as reflected in a spectrum of cultural artifacts. Each element of the poetry performance—the garment, the *minkisi*, the water, the bowl—represents constructed moments in time. These objects challenge the viewer to perceive the objects not only in relationship to the facts or records of everyday experience they may represent, but to begin to access their own personal connection to the objects. The performance allows me to gain access, engage, and make connection to my past, posing a contrast to Coco Fusco's critique based on intercultural works by artists positioned outside of ritual experience as an observer.[24] In the poetry of the installation, we witness my search for ancestral reclamation through my character of Joko.[25] Over time, this New World African woman is approached by Western trained doctors intrigued with the power of her medicine; we see that power of her medicine eventually severed by the metaphor of the construction of the "new road": "her pot of indigo dye had been broken by the new road, and that she was leaving Efon to return no more …"

EARTHENWARE RITUALS

Danger lurks in the dark of the river
where even men,
Women and slavery retreat
Night reveals her
Rubbing until smooth
She, knocks on each pot
Listens to their voices
They answer slowly
Deep, deep from each crack in the
Rock of their African clay
"I am Joko." she says
"Are you my mother?"
No answer comes.

This time she knocks
Caressing the spirit jar
Deep, deep from malleable material
Etched a whisper
"Are you my grandmother?"
Prayers in the crack answer.

Kneeling riddles
Clay bowls in need of a drink
Water is short
Too thirsty to wait for
Language to speak
They scream the secret breath to
Rest in the bow of the caldron
The breath of the crack waits to
Tear its edges
Rocks root the clouds

In a back cabin Benah cradles
Her sickly baby
Joko stands on marked cross in the rice field
Hurls her rice bowl to the wind of the suns imagination
The Cabin door flies open

That North wind breathes for the baby
The bowl sinks to the bottom of the river
As baby's mother smiles

Now Smashing pots ooze soft whispers
"More pots, more crosses
Touch the dust
But do not write on the earth"
Mirrors reflect buried potters hands
Burnished with black stones

Among the dirt some of these potters
Are honored
Some of these honored are dark hands
Some of these dark hands knew signs
Some of these signs were trysts of winds
And air turning back on itself and back on itself again
The relocated air—fleshy
As if inside bone marrow
Breath comes home to resuscitate the dead

Spirit jars break
The doctor comes to beg her remedy
Joko's pot of indigo dye now broken by the new road
Vows "I leave Macon to return no more …"
I throw stone into water
Ripples come back to me
Cipher from the center of my rose
My petals fall
Into red wrappers
Heard in Cairo
Georgia magenta bowl
Clay layers in smooth agreement
Here, now, whisper
"I am Atta. Drape me in
Three white cloths facing Mecca.
More pots, more crosses
More pots, more crosses
In the red dust yellow flowers bloom[26]

The conference panel, "Ritual and Performance," celebrated women, ritual and performance art, and posed questions about personal quests, reflection, and significance. My research to link my past with my present, provided the spark leading to my participation. It is my hope that this performance installation provided an introspective moment for participants to find something of themselves among these artifacts: a sense of memory regained, healing, connectedness, and community.

Space and Ritual Performance: *Sheraton*—A Performance for Video—Catherine McGregor

I am intrigued by the notion of ritual as something that interacts within a space and is refracted through the female body. The idea of rituals as reflected through the experience of being a woman reminded me initially of Faith Wilding's seminal performance "Waiting."[27] Space and ritual are also prominent in the work of conceptual artist Marina Abramovic, whose work has influenced my performance work.[28] Abramovic's earlier work includes "Role Exchange," where she swapped places with a sex worker in Amsterdam for her gallery opening by placing herself in the woman's "window" in the red light district. The sex worker then greeted visitors in the gallery. During the 1970s and 1980s, Abramovic's work explored the body, its extreme states of consciousness, and its relationship to architectural space. This theme has continued throughout Abramovic's work even in recent pieces, such as in 2005 with *The House with the Ocean View*,[29] where she placed herself in a platform constructed in a New York Gallery. Her every action was observed by an audience, and she was able to interact with her audience through non-verbal communication.

In creating *Sheraton*, I focused on rituals inscribed by spaces upon the body. Placing myself in a particular space of the Sheraton Boston conference hotel room, I proceeded to examine the site's cultural resonances for women: objectification, isolation, and discomfort, alongside personal narratives of pleasure and pain. The WCA conference took place in a bland, corporate chain hotel. I subverted the nearly "non-space" of this bland, corporate chain hotel into a performance site. Same hotel space, different cities, different countries. These spaces appear void of meaning but are often the site of deeply felt emotions: from extreme loneliness to passion, violence, and excitement.

I conceived of using the hotel room as a ritual space—embracing the fact that it was a liminal space. Many large American chain hotels create a "limbo," aiming to provide the same impersonal "home-away-from-home" experience, whether one is in Mumbai or Minneapolis, Tokyo or Tahoe. I experience a sense of disassociation when I stay in such places.

Liminality is an ambiguous location/period characterized by humility, seclusion, tests, sexual ambiguity, and *communitas.*[30] Victor Turner defines liminality as "a stereotyped sequence of activities involving gestures, words, and objects, performed in a sequestered place, and designed to influence preternatural entities or forces on behalf of the actors' goals and interests."[31] The liminal potential of a hotel arises from its very anonymity. For example, it has been estimated that hotels gain 60 to 80 percent of their video on demand revenue from porn.[32] The hotel room is also apocryphally the venue for adulterous liaisons, interactions with sex workers, and suicides.

My video performance, *Sheraton*, developed as an idea of going into a sequestered space. I checked into the Sheraton Boston at lunchtime on February 8, 2006, with only my handbag and video camera. I spent the next 20 hours in the hotel room. My only interactions were with the hotel staff and my video camera. I did "crack" and called my partner in the evening: this is the moment when the video performance actually "began."

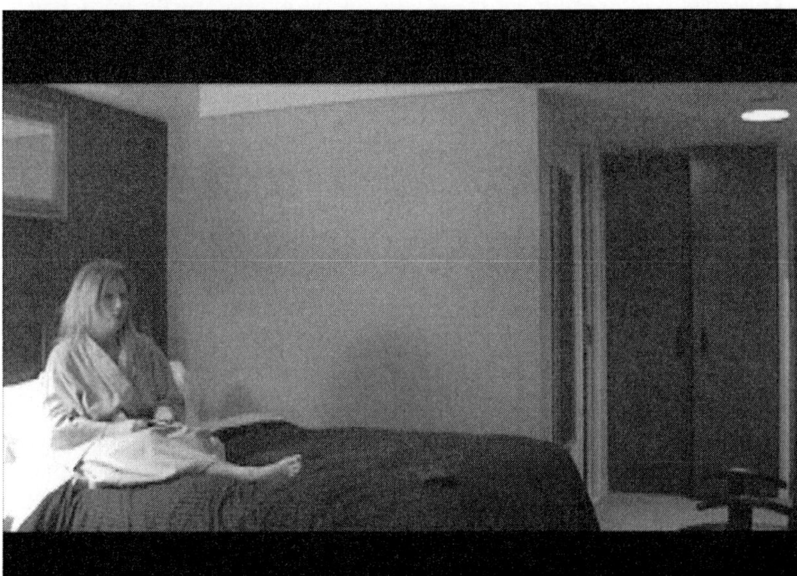

Fig. 2-4
Sheraton. Photograph copyright Catherine McGregor 2006

I decided that every hour, apart from when I was sleeping (which ended up being 6 hours out of the 20), I would perform an "action" for the camera..This might involve speech, performative actions, or simply watching footage of myself watching TV in the room (Fig. 2-4). By setting up the shot of having the camera's eye upon me, I made this a performative action in its own right

I was surprised by how this sequestered space affected me. I began to delve into memories of being in hotel rooms, excavating painful memories (of which I did not usually think). I also became very aware of being a woman alone, under self-imposed surveillance, within the seclusion of a private room. Twenty-first century hotels can be difficult spaces for women to negotiate. This fact that was brought to bear by the security warning on the door of my room and the noisy male occupant of the room next door who sounded as if at any moment he would come barging through into my space!

The condensed nature of a 15-minute video meant that my mood appeared to change rapidly. As the evening wore on, I found it harder to speak to the camera. I was full of emotions that I wished to express. I did so ultimately by writing out these feelings on my body with lipstick. The main body of the video is in black and white, however this particular sequence I left in color. This was due in part to the vividness of the red lipstick and also in part because of the symbolism of this moment when I was at a crossroads, ready to leave, and go back home. At that moment, I felt very wrapped up in the energy of the room. My feelings were exacerbated by the fact that I was choosing to do this of my own free will and that I only lived five minutes away. I ended up staying the night: only coming out of "limbo" the next morning, changed by my experiences at this liminally bland chain hotel.

Civil Case No. 93–0909-F—Anna Wexler

My performance, *Civil Case No. 93–0909-F*, developed out of conversations with Catherine McGregor about generating site-specific work based on the Sheraton Boston hotel as the WCA conference venue. I have participated in countless academic gatherings, often with politically progressive and culturally informed agendas, in corporate hotels whose labor practices are antithetical to the values espoused in such conference discourse. In the process of doing research on labor relations at the Sheraton Boston, I learned that in 1998, the hotel had paid over $200,000 (US) to settle a lawsuit brought against them by the Hotel and Restaurant

Employees' Union for illegal secret videotaping of male workers in its employee locker room seven years earlier.[33]

Unexpectedly, I again found myself at a charged intersection between my artistic/intellectual responsibilities and Haitian realities. Court documents I examined at the Suffolk County Massachusetts Superior Court[34] revealed that the chief plaintiffs in the case against the hotel were two Haitian workers, a dishwasher and a room service busperson, who had fled Haiti during the 1980s as a result of intimately traumatic experience of the surveillance and secret abductions carried out by the repressive paramilitary apparatus of the Duvalier regime. Their depositions contained overwhelming descriptions of re-traumatization caused by knowledge of the videotapes that had recorded them undressing and changing into their hotel uniforms as well as studying for courses during their breaks in the locker room. The sense of being physically and psychically violated by an omnipresent gaze, so intrinsic to feminist concerns, permeates their testimonies. One of the workers reported feeling as if he were being followed, even "haunted," by cameras everywhere he went, even in the bathroom.[35]

I was struck by the courage of these workers, whose vulnerability due to immigration status, ethnicity, and prior experiences of violent repression had not deterred them from taking a public stand against the hotel's secret videotaping and infringement of their privacy rights. On the contrary, these factors intensified their consciousness of the ominous consequences of surveillance practices in an ostensibly democratic society and their commitment to exposing them. Seeking to bear witness to their leadership and eventual victory against hotel management in my piece, I turned, as I have in past work, to the ritual vocabulary of *Vodou* as an ancestral conduit for actualizing legacies of struggles against slavery, colonialism, and imperialism/globalization.

After other preliminary ritual actions, while information I had prerecorded on the case was playing, I drew the word "haunted," used in one of the depositions, in cornmeal flour on the hotel carpet. When this word occurred in my taped reading, my voice stuck there, repeating it again and again, breaking it down into distressed, sonic fragments that eventually moved into the back of my throat as if they were choking me. As this part of the tape played, I rolled across the word as I had drawn it on the carpet so that the letters were temporarily imprinted on my body. Both sonically and graphically, my body bore witness to the traumatic aftermath of video surveillance. In *Vodou* ceremonies, emblems for the spirits are drawn in cornmeal flour on the ground, danced across, and eventually obliterated in the course of ritual time. Often, when particular spirits communicate through their human vessels, they do so in stuttered vocalizations and other sounds that transmit current and submerged states of shock more powerfully than words.[36]

Working within the ritual traditions of *Vodou*, in this piece, was more than an aesthetic choice. I am familiar with *Vodou* as a source of liberatory, protective power from its role in launching and sustaining slave revolts that culminated in the Haitian Revolution to contemporary ceremonies in which embodied ancestral spirits counsel participants in AIDS prevention and other strategies for survival and resistance in the battlefields of urban Haiti and the United States. Having worked with a Haitian performance artist/*Vodou* priest on my piece exploring my New England ancestors' complicity with slavery, I am also familiar with the power of the ritual forms, even in a performance context, to unearth deeply repressed legacies of oppression. In *Civil Case No. 93–0909*, I marked the hotel as a site of violation while ritually honoring the courage of the Haitian workers as a lifeline for inevitable future labor struggles there. This is not to claim that I escape, on any level, the contradictions in intercultural performance work so powerfully formulated by Coco Fusco. They work on me. They are my work. They haunt me at every turn.

Conclusions

As a collective inquiry, the texts above suggest that ritual continues to provide compelling modes for contemporary women performance artists exploring possibilities for transformation within explicit legacies of oppression based on gender, class, racial, and ethnic positions. Each artist consciously locates herself in relationship to Coco Fusco's critique of cultural appropriation in neo-primitive, ritually based avant-garde performance, a perspective that also problematizes some feminist work of the 1970s and beyond as discussed in my introduction above. This awareness then becomes a generative source for more critical, situated ritual vocabularies and actions that intersect multiple, gender-specific historical, socio-cultural and spiritual realities.

Using rituals of domesticity to intervene at the conference site, Mari Novotny-Jones reveals class barriers and fractures within the feminist community gathered there while maintaining acute awareness of the contradictions between her own working class background and her present privileged status as a highly educated artist/teacher. In her site-specific video piece, Catherine McGregor focuses on the vulnerability of the female body in the corporate hotel room with ritual actions that include emerging painful memories of her own prior encounters in such spaces. As a white artist/scholar in but not of the tradition of Haitian *Vodou*, I honor the hotel workers' courage to contest illegal management surveillance practices with a ritual vocabulary through which my own ancestral guilt surfaces, implicating me in the cycles of exploitation and resistance represented in my piece. Janet Gillespie, a white dancer/choreographer, demonstrates the dynamic of her own, deepening critical awareness of the simultaneous absorption and erasure of African dance influences within U.S. modern dance vocabularies and mainstream histories. Finally, in stated contrast to the dynamics of exploitation in intercultural performance work explored by Coco Fusco, L'Merchie Frazier bases her artistic project in ritual forms that evoke genuine, ancestral legacies of oppression and healing for her as a woman of African descent. From this ground, she extends the transformative power of her work outwards to invite participants, regardless of background, to reconnect with themselves and their pasts. As such, her contribution takes us collectively to another point of possibility in our inquiry on ritual and performance—one that is both more critically positioned and more consciously compassionate in its inclusive spirit.

---

[1] Thomas McEvilley, "Stages of Energy: Performance Art Ground Zero," in *Artist Body: Performances 1969–1998*, ed. Marina Abramovic, (Milan, Italy: Charta, 1998), 23–25; and Peggy Phelan, "On Seeing the Invisible: Marina Abramovic's 'The House with the Ocean View'" in *Live: Art and Performance*, ed. Adrian Healthfield (New York: Routledge, 2004), 21.

[2] RoseLee Goldberg, *Performance Art: From Futurism to the Present* (New York: Thames and Hudson, 2001), 9. Wexler uses RoseLee Goldberg's encompassing definition of performance art:

> The history of performance art in the twentieth century is the history of a permissive, open-ended medium with endless variables, executed by artists impatient with the limitations of more established forms, and determined to take their art directly to the public… By its very nature, performance defies precise or easy definition beyond the simple declaration that it is live art by artists. Any stricter definition would immediately negate the possibility of performance itself. For it draws freely on any number of disciplines and media for materials—literature, poetry, theatre, music, dance, architecture and painting, as well as video, film, slides and narrative—deploying them in any combination. Indeed, no other artistic form of expression has such a boundless manifesto, since each performer makes his or her own definition in the very process and manner of execution.

[3] McEvilley, "Stages of Energy: Performance Art Ground Zero," 1998.

[4] Jayne Wark, *Radical Gestures: Feminism and Performance Art in North America* (Montreal, Quebec: McGill-Queen's University Press, 2006), 62–73.

---

[5] Coco Fusco, *English is Broken Here* (New York: The New Press, 1995), 37–63.
[6] Ibid., 47–63. See Fusco's extended discussion in this chapter of audience responses to her performance piece with Guillermo Gomez-Pena, *Two Undiscovered Amerindians Visit...*, based on this legacy of coerced, ethnographic display.
[7] Ibid. 46.
[8] Wark, *Radical Gestures*, 62–73. Jayne Wark carefully examines these contradictions through discussion of ritualized intercultural performances by Carolee Schneemann, Betsy Damon, Mary Beth Edelson, and Donna Henes, among others active in the 1960s and 1970s. Ana Mendieta's ritually informed work, in this context, becomes a counterexample because of its direct connection to her Cuban cultural heritage and its undermining of female archetypal presence through afterimages of her body as vanishing trace in nature. Mendieta was critical of the predominately white middle class women's movement, and its artistic configurations, for marginalizing women of color and their concerns.
[9] Ibid. 6–7
[10] Ibid. 6.
[11] Ibid.58–59. Wark eloquently describes early feminist thought in terms of a cultural feminism that sought to define all women in terms of a male-oriented discourse. Women could only be included in opposition to patriarchal oppression in terms of their homogenous identity as women, void of differences, lacking nuance: "it could be in terms only of sameness not difference, that is, within frameworks which could discuss women only in terms of a common, male-referenced humanity… not specifically as women."
[12] Ibid. 64–66.
[13] Ibid. 6–7. Wark returns to this notion of the essence of what is considered female throughout her book but most notably explains that once differences between men and women were identified along these gender lines, women's experiences were then considered distinct from men's and this distinction became the bases for a unified women's movement.
[14] See Global Feminisms, New directions in Contemporary Art for feminist history, http://nymag.com/arts/art/reviews/29707/. Access date June 10, 2007.
[15]Erika Suderburg, ed., *Space, Site, Intervention, Situating Installation Art* (University of Minnesota Press, 2000), 335–37.
[16] Ibid. 335–37.
[17] Referenced in this essay's introduction Coco Fusco, *English is Broken Here* (New York: The New Press, 1995).
[18] Ballet dancers rise to dance on the tips of their toes when "en point."
[19] Fusco, *English is Broken Here*, 15.
[20] Susan Bordo, *Unbearable Weight: Feminism, Western Culture, and the Body* (Berkeley: University of California Press, 1993), 134.
[21] Susan Manning, *Modern Dance, Negro Dance: Race in Motion* (Minneapolis: University of Minnesota Press, 2004), 42.
[22] Maude Southwell Wahlman, *Sign and Symbols: African Images in African-American Quilts* (New York: Studio Books, 1993), 80.

[23] Leland Ferguson, *Uncommon Ground: Archaeology and Early African America 1650-1800* (Washington, D.C.: Smithsonian Institution, 1992).
[24] Fusco, *English is Broken Here.*
[25] "Joko" is the author's fictional character that allows her reference to West Africa, i.e., Nigeria and the trans-Atlantic travel of enslaved Africans through the "Middle Passage. The name Joko is of Yoruba origin. Joko is in search of reclaimation and link to Africa through ancestral voice and practice.
[26] L'Merchie Frazier, 2006, previously unpublished text of "Earthenware Rituals" performance.
[27] Faith Wilding "Waiting," Performance Photo and Text, in *The Artists' Body* Tracey Warr and Amelia Jones eds. (London,UK: Phaidon, 2000).
[28] Marina Abramovic ed., *Artist Body: Performances 1969-1998* (Milan, Italy: Charta, 1998).
[29] Peggy Phelan, "On Seeing the Invisible: Marina Abramovic's 'The House with the Ocean View'."
[30] *Communitas* is defined as an unstructured community where all members are equal. In a sense, *communitas* could refer to the stereotypical image of the traveler freed from day-to-day constraints, in hotel rooms that look the same. See http://www.anthrobase.com/Dic/eng/def/communitas.htm. Access Date June 10, 2007.
[31] Victor Turner, "Symbols in African ritual," in *Symbolic Anthropology: A Reader in the Study of Symbols and Meanings*, ed. J. L. Dolgin, D.S. Kemnitzer, and D.M. Schneider (New York: Columbia University Press 1977), 183.
[32] Public Broadcasting System news programming "Frontline."
http://www.pbs.org/wgbh/pages/frontline/shows/porn/interviews/mcalpine.html#hotel. Also http://www.msnbc.msn.com/id/14468659/,
http://www.nationalcoalition.org/resourcesservices/stat.html. Access date June 10, 2007.
[33] "Boston Sheraton Settles Employee Spying Case," *ACLU News* January 14, 1998. http://legalminds.lp.findlaw.com/list/news/msg00012.html. Access date June 10, 2007.The case is often cited in discussions of electronic monitoring in the workplace and privacy law. See, for example, National Workrights Institute, "Privacy Under Siege: Electronic Monitoring in the Workplace." http://www.workrights.org and "Introduction to Electronic Monitoring in the Workplace," American Civil Liberties Union, Legal Briefing Kit for Electronic monitoring. http://www.aclu.org/workplacerights/spying/13387res19981231.html. Access date June 10, 2007.
[34] Suffolk County Courthouse, Boston, Massachusetts. Civil Case No. 93-0909-F
[35] American Civil Liberties Union, Legal Briefing Kit for Electronic monitoring. http://www.aclu.org/workplacerights/spying/13387res19981231.html. Access date June 10, 2007.
[36] Kathleen Crown, "The Spoken Word Poetry of Tracie Morris," in *We Who Love to Be Astonished: Experimental Women's Writing and Performance Poetics*, ed. Laura Hinton and Cynthia Hogue (Tuscaloosa, AL: University of Alabama Press, 2002), 222. She has pointed out that "the disintegrating language of Morris's

sound poems" is an instance of "disarticulated language as a means to cultural memory and recovery" within African Diaspora tradition. Spirit possession within Haitian *Vodou* is mentioned as a core site of communicative power emanating from stuttered, sonic fragments open to collective interpretation.

Works Cited

Abramovic, Marina, *Artist Body: Performances 1969–1998.* Milan, Italy: Charta, 1998.

American Civil Liberties Union, Legal Briefing Kit for Electronic monitoring, http://www.aclu.org/workplacerights/spying/13387res19981231.html.

Anthrobase, Kari Helene Partapuoli and Finn Sivert Nielsen, http://www.anthrobase.com/Dic/eng/def/communitas.htm.

Bordo, Susan. *Unbearable Weight: Feminism, Western Culture, and the Body.* Berkeley: University of California Press, 1993.

Crown, Kathleen. "The Spoken Word Poetry of Tracie Morris." In *We Who Love to Be Astonished: Experimental Women's Writing and Performance Poetics*, edited by Laura Hinton and Cynthia Hogue, 222 Tuscaloosa, AL: University of Alabama Press, 2002.

McEvilley, Thomas. "Stages of Energy: Performance Art Ground Zero." In *Artist Body: Performances 1969–1998*, edited by Marina Abramovic, 23–25. Milan, Italy: Charta, 1998.

Ferguson, Leland. *Uncommon Ground: Archaeology and Early African America, 1650–1800.* Washington, D.C.: Smithsonian Institution, 1992.

Fusco, Coco. *English is Broken Here.* New York: The New Press, 1995.

Goldberg, RoseLee. *Performance Art: From Futurism to the Present.* New York: Thames and Hudson, 2001.

Gottschild, Brenda Dixon. *Digging the Africanist Presence in American Performance: Dance in Other Contexts.* Westport, Conn.: Greenwood, 1996.

——. *The Black Dancing Body*. New York: Palgrave Macmillan, 2003.

Manning, Susan. *Modern Dance, Negro Dance: Race in Motion.* Minneapolis: University of Minnesota Press, 2004.

National Coalition for the Protection of Children and Families, http://www.nationalcoalition.org/resourcesservices/stat.html.

National Workrights Institute, http://www.workrights.org.

NY Magazine, Mark Stevens, "The History of Herstory, Global Feminisms, New directions in Contemporary Art for feminist history," http://nymag.com/arts/art/reviews/29707/.

Novotny-Jones, Mari. *The Nature of Transformation in Ritual and Performance: A Study of the Relationship between Performer and Audience.* Unpublished Independent Study Master's Thesis, Cambridge, MA: Lesley University, 2005.

Phelan, Peggy., "On Seeing the Invisible: Marina Abramovic's 'The House with the Ocean View'." In *Live: Art and Performance*, edited by Adrian Healthfield, 21. New York: Routledge, 2004.

Public Broadcasting Service, "Frontline, American Porn, Interview with Dennis McAlpine," http://www.pbs.org/wgbh/pages/frontline/shows/porn/interviews/mcalpine.html#hotel.

Suderburg, Erika, ed. *Space, Site, Intervention, Situating Installation Art*. Minneapolis: University of Minnesota Press, 2000.

Turner, Victor. "Symbols in African ritual." In *Symbolic Anthropology: A Reader in the Study of Symbols and Meanings*, edited by J. L. Dolgin, D. S. Kemnitzer and D. M. Schneider. New York: Columbia University Press, 1977.

Wahlman, Maude Southwell. *Sign and Symbols: African Images in African-American Quilts*. New York: Studio Books, 1993.

Wark, Jayne. *Radical Gestures: Feminism and Performance Art in North America*. Montreal, Quebec: McGill-Queen's University Press, 2006.

Warr, Tracey and Amelia Jones, eds. *The Artists' Body*, London: Phaidon, 2000.

THE COW CULTURE: A DILEMMA IN PUBLIC ART

JOAN RYAN

The art world has a long and varied tradition of public art. In the past, public art functioned as an inspirational social tool that inspired and perpetuated traditional values. Since the advent of postmodernism, the world of public art has entered a new phase, with new objectives and new audiences.

Work for the public is no longer judged solely by its esoteric or esthetic merit; nor does public art create the same assumptions it did for past viewers. There is an ever-increasing focus on reaching a broader-based audience, and engaging audiences in issues directly relating to their lives. The questions we must now ask are whose aesthetic is reaching the public, and how do artists maintain a strong presence in a developing world faced with these aesthetic challenges?

A new public art trend in many of the major cities in United States and Europe embraces the use of an iconic sculptural cow.[1] In Boston, Massachusetts, these life size sculptures were painted by local artists, community, and school organizations, and then placed throughout the city in prominent public spaces. After being exhibited for four months, the cows were auctioned off to benefit the Jimmy Fund.[2] The cows themselves were part of a marketing firm's concept for civic activities sold throughout United States.[3]

This article will look at controversies over public art in Massachusetts while addressing the implications of cow culture on the genre of public art. The recent history of public art is a controversial story between artists' rights and visions, and the needs and taste of the general public. In Massachusetts alone, the conflict between artist and the general public has occurred in three high profile cases: Mags Harries's "Shaman Hat"[4] at the Massachusetts Institute of Technology Student Center, her "Glove Cycle"[5] in Cambridge, and Robert Shurs's "Irish Famine"[6] in Boston.

Historically, one of the longest controversies in public art involved Adelaide Johnson's "Portrait Monument" in Washington, DC. The sculpture was commissioned in 1920 to honor the first members of the women's movement and finally, after 76 years of debate, installed in its intended location in May of 1997.[7] Another excellent example is found in one of the most emotionally charged controversies, the Maya Lin's "Vietnam War Memorial"[8] in Washington, DC.

These are both examples of a commissioning process out of step with the needs of its citizens: the esthetic merit of a work questioned as a result of a closed process due to private funding, and removal or cancellation of a project due to poor planning in the placement of an artist's work. Whether it is the commissioning process, aesthetic issues, or spatial concerns, the dilemmas facing public art are many, and issues of political representation that run deep throughout the art world.

Public art must address issues of space and contextual relationship with the public, who will share the environment with the installation on a daily basis. This is the major dilemma facing our public art programs. Who exactly will live with the work on a daily basis? Such issues become problematic when the majority of the public has been fed trite, sentimental concepts of art through the media and commercial culture. As the art of postmodernism no longer operates with one defining paradigm, and boundaries between high and popular cultured are blurred, how does the average citizen derive meaning from public art? In 1985, the Getty Center for Education "found that 80 percent of all individuals in United States graduate from high school with out any art education (including studio, art appreciation or history)."[9] If the public has not been exposed to aesthetic quality, how are they to know what is missing?

The need for our culture to maintain the arts in society has never been more imperative than it is now. Our environment has become more and more cluttered with commercial images, sound bites, blogs, and video images. We all see them at the pump, the checkout, the stadium, the theater, and the crossroads, on our phones, on our screens, and on our clothing. I question what effect this oversaturated visual culture has on our responsibilities as artists. How do we maintain a voice that can excite, inspire, and challenge the public while still providing a transformative experience?

Arthur Danto, in his essay "Tilted Arc and Public Art"[10] suggests that Richard Serra's sculpture commission for the Federal Plaza in lower Manhattan succeeded as a work of art but failed as public art. The current trend of life-sized cows decorated by local artists is working in reverse of this theory. Cow art may succeed as public art, but may not as a "work of art." At this juncture, what may become irrelevant is the aesthetic criteria. Harriet Senie observes that, "Conversely. . . it is possible that a work of art may be good public art, though bad or indifferent art which would then make esthetic criteria irrelevant to the matter."[11] The present trend does arouse the public with enthusiasm, but its aesthetic value is negligible. As entertainment it excels; as art it fails.

Unfortunately, it appears that aesthetic values are not our society's deepest concern. How can public art provide an aesthetic that has the potential to reveal the spiritual content of a culture, rather than merely manifesting kitsch, or a narrow and simplistic expression of personal experience? It would be hard to answer this question without examining the concept of kitsch as an aesthetic category.[12]

Traditionally, kitsch is considered to be tastelessness in the art world, recognized for its cheap, or sentimental qualities. However, its prevalence cannot be denied as a persistent voice in the art world. "In the best scenarios while addressing stereotypes Kitsch can be a powerful social and political statement."[13] In Kristin G. Congdon and Doug Blandy's article "What? Clothesline and Pop Beads Aren't Trashy Anymore? Teaching about Kitsch" they see kitsch as integral in the study of popular and mass culture:

> Clearly what has been called kitsch is deeply rooted in issues related to esthetics, gender, culture, class, economics, race, ethnicity and politics; all of which are integral to the study of material and visual culture. Even if one thinks of it as "bad art" its prevalence makes it relevant . . . [14]

The prevalence of this cow trend appearing in major cities across United States makes an aesthetic discussion imperative. In defense of the authenticity of kitsch, Congdon and Blandy go on to say:

> Kitsch should recognize that it will be understood and appreciated variously depending upon the historical, political, economic, social, and cultural contexts in which it is being discussed and created. Our learning must also recognize new ways of thinking about kitsch and the appropriation of kitsch for a multitude of purposes.[15]

Kitsch, when used with the persuasive power of sentimentality, combines content, humor, and irony to critique culture. Using kitsch, artists can create work that engages the viewer aesthetically and contributes to a deeper understanding of his or her environment. An example of this is Judy Chicago's *Dinner Party*, which is now permanently located in the Sackler Center for Feminist Art at the Brooklyn Museum. This triangular table—with 39 place settings, each depicting either a historical or mythical woman in history—addresses the omission of women throughout history. The *Dinner Party* is a powerful example of how kitsch can critique both culture and social systems, maintain accessibility, while also elevating awareness and developing a sense of pride.

Conclusion

Has art, like so much in our culture, yielded to corporate ambition and become another arena of professional entertainment? Art reflects society's values. How then do artists sustain their vision? When curatorial processes, funding, and politics challenge artistic vision, it becomes even more imperative that artists work to find ways to engage the public in a more sustainable experience. Hence, it becomes essential that artists' voices be heard in all the decision-making processes of public art.

The cow sculpture project in Boston was presented as a synthetic form that embraced both the historic and the sentimentality of the general public, while having less to do with the identity of the contemporary urban culture in which it was placed. By supplying artists with prefabricated cow, the relationship between artist, site and community, intersecting with idea, was diminished, and dialog was pre-empted.

The arts are an essential part of a society's survival and growth. In the creative process, there is an act of discovery that reveals and reflects not only the reality of humanity, but also the potential of humanity. It is this function that provides a unique insight into unrealized areas within a culture's spiritual arena. Public art has the potential to provide an enduring experience that illuminates the human condition:

> …art was and is crucial to the cerebral evolution of the human organism …and is the essential means by which humans develop and extend their consciousness (and self-consciousness), enabling them to develop special skills, sharpening their essential facilities, giving them an increasingly firmer grasp on reality.[16]

If artists embrace this idea, they must strive for significant work that allows the general public to view and understand their environment through substantial experiences. This experience must transcend cultural limitations, leading the public to embrace a shared realization of common experience through personal exploration.

---

[1] Although other animal forms are available the "cow" was selected in Boston for its connection to the early days of agriculture.

[2] Charitable organization founded in 1948, focused on raising funds to fight cancer in children; see http://www.jimmyfund.org/.

[3] For information on the artist selection process please refer to the Jimmy Fund Cow Parade at http://www.jimmyfund.org/eve/event/cow-parade/default.html.

[4] Mags Harries, *Shaman Hat* (proposed for the Stratton Student Center, Massachusetts Institute of Technology, Cambridge, Massachusetts, 1990).

[5] Mags Harries, *Glove Cycle* (Porter Square, Cambridge, Massachusetts, 1978–84).

[6] Robert Shurs, *Irish Famine Memorial* (Washington Street, Boston, Massachusetts, 1998)

[7] *Portrait Monument to Lucretia Mott, Elizabeth Cady Stanton, and Susan B. Anthony* (Capital Rotunda, Washington, DC, 1920).

[8] Maya Lin, *Vietnam Veterans War Memorial* (Washington, DC, 1982)

[9] Harriet F. Senie, *The Tilted ARC Controversy: Dangerous Prececent* (Minneapolis, MN: University of Minnesota Press, 2002), 42.

[10] Arthur C. Danto "Tilted Arc and Public Art, " in *The Wake of Art Criticism, Philosophy, and the End of Taste*, ed. Arthur C. Danto, Gregg Horowitz, and Tom Huhn, 147–152 (Amsterdam B.V.: Overseas Publishers Association, 1998).

[11] Harriet F. Senie, "*The Tilted ARC Controversy: Dangerous Precedent* (Minneapolis, MN: University of Minnesota Press, 2002), 139.

[12] "Kitsch: 1. Art or artwork characterized by sentimental, often pretentious bad taste: the aesthetic or mentality in which such art is conceived or appreciated: " a movie that sets out to expose the kitsch of Hollywood fantasy" (Vincent Canby) 2. Culture or civilization in a degraded state of sentimentality and vulgarity." *American Heritage Dictionary*.

[13] Kristin G. Congdon and Doug Blandy, "What? Clotheslines and Popbeads Aren't Trashy Anymore? Teaching About Kitsch," *Studies in Art Education: A Journal in Issues and Research* 46, no. 3 (2005): 200.

[14] Ibid. 208.

[15] Ibid. 208.

[16] Ellen Dissanayake, *What Is Art For?* (Seattle and London: University of Washington Press, 1998), 67.

Works Cited

Congdon, Kristin G. and Doug Blandy "What? Clotheslines and Popbeads Aren't Trashy Anymore? Teaching About Kitsch." *Studies in Art Education: A Journal in Issues and Research* 46, no. 3 (2005): 197–210.

Danto, Arthur C. "Tilted Arc and Public Art." In *The Wake of Art Criticism, Philosophy, and the End of Taste* edited by Arthur C. Danto, Gregg Horowitz, and Tom Huhn, 147–152. Amsterdam B.V.: Overseas Publishers Association, 1998.

Dissanayake, Ellen. *What Is Art For?* Seattle and London: University of Washington Press, 1998.

Senie, Harriet F. *The Tilted ARC Controversy: Dangerous Precedent?* Minneapolis, MN: University of Minnesota Press, 2002

VERACITY

LAURIE BETH CLARK

After my father died, I became interested in making a video about my relationship with him. At the same time, in my work as an artist and a teacher, I had grown increasingly skeptical about a mode of confession that was pervasive in contemporary (feminist) video art. I therefore approached this project as a concurrent exploration of women's relationships with our fathers and an investigation of testimony and its critique. As part of this project, I interviewed six women working in truth professions (Law, Literary Criticism. Psychoanalysis, Religion, Theatre, Videography) about their engagements with veracity: professional truth, practice, credibility, lying, personal truth, core truth, confession, artistic truth, and relative truth. For the video, I edited these interviews into a conversational format. A partial transcript of that dialogue follows. Susan David Bernstein, Rosemary Bodolay, Patricia Boyette, Rita Clark, Mary Catherine Fons, and Clare Wagner played the participating roles (fig. 2-5):

Dominican Sister: The question of truth is very important for me. I belong to a Dominican order whose motto is *veritas*, which is the Latin word for "truth." It's in our documents, "Participate in the unfolding of truth." From the time many, many years ago when I was eighteen years old and joined this community, that has been held up for me: "Search of the truth. Go for the truth."

Psychoanalyst: In my work I deal with truth all the time, because the question of different perceptions comes into it and each player in a situation usually feels that they have some aspect of the truth, in fact, a bigger part of the truth than the next person. There's a way of doing psychotherapy which involves you and the patient together constructing a narrative that feels truthful Sometimes I do this with patients, but the thing that I make sure that they understand is that what we're doing is not arriving at some absolute truth, but that we're doing something that's going to help them feel better and give them a rationale—

Attorney: Truth is vital in the work that I do in terms of being a lawyer. People think about lawyers as being those trying to find the truth, trying to determine the truth, trying to prove that in a courtroom. In law school, we are indoctrinated to learn that there is a truth in every case that you are working on; there is a truth and you need to figure out what that is. That's going to get you to win this case. If the truth is on your side, then you are going to win.

Literary Critic: Truth, per se, isn't something I would identify as an abiding interest but power relations were really central to that. I would say that a certain kind of truth, political truth, or truth of power dynamics, shape the disclosure of some kind of transgressive or disruptive information or revelation. The idea of fixed truth is something that I am always working against or trying to trouble with my students in the classroom and also in terms of the research and writing that I do.

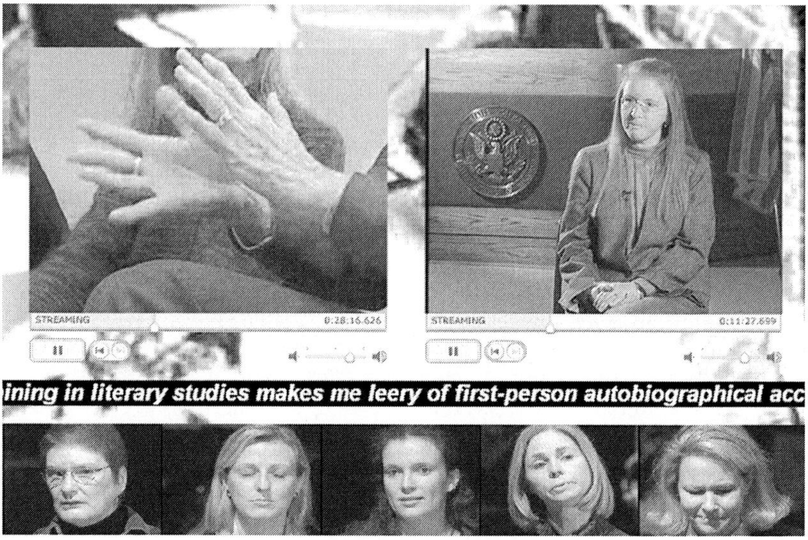

Fig. 2-5
Veracity video still. Image copyright Laurie Beth Clark 2005.

Actor: Acting is creating the illusion of truth, hopefully to get to a deeper truth. A lot of people think of acting as wearing a mask, lying, manipulating, essentially tricking them into believing. I think it's quite the opposite. I don't think there is a lot of difference between coaching someone to be an effective actor, to create an effective character, and coaching someone to communicate more effectively in different situations.

Videographer: As a media maker I'm interested in thinking about what's in the frame as well as what's not in the frame. Documentary work is more interesting with multiple truths complicate a subject than point counterpoint. A tape with multiple perspectives is more truthful.

Attorney: In my work as a lawyer it's important that I am truthful and that I feel that I am being truthful. Those are two different things.

Psychoanalyst: I do some courtroom work, testimony, and it's always a little bit funny to me when they ask me: "Are you going to tell the truth, the whole truth and nothing but the truth, so help you God?" And I always say, "Oh yes. I do. You know. I give them the required answer. I guess I'm giving them a truthful opinion."

Videographer: I think that there are certain contexts where I wouldn't tell the whole truth, not all the details about my past, but I hope I would express truthfulness.

Dominican Sister: Truth is more than just facts or congruency. Truth is the probing of mystery of oneself and the universe.

Actor: When I'm teaching, that is where I feel I have the greatest responsibility to being truthful.

Literary Critic: It depends on what kind of truth you are after. Are you talking about personal disclosure, truths of one's life, or are you talking about professional truth?

Actor: If there is someone that I find very believable, I don't think about believing them, it's very easy.

Attorney: I follow the feelings I get from them when I first meet with them. What they tell me. Whether what they tell me rings true with my experience as a lawyer and as a person.

Psychoanalyst: You know, you can tell if somebody is sincerely believing what they're trying tell you about, something they're trying to sell you, is, if they're really enthusiastic, or if it's something they're doing just to manipulate you.

Dominican Sister: Ordinarily, when someone looks me in the eyes I can intuit if what they are saying is coming from the heart.

Attorney: When I believe , I suppose it's a lot of different factors why I believe them. I suppose it's the way they hold their body and their smile and if they look me in the eyes.

Videographer: Something that would make me believe or not believe would be how often someone is willing to make eye contact.

Dominican Sister: The lack of willingness to look into my eyes when we are dialoguing in my profession and the constant looking around or out the window rather than making eye contact…

Literary Critic: I can imagine all sorts of circumstances where a person is relaying a very difficult truth and would need to look away for all sorts of reasons from the eyes of their listener.

Attorney: I think it would happen quite frequently that someone is telling the truth and would not be believed. That's very common in the context of my work.

Actor: A lot of times there's an overcompensation in some way. It could be with the voice. It could be with the body or the manner. It can be in being oversold, over-intellectualized. It can be in appealing to sentiment. There's something that is over the mark.

Attorney: Being thoughtful can be a good thing and looking like you are thoughtful. However, in a courtroom that can come off like you are in the process of making up the story as you are sitting there.

Literary Critic: I think there are so many different ways of performing what one knows from laughing to seeming very uncomfortable to speaking in a very compelling way. There are all sorts of ways of explaining where those different levels of performance comfort come from.

Actor: I think that the actor, or the person who is not an actor, has to really believe in what they are saying to be believed by someone else. I think that's the way communication works. If they don't really believe it, there is going to be something that's less than complete, there is something held back. They are communicating only 70 percent and I think we pick up on that.

Attorney: They have to be able to tell the story first of all. Some people even though the truth is in there, they aren't able to convey it. They have to be able to explain what happened. They have to be wounded, but not whiners. They have to be able to convey accurately what their story is, but not sound like they are overdoing what has happened to them.

Literary Critic: How you are able to command language and execute your particular word has a lot to do with how that particular truth is understood.

Videographer: There's lots of cultural differences in the ways people think about sharing truth.

Psychoanalyst: In certain cultures, people don't like to come out directly with unpleasant facts. They work around them.

Literary Critic: Relaying a particular kind of truth could be very difficult for somebody, and yes, it could be extremely true.

Attorney: We don't believe people if our experience of what they are telling us doesn't ring true and if they don't look like someone we have been brought up to think tells the truth. We have prejudices against teenagers, against people who have too many tattoos, against people whose hair is purple, or maybe their skin isn't the same color as all the people we have been brought up with.

Videographer: Where you put someone in the frame tells a lot about their expertise or believability as a storyteller.

Literary Critic: Then you have to pay attention to what is the scene of confession, who is making the disclosure, what are the assumptions that frame that disclosure. What are the relationships involved?

Actor: The people being spoken to are part of this–what their expectations are, what they are willing to accept or not accept, what happened right before or right after.

Psychoanalyst: It's not just the person, you are dealing with an interaction, you've got a total structure there with let's say two people. You have to tell the truth and the person has to want to believe that's the truth and then it goes very smoothly.

Actor: The most conflict is when there is someone we actually believe and then the rug is pulled out from under us.

Videographer: I feel sick if I have a sense that somebody's not being truthful or a situation is not revealing itself in a truthful way.

Psychoanalyst: People do lie consciously or unconsciously.

Dominican Sister: There are times when all of us seek cover out of embarrassment.

Videographer: I think if I had a sense that I wasn't sure about the believability, I would just keep coming back at it.

Psychoanalyst: You never would say to someone, "I think you're lying to me." Not usually.

Actor: Someone who is a good liar believes in what they are saying. I think they are also able to drop out of it and not have a conscience that bothers them in terms of inconsistency in dropping in and out of the lie.

Psychoanalyst: I think we've seen a lot of that in public officials and certain business men who look so sincere and they're lying.

Actor: Politicians sometimes really believe what they are saying or alcoholics really believe when they are under the influence and then afterwards say, "Oh I never said that."

Attorney: I expect other lawyers to be lying to me. I expect sometimes clients to be lying to me. I expect other people's clients to be lying to me and I have to sift through.

Psychoanalyst: When a patient comes to me for help and then they lie to me, and I'm talking about conscious lying, I'm not talking about unconscious defenses like denial, I am very concerned because they are violating the basic premises of the treatment which is some truthfulness between them and me.

Attorney: In my agreement that I have when a client hires me, it says that if I find out that something they told me isn't true, I can no longer represent them. I believe that breaks the bond I have with them, and my ability to be an effective advocate for them.

Psychoanalyst: I have to make them see the tremendous disadvantage that they are creating for themselves and if they don't see it, and can't get past it, and we can't form a therapeutic alliance and that's the end of the treatment. I just can't treat someone who is going to continue to lie to me.

Attorney: I expect much more truthfulness in my personal life than I do in my professional life.

Psychoanalyst: I think I'm more off guard when I'm dealing with family or friends, or anybody not in the office.

Attorney: In my personal relationships with my family and my friends I always expect that everything they tell me is the truth.

Psychoanalyst: With a friend, if I think they are doing something that I would consider less than honest, I would probably just let it go.

Literary Critic: I don't make a big distinction between truth telling at work and at home.

Psychoanalyst: I expect that people will be telling the truth unless proven otherwise. I think I have that assumption, that most people are truthful except for certain kinds of salesmen.

Attorney: I doubt the words that anyone says, that is trying to sell me anything.

Literary Critic: When there is not a clear motivation for dissembling then I don't really question whether somebody is telling the truth or not.

Videographer: I hope that in my life every circumstance that I come across I am working at being truthful and honest.

Dominican Sister: I keep myself honest, moving toward the truth, in a couple of ways. I listen to my friends and ask for their feedback.

Attorney: I have an inner code. I have an inner feeling that requires that I tell the truth.

Dominican Sister: I do pray a lot and I'm especially prone to a kind of silent Zen-like prayer in which I find myself trying to reach deeper and to find the place in myself where the truth lives.

Videographer: Part of my work as a maturing human being is that everyday is constant work on myself, approaching a life of honesty and truthfulness.

Psychoanalyst: When I say truth is really a thing and I talk about somebody being truthful what I mean is that they are saying something that they believe is truthful, they're not consciously distorting or lying. That's truth.

Attorney: Truth telling can be very powerful.

Dominican Sister: Every person carries around a spark of the truth and an evolving understanding to the truth.

Actor: There's a truth that's hard to articulate, but it is absolutely understood when it is experienced.

Dominican Sister: I think what I talk about more is the truth that involves the mind and the heart.

Actor: When it's experienced it's unmistakable. It gives you goose bumps. It makes the hair on your neck stand up, when you experience something that is truthful to the core.

Dominican Sister: You go layer by layer, and if a person is willing to open up what is it that you want more than that, then you get to the place where truth lives.

Psychoanalyst: Part of my job is to help them get through that and just get to the simple truth in quotation marks.

Dominican Sister: Maybe, if you wanted to say truth with no quotes, we'd almost have to say divine mystery or the sacred presence in the universe or whatever and then we could say truth with a capital T.

Actor: It's as though our reality that's experienced is only the tip of the iceberg. It's what is underneath that I think is really interesting. It's what's not said as well as what's said. It's what resonates.

Dominican Sister: There are moments when a person finds truth in a very low point in life, in a great struggle, in a great crisis, even in grieving, and the moment when they start to see hope is another illuminating moment.

Literary Critic: I have found a way into an actively religious life that doesn't revolve around certain larger order truths.

Psychoanalyst: There is a core belief I have in my own ability to adapt and survive, not anything, but many things. I have seen this through my life, that I can call on resources from within myself to manage certain things, and I guess that's about as core a belief as I have. I certainly have no core belief in anything outside that is going to help me.

Actor: I think for me the theater has been a substitute for religious experience because it is dealing with the same things that churches are dealing with. It's a searching for deeper truths, that is what art is about.

Dominican Sister: The imagination is key in the pursuit of truth. When someone ponders (the way a fiction writer or a poet would) a piece of reality, and then crafts it into something beautiful, there we have an emblem of truth.

Psychoanalyst: It's all in the details. They become three-dimensional. You don't get a shadow puppet figure just giving you a line. But the way they look, their body language and the details of the scene they may be set in, it's all contributing very, very much to the performance, at least the kind of performance I like to go to. It all works together. It hits all the senses.

Actor: You really do find a way in the way a child would do when playing make-believe. Essentially, it's the same thing, so that you really can, through your imagination, see out of a another person's eyes and walk in their shoes.

Videographer: I'm interested in the feeling when you are done with a novel, or a film, whether you feel that you actually have discovered a truth.

Attorney: I look to novels, I look to movies for truth. I get totally immersed in the theatre or when I'm reading a book. I believe the character. I believe they are representing somebody's life.

Actor: I think that there is a lot of correlation between truth and art.

Psychoanalyst: I am never looking for the truth when I go to a film or read a novel. I'm looking for maybe some insights into human behavior. I'm looking to be entertained, maybe to have some catharsis. I'm not looking for the truth in that setting. Not at all.

Actor: If you are in a theater, and seeing a play, obviously that play is not what is happening in the world, it's a representation.

Videographer: Whether I feel like I've learned something about a truth might be different from whether individual characters were believable.

Actor: I think sometimes when we experience art it becomes a truth that is more real than most of the things that actually happen to us in our real life.

Literary Critic: I'm interested in this phenomenon of reading or viewing a film or television in which one crosses a line from seeing this as a fiction or a performance to believing that it is real.

Psychoanalyst: What has happened with the recovered memory movement is that people get this memory and then treat it as if it's an absolute truth and then go and do all kinds of things in the real world, like seeking revenge or restitution. They're giving it more solidity than they really should, and they're getting other people involved, which they really should not.

Actor: When I was in grad school, I ran across some information about a group of students in the inner city, who had taken an imaginary fishing trip, who could remember the trip with as much detail as those who had gone on an actual trip.

Literary Critic: And of course this is the power of fiction, of all sorts of creative performances, textual or visual. But I think there is also value in stepping back and looking at what's involved in that process of identification rather than just taking it as a given.

Videographer: I think I'm finding that I'm more interested in and attached to reading fictional accounts for some of the kinds of truths that I'm interested in. I'm very interested in the subjective notions that surround truth and people finding their way to their personal lives and finding truth in their life or in the world.

Literary Critic: I think that fiction provides a variety of different kinds of strategies to get at a kind of truth that is not evidentiary. It's not based on real fact that happens in the real world but something that is hard to articulate that has to do with the cadence of reality.

Videographer: Perhaps art making has to do with truths and what are those truths. Are those truths a little more metaphysical? Are those truths more in the world of philosophical truths?

Literary Critic: I think that the status of truth has been so interrogated, so dismantled, so questioned from so many different directions, that the idea that there are fixed truths in the world doesn't seem like a particularly useful theoretical concept.

Attorney: Every political belief I hold dear, and know to be true… But I have friends who believe the opposite and they believe it. It's the truth.

Dominican Sister: It's very dangerous about truth to say we've got a hold on one truth and no one else has the truth we have.

Psychoanalyst: I say true to whom and when and why?

Actor: I don't have a lot of absolute truths.

Videographer: Truth shifts over time.

Psychoanalyst: I'm not uncomfortable with the idea of changing belief systems as life goes on.

Actor: It's not something that's set and static at all.

Videographer: What for me seems to be true in a moment is not necessarily the truth.

Psychoanalyst: Truth is a relative concept. It's something that can be very useful but I wouldn't use it as a stick to beat anybody with.

Literary Critic: There are no whole truths or whole knowledges or complete knowledges but there are partial situated knowledges that one can collect different pieces of knowledge and assemble some sense of what truths there are.

Videographer: I think that the word truth for me is problematic.

Literary Critic: People define truth in so many different ways. There are so many examples.

Actor: It's just overwhelming because if you start by talking about definition of truth, is that there are so many different definitions.

Videographer: I don't believe there is "the truth." I believe there is a truth that is mine and a truth that is another person's.

Dominican Sister: If a person is looking for truth and reaches a point where they can dialogue with another person, that's a breakthrough.

ANONYMITY AS A POLITICAL TACTIC: ART BLOGS, FEMINISM, WRITING, AND POLITICS

MIRA SCHOR

> "I would venture to guess that Anon, who wrote so many poems without signing them, was often a woman."
>
> *A Room of One's Own*, Virginia Woolf[1]

In the historical situation named by Virginia Woolf, writing in 1929, at the end of the first great wave of the suffrage movement, anonymity was the tragic fate of the brilliant woman whose existence one can only deduce based on the laws of chance and general experience of human talents, just as one deduces the existence of dark stars by the gravity that veils their presence from our traditional measuring devices. If ever, or whenever, genius existed in a woman and made its way into cultural form, it was reattributed to a named man or relegated to "Anon," her name erased by propriety, misogyny, and neglect.

In recent years, anonymity has been used as a protective political tactic: for instance in the 1980s and 1990s, the Guerrilla Girls chose anonymity in order to foreclose on career retribution and the danger of being individually dismissed as untalented artists operating out of a sense of sour grapes in their critiques of inequitable representation of women and artists of color in the art world.[2]

The question of anonymity as a political tactic is of particular interest when discourse occurs in a space without physical presence. Debate and discourse on art now frequently takes place on blogs, which often rely on anonymity to enable uncensored speech. These new blogs and Web sites, with varying degrees of intellectual ambition, political focus, and textual informality, suggest a reconsideration of the role of anonymity as a political tactic for any political cause, but here specifically as it relates to feminist activism at a time when there seem to be fewer public voices for feminism, in a media atmosphere that is generally repressive of alternate points of view, and where collaboration-ist dissimulation of a clear feminist position may be seen by younger women as necessary for career survival.

My interest in these sites, particularly those run by artists, develops from my own experience as an artist/writer and as the co-editor, with the painter Susan Bee, of *M/E/A/N/I/N/G*, an art journal that was published between 1986 and 1996 and which itself now has a presence on the Web at http://writing.upenn.edu/pepc/meaning/. Bee and I began from a position of relative anonymity: that is, our identities were public but relatively unmarked in the art world. On the other hand, by creating a space for cultural discourse, we staked out a certain visibility and associated ourselves with and also against various figures and institutions in the art world, with corresponding rewards and risks.

In January of 2006, we put back online two issues of *M/E/A/N/I/N/G* that we had originally created in 2002–2003 for Artkrush, online at artkrush.com.[3] A few days later I updated our site with "She Demon Spawn from Hell," a brief essay I wrote about the artist Tamy Ben-Tor's anti-feminist statements on the *New York Times*-sponsored panel, "'Feminisms' in Four Generations," held in New York City on January 7, 2006. This in turn sparked a lively debate on a new blog, anonymousfemaleartist.blogspot.com/ "A.K.A. Militant Feminist Bitch," run by an anonymous woman artist, self-styled as "Miss Edna V. Harris." Through this blog, I was made aware of a network of art blogs, including artsoldier.blogspot.com, painterny.com, and brainstormers.com, among others, and have followed them over a period of months. Among the 20 or 30 blogs that constitute this nodule of the Web, "anonymous" was the only one that focused on feminism and art. I was interested in what these blogs might reveal about the strengths and the pitfalls of blogs as a medium for discourse, and for what they suggested about anonymity as a political strategy.

Further, art writing on blogs presented the possibility of an alternative to mainstream art media's reluctance to publish much in the way of negative criticism, given that the editorial space in major publications such as *Artforum* is essentially bought back from the advertising space, and the advertisers, including most of the art industry, obviously don't want truly negative criticism of their product. The question of negative criticism comes up a lot when art criticism is discussed: at a panel on art criticism at School of Visual Arts (SVA) in March 2004, entitled "The Crisis in Art Criticism", with Saul Ostrow, Nancy Princenthal, Raphael Rubinstein,[4] Jerry Saltz, and Katy Siegel, there was consensus that, overall, they favored writing positive criticism, citing as their reasons the importance of supporting work that they liked, especially given that their opportunities to publish and space for their writing was limited so why waste it on negativity.

But a distinction was not made between negativity and criticality. Yet there may be aspects of contemporary art works and discursive/market patterns that must be discussed and analyzed even if that analysis may be negative from the point of view of the market. One would hope to encourage curiosity and skepticism but not cynicism, which would mean just staying at the level of "that sucks" or "it's all bullshit." This is just a micro version of the condition of political discourse in America today where the dominant media format is *sucks/bullshit*, and you don't hear longer format thoughtful criticism of the regime from the mainstream media while the rhetoric of the regime is that criticism equals treason. Thus the non-commercial aspect of blogs and the anonymity of many of the participants held the possibility of a freer environment for criticism, but, as further experience proved, the *sucks/bullshit* mode surfaced all too often.

Anonymousfemaleartist had begun on a high note, forthrightly taking to task Chrissie Iles, co-curator of the 2006 Whitney Biennial, over the poor representation of women in the show. Anonymity enhanced the cheeky energy of this intervention. But in the months to come a number of themes could be observed in her posts and the resulting comments. Miss Edna's initial response to the fracas over Ben-Tor's anti-feminist comments on the panel, "Tamy Been-Torqued,"[5] and the comments for that blog posting focused on Ben-Tor's anti-feminist views, as I had reported them. Debates on blogs rage like wild fires and flame out even more quickly. But, while it lasted, the discussion was indicative of the state not just of "feminist discourse," but of discourse, period, at this time.

Miss Edna began by noting something that "Ben-Tor didn't (and doesn't, to my knowledge) specifically present an anti-feminist viewpoint in her work," something I had myself stressed. She continued:

> Of course, the older female artists (who are all prominent enough to automatically, at least professionally, transcend bitterness) tried as best they could to remind Ben-Tor that they laid the groundwork for her acceptance in the art world. They were shocked and dismayed when she cast them off, and most of what I've read focuses on the fact that she dissed them.
>
> But I don't think that's what she did, or at least meant to do. I don't think that even interests her. That would make her merely rebellious, resulting from not wanting to be associated with feminism's bad rap. Instead, I think she symbolizes a 'moving on'—but it's flawed, scary, and all twisted up with issues. It's unsynthesized, and because of that, I think Ben-Tor is

rejecting symbolism more than anything.[6]

Thus, she seemed to applaud Ben-Tor's behavior, as evidence of a new direction for feminism, even though that behavior flouted the very premise of her blog (militantfeminist). Her comments were contradictory, I think precisely because she was unwilling—as a number of her readers were too—to find herself in agreement with a previous generation of feminists—whose work, aspirations, ideas, and even appearance were largely described in the most stereotypically negative terms:

> Artists like Ben-Tor don't seem to think existing issues-related artwork is badass *enough*. I think her refusal to align herself with the other women on the panel wasn't because she wanted to react against them (and their ideas), but because she wanted to react against their *art.* She doesn't want to be in their club because she doesn't like their version of cultural commentary. Isn't that what she thinks is 'weak?'[7]

Paradoxically, another—male—art blogger responded to Miss Edna's post on his own site, artsoldier.blogspot.com, showing much clearer understanding of my arguments:

> What shocked me the most about Edna's post was how sympathetic she appears to be to Ben-Tor's anti-feminism, especially considering that her 'Militant Art Bitch' blog takes a decidedly feminist approach in combating gender discrimination in the artworld. Yet, she writes: 'When Schor then poses the question, 'why is it that young women who are not feminists are the ones so often selected to publicly represent their generation in these contexts?' my answer is: because, issues aside, they are making more exciting work…Ben-Tor's stated reason for not being sympathetic to feminism (according to Schor's notes of the event): 'It's fine if it serves the weak but I don't feel affiliated with it…many women in the world are oppressed, that's where feminism has to struggle, it doesn't have to struggle for me.'
>
> Wow. 'It doesn't have to struggle for me.' It's a good thing that so many women have struggled before her, so that she can feel so unoppressed now.[8]

The discussion continued with an exchange in the comments about which women artists were feminist and which were doing interesting work. The listing of names ended with the following all too predictable development:

> Anonymous writes: 'i feel like your explanation of t.b-t is a little too

> lenient. your blog name is 'militant.' i say: if you dont want to call yourself a feminist or dont want to BE a feminist that's fine but if you're just flat out insulting to feminist history then FUCK YOU. and i think that's a more militant stance toward t.b-t.'[9]

Here I have to interrupt my reportage to call attention to the language and tone of blogs. On the one hand, discussions may reveal passionately engaged people, some of whom are knowledgeable in a substantial manner. On the other hand, many lapse into a more vernacular form of address—"FUCK YOU" was the least of it. I found that many of the women here took on a kind of hip-hop *gangsta feminisma* bravura, "badasses," "long-ass," "screw-the-voyeur" kind of thing. And, as others have noted, anecdotally and in print, it seems like each conversation online rapidly disintegrates into unflattering comments about other people's "dick size."[10] It took only about twelve interchanges in the comments to a May 24, 2006, interview with Miss Edna, which I will discuss a bit later in relation to the issue of anonymity, for the participants to get to the "dick size" discussion.

Certainly, the vulgarity of this posturing is enabled by the condition of anonymity: the rules of civil behavior are suspended when you are basically talking to yourself as you type alone at three in the morning. This posturing style may emerge from the speed demanded or at least enabled by the form, as well as influenced by the pervasive influence of hip-hop culture. The Howard Stern (shock jock) factor further erodes ordinary courtesy. Blogs encourage relatively unmediated writing. If hard copy journalism also is written for the moment, there is still some kind of editorial or institutional control, whereas the beauty of blogging is that not only is the writer is free of editorial interference, but also the writing is only as polished as the writer wants and can accomplish alone. A lot of the writing is good, if a bit loose. Most often, it's fairly un-theorized. A lot of it is fun, and I admire the energy that goes into writing so much and at such a pace, but some it comes across as the end of reasoned thought as we knew it.

The flipside of "badass" posturing is the highly theorized and academized techno-corporate language that often bedevils online forums such as The Institute for Distributed Creativity (IDC) e-mail list conversations on topics such as activism and new media, a disembodied language that may be one of the factors alienating women participants on the IDC list: a discussion thread in the summer of 2006, "Where have all the women gone?" focused on the problem of the paucity of women actively participating in the email discussion, instead acting as "lurkers," theoretically proficient and, in theory, capable of participating but not finding a place for their voices to be heard. One might even suspect that on an art blog, the use of profanity and a low level of discourse would be a reaction formation to the more off-putting aspects of academic discourse.

The issue of who are the good women artists who are also feminists came up again in one of the comments to a March 7, 2006 posting of Miss Edna's, "Girl Art Recession," where she mournfully asked, "Exactly why are we in this Girl Art Recession? Are there specific reasons, beyond the subjective, that women do not get equal billing in galleries, museums, collections, and art magazines in 2006?" If the facts are almost tragic, given all that has come before, Miss Edna's sorrow seemed quite ironic given the ambivalence she herself evidenced in her earlier defense of Ben-Tor's anti-feminism as a "badass" next wave feminist gesture. The discussion was an eerie echo of the Guerrilla Girls' first posters: when dealers began to say that there were no women artists worthy of being exhibited in their artistic stables, the GG answered with the 1989 "GUERRILLA GIRLS' IDENTITIES EXPOSED!" listing 500 women artists; if this poster wittily foiled curiosity about their identities, it also pointed to the existence of a surplus of women artists every bit as accomplished and deserving of exhibition as male artists.

At brainstormersreport.net, a mission statement announces their purpose:

> 'Brainstormers' Report is a performance art collaborative. Founded in March of 2005, we came together to protest the lack of women artists represented in the P.S.1 Greater New York show. Since that time we have been conducting research regarding the representation of women artists in the public sphere. The Brainstormers are Maria Dumlao, Elaine Kaufmann, Danielle Mysliwiec, and Anne Polashenski.[11]

Their site includes a humorous video on gender discrimination in the New York art world, and they begin the process, yet again, of documenting the lamentable statistics of representation and exhibition of women artists in the New York art world, galleries, and museums. In making their names and faces visible, they return to earlier activist models: the artists coalition of the Vietnam War era such as the Art Workers' Coalition (AWC), the Guerrilla Art Action Group (GAAG), followed by groups involved with bringing the women's liberation movement into the art world, such as Women Artists in Revolution (WAR) and the Ad Hoc Women Artists' Committee, which in 1970, among other projects, famously targeted the Whitney Annual. In all these cases artists, writers, and curators, all named, worked in a multi-tactical manner, incorporating statistical research, letter writing, picketing, protests, collective exhibitions spaces, exhibitions, and guerrilla theater.

While the view of the Web as inherently anonymous is problematized by the negative effects of the kind of exhibitionism that the Web also facilitates,[12] even if the participants are named, one cannot verify their identity and, by definition, the discourse takes place in an undefined space. Although the Guerrilla Girls were anonymous, their posters were plastered on the outer walls or as close to the actual locations of the galleries being targeted. That created a kind of specificity of place—the criticism was in the dealers' faces, anonymity was turned on its head: the criticism worked because the dealers were not anonymous and their neighborhood was defaced. Posting on city walls is illegal and the galleries pursued the miscreants. The Web, at least for the moment, creates less physical risk.

There is very little personal risk for Miss Edna and her readers. Her anonymity allows her to be completely free in her views and style, including how contradictory and sometimes confused she seems at time about feminism—engaged in feminist action so long as she is not pinned down to an identification with a phantasmic image of what a feminist is supposed to be, to look or act like. Her anonymity leaves her unmarked: her "portrait," a drawing like the little sketches that accompanied newspaper bylines in the earlier years of the twentieth century, such as the Miss Lonelyhearts columnist's little face with butterfly glasses, is one of the most endearing aspects of her blog site.

She subscribes to the idea that anonymity gives her and others the freedom to express subversive views that might put them at some risk if expressed in their named identity:

> Well, if you're someone who might be jeopardizing your career by speaking out (i.e. all women), you can certainly be more honest when no one knows who you are. When women speak up, they are called bitches, or crazy. In the artworld, there are very few female critics who aren't pandering to men. No one wants to believe it, but it's a fact. It's engrained and somehow accepted. That said, my main reason for staying anonymous is that I'm not interested in any sort of recognition. The downside is that people view that as cowardly.[13]

It is in the comments from men (some of them self-identified by name, some also anonymous) that the greatest criticism of her anonymity is expressed. Thus, artist Chris Rewalt said: "That said, I still don't think, Edna, you need to be anonymous to do what you do—on the outside." And, "Be careful who you pretend to be, because you *are* who you pretend to be." On the same theme, "Tim" writes, "And, it isn't a fake personality, just a fake name."[14] It is interesting to note that "art soldier," without fanfare or discussion of repercussions if any, quickly decided to reveal his identity as artist Jason Laning (although retaining his blog avatar as a painted self-portrait, with his actual appearance veiled by a blurred photograph posted on his Web site). It would seem that to men identity and name count, and on the other hand, men may risk less and have more to gain from identity.

One may wonder what Miss Edna's anonymity allows? Does the actual named identity of Miss Edna, her "real" persona voice the same slightly intemperate and contradictory but basically feminist views when she functions in the every day world? What is the risk differential if the behavior in fact is generally the same? Or is her public, named, behavior *less* feminist, in order to preserve career viability? If so, does she question the system that would force her into such a suppression of self?

It would seem that Miss Edna's freedom, in the present state of political affairs in America, is a useful tactical avoidance of personal risk but also a problematic avoidance of public identity at a time when that might be as necessary and effective as anonymous activism was for the Guerrilla Girls (or as the Guerrilla Girls' activism, based on their anonymity, worked effectively for political change). Many of my women students found Miss Edna's "a.k.a."—"militant feminist bitch"—disturbing. I am not sure which disturbed them more: the danger of being perceived as a "militant feminist" or the self-hatred possibly lurking behind the adoption of the slur "bitch," although some have seen the use of "bitch" as the recuperation of a derogatory term, in much the same way feminists previously sought to revalorize "cunt," blacks have re-marked the word "nigger," and more recently women are said to have recuperated the word "slut."[15] My own argument leans towards the wish that Miss Edna would have changed her Web site name to "militant feminist artist" and spoken from her real name and identity.

Over the next months, artsoldier articulated a more overall political viewpoint and consciousness on his site, often writing about contemporary international political events and critiquing the Bush administration, rather than limiting his focus to the confines of the New York art world. As of July and August 2006, each had effectively moved on: on August 2, artsoldier claimed that, "This blog is finished, but I shall not leave thine prying eyes fodderless. I have refocused my efforts elsewhere," ("The End"). He started a more purely politically focused blog, dailyremedia.blogspot.[16] At the same time, Miss Edna seemed to implode and gave over her posting to guest bloggers:

> I was minding my own business (not really, but whatever) writing stupid senseless stuff on this blog. I never really hurt anyone. I even gave some

> love here and there. Once in a while a good discussion would ensue. So Chrissie Isles probably got her feelings hurt, but she deserved it, and besides—that show was a serious pile of crap. At any rate, I was just plugging along until I realized I was...LIVING A HUGE FUCKING LIE. Dot com.
>
> About a month ago (when you may have noticed I stopped posting) I had a small but sustained IDENTITY CRISIS. I would talk about myself in the third person. I took naked pictures of myself for my own enjoyment. I fantasized about being "found out," hog-tied and violated by angry lesbians. I was falling behind in my work and daydreaming a lot.
>
> Then it occurred to me that I'd created Edna and I could just kill her off. But how? Just stop posting. It'll be so EASY. Just stop going to the blog. Who gives a fuck, I thought. LET THE BITCH DIE. And I have to say, I think it was the best decision. I have lots more time now that I'm not crusading against anything. Hell, I hardly notice any problems anymore. Seems like everything's on track. Good-looking chicks under 25 are getting shows. Things are nearly 70/30%. Everything's fine. (Wednesday, July 05, 2006, "So here's the deal.")[17]

In the winter of 2007, anonymousfemaleartist posts were rare and mostly by the substitute blogger, "rebel belle." The site did not address major events related to feminist art during this time period, including "The Feminist Future: Theory and Practice in the Visual Arts," a major two-day symposium held at Museum of Modern Art in January, and the openings of two major museum survey exhibitions on feminist art, WACK! Art and the Feminist Revolution, at the Geffen Contemporary at Museum of Contemporary Art in Los Angeles, and Global Feminisms at the new Elizabeth A. Sackler Center for Feminist Art at the Brooklyn Museum. The latter was mentioned on the blog, but peripherally and dismissively, in the comments section on a story about an older, and anonymous, woman artist in Los Angeles deciding to create a fake, younger alter ego with a fake body of work for inclusion in a group exhibition, in response to ageism in the current art market as described on other blogs such as Edward Winkleman.[18]

This implosion of a blog that had begun by boldly staking a feminist identity may have a personal dimension in terms of unknown stresses on the individual known as Miss Edna, but may also reflect on some of the troubling aspects of anonymity in relation to feminism and activism. Possibly in the long run public identification would have been a safer, more stable position from which to mount an ongoing feminist critique of power.

We have few public feminists of any stature today, few figures with a significant national profile as a feminist seem to exist as potential talking heads on current affairs or as potential figures to be feared for their point of view—that there are few public intellectuals visible at all, and few "left" or even "liberal" voices, is perhaps the meta-problem. While being identified as a feminist, or as a nonconformist political entity with a feminist view, can have serious repercussions on one's STET career, at least it creates a genuine identity that might have eventually carry enough gravitas to function effectively in a public forum.

---

[1] Virginia Woolf, *A Room of One's Own* (New York: and Burlingame: Harcourt, Brace & World, Inc., 1929), 50–51.

[2] More recently two Guerrilla Girls outed their identities in a lawsuit, as a sad coda to the history of their collective. However this partial unveiling arrived long after the most significant and risky part of their intervention into art world politics, which began in 1985 with two posters pointing to the poor to downright scandalous representation of women in specific important galleries in New York. See Jeffrey Toobin, "The Bench: Girls Behaving Badly," *The New Yorker*, May 30, 2005, 34–5; Mira Schor, "Just the Facts, Ma'am," *Wet: On Painting, Feminism, and Art Culture* (Durham: Duke University Press, 1997), 87–97. In much the same manner that the long awaited revelation, in 2005, (see David Von Drehle, "FBI's No. 2 Was 'Deep throat,'" *Washington Post*, June 1, 2005, A1) of the identity of the Watergate figure, "Deep Throat," as former FBI official Mark Felt was anti-climactic, the revelation of the two GGs did not really penetrate the public awareness of the group as a political entity.

[3] The *M/E/A/N/I/N/G Online* material was de-archived in 2004 when Artkrush sold its name to another online art related magazine.

[4] For further discussion of the current conditions of art criticism, see Raphael Rubinstein, *Critical Mess: Art Critics on the State of their Practice* (Lenox, MA: Hard Press Editions, 2006).

[5] "Tamy Been-Torqued," *anonymousfemaleartist*, entry posted January 23, 2006, http://anonymousfemaleartist.blogspot.com. With comments through the January 24, 2006. Access date June 22, 2006.

[6] Quotes from Miss Edna V. Harris, "Tamy Been-Torqued" and comments, on http://anonymousfemaleartist.blogspot.com, entries posted January 23–24, 2006, and by art soldier (Anonymous) at http://artsoldier.blogspot.com/, entry posted January 24, 2006.

[7] Ibid, Miss Edna V. Harris; art soldier.

[8] Ibid, Miss Edna V. Harris; art soldier.

[9] Ibid, Miss Edna V. Harris; art soldier.

[10] Charlie Booker, "Supposing … there's only one thing worth debating online," *The Guardian*, June 2, 2006. *Guardian* columnist Charlie Booker, writing about the blog-o-sphere response to one of his columns, concludes that

> The internet's perfect for all manner of things, but productive discussion ain't one of them." In particular, he notes that "In the debate sparked by my gibberish outpouring, it wasn't long before rival posters began

speculating about the size of their opponents dicks…. Anyway, if we must debate things online, we might as well debate that. It's not like we'll ever resolve any of that other bullshit, is it? Click. Mine's bigger than yours. Click. NO it isn't. Click. Yes it is. Click. Refresh, repost repeat to fade.

On another blog, painter.com, when "Painter (host blogger)" asks why the level of discourse isn't higher,

> It seems that you're satisfied with a blog full of mostly lazy, immature, and uncritical comments -- the status quo being exemplified by such witty banter as "this sucks" or "i love it" or "this is lame." Thoughtful, engaging comments are rare, although I'd guess that most who participate here would be capable, if pressed. Is this representative of how NYC painters discuss painting away from this blog? Perhaps this explains why so much bland painting continues to be made.
> Why not raise the level of dialogue here by somewhat directing the conversation to a higher critical plane. Or, at the very least, you could set a rigorous, knowledgeable example with your own comments that would not only serve as a positive model for others to follow, but would also be a discouragement to navel-gazing blog saboteurs whose only goal is to impress themselves with name calling and circle-jerking (hint: they become bored and tend to go away when ignored).

To this, another "anonymous" blogger answers:

> jeezus christ, critics, it's not SCHOOL--
> why does everything have to be an "improving" "higher" conversation? do we ALWAYS have to raise the fucking bar?
> cant you conceive of something between a circle jerk and a seminar?
> what i like about this blog is you can get on and say what you'd say to a friend while walking down the street as you leave the gallery. ok it's not the middle or end of the conversation, but just a first hit.
> havent you left galleries and turned to your friend, and said, that sucks? or wow that was great. this blog is just a first hit. maybe get a small conversation going.
> i for one dont need an mfa discussion everytime i come on here.

(http://painternyc.blogspot.com/2006/03/cheyney-thompson.html, entry posted March 3, 2006. The person who asks to raise the discussion level is "satan (the devil)." The person who answers is "anonymous". Access Date March 3, 2006. See "Damien Hirst Apparently Has the Smallest Dick Ever; But We Kinda Knew That Already," http:// anonymousfemaleartist.com, entry posted June 22, 2006.

[11] http://www.brainstormersreport.net. Access date June 22, 2006.

[12] Employers have learned to look up prospective young employees on sites such as "Facebook, MySpace, where said college students often post risqué or teasing

photographs and provocative comments about drinking, recreational drug use and sexual exploits." Alan Finder, "When a Risqué Online Persona Undermines a Chance for a Job," *New York Times*, June 11, 2006, 1.

[13] John LeKay, "Edna V. Harris Interview II," in *Heyoka*, an online magazine with art, music and other cultural features, with a high production value and a slight new age tilt, Volume 4, Spring/Summer 2006, http://www.heyokamagazine.com/HEYOKA.4.Artviews.htm. Access date June 22, 2006.

[14] "Comments" to "Heyoka Magazine Interview," posted May 24, 2006, http://anonymousfemaleartist.blogspot.com. Access date June 22, 2006.

[15] Stephanie Rosenbloom, "The Taming of the Slur," *New York Times*, July 13, 2006, and Maureen Dowd, "What's Up, Slut?" *New York Times*, July 15, 2006, A15.

[16] http://dailyremedia.blogspot.com/. Access date June 22, 2006.

[17] Quotes from Miss Edna V. Harris, "Tamy Been-Torqued" and comments, on http://anonymousfemaleartist.blogspot.com, entries posted January 23–24, 2006, and by art soldier (Anonymous) at http://artsoldier.blogspot.com/, entry posted January 24, 2006. Access date June 22, 2006

[18] Rebel Belle, "She's Not Taking This Shit Anymore," entry posted March 25, 2007, http://www.anonymousfemaleartist.blogspot.com. See also Edward Winkleman, "Something (Slightly) Naughty; Something Very Nice," entry posted December 22, 2006. Access date June 22, 2006. http://edwardwinkleman.blogspot.com/2006_12_01_archive.html. Access date June 22, 2006.

Works Cited

Anonymous Female Artist ("A.K.A. Militant Art Bitch"), http://anonymousfemaleartist.blogspot.com.

Booker, Charlie. "Supposing…there's only one thing worth debating online." *The Guardian*, http://www.guardian.co.uk/Columnists/Column/0,,1788773,00.html. Posting date June 2, 2006

Dowd, Maureen. "What's Up, Slut?" *New York Times*, July 15, 2006, A15.

Finder, Alan. "When a Risqué Online Persona Undermines a Chance for a Job." *New York Times*, June 11, 2006, 1.

LeKay, John. "Edna V. Harris Interview II," *Heyoka* 4 (Spring/Summer 2006). http://www.heyokamagazine.com/HEYOKA.4.Artviews.htm.

Painter (anonymous), http://painternyc.blogspot.com

Rebel Belle, "She's Not Taking This Shit Anymore," http://www.anonymousfemaleartist.blogspot.com. Posting date March 25, 2007.

Rosenbloom, Stephanie. "The Taming of the Slur." *New York Times*, July 13, 2006.

Rubinstein, Raphael, ed. *Critical Mess: Art Critics on the State of their Practice*. Lenox, MA: Hard Press Editions, 2006.

Schor, Mira. "She Demon Spawn from Hell." *M/E/A/N/I/N/G Online* 3, http://writing.upenn.edu/epc/meaning/03/index.html (January 2006).

Toobin, Jeffrey. "The Bench: Girls Behaving Badly." *The New Yorker*, May 30, 2005, 34–5.

Von Drehle, David . "FBI's No. 2 Was 'Deep throat.'" *Washington Post*, June 1, 2005, A01.

Winkleman, Edward. "Something (Slightly) Naughty; Something Very Nice," Posting date December 22, 2006. http://edwardwinkleman.blogspot.com/2006_12_01_archive.html.

Woolf, Virginia. *A Room of One's Own*. New York and Burlingame: Harcourt, Brace & World, 1929.

PART III: COLLABORATION

THE TIPPING POINT PROJECT: A CASE STUDY IN THE COLLABORATION BETWEEN MEDICAL ANTHROPOLOGY AND ART

ELLEN S. GINSBURG AND JENNIFER HALL

Project Development

The *Tipping Point Project* brings together the collaborative efforts of Professor Ellen S. Ginsburg, medical anthropologist, and Jennifer Hall, information artist, to create a new paradigm that merges anthropological investigation with art practices. The project began in 2004, with lengthy discussions and a collaborative vision and goal shared by Ginsburg and Hall to bring together the disciplinary voices of anthropology, art, and technology that would result in a multilayered work culminating in seven interactive sculptures. The project pivots around the assumption that small/large changes in health status can, over time, have a significant impact on the lives of artists and their community. Ginsburg's collections of health narratives from artists having ties to the South End community in Boston, Massachusetts, serves as the content to inform Hall's kinetic sculptures with "tipping points" or triggers where change would take place through interactions provided by the viewers.

The Anthropologist as Artist: The Artist as Anthropologist

In recent decades anthropology, along with other intellectual disciplines, has been overwhelmingly concerned with meaning, a topic that is likely to remain near the center of anthropological study of art for the foreseeable future.[1] As a collaborative venture, our project provided a unique venue to exploit the synergy between medical anthropology and contemporary (new media) art, not as fields, which create products, but as processes, which explore how people generate, organize, and transfer their knowledge of the world. Our collaboration between anthropologist and artist uniquely identifies both as practitioners, who, in this case, appropriate and represent others. Since its inception, anthropology has drawn from a variety of methodologies and theories from other fields, such as literature, biology, linguistics, history, geography, and theater; however, anthropological work in the field of art has tended to treat visual culture as the object of investigation. Contemporary art is based in the conceptual and is most often, interdisciplinary. Setting a framework for the interdisciplinary nature of art becomes part of a narrative that contextualizes art as a product unto itself. The *Tipping Point* collaborative navigates outside a singular discipline and seeks to form a new construct, a hybrid that combines expertise and redefines the language of each individual discipline. In the *Tipping Point Project,* anthropology and art no longer occupy opposing sides of a subjective/objective divide. Through this collaboration, the representational strategies of both anthropologist and artist have been altered, and differences and similarities between ethnographic authority and artistic authorship have been refigured. "Anthropology, traditionally, has been a discipline of words."[2] Specifically, anthropology has been rooted in text. However, at times it has incorporated film, photography, and audio recordings, either as a featured format such as ethnographic film, or to supplement writing for fieldwork reports or publication.

Contemporary art also incorporates many media and extracting product from concept requires the use of a variety of research methods. The collaboration asks and attempts to answer the question as to what differentiates the work of the anthropologist and artist. We discovered that the answer does not lie in the methods (what media are employed or who talks to whom), but rather each respective professional field defines the outcome. These expectations then guide both anthropologist and artist to create product that fits the requirements of their practice, often missing the opportunity for authenticity of experience. Arnd Schneider and Christopher Wright report: "Anthropologists have remained largely unconcerned with these processes, or even actively hostile to them, in creating their own works, whether films, photographs, or books."[3] It is safe to say that most anthropologists use new media data in the objective form, producing synthetic or clinical documentation of their work. The *Tipping Point Project* represents a new way of addressing the meanings health issues have in our experience, notably the significance of objects, events, tools, the flow of time, the self, and others.

In a similar vein, contemporary artists have been known to use data collection methods developed by anthropologist. The artist is expected to further manipulate their findings to fit the contemporary art constructs of late twentieth century art. Michael Rush considers, "The viewer and voyeur are interconnected".[4] The issues of real versus artificial, physical versus virtual, authentic versus manipulated are familiar art consequences. In the context of this understanding, the focus of artwork returns exclusively to process and loses the opportunity to reconnect with the original threads of research. A positive outcome of interdisciplinary projects is that it allows participants to revisit their own disciplines while exploring particular concepts from the other.

Methods

Ginsburg used traditional ethnographic anthropological field methods collected the health narratives over a period of seven months. Ethnographic fieldwork requires the researcher to become part of the unit of analysis, in this case the community of artists living and working in and near the South End. To a great extent, the strength of this method (participant observation) is that the researcher becomes the instrument for both data collection and analysis through her own experience: first and most important is establishing rapport with the informants, getting close to the people to be interviewed in the community, and making them feel comfortable with the anthropologists presence. Specifically, Ginsburg's goal with this community of artists was to collect data, analyze it, and synthesize it for Hall. Fifty narratives were collected over a period of seven months. The data was collected by means of observation, natural conversation, and various kinds of interviews (structured, semi-structured, and unstructured). These data are then subject to qualitative analysis, where Ginsburg examined the collected information to discern patterns and arguments that would help explain the patterns. Ethnography typically relies on a few key informants rather than on a representative sample. The informants were selected from volunteers based on their willingness to share their stories. Criteria for selecting the informants were that they were artists that had worked or lived in the South End community.

Out of the 50 narratives that were collected, a decision was made to use seven. This decision was made not only for methodological reasons, but logistical ones—a need to conform to space constraints that would be necessary to exhibit the sculptures. Once a number was agreed upon, Ginsburg, Hall, and Blyth Hazen (robotics system's lead) examined all the narratives looking for patterns and goodness of fit. It was agreed that seven sculptures would be sufficient to represent a community and enable a full representation of the health narratives. The narratives collected by Ginsburg focused on discovering if a tipping point existed for the artist, a point in the artist's life where change took place as a result of a change in health status. The narratives ran the gamut from the powerful, provocative to the mundane. As Warhol suggests, "Narrative, of course, is among the most common and most powerful instruments we possess to confer meaning upon experience."[5] Some of the narratives were self-conscious, e.g., illness told as a personal liberation; some provided insight, grant permission, and absolution. The interesting point, as it relates to our project, is the telling of the story offers the informant an opportunity to employ the full resources of narrative reconstruction. It is also important to consider that the experience of illness is always framed in the culture in which it occurs.

The processes of observing, collecting, and editing may be similar in anthropology and art, while the interpretation and subsequent creative directions chosen may be particular to the discipline. Personal narratives have been thought to be the domain of both the anthropologist and artist. Narratives provide a kind of raw material of the world that both anthropologist and artist can sift through, making meaning by personalizing or subjectifying their collection.

All of the artists one way or another had recast their lives' story in response to certain tipping points. In all of the narratives it was my aim to accommodate mutuality, sharing attentiveness to the experiences of the informants as they shape their stories. As the project team came to quickly learn, narrative is often indispensable in helping us grasp what our deepest values are. Important values often are discovered unintentionally and emerge as the twists of a particular life story. The narrative approach focused on the artists themselves as agents who enact choices. Of significance is how their lives are changed by a transformative or series of transformative events.

The phenomenological approach as Woodruff Smith states in the *Stanford Encyclopedia of Philosophy* seemed well suited for our research, in that it is designed to "study structures of experience, or consciousness, Literally, the study of "'phenomena': the appearance of things, or things as they appear in our experience, or the ways we experience things, thus the meanings things have in our experience".[6] The descriptions, analyses and interpretations of the artists' journey became our tradition represented in their art. This method was ideal for Hall and Hazen as the material translated into a coactive experience. The health narratives were configured into an interactive art installation of seven sculptures that are represented by mechanical tipping points. Robotic elements served to reflect the flexible relationship between such issues as body/health, community/individual, and public/private self. Interactive software enabled the sculptures movement both independently and collectively. Ultimately the installation, *The Tipping Point: Health Narratives from South End Artists*, involved gallery goers in a cumulative expression of community.

How The Tipping Point Project Works

When a person entered the gallery, in the blink of an eye, his or her movement was collected and stored; seven passive infrared sensors sited at various heights on the door accomplished this (fig. 3-1). The sensors captured the speed and mass of individuals entering and leaving the gallery. The data collected by these sensors was sent to a central compilation point and retransmitted to each of the seven sculptures. Within a few seconds the tipping machines began to move. The movement of the machines was the difference of motion pattern from the person

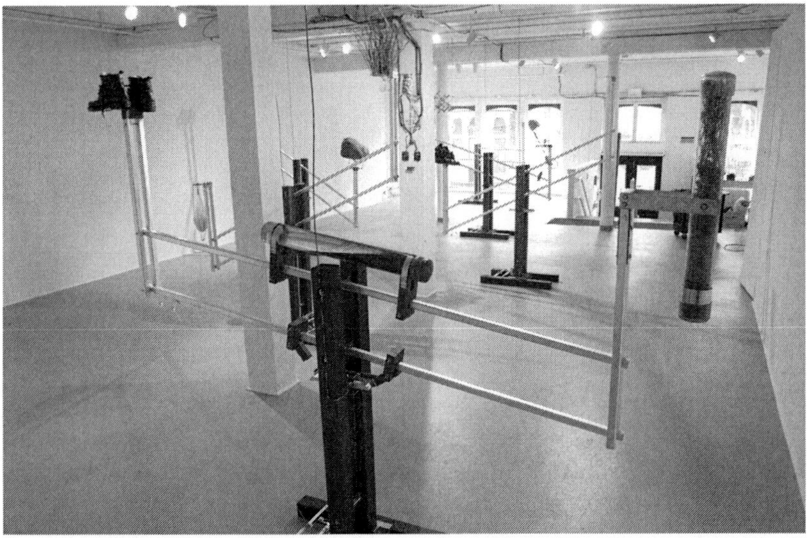

Fig. 3-1
The Tipping Point Project Scupture. Overview at the Mills Gallery, Center for the Arts, Boston, Massachusetts. Photograph courtesy of Jennifer Hall. Photograph copyright Arnaldo Hernandez 2006.

entering the gallery and the entered state of the gallery before that person entered. When another person the gallery, who walked exactly the same way, was exactly the same height, or was similar in volumetric ways, there would be no difference to the master machine doing pattern recognition, and therefore, the movement of the tipping machines would find stasis. If three people entered the gallery in relative succession, the pattern they created was now different from the pattern established by those already in the space, that a change would be triggered. In fact, few people are the same and more people entering or exiting the gallery would create some differences that signaled movement to the tipping machines. Furthermore, the master board retained several differences of time in a cumulative way. Through this robotic/software interface people became part of past gallery goers and affected future gallery goers. Each visitor left a trace that affected the space, and hence the experience of succeeding visitors.

The community of motions is not a series of individuals who have activated each tipping machine but rather a collective gesture where an individual can create great change in the larger pattern of motion. This pattern stays true to how tipping points are identified in many disciplines such as health, economics, and group dynamics.

Conclusions and Challenges

This interdisciplinary collaboration presented many challenges. It required crossing professional boundaries into what is often unfamiliar territory and challenged us to drop preconceived notions of understanding, learn new languages, and most importantly to see problems through a new lens. Our collaboration required work teams from different disciplines to push through the boundaries of any one particular profession.

Perhaps most critical, was establishing a consistent philosophy and set of personal values among team members that were in sync with each other. All the project participants agreed that the success of the project would be enhanced utilizing the diverse perspectives, expertise, and resources of the team which required members to relinquish control of the project and share ideas with others. Hall and Ginsburg called on the expertise of Blyth Hazen as systems robotics lead and later, Arnaldo Hernandez, software programmer, to round out the team.

Recently, educators, and in particular contemporary anthropologists, have been challenged to develop innovative approaches for using texts in the classroom. Many academic texts conform to linear forms of representation, allowing for a minimal amount of interactivity with material under study. The *Tipping Point Project*, which is ethnographically based, offers a format for learning that is reliant on different data and different media, the sequence of which is not fixed, and which do not impose restrictions on the ways in which the data are assessed. No piece of scholarship exists without authorship or narrative, but in regard to this project it is important to understand that these usual hallmarks of ethnographic authority remain implicit as opposed to explicit within the body of the work. The strength of doing away with an anthropological reliance on explicit, linear narration (such as with text) is that taking this risk may enhance the user's ability to sift through the material by their own directives, and to formulate their own analysis of the material without being constantly exposed to various indicators of authorial control.

The interdisciplinary collaboration between the anthropologist and artist creates a mechanism that allows users to subject the data to multiple interpretations. Clifford Geertz, in commenting on ethnographic methodology, suggests that we look at culture "as an assemblage of texts to be interpreted."[7] While Geertz presumes that the ethnographer should remain the expert, providing the interpretation, in this project the ethnographer's analysis acts simply as a meta-referent. Thus, our work reflects the ethnographer's experience of a cultural encounter, while making available a multiplicity of possible readings, to which users bring a variety of approaches and out of which the users build their own analysis. The collaboration between author and reader requires the former to relinquish control to some extent over how information can be manipulated. This project opens up discourse on the reflexive nature of ethnography and goes beyond the linear format of a "thick description" of culture.[8] It is hoped that the installation evokes such questions as: How can we decipher the ambiguities surrounding the body? How do we obtain precise inform about ourselves? How can we maintain our individual integrity? The investigation of these issues regarding the body politic-objectification of the individual, and sometimes contradictory discourses surrounding certain technologies is essential to reinterpreting the place of the individual as a corporeal entity in society. The gallery exhibition and incorporated narratives posit some of these questions in the examination and representation of how we can all perceive the tipping point as an agent of change. The project represents the participating ongoing interest in ways in which technology intersects with and affects our perception of our bodies, our lives, our imaginations, and our culture. More specifically, this project explores how contemporary culture is reconfiguring the dichotomies of nature/artifice, real/virtual and body-embodiment.

---

[1] Jeremy Coote and Anthony Sheldon, eds., *Anthropology Art and Aesthetics* (Oxford: Clarendon Press, 1992). Introduction, 4.

---

[2] Margaret Mead and Rhoda Bubundy Metraux, eds., *The Study of Culture at a Distance* (Oxford, New York: Berghahn Books, 1973), 18.
[3] Arnd Schneider and Christopher Wright, eds., *Contemporary Art and Anthropology*. (Oxford, New York: Berghahn Books., 2006), 26.
[4] Michael Rush, *New Media in Late Twentieth Century Art*,(London: Thames and Hudson Publishing, 1999), 32.
[5] Andy Warhol *The Philosophy of Andy Warhol From A to B and Back Again* (New York: Harcourt Brace Jovanovich, 1974), 12.
[6] David Woodruff Smith, "Phenomenology", *The Stanford Encyclopedia of Philosophy,* Edward N. Zalta ed., (Winter 2005).
[7] Clifford Geertz, *The Interpretation of Culture: Selected Essays* (New York: Basic Books, 1973), 10-14.
[8] Clifford Geertz, *Works and Lives: The Anthropologist as Author* (California: Stanford University Press, 1988), 46-5.

Works Cited

Coote, Jeremy and Anthon. Sheldon, eds. *Anthropology Art and Aesthetics.* Oxford: Clarendon Press, 1992.

Geertz, Clifford. *The Interpretation of Culture: Selected Essays.* New York: Basic Books, 1973.

——. *Works and Lives: The Anthropologist as Author.* California: Standard University Press. California: Stanford University Press, 1988.

Mead, Margaret and Rhoda Bubundy Metraux, eds.. *The Study of Culture at a Distance.* Oxford, New York: Berghahn Books, 1973.

Murphy, Howard and Morgan Perkins, eds. *The Anthropology of Art: a reader.* Boston: Blackwell Publishing, 2006.

Rush, Michael. *New Media in Late Twentieth Century Art.* London: Thames and Hudson Publishing, 1999.

Schneider, Arnd and Christopher Wright eds. *Contemporary Art and Anthropology.* Oxford, New York: Berghahn Books, 2006.

Smith, David Woodruff, "Phenomenology", *The Stanford Encyclopedia of Philosophy.* Edward N. Zalta ed., 2005. http://plato.stanford.edu/archives/win2005/entries/phenomenology.

Warhol, Andy. *The Philosophy of Andy Warhol From A to B and Back Again.* New York: Harcourt Brace Jovanovich, 1975.

DEFINING PLACE: BUILDING COMMUNITIES THROUGH PUBLIC ART

CHRISTINA LANZL

Introduction

Public art or art in public places can be defined as art with a civic purpose. Public art enhances relationships, between individuals as well as people and places. It brings people together and serves as a tool for communication. Many communities have realized the great potential of the arts and culture as a vehicle and centerpiece in connecting individuals to each other and to their localities. Public art has proven an excellent tool in invigorating neighborhood activity and identity.

For more than two decades, I have been immersed in creating, shaping, and advancing the artistic and cultural life in my local community, and at the state, national, and international levels, as creator, manager, and consultant. I am pleased to share direct observations and experiences gleaned from recent public art projects. Since Boston, Massachusetts, is my home—and was the site of the 2006 Women's Caucus for Art (WCA) national conference—I have selected Boston-based projects as case studies and as opportunity to highlight successes and challenges. I invite the reader to keep in mind the following recurring themes while traversing the neighborhoods with me:

- Place-making, community building, and quality of life
- Planning within the context of the urban fabric
- Best practices and creation of a supportive framework for public art
- Application of sustainable methods and materials
- Integrated design team approach

"Site-specific" Public Art

Tying art in the public sphere to its location begins at the planning stage to create a local context and ideally involves the resident community. With increased understanding of the importance of community and urban context, there has been a noticeable shift from installing *individual* works—often decried as "plop" art—to creating *environments,* where public art is a part of a whole, and each part has a role and functions within visual and conceptual contexts. The term *site-specific* (along with several permutations) has commonly been employed to define this approach. Recent writings caution that the term is beginning to be applied rather indiscriminately and warn of a weakening and redirection by institutional and market forces.[1] With this warning in mind, let us proceed.

Community and Culture

Although art in public places has been created since the prehistoric age, functioning as a centerpiece that references historic events and identity across cultures, the critical analysis and institutional facilitation of public art as a coherent field of study only evolved within the past 40 years. The second and third generations of professionals working in the field are now building on past research and "trail-blazing" projects, such as Philadelphia's Fairmount Park sculpture program or Boston's subway art program, setting the stage for advancements in theory and practice. The Works Progress Administration (WPA) of the early 1930s can be seen as an early large-scale, federal effort that employed artists to create work in the public sphere, though much of it inside buildings, such as post offices and other civic facilities. A crisis management tool in its day, the program has been superseded by the Federal Project Administration's percent-for-art policy.[2]

Even though there have been setbacks, a renaissance of cultural awareness and civic engagement is evident in the many flourishing public art programs around the country and internationally. Formerly restricted to the recognition and expression of ruling factions—equestrian monuments are a prominent example—public art has more recently morphed into an egalitarian vehicle for local, individual, and neighborhood identity by involving the "community"—in the widest sense of the word—in its planning and creation.[3] My own work is permeated by formative experiences with *community*, in the roles of visual artist, public art project manager, and active citizen. Public art can introduce positive change on many levels, and I will outline a few firsthand experiences.

As long-term resident of Boston's Fort Point Arts Community (FPAC), I have been observing the fundamental changes brought about by the rapidly changing urban landscape, a process that is ongoing in many places, both urban and rural. Fort Point is a story full of successes and losses, and I have been an active participant in the attempt to shape its future as part of the resident arts community. Partly, my presence in Fort Point triggered my involvement in public art. Carrying out projects beyond my own neighborhood both as public artist and as public art administrator has confirmed and augmented knowledge that has now accumulated to two decades of professional practice and quite a few anecdotes. In 2000, I joined the UrbanArts Institute at Massachusetts College of Art.[4] As project manager, I have been part of this nonprofit's mission to incorporate the arts and cultural programming into urban design and community revitalization efforts. Founded in 1980, the organization's efforts are "based on the belief that cultural vitality depends on a more active role for the arts in shaping the urban landscape, with greater involvement by artists and citizens as participants in this process."[5]

The Quality of Enabling

Successful public art requires the combination of creative talent with managerial dexterity. Are there key requirements for public art-related job descriptions? To me, anyone who takes on a role in facilitating art in the public realm—be it artist, fabricator, administrator, community activist, or sponsor—needs to be an *enabler.* A person with a positive, can-do attitude will make all the difference when being confronted with complex administrative processes usually involving multiple stakeholders, permitting agencies, and restrictive funding sources. Outstanding communication skills, a penchant for challenges, flexibility, and a sense of humor are absolutely essential. Qualifications also include a willingness to face the odds, setbacks, and surprises that will invariably occur. Negativity and misguided, incompetent bureaucracy are the most common and worst enemies of public art process.

The managerial skills of the public art administrator are directly tied to administrative structure, process, and funding. A formidable number of public art projects by internationally acclaimed artists have been dedicated since Berlin became the new capital city of the reunified Germany. Both public and private investment funded significant works by Jonathan Borofsky, Jeff Koons, Claes Oldenburg with Coosje van Bruggen, and

Robert Rauschenberg, to name a few. Noticeable is the lack of women artists in the lineup. Of note also is the fact that many American artists have been commissioned to install work at prime locations. Berlin's office for art in public space does have a highly efficient structure of a main office for public art that delegates implementation to local neighborhood offices. By comparison, American public art agencies' operations tend to be more centralized.

Placemaking and Quality of Life

Why is there a need for art in the public realm? The argument is that appropriate incorporation of art in public environments greatly enhances not only the visual qualities, but actually improves the *quality of life.* Historic cities and town centers, well known for their active public use, are ardent proof of this theory, because they invariably feature central public plazas and streetscapes adorned by statues, fountains, and other well-designed and integrated amenities for the user. As we study these often centuries-old accomplishments, we also need to remind ourselves of the dearth of public art designed by or featuring women and minorities. This consideration should be ever-present with every new proposal entering the planning stage.

Urban planner and theorist Jan Gehl has extensively researched the psychology of public space. He categorizes outdoor activities into three basic groups: *necessary*, *optional*, and *social activities.* Physical appearance directly impacts use of public space:

> When outdoor areas are of poor quality only strictly necessary activities occur. When outdoor areas are of high quality, necessary activities take place with approximately the same frequency—though they clearly tend to take a longer time, because the physical conditions are better. In addition, however, a wide range of optional activities will occur because place and situation now invite people to stop, sit, eat, play and so on. In streets and city spaces of poor quality, only the bare minimum of activities takes place. People hurry home.[6]

What makes places special and therefore worth visiting or worth living in? For most of us, it is the rewarding experience to feel a *sense of place.* In many public environments, there is a dire absence of these qualities. For almost a century, particularly following the invention of the automobile and modern urban renewal practices, our public spaces were either endangered or actually sacrificed to progress. In her bestseller, *The Death and Life of Great American Cities*, architectural critic and urbanist icon

Jane Jacobs eloquently writes about her own battles to save New York's West Village neighborhood from highway construction. Many cities are now working to correct various depravations, usually at high costs. Boston is one such city, where the elevated I-93 expressway that dissected its downtown beginning in the 1950s turned into the Central Artery/Tunnel project just one generation later, as the largest public works project in U.S. history.

Public Planning for a New Greenway

Planning for the Rose Kennedy Greenway, the new public park that sits atop the new highway tunnel, became one of the most intensely discussed topics in the City of Boston. In 2002, the debate found a public outlet at large-scale community meetings aimed at getting input from the public on what the park should be.[7] Central Artery park forums were sponsored by the Boston Society of Architects and the Boston Foundation. More than 350 people took part in a pair of public events, called *Creative Community Conversations.* Media sponsors and Web sites carried the conversation into millions of homes, complemented by hundreds of other, smaller meetings sponsored by other organizations. Participants shared ideas for uses of the Big Dig parkland, with special emphasis on what would keep them coming back again and again. At the top of the wish list were public amenities that offered something for everyone during the day and at night, such as *inspiring sculpture and modern art, fountains, creative lighting design, and performance areas.* It remains to be seen if the residents' dreams will be fulfilled, since neither city nor state have been willing to set aside public funds for this most public new parkland. Critics warn that relying on private funding will lead to private interests controlling the Rose Kennedy Greenway.

When planning public art, a distinction has to be made between temporary and permanent projects. A healthy, active community offers high quality programs in both genres. While permanent projects provide the framework and focus of a public space year-round, the nature of temporary work is ephemeral. The former generally has substantial planning and implementation phases, and is more restricted by permitting and issues of longevity. Temporary programs, on the other hand, can be more experimental and realized within shorter timeframes. This insight has been effectively employed by Boston's Fort Point arts community.

Fort Point: No Art / No Point

Just blocks away from the new Rose Kennedy Greenway, in Fort Point, several hundred artists have worked in their studios for several decades. The artist community in Fort Point quietly grew on the east side of Boston's Fort Point Channel, a district of historic warehouses that thrived during the heyday of Boston Harbor in the nineteenth century, whose industry has long since left New England. Beginning in the 1990s, major infrastructure improvements introduced the new underground highway system and new public transportation service to the airport, followed by the largest convention center in the Northeast and cleanup of Boston Harbor. These public investments led to a surge in popularity of Boston's waterfront, both for office and residential development. The formerly isolated seaport district became a prime real estate opportunity. These outside influences resulted in an imminent threat of displacement to the resident artist population, which was thriving unnoticed by many up to that point. Well organized since the early 1980s through the Fort Point Arts Community[8] (FPAC), a not-for-profit organization, the community realized that the only way to stay put in the neighborhood was to acquire its own real estate. Today, three complexes offer roughly 150 affordable legal live-in units reserved for artists, while rentals in the area are commercially zoned non-live-in units. The first live-work artist coop was purchased and refurbished in the 1980s, followed by the Artist Building in the 1990s. In 1999, the Fort Point Cultural Coalition (FPCC) was formed as an independent 501(c)(3) non-profit organization, in part as an outgrowth of FPAC's building search committee. Midway, a three-building warehouse complex, was acquired and built out as artist live-work space with both affordable and market-rate lofts.

At the same time, a campaign was launched to increase visibility of the artist community in Fort Point. Driven by artists and art advocates, the resident artist community did what they do best: they utilized their creative skills to bring their cause to a larger audience and to build awareness and support at all levels of public opinion, as well as in city and state government. The *Fort Point Public Art Series* of 2001 and 2002 were a grassroots initiative born out of a need to create awareness and visibility for a community of artists under threat of displacement. I launched *A Fort Point Vision for Public Art* as part of this initiative, geared directly towards integration of long-term public art planning for the neighborhood.

How did it work? FPCC secured grant funding from the Boston Foundation, New England Foundation for the Arts, and the LEF Foundation. Through an open call to artists in the Fort Point community, small project grant proposals for up to $2,000 were solicited and reviewed for approval. The series began in the fall of 2000 with an outdoor public forum, concert, and video screening. In the catalogue *No Art/No Point* (2004), Fort Point Public Art Series coordinator Jed Speare writes:

> The forum, *Let's Get to the Point,* was meant to bring artists' housing issues to the fore. Further programming then commenced over the winter through community meetings at Mobius, introducing the project, and creating a dialogue with and encouraging artists with their ideas, several of whom had not ever made public art.[9]

Anita Lauricella, Fort Point Cultural Coalition (FPCC) president, summarizes the outcomes. The Public Art Series:

- Got three Fort Point organizations to work together, namely FPCC, FPAC, and Seaport Alliance for a Neighborhood Design (SAND)[10]
- Put the neighborhood on the map for many who had never heard of it before
- Brought people together, both in creating and experiencing art

A Fort Point Vision for Public Art

Public space is a system of interconnected, highly unique sites that need to be seen within an overarching framework. I see a great need to plan within a larger context when attempting to create a more successful public realm: the parts make the whole and vice versa. A sound, well-versed plan begins with good communication and the recognition that good process is crucial for successful outcomes. Community-oriented urban planning theory and tools offer the best practices for this process. I initiated *A Fort Point Vision for Public Art* within this conceptual structure. At the outset, I forged partnerships with two key organizations—with a competent public art agency, UrbanArts, under the directorship of Ricardo Barreto, and with Mobius, an alternative performance art space located in Fort Point with a long history of temporary public performance art, led by Jed Speare. Mobius became our headquarters and UrbanArts provided public art expertise.

A Fort Point Vision for Public Art was both open forum and public art project and was conceived as a community-driven response to Fort Point development with the goal to discuss the future of public art in the neighborhood. The project took place as a four-day community-driven think tank comprised of a diverse group of over one hundred participants from Fort Point and Greater Boston, including artists, arts administrators,

City planners, architects, and corporate representatives. Ten temporary public art projects complemented the think tank in multiple locations in the Fort Point district. Art installations were created by artists from Fort Point and the metropolitan Boston region: namely Caroline Bagenal, Terry Bastian, Yani Batteau, Alison Canfield, Leslie Clark, Shauna Gillies-Smith and Lisa Roth, Danielle Krcmar, Melora Kuhn, Ruth Mordecai, Jessica Poser, John Powell, and Reclamation Artists. These temporary art installations can be seen as a pilot project and point of departure for future permanent work. Temporary projects have the advantage that creative ideas can be implemented quickly and without concern for long-term implications. Charrette findings and art projects were documented in a brochure that was forwarded to participants, planning agencies, and developers as a resource. Ultimately, success of the project will be evident in the creation of policies that integrate the arts, artists, and open space in the planning of Fort Point and the parks corridor on the depressed highway.

In summary, Fort Point's efforts can be viewed as a model for community building through public art. Long-term development of the Fort Point arts community will be living evidence to the success of the project and the idea that public art enriches the urban cultural experience, not only for the community, but for the entire city and visitors alike. Much work needs and continues to be done, much of it by engaged citizen volunteers. The outcome of the *Fort Point Vision for Public Art* sessions was the vision for a cultural district and the call for a cultural master plan. The community and affiliated cultural planners continue to pursue this initiative to benefit the neighborhood as it grows and continues to develop. With arguably New England's largest community of artists, the Fort Point district is in the enviable position to draw on extraordinary local talent, which in turn will help guarantee the future success of the district for both residents and visitors alike.

Integrating Public Realm Planning and Public Art

The development of a high quality visual environment makes great sense and is increasingly supported by scientific research and discourse. Yet, there still is a great need for professionals who design the public realm to think and act collaboratively and in a cross-disciplinary fashion. The City of Boston, for example, would certainly benefit from an increased interface between urban planners and public art professionals. For one, both the City of Boston and the State of Massachusetts lack a "percent-for-art" policy, which would mandate incorporation of public art into the public built environment. By the same token, much development is private and there continues to be a dearth of well-designed public space. In my experience, it often takes the initiative of an enlightened individual or community to change the status quo.

UrbanArts advocates for an *integrated design team* approach, so that architects, planners, and artists work collaboratively from the beginning stages of a design project. This process is still underdeveloped when it comes to planning and designing the public realm. Partly, this can be attributed to oft-quoted funding constraints, though one might intone the old adage, "Where there is a will there is a way." Another hindrance is professional barriers and unfortunate turf-wars between the architecture and art disciplines, leading to fears of contact.

A Sustainable Approach to Public Art and Design

Employment of *sustainable practices* has been a longtime, dedicated personal cause.[11] Sustainability of our basic resources becomes an ever more urgent question as resources dwindle and pollution increases. Opportunities are twofold: public artist and landscape architect apply best practices and state-of-the-art, ecologically sound products and processes to minimize negative impacts on the environment; secondly, this application can offer a crucial link to increase awareness and to instigate change in communities' approach to sustainable methods. New commonsense principles are being adopted by both private initiative and governing agencies, including mandates to be fair, restore, and enhance the environment, conserve natural resources, and implement overarching planning. In 2005, UrbanArts adopted an expressly stated commitment to promote sustainable approaches and to mandate employment of sustainable methods and materials whenever possible. My own environmental efforts have found expression in several nest box projects for endangered cavity breeders, including an urban wild installation on Boston's Mission Hill, a hillside neighborhood of primarily double and triple-decker homes.

These initiatives are in response to and investigate the effects of urban development on the environment, urban culture, and the individual experience. The project consisted of individually designed nest boxes for screech owls who lack breeding opportunities. Large cavity breeders and other wildlife face increasing difficulties as rapid development diminish their habitat.

Some important principles regarding sustainable approaches were gleaned during prior international research on the subject.[12] I surveyed leaders, practitioners, and students in the field of public art to reflect on sustainable approaches to public art, landscape design, and art in the community. Their responses may be summarized as follows:

- Professionals tend to reject the notion of sustainable approaches as a means to an end.
- Since public art is often seen as the *voice of the community*, practitioners must avoid being reactive rather than proactive when it comes to sustainability and ecology.
- Scientific discourse is crucial to advance the field and benefit the public at large.
- The sustainability discussion is closely tied to the leadership and philosophy of individuals.
- Public opinion, government, and educational efforts most effectively evolve hand-in-hand in order to develop best practices and policies.

---

[1] Miwon Kwon, *One Place After Another* (Cambridge: MIT Press, 2002), 1.

[2] President Franklin Delano Roosevelt launched the Works Progress Administration (WPA) in the spring of 1935 as a massive employment relief program of the Depression era. WPA was the largest and most important of the New Deal cultural programs, aimed at putting the unemployed back to work in jobs that would serve the public good and conserve the skills and the self-esteem of workers, artists and artisans throughout the United States. Detailed historic overview at http://www.wwcd.org/policy/US/newdeal.html#TREAS Access date May 24, 2007.

[3] The *AIDS Quilt* is a prominent grassroots example. Initiated in San Francisco in 1987, the project documents the lives of those lost to AIDS and educates the public on the devastating impact of the disease. To date, more than 44,000 individual 3′ × 6′ memorial panels have been sewn together. See http://www.aidsquilt.org. Access date May 24, 2007.

[4] The UrbanArts Institute (UA) works to promote excellence in public art and design. UA is an independent non-profit organization affiliated with Massachusetts College of Art, the only *public*, independent college of art and design in the United States. UA incorporates the arts and cultural programming into urban design and community revitalization efforts by offering services in three key areas: (1) *Art in Public Places*: Providing services to implement public art projects for private and public-sector clients. (2) *Arts and Community Development*: Creating neighborhood-based collaborative design projects that involve citizens in planning for the future of their communities. (3) *Education and Resources*: Offering educational programs for the public; access to resources for artists, community groups and design professionals seeking to implement public art programs, including UA's national artist registry of more than 2000 artists. See http://www.urbanartsinstitute.org. Access date May 24, 2007.

[5] UrbanArts mission statement.

[6] Jan Gehl, *Life Between Buildings* (New York, NY: Van Nostrand Reinhold, 1987), 13.
[7] Central Artery park forums were the brainchild of Thomas Piper, Principal Research Scientist at Massachusetts Institute of Technology's (MIT) Department of Urban Studies and Planning. Detailed account of events at http://www.boston.com/beyond_bigdig. Access date May 24, 2007.
[8] Annual events include open studios weekends, first held in 1978. This and other events bring thousands of visitors to the neighborhood, directly contributing to the district's revitalization. See http://www.fortpointarts.org. Access date May 24, 2007. Now popular across the country, the concept of open studios originated in Boston's Fort Point.
[9] The Fort Cultural Coalition Point Public Art Series. Introduction to *No Art / No Point* (Boston, MA: Fort Point Cultural Coalition, 2004).
[10] Fort Point's Seaport Alliance for a Neighborhood Design (SAND) was founded in 1998 to advocate for long-range planning ideals, envisioning the South Boston waterfront as a vibrant, diverse *community* with a distinctive character and sense of place.
[11] Sustainable growth theory began with the landmark publication, *The Limits to Growth: A Report for the Club of Rome's Project on the Predicament of Mankind.* (New York: Universe Books, 1972), 39. Over one million copies have been sold worldwide. The Club of Rome was formed in 1968 by and as "an informal, multinational, non political group of scientists, economists, planners, educators, and business leaders." Commissioned by the Club of Rome, a research team at MIT analyzed existing data and published them in this highly controversial report. This book marks the beginnings of the sustainable development concept in light of the exponential increase in human population and the finite size of resources on our planet. As a result of the report, the unquestioned belief in economic growth and technical progress of the 1950s and 1960s began to be regarded more critically.
[12] Christina Lanzl, "A Sustainable Approach to Public Art Education," *Public Art Review.* 34, 42–44 (Spring 2006): 42.

Works Cited

About the Quilt. Atlanta, GA: Names Project Foundation, 1987–2007. http://www.aidsquilt.org.

About UrbanArts. Boston, MA: UrbanArts Institute. http://www.urbanartsinstitute.org.

Adams, Don and Goldbard, Arlene. *New Deal Cultural Programs: Experiments in Cultural Democracy.* Talmage, CA: The Institute for Cultural Democracy, 1986, 1995. http://www.wwcd.org/policy/US/newdeal.html#TREAS.

Beyond the Big Dig. New York, NY: New York Times Company, 2002. http://www.boston.com/beyond_bigdig.

The Fort Cultural Coalition Point Public Art Series. *No Art / No Point.* Boston, MA: Fort Point Cultural Coalition, 2004.

Gehl, Jan. *Life Between Buildings.* New York, NY: Van Nostrand Reinhold, 1987.

Jacobs, Jane. *The Death and Life of Great American Cities.* New York, NY: Random House and Vintage Books, 1961.

Kwon, Miwon. *One Place After Another.* Cambridge: MIT Press, 2002.

Lanzl, Christina. A Sustainable Approach to Public Art Education. *Public Art Review,* 34 (Spring 2006): 42–44.

Meadows, D. H. et al. *The Limits to Growth: A Report for the Club of Rome's Project on the Predicament of Mankind.* New York, NY: Universe Books, 1972.

What We Do. Boston, MA: Fort Point Arts Community. http://www.fortpointarts.org.

MENTORS AND MENTORING: THE WOMAN'S WAY

ELINOR W. GADON

One of the most fruitful developments of the Feminist Movement has been the role that the female mentor plays in the empowerment of women in the academic, art, and corporate worlds. Mentoring has traditionally been associated with the male—fathers mentor sons, bosses mentor subordinates, gurus mentor disciples, and professors mentor students.

Women, on the other hand, did not mentor per se. Indeed, while mothers instructed their daughters in the domestic arts and marital duties, they seldom transgressed the boundaries of the private world to model behavior in the public domain. The first women to scale the heights of the so-called professions—law, medicine, the academy, and the corporation—had no female mentors. A former president of a woman's college once told me that no women could achieve such a high position without the support of a powerful male.

One formidable problem for young feminists seeking equal opportunities in entering the professions was the dearth of female mentors. What was needed and sorely lacking for most was a same sex role model for our time, which is the feminist era—the epoch of rising female agency. It is difficult for the inexperienced to step into roles for which there are not blueprints. The prescribed role models for women, centuries-old and millennia-old, have been imprinted on our consciousness since birth, perhaps even encoded in our genes. Mothers, who traditionally have served as models for their daughters, are no longer deemed adequate. Women who haven't been raised by feminist mothers claim that theirs don't know anything. As poet/philosopher Adrienne Rich claimed 30 years ago, "The mother I needed was yet born."

For lack of a role model, I opted out from my undergraduate pre-med program. I had never met a women physician. Years earlier, during my first foray with career planning while in middle school, I choose scientific research as my future destiny. Having read the biography of Marie Curie, I identified with her heroic path, which included a research partner who was also her lover and mate. Heady stuff for a romantic adolescent. I would be a research scientist and find my true love in the laboratory. Together we would make great discoveries. I saw us as equals rejecting the traditional role of wife as helpmate. The man I married was locked in the old paradigm. He could support the empowerment of his daughters and women students, but not his wife.

Even years later when I came to understand the importance of power within, self-knowledge, and agency, I continued to look to male mentors—mostly my professors. After all, they were the ones who had the power. I did, however, choose the most empowered women I had ever encountered for my dissertation chair. She was most helpful in advancing my research, but when I came into a time of personal crisis, family tragedy, and depression, she lost interest in me, seeing me as weak.

My next mentor was the director of the women's studies program in which I was teaching. She understood me better that I did myself and tried to point me in a career direction more suitable to my personality and creativity that of curatorial work in an art museum. But I was stuck in my stated goal of teaching art history at the college level, unrealistic about the incompatibility of my free spirit in the hierarchical, patriarchal academy.

It was easier for me to identify with the elderly anthropologist for whom I did some editorial work. Although she was the same age as my mother, we became fast friends. Unlike with my mother, we shared both intellectual interests and social values. We could talk about feelings, anxieties, and personal as well professional. These were intertwined for us as they are for so many women. We could be vulnerable.

When I had the opportunity to develop and direct a graduate women's studies program, I built mentoring into the very structure of the curriculum and pedagogy. We were building a learning community. My students were all professional women, feminists returning to the academy for training as change agents. Faculty and students could learn from each other. I called this a relational pedagogy. I was making revolution, and as an administrator without a mentor, it was often rough going.

It is only now as a resident scholar at a women's studies research center, that I have had the good fortune to find a mentor in the director of the program who not only understands my intellectual and personal strengths and limitations, but who also fully appreciates my contribution to our academic community and to scholarship. In this ambience and under her leadership, I am flourishing, fully able to utilize my life experience and creativity.

Through trials and tribulations, I have come to understand the role of the female mentor and the paramount value of such a relationship in both professional and personal life. It is never easy to go it alone. Most of us need the support and confidence of an experienced woman to whom we can turn for guidance. I hold that women are different from men; they have different needs and ways of relating. It is still mostly a man's world out there, and we gain in strength through solidarity.

There is a time and place for the mentoring relationship. For men it has often been the golf course or locker room where women cannot trespass. Women too, need their safe spaces for intimate dialogue.

I suggest that the mentor we seek should be:

—Well established in her profession and knowledgeable about the rules of the Game
—Willing to engage in open-ended discussion on both professional and personal levels
—Non-judging, generous in spirit, open-minded

Good luck! Don't try to go it alone.

Transforming Personal History into Paintings

Thea Paneth

Dedicated in memory of Elma Paneth, March 1, 1926—January 15, 1987

Four paintings tell a story about my family. Memory, a dream, family mythology and photographs, as well as a movie, are interwoven and form the basis for these works of art.

One painting is a portrait of my grandfather that my mother painted.

My mother had a considerable talent for drawing and painting; she painted sporadically throughout my childhood, working on canvases of flower arrangements and a portrait of her father that is very important to my family. She left developing her art to "old age," as she put it, but she died at the relatively young age of 60 from cancer.

My grandfather came to the United States in 1908 using false papers. He had to flee Russia when a "tsarist agent" was killed where he lived. This was a commonly told immigrant story a hundred years ago. Today, my grandfather would be considered an illegal immigrant. He worked all his life in the garment trades and was a charter member of the International Ladies Garment Workers Union (ILGWU). My mother was always proud of his union activity.

My mother painted a portrait of him at the end of his life, seated in his wing chair. She felt that his portrait was a visual portrayal of the of the immigrant experience. "The painting of papa is every Jewish immigrant," she said.

On this same grandfather's side of the family, we hold on to our mythology that we were expelled from Spain during the 1492 Inquisition and migrated across Europe to Russia.

Ten years after my mother's death, I traveled to Spain to imbue myself with a sense of the country in preparation for making paintings about her. I wanted to be in the country of flamenco music and dance.

I made three paintings: a stylized portrait of my mother and her sister and two paintings about my mother's death.

When I made the portrait of my mother and my aunt, I took the title of *Las Dos Hermanas (The Two Sisters)* from the nickname of two perfectly white slabs of marble that are set into the floor of one of the chambers in The Alhambra, a Moorish palace in Granada.

The portrait I made of my mother and her sister is based on several photographs in which each sister is wearing a gray suit and posing outdoors for the camera. I painted them at the beginning of their adult lives, before they were married. At the bottom of the work, I incorporated text tracing the immigrant journey of our family, and I also put their first names and years of birth and death.

Once Upon a Time in the Hospital and *Dancing Shoes* incorporate flamenco imagery and hospital images. To make these two paintings, I reached back into my memories of the real-life experiences of the last days of my mother's life and incorporated elements of her dream with images from the hospital.

My mother suffered from a radiation-induced breast cancer that was caused by X-ray treatment for mastitis, a common nursing infection that could have been treated with penicillin. She received the X-ray treatment in 1963, was diagnosed with cancer, and went through surgery and chemotherapy in 1981. In the fall of 1986, her cancer returned and early in 1987, my mother died.

Once Upon a Time in the Hospital shows a person in a hospital bed in the center of the canvas and monitoring equipment in the lower right corner. A medical device that measures diastolic and systolic blood pressure is attached to ICU patients. When a person dies, the numbers go to zero.

I painted two red squared-off zeroes on a black box to represent the device. In the top right corner of the painting there is a flamenco dancer with a couple of guitar players.

The title of this painting comes from a 1968 spaghetti western movie directed by Sergio Leone called *Once Upon a Time in the West.* It is a classic tale of good and evil, set in the mythic American West. It has a great cast—with an evil railroad mogul played by Henry Fonda and an archetype widow, whose homestead lies in the path of the railroad, played by Italian star, Claudia Cardinale. Jason Robards is the leader of an outlaw gang who goes off to die alone when he is belly-shot, and Charles Bronson has a non-speaking part as a character who plays his harmonica throughout the film. This movie, especially the Jason Robards character, was a favorite of my mother's, and it was playing in New York the day she died.

After six straight days in the hospital, we were told that she was "improving" and my brother and I went to see this movie. We told her where we were going. She was in a coma, on a respirator and during the hours we were gone, her BP numbers went to zero.

The relationship of the film to the events we lived through is significant because my mother held on to life while her children were at the hospital around the clock; she knew the length of the film and that her favorite character died alone in the desert. While we were at the movie, she could let go.

Dancing Shoes, and the flamenco section of my painting *Once Upon a Time . . .* , are both based on a dream that my mother told me about in the days before she died.

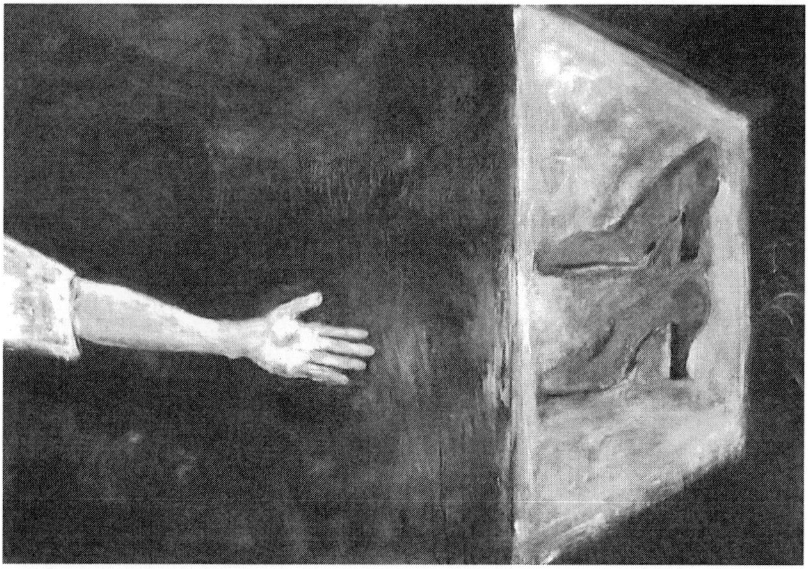

Fig. 3-2
Dancing Shoes. Painting copyright Thea Paneth 2006.

My mother loved flamenco dance. She felt that in a past life she had somehow offended a "gypsy queen" who had put a curse on her, which was why her life was so difficult in the present. Shortly before my mother died, she had a very interesting dream about a gypsy: My mother dreamed that she was dying in a hospital. As she lay dying, she knows that a young man, a gypsy, is looking for her. The young man is searching up and down the corridors, carrying dancing shoes. When he finds her, he places coins in the hand of the older woman dying in the hospital bed, and says, "The debt is paid now." At the same moment that the older woman dies, a young woman is released from her body to claim the dancing shoes and go off with the young man. When my mother told me about the dream, she said, "Don't grieve too much when I'm gone because I've got my dancing shoes."

Dancing Shoes is a vertically divided canvas; (fig. 3-2) one half shows an outstretched arm in a hospital gown, with coins in the palm, on a black ground. The other half shows a pair of red high-heeled pumps such as flamenco dancers wear, set against a white shape that narrows as it approaches the right edge of the canvas and can be read visually as a partly open door. I think of it as the gateway to the world of imagination and memory.

When I made these three paintings I found a way to resurrect my mother and tell some of this story.

The portrait of my grandfather by my mother is an important record from her generation—there are not many portraits of a Jewish immigrant painted in a formal or traditional way.

These four works exemplify the creative struggle in which my mother engaged, and that I took up as well.

IMAGISTIC IMAGERY EXCHANGE IN MOTHER-DAUGHTER ART MAKING

DENISE MALIS AND SIMONE ALTER-MÜRI

As female artists, our identities hinge on the varied roles we have in our lives. Therefore, the art created by woman is rich and has a broad reach in imagery and art form. For the purposes of this paper, the artwork of women and women collaborating is seen through a psychological/sociological lens. In order to embrace the unique visual language that distinguishes the female from the male perspective, consideration must be given to the contrast between male and female personality development and differences in social development.

Some aspects of women's identity can be regarded as unique in formation. Our initial group experiences are based in family; connections to others and to ourselves stem from these early interactions and communications. Family-as-imagery often marks an interesting juncture in the lives of female artists because it attempts to define the psyche and the relational base of women's social and psychological stages of growth.

Women artists have primarily been deemed less than their male counterparts, despite education and accomplishments.[1] In the history of painting and sculpture, motherhood is a central theme, visually stating that this is women's defined role. The message that being a mother is synonymous with being female further relays that women exist for others and not for themselves. Taking into consideration the historical depiction in art of women's roles, as well as the psychological and sociological view of women, it is with considerable risk that women artists include and depict images of family in their artwork. Incorporating such images is not necessarily a reaction to the role of mother, but rather a depiction of self through relationship. Though progress has been slow, women have gained acknowledgement, particularly in the field of art. The twentieth century marks the progress and blossoming of women, who have developed their own individual aesthetics in the art field

Imagery as Self-Dialogue—Denise Malis

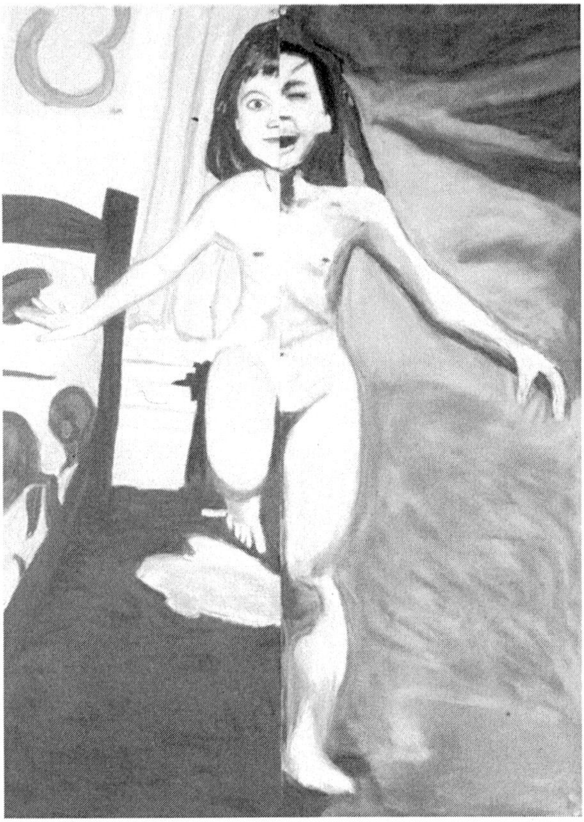

Fig. 3-3
Child of Mine. Painting copyright Denise Malis 1996.

Like many women, Denise Malis straddles several roles: she is mother, daughter, artist, educator, and art therapist. In each role, she accesses different aspects of herself. The art that she creates is a synthesis of these roles. When considering the challenges in her life, she sees art as the essential path in finding her voice. Her artwork from 1995 to 2000 occurred at a juncture in her life when she was examining core relationships. The emergence of images of family paralleled a deep examination of key parental figures in her life. It was a natural occurrence to integrate the visual images of mother, grandmother, daughter, and father. In further examining this body of work, Malis's approach to process and product in this period is in great contrast to her previous work. She experienced the inclusion of images of family as "risk-taking". She identified this dynamic as a struggle, however, she sought to not sentimentalize or personalize her artwork in such a manner that it became irrelevant as "serious" artwork. In examining relationships, Malis was ultimately drawn to the mother-daughter relationship. She found that sorting through the relationship with her mother led her into examining the relationship with her daughter. This is concretized in the many artworks where her daughter's image was central (fig. 3-3). In the artwork produced at this time, Malis expanded on the familial relationship by combining and reframing family images with images of nature.

The mother-daughter theme was realized when Malis recognized the imagistic exchange (nonverbal communication) through artwork done separately by her and her daughter. The exchange occurred during her daughter's adolescence when their verbal rapport was minimal and conflicted. Both the relational model and psychosocial developmental theory identify the developing years of adolescence as a marker in the lifespan.[2] During this time, Malis's daughter, Mekkin, was enrolled in a school-based ceramic class where her main concentration was the use of the potter's wheel to build objects. Her daughter's hand-built pieces stood out as unique. In one piece, she sculpted her hands around the base of a volcano. Both of these symbols—hands and volcanoes—also appeared in Malis's artwork at the time. Malis saw this nonverbal dialogue as an imagistic exchange between mother and daughter.

Contemplating the roots of her artwork has led Malis to view the artwork of other female artists in a similar way. The works of two woman artists stand out. Thea Paneth and Susan Sills had significant experiences that had an impact on the imagery found in their paintings. Sills underwent treatment for early-stage breast cancer.[3] Prior to this, she had painted representational images based on photographs she took. Following medical treatment, she found she was no longer compelled to continue this direction in her artwork. The work she produced was smaller and incorporated photographs of her family. This new direction documented images of her two daughters in relationship with one another. Paneth's significant event was the birth of her daughter.[4] Her imagery prior to her daughter's birth was large scale, politically charged paintings. To balance this, she also produced smaller paintings based on landscape. Paneth's imagery changed following the birth of her daughter, when she felt compelled to paint several large canvases of her mother. It is significant that the urge to paint images of her mother reflects the ongoing nature of the mother-daughter relationship. Paneth's paintings of her mother can be seen as a continuum of communication with her as well as a nonverbal, image-based dialogue. Both artists responded to significant life-altering events with visual responses that were based in intimate family relationships.

Art and Career Choice—Simone Alter-Müri

To understand family influence and its relationship to career choice of women artists, Simone Alter-Müri interviewed several women artists who have a mother, daughter, or father who is/was an artist and who use the theme of family in their art. Alter-Müri is interested in the benefits of collaborative art making as it occurs in mother-daughter relationships. Several of the women whom Alter-Müri interviewed created collaborative pieces with other women who are artists in their family. Women artists such as Anne, Cynthia, and Leslie Packard[5] have supported one another's creativity not only through collaborative art making but through jointly owning and managing a gallery that exhibits their work.

Alter-Müri's interest in women artists and the family is strongly connected to her own story. Alter-Müri and her mother, Harriett, both create art and have collaborated on several paintings. In the late 1940s, Harriett wanted to study the piano. She was also talented as a visual artist and won art awards and contests in her high school. Her parents, immigrants to this country from Eastern Europe, felt that she would not be able to support herself as an artist and encouraged her to become a teacher. Harriett abandoned her artistic yearnings and obtained her master's degree in education, specializing in art education. As an art teacher in a middle school in the Bronx, Harriett had little time for her art. After Alter-Müri was born, Harriett's husband became ill with cancer and died. Harriett remarried, had another child, and created art intermittently. This vignette reinforces information gleaned in the literature that women are socialized to put the needs of others before their own.[6]

The high school guidance counselor discouraged Alter-Müri from choosing a career path as a visual artist. Her mother was informed that Alter-Müri should be on the "Mrs." degree track (i.e., that she should marry). Alter-Müri did not heed the guidance counselor. However, she was influenced by her family's advice to become a teacher. Putting aside her art making to raise a family and continue her education, Alter-Müri remained in the art field as an art therapist and art educator. After the birth of her second child, she earned a doctoral degree and now works as a professor.

Alter-Müri and her mother have created collaborative paintings. Usually Simone would start a painting and would invite her mother to critique and paint on her artwork. Alter-Müri's mother was cautious in their collaborations because she was afraid of "ruining" Simone's work or changing the direction of the painting. When painting together, Alter-Müri and her mother converse more easily. This is related to Malis's concept of imagistic exchange, and allows Alter-Müri and her mother to validate each other through art. Although Alter-Müri can be disillusioned by some of her mother's attitudes, this does not occur in the studio. Alter-Müri has learned about boundaries, validation, and acceptance through the process of collaborative art making. Mother and daughter are able to discuss the aesthetic components of the art-making process and give each other feedback. Creating art in the studio allows Alter-Müri to take risks in the mother-daughter relationship. Although generational issues arise, those issues do not interfere with the creative process.

Family, Career and Art

Linda Klein, an exhibiting artist and a professor, experimented with collaborative art making with her three daughters, all artists. As a young woman, Klein discovered that there were no role models for women artists.[7] She started her career as a nurse and worked hard to get to her dream of attending the Art Institute of Chicago. As her children grew, Klein went on to receive a Master of Fine Arts degree.

Women artists often struggle with time commitments and feelings of guilt: they feel that their time should be focused on the family. Although Klein's first marriage was to an artist, she experienced patriarchal behavior and attitudes towards women artists. Before the women's movement, Klein participated in an exhibit with her husband. The press reviewed her husband's paintings with only a brief mention of her art, even though her art sold and her husband's did not. Klein felt that women artists married to male artists were almost invisible. As a mother with young children, her studio was in a room near the kitchen, and she would move from the canvas to the stove.

In the last few years, Klein and two of her adult daughters have created collaborative art. Like Malis, Klein has experienced the power of imagi-istic imagery with these collaborative pieces. These collaborative pieces had rules and parameters. All three artists had five pieces of drawing paper and each had the opportunity to start the visual dialogue. The drawings were passed from one person to the next. Each artist had one chance to create on the paper, and then she would mail the art to the next artist. The third artist would determine when the work was finished—each piece only went around one time. The original "owner" of the art could not change their original art. The artists had no restrictions of materials or time. At the start of this collaboration, Klein felt that she held back when it was her turn to collaborate on art started by one of her daughters; she did not want to intrude on her daughters' space. Klein realized that she was responding as a mother, rather than as an artist and decided to change her behavior. She did not want to intrude on her daughters' space. Realizing that this hesitancy was due to the role of "mom" rather than fellow artist, When Klein reacted to the art from an aesthetic perspective rather than as a cautious mother, her daughters felt a greater sense of connection.

Anne Packard is a dynamic woman in her seventies who raised her children with a love of the landscape and art.[8] Packard's family of origin is made up of several artists, including her grandfather, Max Bohm, a turn-of-the-century Impressionist painter. Although family and children are important to these women, their commitment and passion for their art is intense and inspiring. Anne and her daughter Cynthia are artists who both work eight to ten hours a day and critique and support each other's artistic processes. Their studios are down the street from each other's and they have had a gallery together for more than 20 years; their relationship is one of mutual respect. Cynthia experiments with media and form in her work, her art is more abstract than her mother's.She encourages her mother to continue to try new approaches and to become more open in her application of paint. Although they approach their work differently, they seek each other's approval and flourish on their mutual critiques. They have a dynamic relationship where mother and daughter tend to push each other to look beyond the surface. Their relationship seems to be enhanced by their roles as artists.

Women artists often incorporate images and metaphors of family as major content matter in their art. Rosa Ibarra is a painter who creates portraits of her children and the strong women that she meets.[9] The figures in her paintings are solid and often outlined, feminine shapes and include mixed media such as fabric, beads, and objects from women's crafts. Brought up in Puerto Rico by her father, Ibarra attended art classes that her father taught. She moved with her father to Paris, where he worked as an artist, while she finished school. Ibarra assisted her father in executing his paintings. Although they worked collaboratively, supporting each other in their respective journeys as artists, this exchange was mainly to help her father during his execution of large murals. As a divorced mother, Ibarra confronted the challenges of being an artist, and a single-parent, struggling economically. Nonetheless, Ibarra's daughters felt they benefited from their mother taking the time and energy to paint their portraits. Ibbara felt that the portraits validated her children's importance in her life and enabled her children to engage in the process of imagistic imagery, which added to their relationship.

Conclusion

Family is a factor in women's ability to maintain energy for the creative process. Although women keep making strides, they still are not able to reach their artistic potential due to economic and family issues. These interviews make apparent that art is important in the relationship between parent and child. Art symbolically becomes a family member, facilitating communication in ways words cannot. Collaborative art creates bonds allowing communication to grow and voices to be heard and respected. These vignettes support the proposition that families are a factor in women's art making. They also augment the discussion of collaborative art making.

Recent research indicates that the mother-daughter relationship extends through the lifespan and is an essential factor in the developing self.[10] The ongoing nature of women's relationships, including the core relationship of mother-daughter, potentially holds a resource for women artists. The imagery that enters the artwork of female artists is often based upon significant events and relationships. This underscores the ongoing impact of relationships that feed women's creative endeavors. Art can be a communicative resource and active ingredient in the relationships of women artists. Looking at the art process and its by-product as a unique visual language can emotionally enrich, and further expand, women's understanding of themselves. Our ability to connect and build meaning and matter from the interweaving of our relationships gives us access to experiencing the power and beauty of imagistic imagery.

---

[1] Elsa Honig Fine, *Women and Art*, (Montclair, New Jersey: Allanheld, Osmun, 1978) and W. Slatkin, *Women artists in history* (Englewood Cliffs, New Jersey: Prentice-Hall, 1985).

[2] Carol Gilligan, "In a Different Voice: Psychological Theory and Women's Development" 31,51,151. Jean Baker Miller, "The Development of Women's Sense of Self."

[3] Susan Sills, personal communication, January 2007.

[4] Thea Paneth, personal communication, February 2006.

[5] Anne Packard and Cynthia Packard, personal communication, July 21, 2006.

[6] Joanne H. Stohs, "Career Patterns and Family Status of Women and Men Artists," *Career Development Quarterly*, 40, no.3 (1992): 223–233.

[7] Linda Klein, personal communication, February 1, 2005.
[8] Anna Packard and Cynthia Packard, personal communication, July 21, 2006.
[9] Rosa Ibarra, personal communication, February 1, 2005.
[10] J. R. Bohannon and P. W. Blanton, "Gender Role Attitudes of American Mothers and Daughters Over Time," *Journal of Social Psychology* 139, no. 2 (1999): 174.

Works Cited

Bohannon, J.R. and P.W. Blanton. "Gender Role Attitudes of American Mothers and Daughters over Time." *Journal of Social Psychology* 139, no. 2 (1999): 173–80.

Fine, Elsa H. *Women and Art.* Montclair, New Jersey: Allanheld, Osmun, 1978.

Gilligan, Carol. *In a Different Voice: Psychological Theory and Women's Development.* Cambridge, Massachusetts: Harvard University Press, 1993.

Miller, Jean Baker. The Development of Women's Sense of Self. In *Women's Growth in Connection*, edited by Judith V. Jordon, Alexandra G. Kaplan, Jean B. Miller, Irene P. Stiver, and Janet L. Surry, 11–26. New York: Guilford, 1984.

Slatkin, Wendy. *Women Artists in History.* Englewood Cliffs, New Jersey: Prentice-Hall, 1985.

Stohs, Joanne H. "Career Patterns and Family Status of Women and Men Artists," *Career Development Quarterly*, 40, no.3 (March 1992). 223-233.

Transnational Metaphors: Receptive Spaces in Public and Private Rituals

C.M. Judge

Today, like every other day, we wake up empty
and frightened. Don't open the door to the study
and begin reading. Take down a musical instrument.
Let the beauty we love be what we do.
There are hundreds of ways to kneel and kiss the ground.

Rumi, stanza one, *Spring Giddiness*[1]

I make art because it transforms my innermost self. When my work travels from my studio into the public realm, a synergistic relationship develops between me and my audience—the work is not complete without audience involvement, and audience involvement hinges on my capacity to truthfully express my experience. The artwork brings us collectively into dialog about our beliefs, assumptions, loyalties, and dreams. In other words, through this shared experience, we co-create our identities. The issue of identity and its creation has been relevant to my art practice for many years, and in particular has surfaced to the forefront of my thinking since I became a mother at the turn of the millennium. It is through this engaging, invitational lens that I organized the panel discussion of the same topic for the 2006 Women's Caucus for Art (WCA) National Conference in Boston, Massachusetts, featuring Cathy McLaurin, Elsa Voelcker, and Paula Rendino Zaentz. In this essay, I present works by the original panelists while further reflecting upon this poetic notion of "co-creation" by sharing my passion for the work of Véronique Sapin, Atsushi Ogata, Josh Friedman, and Todd Drake.

Recently, I took my young son to a "Birds of Prey" live presentation. The awe-inspiring experience of being face-to-face with an adult raptor, a female bald eagle no less, remains seared in my memory. The presenter lovingly spoke of the sanctuary for injured birds that he runs in New England. Some birds can be rehabilitated to the point where they can be reintroduced to the wild, while others need to remain in captivity. It occurred to him that perhaps the adult eagles that remain in captivity might mate, so he built them an enormous cage, and, sure enough, eggs were laid. In order for the eggs to be cared for properly, he built a wooden box with a mirror and a small opening with a flap along with a hand puppet in the form of an eagle head. As the eggs hatched, he fed the chicks by poking the puppet into the box to drop the food in their mouths. He knew how critical it is for the chick to "imprint" with the image and likeness of a parent eagle during its initial introduction to its new world. The last stage is to bring the healthy eaglet to an eagle nest in the wild for adoption; fortunately, parent eagles aren't able to count, and they simply feed the new sibling, treating it as their own.

Artists inevitably create such boxes, often containing mirrors and openings with flaps. They interject through them what they intuitively feel is needed in that particular moment under those particular circumstances, and the effect is similar. Those of us who enter the box risk being "imprinted" with a vision of a world seen anew, or perhaps even a world seen for the very first time. The artworks presented create compelling new worlds. The artists responsible for these artworks embrace this notion, expressed by artist Miriam Schapiro:

> I set myself free in the studio, inventing ways to bring out the hidden crevices of my heart: that which is stubborn and which asks for more and more strength and discipline for the extraction. If I make shifts, I do not see myself as following trends—I see yet another aspect of myself that needs definition.[2]

Puppet Master

A moon, a mirror, a glance,
a shiver of intention
begs us
to invite ourselves home,
into the exquisite reality
of our hearts[3]

One of France's premiere video artists, Véronique Sapin, creates single channel video art and installations that create spaces where the vulnerability of the human experience can be contemplated. Focusing on the human form, solitary and in tandem, she places them in carefully selected and seemingly unique, time-expanded moments. Through the use of slow-motion and long shots that heighten the ability of her audience to delve deeply into this extended experience, she reaches for moments that extend beyond what one can encounter in "real time" by offering us a world that is filled with both spontaneity and contemplativeness.

As artist Diego Velázquez gives us an arrested moment in time in his 1656 painting *Las Meninas* [*The Maids of Honor*], Sapin offers us a further reflection in her video installation, "Variation vidéo autour des 'Ménines numéro 1." The dynamic positioning of figures in space and multiple points of view offered by Velázquez is the same spatial device that Sapin chooses to occupy. The video installation is comprised of ten video monitors each depicting an actor's face that represents those persons in the painting. For example, the dwarf girl, in charge of entertaining the king and his court, transmutes into the face of a contemporary television station director—who, by the way, has that similar function in today's world. The monitors are set up on pedestals of varying heights within the installation to reflect the position that each character occupies in the painting. An eleventh monitor plays real time video of onlookers of the installation thereby acting like the mirror in the painting that reflects the king and queen whose portrait is being painted. The painter and videographer have exchanged positions and, in Sapin's rendition of this moment (in the artist's own words), she "assumes the role of puppet master letting the visitors come into the showroom as if to lead them into a gallery wherein the figures are offered for viewing in a well-established order."[4]

The installation is arranged in such a way as to allow viewers to move freely among the monitors. Occasionally, the figures turn and look at each other, lending an added spatial as well as psychological dynamic to the installation space. Riddled with unexpected glances, deep gazing, and unspoken narratives, one is drawn into a drama that requires one's own extended glance both outward and inward. Sapin invites her audience into this carefully crafted moment knowing that what we bring into the room will be reflected back to us in the mirror on the far wall. The inspiration continues as Sapin has realized three other variations of the project with each variation building from the last; she describes this process as being like "nested Russian dolls (a doll inside a doll inside a doll)."[5]

Representing France in the FemLink international video collage, Sapin created a video short titled *And Then, the Total Blank*. The theme of the collage, featuring 39 women video artists from 39 countries, is fragility. A black and white image of a woman's hands is seen. Her index fingers and thumbs are gathered. Slowly, she tears a piece from the paint chip she is holding and lets it flutter to the ground. The moment is enduring and inevitable, poetic and mundane, fragile and tender. Sapin writes, "I wish for the viewer to share in the same vulnerable space that my videos try to create. Tranquility on the surface is pitted by the turmoil underneath that bubbles up serendipitously through the thin surface of the image."[6]

Inviting Moments

My tears flow
into ink that makes
paper hanging on your walls
stare back at you.[7]

Cathy McLaurin embraces her audience with participatory projects by inviting them to join her in the discovery process. McLaurin's national exhibition record is peppered with participatory works that focus on human interaction. She explains:

> I explore and investigate the world around me through the work that I make and the projects in which I engage others. In this way, my process is not unlike that of a scientist doing research, gathering information and documenting those findings. I am curious about people—human behavior and interaction—most especially, that behavior and interaction that manifests as a result of experience of pain and loss.[8]

In 2001, she began inviting people to anonymously send her their secrets written on small pieces of newsprint for her installation *what haunts . . . ?* Her intention to display the secrets has brought her work to a wide range of public places including pubs and churches. Along with the 2,500 plus secrets—her collection continues to grow—she provides a wooden booth with a curtained entrance, where one can record one's where one can record one's own secret and then drop it into the collection box.

Your secret defines me

The "private confessions" made public take many forms from the humorous to the tragic. One participant writes, "I used to pick my goldfish up out of its fish bowl and hold it by the tale." Another reflects on the notion of privacy by relating, "I read several pages from my daughter's private diary. . .and don't feel guilty about it. I admired and appreciated her more after reading it, though I think I was wrong to read it." Yet another tells us, "I woke up one night while staying at my grandmother's to find her topless painting her nails at the kitchen table. I'm still in therapy."[9]

McLaurin speaks about the personal responsibility she felt to ensure that the secrets were safe and for some time carried them with her wherever she went. The note-sized pieces of newsprint are placed side by side on the wall without regard to the content. Visually alluring with subtle color variations of the paper and a study in penmanship, the wall begins to breathe with layers of intersecting intentions—intentions that lead us to reflect upon our own. Creating a safe, private place for reflection while facilitating public reflection and dialog is at the heart of altering perception, and thus, identity.

As her desire to make daily mediation a part of her life increased, McLaurin developed the collaborative project, *Still busy. . .Sitting still.* She put out a call to the community to e-mail her with meditation requests and to send her objects that have a connection with each request. Each day, during a month-long residency, she chose an object to hold while meditating on the request. During each session, she made a small drawing that was later given to the participants. The small drawings are related to the final manifestation of this project, which is a floor drawing in chalk dust based on traditional Indian *kolam*s (or *rangoli*).[10] Symbolizing mediation energy, the series of interwoven line patterns create a matrix for the objects that have been placed on the floor in the interior of the drawing.

Ten Thousand Gestures

> It is the smallness that I want to celebrate and elaborate. I am forever changing my past by my present. The circularity of objects to life to art means that I do not have to leave well enough alone.
>
> Lisa Hoke[11]

Revelation, for visual artist Josh Friedman, takes many forms: the enduring beauty of simple body gestures, meaning that springs forth from old objects, hidden histories, and edges. Friedman writes, "The physical residue of my studio activities solidify observations and responses to the internal landscapes within my body and the external world. They are influenced by life experience; punctuated by travel and language."[12] Friedman's artistic identity is intimately linked to simple body gestures of everyday life that we all share. These human gestures take on a ritualistic overtone when performed over and over again throughout the course of a day, week, or year. Friedman's continually contracting and expanding sense of self informs the kind of meaning gleaned from daily gestures and helps us extract meaning from our experiences.

As a farewell gesture to his beloved Japan (he lived In Tokyo, Japan, for three years), Friedman created an installation titled, *Between Spaces*,

Your body calls to mine
My body calls to yours.
We are locked into
knowing each other.

which is composed of ten thousand sculptures he made by pressing clay between the hollow of his two clasped hands. He writes, "I lived amongst forty million people in the Tokyo metropolitan region of Japan. References in the work to density and compression became unavoidable and made the decision to work with clay most appropriate."[13] The result is a stunningly beautiful visual *mantra*. The natural contour of the clay divulges its history of being formed by the hands. Variations in color, texture, and definition tell a story of movement from the current moment backward and then from the current moment forward. The artist has created a lovely measuring tool for us as we interact with the sheer volume of this work. And it is work with all the sameness and repetition that the word *work* implies. Yet, the spirit of intention in this work of human hands conjures an entire world, from the earth itself to the yearnings of the heart.

Friedman writes, "While working, I enter, for lack of a better word, a zone, a place where the work creates itself and I have the privilege of being present, doing what the drawing tells me to do and observing it reveal itself."[14] This willingness to let the work shape and inform us is intimately linked to a wall piece created with cooking paper, fire, and incense, titled *Flow*. Exploring the edge between the forces of creation and destruction, Friedman creates six elegant vertical paper scrolls suspended from a rod. The surface pattern of billowing smoke-like forms sweep smoothly from one panel to the next. It's not until one is very close to this work that one sees the drawing is created by thousands of impressions of the tip of an incense cone or stick deftly leaving coffee-colored circular marks of various values on the cooking paper. The hand, the fire, the paper tells us a story as we enter into a place where a common everyday gesture is celebrated by an artist who keeps on looking for the edge of meaning.

Body as Canvas

The great earth innocently
nurtures the flowers of spring.
Birds trust freely
the strength of the wind.
All this derives from the power of giving
as does our self, coming into being.
John Daido Loori[15]

Photographer Elsa Voelcker has been creating portraits and nature images for nearly forty years. As a girl, she often felt like an outsider. Her curly vibrant red hair was a distinguishing feature that called attention to her otherness. She felt socially awkward most of her life and then as a young woman; Voelcker found she could make connections with people by taking their picture and giving them a print. Often the ensuing conversation about the picture would form the basis of a friendship. Family, particularly her children, friends, and the natural world form the central subject matter of her work.

The idea of mutual exchange, creating art that functions as a personal and cultural bridge, remains central to Voelcker's process and is evident in her newest project, *PIERCED, body as canvas*. A poet friend approached her with the idea to shoot images of persons with body piercing. He was hoping to write about his perceptions of this growing phenomena. Voelcker agreed with some hesitation, questioning the medical wisdom of the practice.

Your eyes
Change me

Each sitter is given a print in exchange for his or her time and a dollar to formalize the model release. As the series of black and white images evolved, Voelcker began to see her investigation and her subjects in a new light. They were relaxed because they saw her as documenting their body piercings and not necessarily themselves as individuals. Her sensitively shot images, of course, do both by capturing their aesthetic choices as well as their humanity. Her images are of the elderly: 81-year-old "Conrad," whose nose ring tucks conveniently into his nostrils when he desires an alternative look; the young, "Pat" whose 25-plus facial piercings include a nose and lip rings, as well as multiple earrings, including lobe extenders that outshine his short buzzed hair cut; and a mother in *My Daughter's Canvas*, whose daughter is a student of piercing and tattooing and whose torso is adorned with her daughter's work (Fig. 3-4).

The movement of the practice of piercing from its sadomasochistic sexual associations into the mainstream of youth culture became a focus for the series. Issues surfaced around personal identity and the potentially addictive quality of being pierced. Rather than imposing a "voice" onto the series of images solely from an external source such as that of her poet friend, she understood the value of hearing from the subjects themselves. She began to ask them questions that illuminated their attraction to the new wave of interest in this historical ritual. The interviews became a crucial element in the overall design of the project, which creates a cultural bridge of understanding between the general public and those with

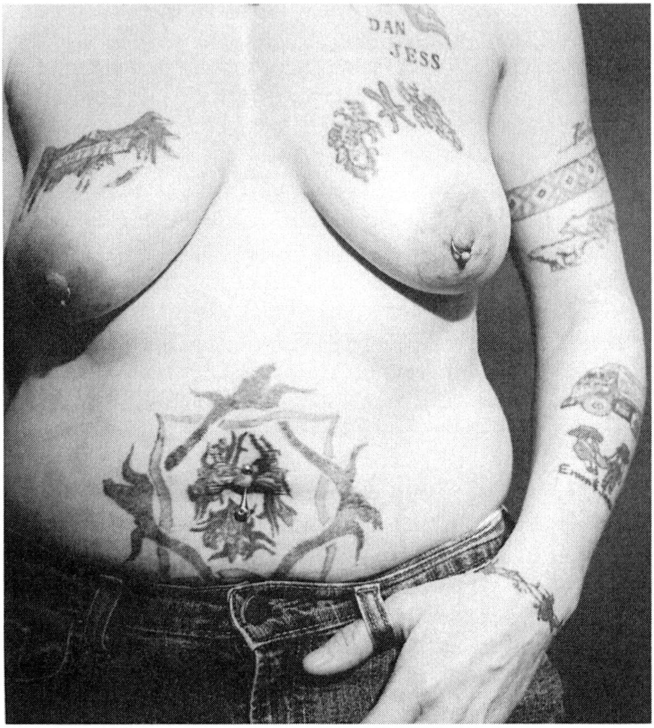

Fig. 3-4
My Daughter's Canvas. Photograph copyright Elsa Voelcker 2006.

body piercing. Voelcker declares, "I have a romantic gaze that takes potentially provocative subjects and makes them into an experience that leaves the viewer room to become tolerant if not appreciative of other people's choices and aesthetics."[16]

Peace Through Beauty

I have placed in my hands
all that is good[17]

Photographer and installation artist, Paula Rendino Zaentz, and I met in 2002, at the WCA National Convention in Philadelphia. We were drawn to each other's work. A natural conversation unfolded concerning our mutual interest in seeing art's potential for expressing the confluence of the spiritual, emotional, and physical realms through imagery that is simultaneously concrete and symbolic. Our mutual interests include patterns of human spirit as expressed through the generations, a reverent attitude toward the female body as a vessel of beauty and knowledge, and holistic energy patterns in the realms of the psyche, body, and natural substances.

Rendino Zaentz's interest in dowsing and healing arts brought her to the medium of black-and-white photography. She is most well known for photographs in which she takes images of her own hands aiming to capture energy and emotion, while exploring *mudras* (a Sanskrit word for any action that seals in strength). The images are strikingly beautiful evoking a heightened sense of the piercing kind of human intentionality that illuminates the human capacity to embrace vital energy.

At the same time, I had been working on a series of images of the human face inspired by the birth of my son. Maskless, every emotion he expressed in his face during those first several months was complete, intense, saturated, and openhearted—a daily poem that called to me. A synergy occurred when our images were combined, illuminating many "veils" of consciousness. The ensuing collaborative montage, *Veils of Anima: mapping the soul's journey* is comprised of hand and face images placed side by side positioned in a grid.

Take my breath
Use it to heal.

Envisioned as a worldwide network of cleansing rituals, our second project, the *Stream of Atonement* series *On Mine Hands, On Thine Hands* explores all humanity's role in bloodshed. It is our visual prayer for peace and an invitation to the community to look to the past, to make peace, and to move on. Each time the work is installed/performed, the intention is to address the history of that place and its inhabitants.

This series is comprised of a video installation, a performance work, and a photomontage printed in tabloid format. The American project depicts a middle-class, colonial woman of eighteenth-century America portrayed by Rendino Zaentz. Drenched in natural sunlight, she cleans and cleans, as women have for ages. We watch the pattern of her motions, her hand caressing a bowl of water, the weight of her body as she descends to her knees. She becomes a silent vehicle of atonement for the United States in its infancy for the massacre of the native peoples and for all wars, both just and unjust, including, of course, the current conflict in Iraq. While all nations share in bloodshed, this work invites us to take a deep breath and close our eyes to envision a graceful peace, an inner peace that endures, that brings us together in common spirit.

Bowing to Each Other

Tracing your footprints,
I see a path
that becomes my path
that becomes my being.[18]

Inevitably, artists bring evidence of our internal life forth into the public realm. Japanese video artist, filmmaker, and writer Atsuhsi Ogata and I have been creating video installations together for 20 years. Our diverse yet complementary sensibilities come together lending a layered resonance and improvisational character to our creative process. It's familiar and reassuring, yet dynamic.

We created a site-specific, community-specific video installation titled *Step in/Step out* for the 2003 Echigo-Tsumari Art Triennial. Festival Director Fram Kitagawa believes that art has the capacity to bridge cultural differences; thus his idea of bringing contemporary artists to the rural, agrarian, "snow country" region of Japan[19] to create site-specific works. Intended to revitalize the economy of the region, which suffers from depopulation, the festival brings people together from many diverse backgrounds all crossing over into relationship with one another through the necessity of art.

Each step we take while walking reaffirms our connection to the earth. This simple idea became the focal point for structuring the *Step in/Step out* project while the people of the region and the intimacies of their daily routine became our inspiration. Ogata shot video images of the area residents walking in their daily life. From young to old, the repetitions of their movements were captured by his camera held just inches from the ground. These 21 videos were then integrated into a vacant, lifeless two-story house in Tokamachi, a place where our grandparents might have lived. We invited residents to donate old shoes that would become a sculpture on an interior wall of the house, and I asked for volunteers to have their feet cast for sculptures that would be displayed in the house. The house became lively again with neighbors stopping by to help and to see the progress of the work.

Walking behind
each other,
We find our way

Eventually, this empty house became further invigorated, breathing with video images, sounds, colored light, residents' shoes/boots, and cast sculptures of residents' feet. *Tatami* mats and *shoji* screened rooms reflected images of feet walking on moss. Piercing sounds of cicadas resonated in the space; chocolate colored, feather-light soba hulls from the region graced the floor. A large sculptural wall of shoes traced residents' footprint paths. Images of children's feet playing in kindergarten were projected inside a bathtub, their squeals of delight echoed throughout the room. Above, firemen practiced their drills. In a tearoom with an orange hue, a woman in *kimono* elegantly walks and engages in a tea ceremony. In a long corridor with a light green hue, figures walk inside a tunnel carved through a mountain traditionally used during heavy snow. Walking through the house, visitors discovered hundreds of moments celebrating the vitality, beauty, and diversity of the region. As artists, we became their audience.

At the opening reception, a young woman ran up to me with outstretched arms. She filled my arms with freshly picked vegetables from her garden. Although we didn't share a common spoken language, her kind gesture spoke resoundingly. In gratitude, we bowed to one another.

Reaching Out

Let the paint
tell us what we need
to know, to embrace, to see, to taste
to let go of, to admonish, to defend, to love.[20]

Community activist and artist Todd Drake aligns his creative process with the notion that our identity is intimately linked to person-to-person contact; thus his projects are often structured around creating the possibility for interaction with others. He explains:

> In a search to paint more honestly, I have opened my art making process to the influence of others. This may seem a contradiction but this duality more completely represents who I am and what I believe is most important; that who we are is shaped by who we come into contact with over the span of our life.[21]

In his twenty 20′ × 32′ mural, *OPEN at SECCA* (2004), Drake drew and painted on the top half of a canvas that was installed in the South Eastern Center for Contemporary Art, in Winston-Salem, North Carolina, while visitors were encouraged to contribute doodles on the bottom half. Creating the work on site over a three-month period, Drake took the lead from the visitor participation to "inform" the progression of the mural's content and design. Rather than longing to create a "finished" work, he continued taking inspiration from the public, letting the piece evolve and change until its scheduled removal and demise. In reflecting on the process, he writes "In a sense it will never be finished, just as we as humans are never finished growing and changing." [22]

Meshing the tenants of abstraction with integrated narrative elements, Drake uses animated gestural brush strokes. He enters into communities to foster connections. The connection is the starting point for his paintings that are both personal expressions and "tributes" to the particular experiences of the community. From his painting series *Et Al #6: A Collaborative Painting With The Montagnards*, Drake reflects on the experience of the Montagnards, aboriginal peoples from Vietnam, who sided with the United States during the Vietnam War. He spent a Sunday afternoon collecting doodles at Pastor Y Hen Nie's church in North Carolina. Drake describes the painting:

> I have chosen to visually reflect their struggle for survival by creating a vine or snakelike figure running through it. This vine represents the attack on their way of life from the war, Communism, and now life in the USA . . . Some recognizable images in the work include their traditional home on stilts, chickens, a well, a tree stump, rain cloud, skull, and soldiers fighting. The latter was provided to me by a 10-year-old Montagnard child, who graphically recounted the battles his people have faced with the Vietnamese. The red line running down the middle was something I borrowed from their traditional weavings. They are usually black with a red strip down the middle. If you look closely in the lower right corner you can see an airplane. To me this represents both their travels to the US and the communist bombers who use(d) to attack their villages.[23]

Drake's current project, *What Divides?/What Divide?* takes on international tones as he "examines issues surrounding human conflict and separation."[24] Working both in person and by Internet, Drake is collecting images and comments from "communities that are at odds with one another."[25] Working with both communities, Drake will create a painting inspired by the participants. The two paintings will then be paired together and exhibited as a diptych. His first diptych in the series will center on the issue of illegal immigration along the United States/Mexico border. The paintings not only translate community experiences into visual form but also act as mirrors into the world of "the other."

A Box, a Mirror, an Opening

A strong thread moving through each of our creative paths is the willingness to let chance mark the artwork and its outcome. Whether it is

McLaurin waiting for a meditative object to arrive in her mail box, Drake waiting for a doodle to appear, Friedman listening for the history of an antique to reveal itself, Sapin observing the pattern of a visitor's pathway through her installation, Ogata reacting to the nuances of his subject's gait, Voelcker stepping into a piercing parlor, or Rendino Zaentz finding yet another gesture of strength, the art reflects acts of co-creating. Each provides an entry point for us to step into "the black box" through a door of our own choosing, with a gaze into a mirror of our own making.

These actions, performed with intentional vigor, over time become personal rituals that lead artists and their audiences into new worlds. Actor Eric Booth, who advocates awakening powers of creativity in all people, affirms this idea, "In a very direct way, the connections we make while exploring a worthwhile world reconfigure our inner scripts; the fresh understandings provide more satisfying ways for us to encounter what we meet in life."[26]

---

[1] John Mayne and Coleman Barks, trans. *A Buddhist Library*. August 27, 2006.
[2] Miriam Schapiro. Over Time: A Forum on Art Making, in *M/E/A/N/I/N/G,*. Susan Bee and Mira Schor eds. Durham & London: Duke UP, 2000), 247.
[3] C.M. Judge, *Untitled*, previously unpublished, 2007.
[4] Véronique Sapin, "Artist's Statement," e-mail to the author. August 9, 2006.
[5] Ibid.
[6] Ibid.
[7] Judge, *Untitled.*
[8] Cathy McLaurin, "Artist' Statement," e-mail to the author, August 10, 2006.
[9] Ibid.
[10] South Indian designs.
[11] Lisa Hoke, Working Conditions: A Forum on Art and Everyday Life by Younger Arts in *M/E/A/N/I/N/G,* Susan Bee and Mira Schor eds. (Durham & London: Duke UP, 2000), 304.
[12] Josh Friedman, "Artist's Statement," e-mail to the author, April 9, 2006.
[13] Ibid.
[14] Ibid.
[15] John D. Loori, *The Zen of Creativity: Cultivating Your Artistic Life* (New York: Ballantine Books, 2005), 150.
[16] Elsa Voelcker, "Arts Council," e-mail to the author, April 12, 2006.
[17] Judge, *Untitled.*
[18] Paula Rendino Zaentz and C. M. Judge, Artists Statement, 2005.
[19] Todd Drake, *The et al Series*, Todd DRAKE Community Influenced Art. http://www.tdrake.com. Access date August 10, 2006.
[20] Judge, *Untitled.*
[21] Todd Drake, *The et al Series.*
[22] Ibid.
[23] Ibid.

[24] Ibid.

[25] Ibid.

[26] Eric Booth, *The Everyday Work of Art Awakening the Extraordinary in Your Daily Life* (Lincoln, Nebraska: iUniverse.Com, 2001) 174.

Works Cited

Booth, Eric. *The Everyday Work of Art Awakening the Extraordinary in Your Daily Life*. Lincoln: iUniverse.Com, Inc., 2001.

Drake, Todd. "Artist Statement." Todd DRAKE Community Influenced Art. http://www.tdrake.com.

——. *The et al Series.* Todd DRAKE Community Influenced Art. http://www.tdrake.com.

Friedman, Josh. "Artist Statement." E-mail to the author. April 9, 2006.

Hoke, Lisa. "Working Conditions: A Forum on Art and Everyday Life by Younger Arts," in *M/E/A/N/I/N/G*. Susan Bee and Mira Schor ed.. Durham & London: Duke University Press, 2000. 301-316.

In Motion Magazine. *Alice Lovelace Talks About Community-Based Art*. January 27, 2007. http://www.inmotionmagazine.com/altulsa.html.

Loori, John D. *The Zen of Creativity Cultivating Your Artistic Life*. New York: Ballantine Books, 2005.

Mayne, John, and Coleman Barks, trans. *A Buddhist Library.* http://www.abuddhistlibrary.com/Buddhism/H%20-%20World%20Religions%20and%20Poetry/Poetry/Rumi/Today.

Schapiro, Miriam. "Over Time: A Forum on Art Making," in *M/E/A/N/I/N/G*. Susan Bee and Mira Schor eds. Durham: Duke University Press, 2000.

Zaentz, Paula Rendino and C. M. Judge, *Artists' Statement*, Unpublished. 2005.

COACHTV: COLLABORATIVE PROCESS FOR UNDERSTANDING

EMILY R. EASTRIDGE
AND RAISHAD J. GLOVER

CoachTV is a composite of images, actions, thoughts, sounds, and words created and arranged by Emily Eastridge and Raishad Glover. Raishad and Emily have been working together closely since 2003 and draw upon their contrasting personal histories, current surroundings and mutual brain-picking for inspiration and material. Given their very different artistic approaches and mental techniques, Emily and Raishad have been challenged by their occupation as collaborative artists in understanding and explaining of their collective process to themselves, each other and their audience. Often the initial ideas and interests of the two artists differ entirely in content and finding common ground for united expression is a difficult endeavor. However, by vying to listening to each other with absolute openness, genuine curiosity is often aroused. Similar sympathies are frequently discovered and from there, the artists are able to embark on projects that satisfy their respective absorptions.

CoachTV would like now, to give you an example of the individual interests of its two artists and then display the results of the combined mulling of both. Here at CoachTV, we believe that the employment of openness, cooperation, conversation and compromise are essential to opening new doors to understanding and ultimately, to social advancement.

Raishad J. Glover

Without trash we loose respect
we loose respect of the disrespected
giving credit to the non achievers
it takes garbage to understand life
because life sometimes equals crap
and trash equals love

we need this
so we pray
we bow our heads
and remember
remember to "ask"
meditating on trash

some people call it crap
but
trash and crap can relate
relate to words
words such as
sluts... rags...
and... shacks
begging
'cause, sometimes
we forget
forget our
sluts... rags...
and shacks
"yeah that's right"
trash... crap...
and garbage.

I want that

I want that
that so called
garbage
garbage known from
that
jazz... disco...
and rock
"give me the niggers,"
known with the garbage
including
gooks... fags...
and white trash on the block

no

no longer will i respect
the given
ignore
the struggle

or...
not recycle
the cycle
no more
and no longer may the trash lay
lay in our deceivers hands...
it takes garbage to understand life
because life sometime equals crap
but as for that trash
trash equals love.

Emily R. Eastridge

Smartly dressed in the height of Back-To-School casual fashion, two sweethearts lounged sloppily upon one another, though not so oozingly sweet as to offend their fellow passengers. The undeniably adorable teenagers gazed fondly at each other, oblivious to the rocking subway cacophony surrounding them, their respective heads bobbing and swaying in gentle consent to the beats supplied via their individual headsets. Ubiquitous iPod ear buds dangled from jaws and tangled around the lovers' limbs like smitten fingers and crept eventually into deep, stylish pockets.

After observing this tender duo for just a few brief moments, one may ascertain, most certainly, that they were bedazzled and awestruck by one another. However, this romantic moment existed on two contrary planes of understanding. Rather than sharing a tender experience, the two lovers were conducting and receiving two very different, musically tailored situations. Audible to those within close proximity, the music emitted from the various headphones was strikingly different from its counterpart in regards to color and genre. The tuned-in bodies were subtly responsive to the beats, and as the two beheld and held each other, their gestures articulated independence. Kisses darted and lingered, synchronized with their respective instrumental solos. Hands glided in measures and pre-bedroom eyes of puppy-love adolescence batted in varying tempos. The dramatic soundtracks heightened each lover into star-crossed smiles. Grooving on fabricated space, the pair wallowed in their constructions, oblivious to their partner's particular experience. I do not mean to "tsk" or judge these lovers, but one must wonder at this latest social phenomenon. Could it be possible that there is a trend towards the stringently personal experience? Are portable DVD players, home entertainment centers, Walkmen, Discmen, and iPods seducing us into never ending daydreams? Are we synthesizing our communities? If so, what lies ahead for the communication and perception of technologically modern humanity? One may fancy that eventually MySpace will be MyIdentity, indefinitely. Perhaps, in time, individuals will be able to present themselves to the world framed in their preferences, customized settings to be projected onto other cosmetically digital identities. Screen names, nicknames, and alter egos are interchangeable. Soft and hardware define the moment.

So here I sit, guiltily pondering this notion, typing languidly on a beautiful day amidst the public of the park. My laptop resides with me in the shade and absorbs my imagination. Every so often, the odd Frisbee or rambunctious child captures my withdrawn attention for a few fleeting moments. Ultimately, I enjoy the fresh air from the hermit's vantage of my mental perch. I imagine that if my contemporary "notebook" was a notebook of the traditional sorts, my mind would be similarly inwardly involved. However, the quiet hum of an especially dreamy track resonating off of my machine's internal speakers sets a tone that I find particularly engrossing. All in all, my present reality is a hybrid of digitized reflection, grass, sky and urban society. I find my combination of environmental elements to be soothing, rather perfect actually. I wonder if perhaps this is truly a dismantling of reality, or perhaps a mere luxury to be enjoyed. Then, quite subtly, I stop wondering at all.

CoachTV: The resolve of separate interests

After reviewing the two articles of interest above, one realizes that the artists of CoachTV are drawing upon their fascinations and expressing them in two very different fashions. The initial meeting of these separate minds is, at first, often daunting. Where do the artists begin to find commonality? How will these ideas be developed collaboratively? Discussion, elaboration, openness to difference in personal experience and attentiveness towards a greater picture are a few techniques CoachTV employs to reach understanding. Here, Raishad and Emily have brought their respective focuses to the table: Raishad with his poem about the beauty of trash and Emily about her concern for technology and social relationships. In brainstorming the possible connections between the two subjects, CoachTV identifies technology as a spring for trash. Technology, with its relentless forward motion, consistently discards and outdates itself, often resulting in some of the most beautiful and useless garbage ever. Looking for a connection on the flip side of the issues, CoachTV recognizes the social value in regarding and evaluating trash. Trash is a mass generated by and committed to a whole community. In order to responsibly take care of trash, people must snap out of their privacy and really communicate with each other. Also, trash will not vanish with the press of a button, so stepping outside of the digital realm is imperative for environmental repair.

CoachTV finds its approach to collaborative thought to be equally helpful outside of the realms of art. By simply attempting to look thoughtfully at the entirety of a person's concern, one may discover a common ground, despite initial apprehensions. People rarely agree upon much, which makes finding those threads of understanding all the more important. The artists of CoachTV hope to sustain this mental approach in a world in which people are harshly divided in opinion. Our mutual consents may not be enough to make us all allies, but they will at least keep us human in each other’s eyes, which unfortunately seems to be a goal in and of itself, at this point in history.

PART IV: THE WORK

ARTIST AS SCHOLAR: SCHOLAR AS ARTIST

JENNIFER COLBY

Creating visual art can contribute to our ways of knowing.[1] Digging deeper to understand female experience through the arts is a territory of exploration that is being cultivated by artist-scholars, women who are both practicing visual artists and scholars.[2] In academia we divide the disciplines, in the art world we divide functions: one is a painter or a gallery owner, an art historian, or a photographer. Women who are artist-scholars are both creative producers and reflective scholars, and often they are community art activists and visual art curators. I will explore the contribution of visual knowing and feminist methodologies to scholarship through an exploration of the concept of an artist-scholar, and through the example of my own life as an artist-scholar.

Traditionally within scholarship in the arts, critics and historians take a distanced "objective" view of the artist living or dead whose art they are making meaning from. They explore works of art perhaps without the context of the life of the artist, and may fail to recognize the voice of the artist's own reflection. Feminist methodologies have proposed engagement and respect for the voice of the artist.[3] I am proposing a class of integrated artist-scholars as another means for creating engaged scholarship and meaningful artwork. What happens when the scholar is making meaning out of her own art, or looking at a group of contemporary artists that includes her? In this situation, the scholar who is also an artist brings to her study the unique perspectives she holds as a practitioner of art. Much like the participant observer in anthropology, the positionality of the artist-scholar is complex because of self-identification with the process of making the art. This position presents unique insights, but also the type of issues inherent in the complexity, for example, the question of how the scholar actually influences the research by her participation. I believe the insights gained are worth the risks and create a new way of doing scholarship.

Art inquiry would derive a great deal of knowledge and perhaps be able to escape from its hierarchical claims by examining the methodologies of other research fields, like anthropology, theology, and other social sciences. By investigating the areas where participatory or action research has enhanced the fieldwork of other disciplines, visual arts research could be enhanced. The committed self-aware researcher creates inquiry that leads to action in the world, problem solving for a particular situation. The myth of pure objectivity and the distanced observer-researcher is blown to pieces in this postmodern research paradigm. Feminist discourse has brought to the forefront these types of research methodologies.[4]

Feminist scholarship brings to research an activist stance. Feminist epistemologies acknowledge personal experience as a way of knowing in research methodologies. Through investigation and exploration, women have brought to awareness untold stories from the past and present, from their own experience and the experience of the communities in which they are active. Action research takes inquiry out of the ivory tower.

The artist as scholar also takes the artist out of an isolated studio into a context of investigating the community. Through art making itself, she investigates the world. Scholarship is used to inform her art making, and visual representation of scholarship, interrogatory and provocative, digs deeper into the knowable, offering a visual synthesis of action research. This creates insights into collective histories, with a strong sense of agency, and the outcome of the research will be meaningful to the community and to her own progress as an artist. When teaching and learning about art history, students who are artists want the information for the purpose of improving practice. The very engagement in that practice makes the artist-scholar an action researcher. These great shifts in scholarship have opened the door to women doing research that is personally meaningful, and often about their own subjective experience as an artist. The taboo against the artist being an intellectual engaged in the world rather than being "merely" a producer of content and form, which is analyzed by others, has been lifted. Artist-scholars are defining their own art worlds, curating, writing, collecting, and producing art that is relevant to their communities.

During the 2006 Women's Caucus for Art conference in Boston, I chaired a panel called "Artist as Scholar, Scholar as Artist," where I invited Patricia Rodriguez, artist and curator, to speak about new research she is doing on the inequities in academic jobs for Chicana artists; Kira Carillo Corser to talk about the research that she does as preparation for her photography series on homelessness, healthcare, and drug abuse; Tricia Grame to speak on her scholarship on her own visual work in comparison to poet Anne Sexton; and Elinor Gadon to speak to her role as a scholar in developing a Women's Spirituality PhD program that honors the visual arts.[5] Each woman offered an example of a life as artist-scholar. One of the reactions to the panel was a comment from an audience member who had not imagined that the artist-as-scholar panel would be so much about activism. I realized that I have made a great assumption in my life that activism and social justice is a norm that I work towards, and I have for so many years worked towards a type of scholarship that is grounded in community needs. I forget that others may continue to have a view of scholarship as elite and distanced, which continues to discourage artists and others to take up scholarship. We have constructed an art world with distinct parts, historians, critics, curators, all playing their roles in determining the value of the artists' production. We have created separation and a hierarchy that marginalizes the visual art maker, even though her works are the content of the art critique. This puts the scholar in an ivory tower above the community from which her research is drawn.

Fortunately, artists and scholars have turned this paradigm on its head in many areas, refusing to create work only for the market, creating environmental or community-based art and scholarship with an agenda of problem solving and community building over commercialism. As these strategies intervene in the structure of the market and academe, the artist regains some control over the production of information about her work, especially if she herself writes about it and adds to the scholarship and dialog. It also appears that the disciplinary boundaries are becoming more permeable. I know many women who are embracing all these roles: artist and writer, artist and gallery owner, artist and historian. Although there is still a strong notion that you need to choose art alone to be a great artist, many artists today are more well rounded, pursuing many areas and finding that their gift of being an artist, thinking like an artist with visual literacy, lends itself to important insights in many areas of their lives and in many career paths.[6]

My own life is an example of an artist-scholar. Being an artist has always been a core part of my identity, but it has always intersected with scholarship and activism in some way. I have both written about art and culture and curated exhibitions, and my scholarship and curating is influenced by my identity as an artist. I look at the world with visual literacy. When I studied biology at the University of California, I relied on my visual acumen for my research on invertebrate marine life. I used my drawing skills not only to illustrate marine biology, but also to actually aide in discovering facts about the development of sea urchin larva and the gastronomy of sea slugs. It may have been easier to take photographs of the stages of larval development, but through drawing I was seeing and observing the subtle changes that led to my new knowledge and contributed to my research. I was as a visual problem solver. Realizing that my visual strengths were important, I later shifted to focus on art for its own sake, but I continued to use visual language to research new territory: my own subjective experience and the stories and life situations of human communities.

The visual exploration of human stories captured my attention as I worked in political activism. After viewing museum after museum in Europe, I was given a sense of the purpose of visual art and I pursued my bachelors and masters degrees in painting and printmaking. Meanwhile I was engaging in radical politics during the 1980s, mostly focused on supporting the liberation of women and people of Latin America, as well as that of refugees coming to the United States. In my seminal work "Border Crossings,"[7] I was able to capture the stories of men and women at the three borders I had personally crossed, between Argentina and Chile, Nicaragua and Honduras, and the United States and Mexico. Experimenting with acrylic and collage on 7-foot-high two-sided "banner paintings," I told these stories with visual clues, while attaching written versions of the story to barbed wire and other structures. This visual scholarship was activist in the way that it told the stories and also gave voice to a community. In the viewing of the installation, both the art patrons and the Salvadoran refugees themselves saw the power of visual storytelling. I invited the viewer in through visual beauty to see the hard-to-imagine tragedies of people whose family members had disappeared or lost their lives and yet who struggled to live productive lives despite the political complexities of imperialism in their countries. My inspiration had been working with the poorest women of Buenos Aires, Argentina, during the military regime and later leading trips to Nicaragua to understand the power of the Sandinista Revolution. My activist scholarship contributed to my visual art installation, and my visual ways of knowing contributed to my scholarship.

Next, I was challenged to weave together my art as scholarship by developing theory while a graduate student at the Graduate Theological Union in Berkeley, California, which offered a strand of study in Theology, Religion, and the Arts. Feminist and Latin American liberation theologies offered me a circular methodology for research that engaged the praxis of community or political work in informing one's scholarship.[8] In my thesis, I would add visual art making to that methodological circle. I expanded my banner paintings to include a Midrash[9] on women of the Torah. So my scholarship on biblical women linked to the stories of Latin American women and lead to the installation "Face to Face."[10] I proposed that visual art could be the culmination or expression of the construction of theology or an element that informed the theological task at hand. Even today, after leaving the church and theology for women's spirituality, I find the strength of these feminist and Marxist models helps me to construct research that honors the circle of praxis, inspiration, social analysis, and creative expression to create meaningful scholarship that is both grounded in the community and useful for an activist trajectory. Cornel West and others have been able to glean from this important theological work and apply it to the visual arts.[11] Artists can find their role in the community process to be an important site for engagement. Scholars can articulate the meaning-making process of community praxis in the arts as a site for cultural change.

While continuing my art making, I began to focus more and more on curating exhibitions. I found the scholarship involved in bringing together a vision for an exhibition to be another example of the intersection of being an artist and scholar. After 16 years curating more than a hundred exhibits at the Bade Museum and at Galeria Tonantzin, I find the curatorial process both a unique form of scholarship and an art form, (especially since I hang all my exhibitions). Theme shows have been my specialty, and they give an opportunity to explore an issue that is prevalent in the culture. At the Bade Museum, I was curating for the audience at the Graduate Theological Union. Through the arts, I brought into the theological debate many community issues. A series called Art as a Healing Force led to my teaching a course with that name and using the exhibition series as a "text" for the course. A yearly exhibition at Galeria Tonantzin in San Juan Bautista called Images of the Virgin led to my dissertation topic.[12] I brought together artists and scholars in a yearly conference, and this dialog as well as ten interviews of Anglo and Latino artists was the source material for my exploration of how artists transform the image of Our Lady of Guadalupe in their art. Scholarship on Guadalupe, an important figure in Mexican identity, and feminist questioning of her impact are important explorations at the intersection of religion, art, and feminism.[13] I was able to bring to this discussion the perspective of an engaged artist and a person living in the bicultural area of coastal California, in the northern reaches of Aztlan, the mythical homeland of the Mexican people and source of Chicano pride. By engaging in cross-cultural inquiry, I am able to pose questions for my community and for my students who live in this multicultural reality.

Most recently, my scholarship on Guadalupe in my community, a rural area of California, led to a major humanities project and exhibition on the local watershed.[14] Here, all my previous work as an installation artist and curator, humanities scholar, interviewer, and collector of stories, as well as my early understanding of the natural world through biology and visual inquiry, were combined in collaboration with others in the community who had skills in multimedia. We produced an exhibition and a CD.[15] This project highlighted the stories of children, farmers, native Mutsun Ohlone, sand miners, and biologists, and came to the conclusion that there are many challenges confronting the river and its watershed. From discovering that the river was central to the cosmology of the Native peoples of the area and that the bird habitat was lost in wanton destruction of trees, to stunning the community with the visual impact of painting, photography and video of this neglected river and securing the designation of the Pajaro River as the number one endangered river in America in 2006,[16] this project was activist art and scholarship at its finest. For me, it was also a leap into collaboration and the use of skills in grant writing and holistic visioning of a community and its political processes.

These examples from my life story as an activist artist and scholar can be added to a chorus of other lives of engagement, artists who are writing and curating and engaged in their communities. Each of us is making an impact on how the arts are perceived in our society. I am engaged daily in preparing college students to become liberal arts scholars and multicultural community builders. I introduce research methodology and encourage them to explore their visual acumen. My students are future elementary school teachers and their contribution to future generations having visual literacy and engaging in scholarly inquiry will be great.[17] The more that women and people of underrepresented cultural groups become engaged in inquiry, the stronger our voices will be in the academe. This transformation of scholarship is creating a new view of the world, informed by previously forgotten segments of our society, including the visual artist.

For me, the true test of good scholarship is whether it informs praxis. With this in mind, scholarship that furthers artistic production and scholarship that furthers the progress of a community offers the highest value. The development of this perspective has been the result of feminism and other liberatory theories reaching into academia and breaking down the barriers between the scholar and the community. Obtuse discourse that offers no relevance to living artists or to living communities is self-serving, and not the type of scholarship that will take us forward in the twenty-first century. If we continue to prepare scholars who ignore community needs and do not see the importance of visual literacy, if we continue to prepare artists in a vacuum of visual production without scholarship, we will rob future generations of the richness of cultural production that will come from artists who see themselves as scholars and members of the community with a strong role as creators of culture in our society.

[1] Art as a way of knowing has been explored by Pat Allen, *Art Is A Way of Knowing : A Guide to Self-Knowledge and Spiritual Fulfillment through Creativity* (London: Shambhala, 1995) and others, my understanding is influenced by epistemological studies in women's ways of knowing and explorations of more than human ways of knowing. See Jaggar and Bordo, eds. *Re-visioning Knowledge. Gender/Body/Knowledge: Feminist Reconstructions of Being and Knowing,* (London: Rutgers, 1989), and David Abram. *The Spell of the Sensuous: Perception and Language in a More-Than-Human World* (New York: Vintage Books, 1997).

[2] In my 1987 master's thesis I coined the term artist–theologian. The term artist-citizen is another important construct. The term artist–scholar has been used to describe artists who write about art or are engaged in other fields of scholarship.

[3] Feminist methodologies have proposed valuing subjectivity. See Patricia Hill Collins. *Black Feminist Thought: Knowledge, Consciousness, and the Politics of Empowerment.* (New York: Routledge, 1990) and Uma Narayan and Sandra Harding. *Decentering the Center: Philosophy, Postcolonial, and Feminist World* (Bloomington: Indiana University Press, 2000) and Tracy Ore, ed. *The Social Construction of Difference and Inequality: Race, Class, Gender, and Sexuality* (London: Mayfield Publishing, 2000).

[4] See research methodologies by feminists like Shulamit Reinharz and Patricia Maguire.

[5] California Institute of Integral Studies Women's Spirituality Doctoral program founded in 1994 in San Francisco by Dr. Gadon.

[6] Internationally, the promoters of the concept of the "Creative Economy" have recently recognized that in educating a new work force we need the skills gained in the arts.

[7] Exhibited at Fresno State University Phebe Conley Gallery (1985) and at Nexus Gallery, Berkeley (1986). I studied with Joyce Aiken in the Feminist Art class at Fresno State University.

[8] My contribution to the field of theology and the arts was to make links to feminist and Latin American liberation theologies. For a definition of the field see Doug Adams and Dianne Apostolos-Cappadona, eds. *Art as Religious Studies* (New York: Crossroads, 1987).

[9] I studied with Jo Milgrom who developed the idea of handmade visual Midrash as a way to create visual commentary on scripture. See Jo Milgrom, *Handmade Midrash:Workshops on Visual Theology* (Philadelphia: The Jewish Publication Society, 1992).

[10] "Face to Face" was my thesis project for a Graduate Theological Union master's in Theology.

[11] Important work on liberatory practice in the arts has been developed by Cornell West and bell hooks.

[12] My dissertation: Jennifer Colby, *Transforming Tonantzin/Guadalupe: Cultural and Spiritual Identity Politics in Latina and Euro-American Women's Art in San Juan Bautista, California*, PhD dissertation, California Institute of Integral Studies, San Francisco, 2001.

[13] Guadalupe has been explored by artist-scholar Yolanda Lopez and by numerous feminist scholars. Many have attended the annual "Virgin Image Conference" in December. See http://www.galeriatonantzin.com. Access date June 10, 2007.
[14] Even with a national consciousness, I have chosen to act locally and create art about a sense of place which is both ecological and cultural. See Lucy Lippard, *The Lure of the Local: Senses of Place in a Multicentered Society* (New York: The New Press, 1997).
[15] Jennifer Colby, *Rumme Living River: The Pajaro River Watershed Experience* (Aromas, California: MMPublishing, 2004), see http://www.mmpublishing.com. Access date June 10, 2007.
[16] American Rivers designation; see http://www.americanrivers.org. Access date June 10, 2007.
[17] CSUMB is a 13-year-old state university with a vision for multicultural social justice teaching. My Liberal Studies students are predominantly Latino students looking to enter the teaching field.

Works Cited

Abram, David. *The Spell of the Sensuous: Perception and Language in a More-Than-Human World*. New York: Vintage Books, 1997.

Adams, Doug and Diane Apostolos-Cappadona, eds. *Art as Religious Studies*. New York: Crossroad, 1987.

Allen, Pat B. *Art Is A Way of Knowing: A Guide to Self-Knowledge and Spiritual Fulfillment through Creativity*. London: Shambhala, 1995.

Anzaldúa, Gloria. *Borderlands, La Frontera : The New Mestiza*. San Francisco: Aunt Lutes Books, 1987.

Aquino, María Pilar. *Our Cry For Life: Feminist Theology From Latin America*. Maryknoll, NY: Orbis Books, 1993.

Baumgarten, Barbara Dee Bennett. *Visual Art as Theology*. New York: Peter Lang, 1994.

Colby, Jennifer. "Face to Face: Visual Art As An Element in Feminist and Latin American Liberation Theologies." Master's thesis, Graduate Theological Union, 1987.

——. Transforming Tonantzin/Guadalupe: Cultural and Spiritual Identity Politics in Latina and Euro-American Women's Art in San Juan Bautista, California. PhD dissertation, California Institute Integral Studies, San Francisco, 2001.

——. Rumme *Living River: The Pajaro River Watershed Experience*. Aromas, California: MM Publishing, 2004.

Collins, Patricia Hill. *Black Feminist Thought: Knowledge, Consciousness, and the Politics of Empowerment*. New York: Routledge, 1990.

Dissanayake, Ellen. *Homo Aestheticus: Where Art Comes From and Why*. Seattle: University of Washington Press, 1992.

Gablick, Suzi. "Connective Aesthetics: Art After Individualism." In *Mapping the Terrain: New Genre Public Art*, edited by Suzanne Lacy. Seattle, Washington: Bay Press, 1995.

hooks, bell. *Teaching to Transgress Education as the Practice of Freedom*. New York: Routledge, 1994.

——. *Art on my Mind: Visual Politics*. New York: The New Press, 1995.

Hurtado, Aída. "*Sitios* and *Lenguas:* Chicanas Theorize Feminisms." In *Decentering the Center: Philosophy, Postcolonial, and Feminist World*, edited by Uma Narayan and Sandra Harding. Bloomington: Indiana University Press, 2000.

Jaggar, Alison and Susan Bordo, eds. *Re-visioning Knowledge. Gender/Body/Knowledge: Feminist Reconstructions of Being and Knowing*. London: Rutgers, 1989.

Langer, Susanne K. *Feeling and Form: A Theory of Art Developed From Philosophy in a New Key*. New York: Charles Scribner's Sons, 1953.

Lippard, Lucy R., *The Lure of the Local: Senses of Place in a Multi-centered Society*. New York: The New Press, 1997.

Maguire, Patricia. *Doing Participatory Research: A Feminist Approach.* Amherst: Center for International Education, University of Massachusetts, 1987.

Miles, Margaret R. *Image as Insight: Visual Understanding In Western Christianity and Secular Culture*. Boston: Beacon Press, 1985.

Milgrom, Jo. *Handmade Midrash: Workshops in Visual Theology.* Philadelphia: The Jewish Publication Society, 1992.

Ore, Tracy, ed. *The Social Construction of Difference and Inequality: Race, Class, Gender, and Sexuality*. London: Mayfield Publishing, 2000.

Reinharz, Shulamit. *Feminist Methods in Social Research*. New York: Oxford University Press, 1992.

Schor, Mira. *Wet: On Painting, Feminism, and Art Culture.* Durham: Duke University Press, 1997.

West, Cornel, "The New Cultural Politics of Difference" in *The Cultural Studies Reader* ed. During, Simon. London: Routledge. 1993, 1999.

CONVERSATIONS: THE PARALLEL UNIVERSE OF PUBLIC ART

PAMELA ALLARA, WITH ELLEN DRISCOLL AND MAGS HARRIES

> "The prospect of coming together, all classes largely represented, with a common purpose, not at all intellectual, competitive with none...each individual adding by his mere presence to the pleasure of all others, all helping to the greater happiness of each."
>
> Frederick Law Olmsted on Public Parks, 1870

In her talk for the "Public Memory" panel at the Women's Caucus for Art National Conference on February 20, 2006, in Boston, the artist Ellen Driscoll quoted the founder of America's public park system with approbation. In his rather dreamy statement, Olmsted articulated a utopian vision of community made possible by beautiful spaces accessible to all citizens. But can we imagine such a public space today, where people do not compete for ease of pedestrian access and who cordially acknowledge passers-by—even in the very park systems Olmsted created? Do we ever consider a stranger as adding to our pleasure, much less try to assure that our own public presence contributes to others' happiness? "Community" is something we now speak of in the past tense, something we nostalgically wish to recreate—an impulse that has often resulted in nightmarish, Disneyfied housing developments. What are the implications of this situation for public art at present? Artists practicing in the public arena generally hope that their projects will nurture or even help create a sense of community in the places where they are sited.

Artist-moderator Joan Ryan noted in her introduction to the panel, she remarked that public art is no longer predominately publicly funded in these conservative times. She asked how public memory, as embodied in works of art, might best be defined in an era when history has been reduced to propaganda.

Over the past quarter century, Mags Harries (faculty, Department of Sculpture, School of the Museum of Fine Arts, Boston) and Ellen Driscoll,

(Professor of Sculpture, Rhode Island School of Design) have produced consistently outstanding public art projects, while circumventing the hidebound "turd in the plaza" approach to public art.[1] Despite significant differences in their approaches, both artists have served as "catalytic agents," (in Driscoll's words), who have challenged assumptions about the built environments in which they have worked. For both artists, the element of time—as expressed on three levels: the history of the site, the movement of people's bodies through the created spaces, and the ongoing personal and shared experiences of the works—is essential to linking the present to potentially threatened histories. When so rooted, public art can encourage the healthy growth of communal life.

Despite the achievements of feminist activism during the 1970s, the public realm—representative government and its civic spaces—remains a man's world. Nonetheless, throughout the twentieth century, women artists have confronted the numerous obstacles presented by public commissions to create artworks designed to engage and challenge a broad audience. Beginning in the 1960s, the burgeoning realm of public art offered women artists inspired by feminism an arena that while circumventing the predominantly male-controlled museum-gallery system, simply landed them in the even more male-entrenched realm of politics. Despite the frying-pan-to-fire trajectory, public art offered the possibility nonetheless of a broad forum for the politically or socially concerned art resulting from feminist activism. Moreover, it drew on the skills women have been socially conditioned to develop: listening, working cooperatively, and reaching consensus.

Driscoll began her WCA presentation with a description of a New Yorker cartoon by Roz Chast that depicted the "Parallel Universes" of cookie baking on different planets. For Driscoll, public art is about creating a space where we can imagine lives that are not our own, in other words, a seemingly impossible world where parallel lines may paradoxically converge. The first step into the parallel universe of the public realm begins at the inception of a project, where the concepts are presented to potential funders, collaborators, and supervisors. As she observed during our conversation:

> Very often we are present in a room full of men—engineers, city planners, architects and on and on, and I will be the only female…other than the administrators from an arts agency, who are almost always women. So that's where the frontier is, in that all those guys have to wrap their minds around the fact that you're going to be dealing with them as an equal.

Expressing admiration for Ellen's backbone, Harries noted that she has recently adopted a different approach to confronting the inevitable "room full of men":

> At the beginning I thought I could do a lot, but I found that in a room full of men I was without much power. So I decided in 1990 to work with Lajos Héder [her architect-husband], because he can talk to engineers and architects and thinks of an urban space in a different way…Collaboration has proved very helpful in enlarging the scope for projects that would not have been possible otherwise.

Serving initially as a facilitator and translator, Héder is now a collaborator fully engaged with developing the ideas for their projects.

Whether artists work as a team or independently, public art is always collaborative, and while acknowledging that "collaboration" most often involves surmounting bureaucratic hurdles, both Driscoll and Harries deny that their public art demands a greater compromise than studio art production. As Harries notes:

> Public art is seen as an art of compromise, whereas the compromises needed to succeed in the gallery world are not discussed!...It's not as if you can make the big bucks like in the star system of the galleries. Public art often has to operate under the radar, because otherwise there would be an outcry over the funds spent for art.

In our culture, fine artists seemingly face a stark choice between the stumbling blocks of bureaucracy in the public realm on the one hand, and the raw competition of the market-driven private gallery system on the other. In reality, because the public realm has become increasingly privatized over the past quarter century, the line between the two has become increasingly blurred. (Perhaps the shrinking of public funding helps to explain why, in contrast to the 1960s and 1970s, so little art of protest against the loss of our civil and constitutional rights is being made today.)

Despite their drawbacks, it is important to recognize that collaboration and compromise in the public realm do not necessarily result in the dilution of the artist's original concept. When the creative artist serves as a "catalytic agent," the other team members can be empowered to tap into their own imaginative faculties and to contribute positively to the project's outcome. In contrast, when a private realm artist compromises her vision to gain acceptance by a gallery, the result is a loss of personal integrity and an art object of limited lifespan. As Carol Becker, Dean at the School of the Arts, Columbia University, has observed: "All art is…mystified by its commodification—its real social or anti-social value is obscured."[2] In addition, commodification obscures the fundamentally public nature of all art production.

As educators, Harries and Driscoll place the blame for this narrowing conception of art not simply on privatization and resulting commodification of art, but on the art schools as well, many of which continue to base their instruction on a formulaic, western-European modernist definition of art as "personal expression." Both bemoan the fact that most educational institutions have failed to develop a model of art making that is team based or to require students to read critical writing on public art.[3]

Over a decade ago, Carol Becker asked art educators to "reimagine" art schools. After all, students raised on the Internet simply assume that they will be sharing their work—i.e., collaborating—often over great distances. Yet art schools do not prepare students to understand the marketplace or the networked global culture they are entering, because to do so might "shake the foundations of our institutions in ways they need to be shaken." Becker argues that "…an artist can be formed only when all of the self is considered and placed within the societal context. This type of education…allows for the possibility of a true democracy in which everyone is capable of being, in [Joseph] Beuys's terms, 'co-creator of a social architecture.'"[4] The fact that this call for reform has fallen on deaf ears is exemplified by the uncertain future from year to year of Driscoll's public art course in the Rhode Island School of Design's curriculum. Because art schools have so often failed in their role as educators, it is hardly surprising that all too many art students in our age of hyper-individualism and atrophied communities graduate with little awareness that they have options other than that of entering the closed circuit of the gallery system. Their options, and their imaginations, are prematurely circumscribed.

Whether or not Harries and Driscoll find the term "feminist" to be relevant today, they were certainly inspired by the feminist approach to minimal sculpture developed by artists such as Mary Miss, Alice Aycock, Ursula von Rydingsvaard, and Agnes Denes in the 1970s. Further, both would agree that those basic concepts that critic Lucy Lippard has explicitly defined as "feminist values," including "…collaboration, dialogue, a constant questioning of aesthetic and social assumptions, and a new respect for audience"[5] are central to their practice. Finally, they acknowledge the importance of the artist's role as teachers: an effective public artist must communicate clearly and effectively. The following brief summary of aspects of their WCA papers will help clarify their processes.[6] In their presentations, both artists addressed public memory as a form of collectively held knowledge essential to a vital civic life. In summarizing their presentations, I will isolate one part of a larger work by each for the purpose of brevity; the reader is urged to visit the artists' Web sites for a full description of their projects.

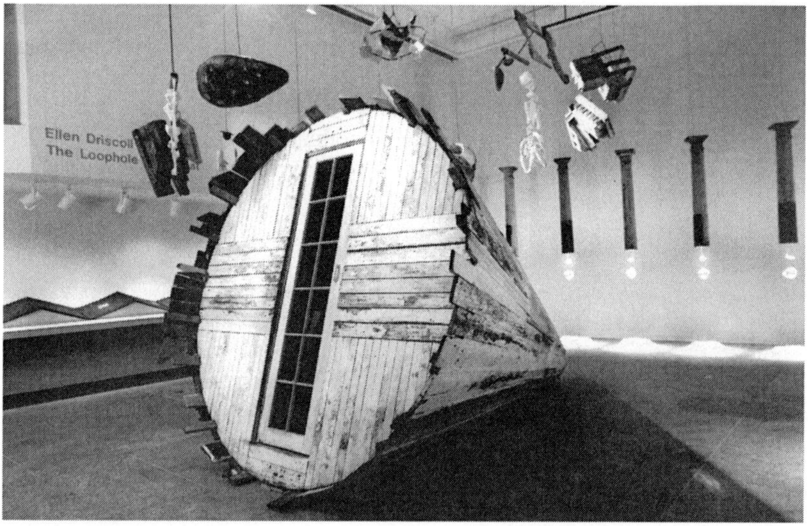

Fig. 4-1
The Loophole of Retreat, copyright Ellen Driscoll, 1991. Photograph by George Hirose.

Ellen Driscoll's *The Loophole of Retreat* (1991) (fig. 4-1), commissioned by the Whitney Museum at Philip Morris, is based on a poetic interpretation of the 1861 slave narrative, *Incidents in the Life of a Slave Girl*,[7] by Harriet Jacobs. Driscoll describes the work as follows on her Web site: "A large cone, constructed of salvaged wooden planks…could be entered through a door…The form and materials invoked the low eaves and claustrophobic space that Jacobs endured, as well as provisional dwellings that homeless women and men build on the street. With a small hole in the wall…the dark interior of the cone was a camera obscura." A cone, which diagrams our line of vision, permits both shelter and seeing when realized in material form. In choosing the title of Chapter XXI of *Incidents* for her sculpture, Driscoll took advantage of the various meanings of the word *loophole*—a small opening through which small arms may be fired; an opening to admit light or permit observation, or a means of escape, as from a contract.[8] In the 1850s, Harriet Jacobs "escaped" from slavery by confining herself in her grandmother's tiny garret for seven years, before finally finding her way north to Massachusetts. Through the hole she had created with a gimlet; she was able to see her children and also her slave owner, Dr. Flint. Her world, and the world of those on the outside, were parallel universes with limited sightlines: Harriet's was the fragmentary, tunnel vision of the hunted alien, Dr. Flint's the blindness of those in power, who choose to be ignorant of what is around them. In short, *Loophole* is a perfect metaphor for social inequalities then and now. By creating a connection with what was during the 1850s the new medium of photography, Driscoll extended the metaphor of the visual/visualizing cone to that of a memory box. Once entered, the shed becomes a camera obscura, reflecting on its back wall the image of the sculpted objects circling it on the outside. Everyday objects such as a shirt or a book are the stuff of Jacobs' world reflected back to us over historical time. In turn, the recreated artifact becomes a photograph, which, set in circular motion, becomes at once a documentary film and Jacobs's personal cosmology. The history of slavery in the United States is literally animated so that it can be experienced both physically (in the claustrophobic interior) and imaginatively, in the mind's eye. The parallel universes of slave and master were structured so that the master never recognized the slave's humanity, but Loophole of Retreat permits the contemporary citizen to experience such oppression firsthand. As Driscoll commented in her WCA talk, "By awakening feeling in the viewer's body, many people, (including school children), are given an understanding of the text"—and, one might add, a visceral understanding of the experience of slavery, which facilitates a connection between past and present and sparks a change in consciousness.

Most works of commissioned public art are meant to be permanently installed, but *Loophole* has traveled widely over the past 15 years to museums around the country, most recently to the New York Historical Society's exhibit, Legacies: Contemporary Artists Reflect on Slavery (June 2006–January 2007). As a migratory artwork, it mimics the diasporic condition of many trafficked workers in the global economy who are themselves reduced to slaves in factories or homes far from their place of birth. In 1991, when it was made, the work referenced the growing national disgrace of homelessness, but today it has the added shock of reminding us that slavery not only still exists but also is in fact a structural part of neoliberalism. Like the shadowy images on its interior, *Loophole* circulates, and as it travels over time, it accumulates meaning.[9]

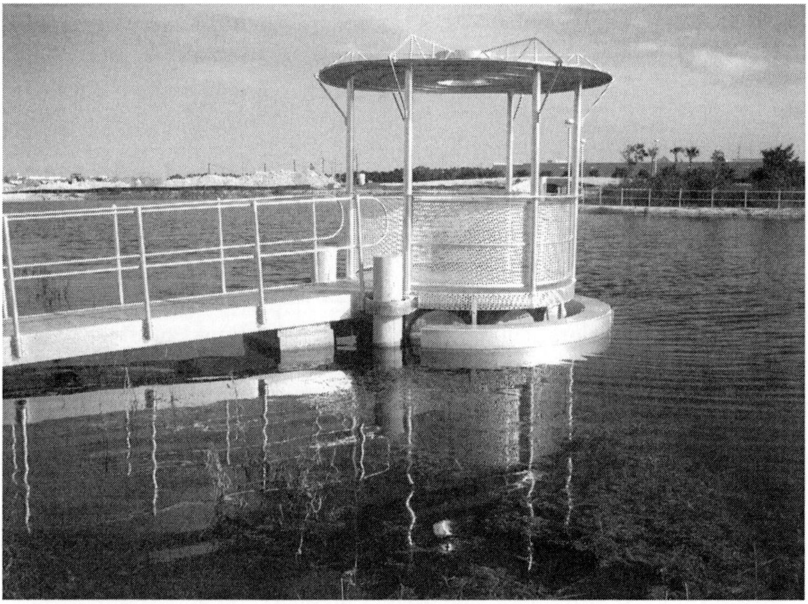

Fig. 4-2
Terra Fugit: Miramar Regional Park 1996–2006, Detail of Floating Landing. Copyright Mags Harries and Lajos Héder 2006. Photograph courtesy of the artists.

Like Driscoll, Mags Harries educates herself about the history of the region where she will be working and then creates art that will educate others. Like Driscoll, the umbrella term "public sculpture" embraces a wide range of projects, from museum installations to civic structures and public parks. If one were to attempt to generalize, however, Harries might be described as an archeologist of modern life, who excavates and reveals our culture to us through its buried detritus. Best known for *Asaroton* (1976), cast bronze garbage embedded in the walkway between the Haymarket food stalls and the Italian North End in Boston, Harries early on established a radically non-hierarchal approach to public sculpture that requires active discovery and interaction on the part of the pedestrian. In her presentation, Harries concentrated on a recently completed work, *Terra Fugit: Miramar Regional Park" (1996–2006)* in Broward Country, Florida. Situated near Fort Lauderdale in a rapidly expanding development bordering on the Everglades, *Terra Fugit (Land Flies)* (fig. 4-2) examines the impact of the newly-built condo units on the land, as well as the differing time frames of human and geological development. According to Harries, "…the town of Miramar is one of the fastest growing towns in the country, with no memory of the land and…no recognition of the value of an eco-system." The pun on "Tempus Fugit" ("time flies") and "Terra Firma" ("solid earth") points immediately to the ecological issues that were raised for Harries when she first came to the site. As she explains, she does not travel to a location "dressed for the occasion," that is, with a pre-existing set of ideas or plans, but rather draws her inspiration from the place itself: the built and natural environment. Harries and Héder began the project in 1996 before excavation had started on the park, so they had the opportunity to significantly shape the site. Development in that region usually consists of "demucking" the land, then blasting the land to create waterways, and finally using the fill to raise the level of the new development to above water level. In the process, the entire ecology of the landscape is changed. As Harries comments, "The scale and totality of these transformations is breathtaking…Even though the site is currently open marshland, its grading, water bodies and vegetation will be completely new, totally created by the hands and the machines, of humans." In the blasting process, boulders are seen as undesirable, and are usually thrown back in the waterway. In *Terra Fugit*, they became one of the elements that shaped the concept of the piece.

According to Harries, the blasted rock that was brought up from 200 feet below the surface was ancient and contained phenomenal fossils, inspiring her to contrast the slow time required to create the Florida landscape with its rapid, greed-driven development/destruction. She therefore insisted that at least one piece of earth, 60 feet in diameter, remain untouched. The resulting garden, *The Preserve*, is situated at the end of a curved walkway around the lagoon created by the excavation. There, each plant is identified and the history of its uses described, thereby permitting a clear contrast with the non-indigenous plantings brought in to "beautify" the park and condo grounds. The boulders themselves were used to create an "amphitheatre of memory" as well as seating. In effect, nature, literally supplanted in the rest of the area, becomes an archeological artifact in the artwork: the indigenous ecology has "flown," to be replaced by man-made development. *Terra Fugit* presents an argument for the recently arrived condo owners to consider: this new residential area cannot be called a community until it understands its eco-history, and addresses the fact that the life forms that previously sustained the environment have now been destroyed.

In this sense, *Terra Fugit* connects past with the future, creating a space from which to contemplate the future demise of the development itself. As Harries argued in her presentation, this part of Florida was under water eons ago, and as global warming increases and sea levels rise, predictions are that it may be re-submerged by as early as 2020. By contrasting human, natural, and fossil time, the humble weeds of "The Preserve" may well plant the seeds of a broader ecological awareness leading to community activism.

In her WCA talk, Driscoll commented that working in the public realm keeps you humble. Both the camera obscura of *The Loophole of Retreat* and *The Preserve* section of *Terra Fugit* are physically small spaces created from humble materials. Neither attempts a grandiose or monumental statement; instead, both create a retreat that permits a change of consciousness, a sort of cultural evolution that can connect to larger concepts. Through engaging in complex ideas, both disperse the media-induced cloud of simplistic, reactionary notions currently passing as history and current events. Both initiate a dialogue between present and past history in order to bring current social and political problems into focus, creating a small opening, a loophole, through which to anticipate alternative futures, new universes. The collision of systems precipitated by their public art projects generate, to borrow the phrase of sociologist Mark C. Taylor, "moments of complexity," of creative tension that can produce positive change.

Is this, then, the role of the public artist today? It is one important role, to be sure. Other activist or interventionist artists, such as Suzanne Lacy or William Pope L., also work with communities, and create events that shift community perceptions, even though they may well not leave a lasting visual object. Harries and Driscoll, on the other hand, are sculptors who create permanent installations. As a result, they must anticipate not just present, but also future readings of the work. By recuperating history, they can also begin to formulate a vision for the future in the memories of those who experience the art. As Driscoll remarked in a recent interview with artist-activist Karen Frostig: "Each piece has a different learning curve attached to it. In every case, I am passing large amounts of information through the eye of a needle. What changes are the things I learn when doing that."[10] That learning curve leaves the ball in the public's court.

---

[1] This essay is based on the artists' presentations at 2006 WCA conference, as well as on our subsequent discussion on April 5, 2006.

[2] Carol Becker, "Reimagining Art Schools," Chapter 7 in *Zones of Contention*, 101 (Albany: University of New York Press, 1996).

[3] Indeed, it is horrifying to observe that even when new studio art buildings are created, architects must follow the faculty decree to chop the spaces into private

studio-rooms, as if a nineteenth century mode of production is relevant to the twenty-first!

[4] Becker, "Re-imagining Art Schools," 103.

[5] Lucy R. Lippard, "Sweeping Exchanges," in *Expanding Circles: Women, Art & community*, edited by Betty Ann Brown, 27 (New York: Midmarch Arts Press, 1996).

[6] The reader is urged to visit the artists' Web sites for a fuller introduction to their projects: www.ellendriscoll.net and www.harriesheder.com. Access Date June 10, 2007.

[7] Harriet Jacobs with L. Maria Child. *Incidents in the Life of a Slave Girl.* (Minneola, New York; Dover Publications, 1861, 2001).

[8] *Merriam Webster's Collegiate Dictionary*, 10th edition.

[9] *Loophole of Retreat* is a multi-part work including projected images on the floor and a monumental book of images; only the central sculpture is discussed here.

[10] Karen Frostig, 2006. "In the Studio, Ellen Driscoll: Transforming Transitory Space," *Art New England* 27 (2): 63.

Works Cited

Becker, Carol. "Reimagining Art Schools." In *Zones of Contention*, 101. Albany: University of New York Press, 1996.

Driscoll, Ellen. "The Spokes of the Wheel: Art Work, 1991–Present," http://www.ellendriscoll.net.

Frostig, Karen. "In the Studio, Ellen Driscoll: Transforming Transitory Space." *Art New England* 27, no.2 (2006): 63.

Jacobs, Harriet, with L. Maria Child. *Incidents in the Life of a Slave Girl.* Minneola, New York; Dover Publications, 1861, 2001.

Lippard, Lucy R., "Sweeping Exchanges." In *Expanding Circles: Women, Art & community*, edited by Betty Ann Brown. New York: Midmarch Arts Press, 1996.

Merriam Webster's Collegiate Dictionary, 10th edition.

PRACTICAL ECOFEMINISM

AVIVA RAHMANI

This essay introduces a term for and theoretical model for ecofeminism in ecological art practice. The term, "practical ecofeminism," is based on an evolution from an innocent, celebratory relationship to the earth, arguably predicated on feminist essentialism, to a recognition of and layered response to environmental damage done. That narrative unpacks a relationship between human rape, human disturbance of nature, and healing models for both. Practical ecofeminism is the work of artful repair to damaged ecosystems: environmental triage. It manifests theory in works, based on careful observations of natural phenomena. In this text, I will examine my own career to illustrate that story.

Women's bodies have always been sites of land conflict, proxies for political power, and fields of competition for resources and genetic domination. We are particularly revolted today over rape victims in Serbia or the Sudan. Yet, one in four women internationally, and one in seven men, even in peacetime, experience brutal private repression and physical rape that parallels the public experience of rape of natural resources.

The night I was raped by my fiancé, there was no blood on my face, as there had been four years earlier, when my father beat me. My mother didn't fly in the door to rescue me in response to my screams. There were no screams. I had learned helplessness in the face of shame and fear. My silence was cousin to the silence in the forest that masks subsonic cries from adjacent trees, when they are felled by clear-cutting, the panicked squeals of livestock led down chutes in slaughterhouses and the melodies of dying songbirds translated for us by Rachel Carson in *Silent Spring*.[1]

Women are affected disproportionately, globally by environmental problems.[2] Women are usually the family nurturers. When pollution and global warming disrupt growing cycles, deplete water, and sicken the environment, women are first responders to the crisis. But women who challenge powerful men and patriarchal systems over land use and land use policy are especially vulnerable. Women such as, Vandana Shiva,[3] Wengaari Maathi,[4] and Judi Bari[5], who have been in the vanguard of protests against environmental degradation, often become targeted for especially violent reprisals.

How might we remodel the aesthetics of land policy? The answers began taking shape for me as a child in a family of developers. I observed how conventional land development is extractive rather than supportive of healthy ecological diversity. I rebelled against how that work cast my father as hero, my mother as housewife-support victim, all at the expense of cherished ecologies. Family context and feminism would make land and gender-role issues inseparable and personal.

Seventies ecofeminism in art evolved from romantic idealism about goddess worship. It rode a buoyant late-century tide of international reformist political optimism. Liberated by birth control from inevitable pregnancies, women foresaw an eroticized and empowered theoretical future. Despite significant progress and earlier historical warnings, as from the trials of American suffragettes, many of us were unprepared for the decades ahead of infighting within the movement and cultural backlash around it. With several major exhibitions, 2007 emerged as a time to consider a more complex historical analysis of how women artists have been and continue to be culturally effective. But the role of environmentally conscious American women artists was scarcely noted. Yet many of those women, such as Mierle Ukeles and Betsy Damon, have been uniquely effective in addressing the ever-expanding list of human-induced ecological disasters.

Early in the century, in Germany's Bauhaus, experimental artists and movements challenged the social and cultural implication of what was good art. In the sixties in New York City and in the seventies, in Southern California, I was privileged to know and work with many of the seminal crossover thinkers who inherited that mantle, influencing my own work and that of others. They informed and re-invigorated my rigorous classical education in Europe and traditional training in the arts. In the late sixties, there were several people who affected me. Those included the writer Anaïs Nin, arguably a mother of the sexual revolution, and philosopher Herbert Marcuse,[6] who analyzed surrealism in the context of merging Freud and Marx. Artists such as Allan Kaprow (father of "Happenings"), John Cage and the Fluxus artists, who introduced Zen chance and ephemerality into art market discourse, were crucial to me as was Peter Schumann of the Bread and Puppet Theatre who worked with ordinary people to merge art and politics and the visionary Billy Kluver whose work with Experiments in Art & Technology (EAT), supported by Bell Labs, revived the tradition of merging art and science that went back to Leonardo DaVinci.

In 1968, I moved with my then-husband from art schools in New York City to San Diego. As a young artist and activist against the Vietnam War there, I set out to apply my theoretical understanding of the parallels between physiological responses to stress, such as, rape and environmental instability caused by human exploitation to performance work.

The American Ritual Theatre (A.R.T) (1968–71),[7] was a group I founded and directed. It led to the communal farming experiment *Synapse Reality* (1970). I called this commune an on-going performance event and sculpture, long before I'd heard of Hans Haacke or Joseph Beuys' "Social Sculpture" movement. I designed other alternative conceptual models, seminal templates for later thinking and work that challenged the land-human models of my childhood. Marcuse's lectures, which I audited at the University of California at San Diego (UCSD), plus his friendship and conversations with other faculty at Scripps and the Salk Institute, inspired me to think ever more boldly. It was at this time that I first became active in what was then called the Women's Liberation Front (WLF). Three feminist groups began in San Diego simultaneously, all of which I became active in. One formed by Martha Rosler was the first consciousness-raising group for WLF at UCSD. The second, called Nine Women,[8] formed by Eleanor Antin and myself, was the first feminist artist's group in San Diego. The third, was the newspaper, *Goodbye to All That.*

The *Synapse Reality* project developed in the midst of that intellectual ferment. It would be the first of a series of three site-models that culminated in *Ghost Nets*.[9] In addition, four more performative-conceptual works from A.R.T. embodied the seeds of practical ecofeminism: *The Meat Piece*, *The Pocketbook Piece*, *The Relationship as Art Form*, and *Stay, Wait, Look, Listen.*

The Meat Piece, filmed in 1969, was a tightly framed, close-up view of two hands manipulating a cow's heart. The raw meat of the dead animal's essential organ all too vividly and disturbingly evoked intimate human relations. The image was a metaphor for all of the disturbed gender-power relationships I had experienced and observed. Audiences responded with initial amusement to the voiceless allusions between the title and then-still shocking-to-see-in-public pornographic films. Giggles quickly segued to chilled silence. The metaphor was a mandala for rape, a dramatic counterpoint to Carolee Schneemann's 1967 similarly framed 1967 film, *Fuses*, celebrating orgasmic genital release.[10] Thirty-five years later, I recycled the *Meat Piece* image again, with the text, "We Raped the Earth" for Waterways, a show adjacent to the 2005 Venice Biennale, Vara Global Fine Arts.

The late sixties and seventies, particularly in California, were the era of encounter groups upon which many feminist consciousness-raising groups were modeled. These movements drew on similar, non-hierarchical models to dismantle repressive social constructs. I threw myself into that experience, researching how to deconstruct "insane" relationships. Consciousness-raising was a fundamental tool of late 1960s feminists. It unearthed rich raw material, including the validation we gave each other's responses to rape and helped launch the early Southern California performance movement that included my work.

Three young women walked out into the audience in 1968. Once seated on the floor, they emptied the contents of their pocketbooks simultaneously. Then each casually described the implications of why they carry each item, in intimate detail, without censoring either the object or context, whether a seduction, rape, divorce, or a one-night stand. For example, they described lipstick worn the night of an incident, or they recounted what they wore to get a police injunction against an ex-husband. As they did so, they made friendly eye contact with each other and the audience. They arose and left when the last woman had described and replaced the last item.

This was a type of collaborative relationship that gave attention to the objects we carry with us. Formally inspired by Cage and Fluxus Art, the stories of "ordinary/found" objects in these performances became audible and visible, enshrining and framing attention and making transparent, our relationships with these things.

The Pocketbook Piece performances were about the dispassionate democracy of investigation. Each element in a system is given equal and relational value. Giving attention creates life as much as it discovers it.

Such attitudes might link us to indigenous peoples and Eastern religions, who find sacred life in air, rocks, and soil. *The Pocketbook Piece* was an abstraction of the consciousness-raising experiences of those times. It was repeated many times, especially in Southern California, between 1968 and 1974, but never scripted or documented. The commitment of those times was to ephemerality. Alison Knowles presented it again in 2005, as an aspect of her *House of Dust* project, for which it had been performed and audiotaped in 1971 at the California Institute of the Arts in Valencia (Cal Arts),[11] the only surviving documentation of the performances.

The night I was raped, I knew there was a moment when my heart stopped. My entire life changed at that moment. The writings of Diana E.H. Russell[12] (1999) document the relationship between brutality, intimacy of connection, duration, and damage to the victim, paralleling what we observe in other natural systems under stress.

Entire biological systems become helpless when a threshold of abuse has been reached and then collapse, just as mine did the night I was raped. I was no longer able to regroup to my previous state. The assault of too many systemic insults rendered me helpless to sustain a spiritual center. Just so, we may consider that there is a "spirit of place". That spirit allows biodiversity, but under the stress of disturbance, it collapses.

Disturbance theory[13] is a branch of ecological and evolutionary biology articulated in the early eighties. It is the idea that systems can only adjust to change to a finite point. With sufficient disturbance, the entire ecology collapses to another state. Disturbance theory implies that just as some people never survive post-traumatic stress disorder (PTSD), neither do some ecological systems.

Synapse Reality, was designed at the same time that I was studying R.D. Laing's[14] theory of insanity, to illustrate a textbook. His premise was that acting out, even schizophrenia, is a message from the disturbed brain, a necessary systemic breakdown, to allow a healthier psycho-social stability to take root. As the Vietnam War wound down, the implied imperative was to create art as conscious antidote to the political insanity I was observing.

Synapse Reality was an exploration into ecological systems as raw material for art making, primed by research into behaviorialism and environmental stability. Besides being my first site-specific sustainable model, it was also the only one designed for a particular group of people: the A.R.T. troupe. All the original A.R.T. performers were also students of Herbert Marcuse at University of California at San Diego. Most of the women, were new-minted Feminists. That contextualized our philosophical approach to all the housekeeping details of daily life, making the household meetings as performative as the tasks.

The research I was doing into the parts of a healthy environment inspired me to create my own mantra: *Stay, Wait, Look, Listen,* a conceptual meditation-event about the ecology of places and relationships. The use of repetitive, text-based meditations became core to my practice. Arguably, that capacity to narrowly focus my attention was a skill that emerged as a survival mechanism, from my early experiences of gender violence. As part of *Goodbye to All That*, I continued to publicly explore and write about new forms to model personal and political change. What slowly became clear, however, was the ambivalence many feminists still feel about owning personal experiences of victimization. Whole bodies of feminist work, embraced by the media, emerged to privilege overt sexual affirmation over erotic ambivalence and the more complex disempowerment issues explicit in rape.[15]

The performance models that emerged from the A.R.T. work, including, *Stay, Wait, Look, Listen*, and what I observed in *Synapse Reality* became vehicles to consider environmental issues in more depth. I imagined, with other ecofeminists, a natural world that excluded rape. That vision included a powerful mix with technology, technology as a force for political inclusiveness rather than resource exploitation.

The Relationship as Art Form project started as a series of conceptual story-events about models for breaking gender conventions, relayed in casual conversations. In the late sixties I studied computer languages. Those schematics were information maps that became the basis of software design. I began mapping the software of relationships that for many women continue to be our primary reality. Those mapping investigations would segue into one of the most significant tools of my present practice.

The Relationship as Art Form went from stories to performance in a series of collaborative experiments. That interest became one of several motivations returning me to school at CalArts in 1971. I was attracted equally by the technology available there, and by many of the teachers. Thanks to Nam June Paik, Mort Sobotnick, and others, CalArts excelled in new electronic technologies. I considered the access I had to technology there to be my access to the future.

The Feminist Art Program at CalArts, in which I participated, had been established by Miriam Schapiro and Judy Chicago. I gained my MFA in 1974, with a double major masters in multimedia and electronic music. My most important mentors there, Sobotnick Allan Kaprow, and Alison Knowles, remained lifelong friends and influences.

The most significant collaborative work I embarked on at CalArts out of *The Relationship as Art Form* was *Ablutions*. That 1972 work about rape emerged from discussions between Judy Chicago, myself, and two other then-fellow students: Suzanne Lacy and Sandi Orgel. *Ablutions* developed content, imagery, and formal means I contributed from previous performance work with A.R.T., especially *The Meat Piece* and *The Pocketbook Piece*.

Arguably my most important ecofeminist work at CalArts was *Physical Education* (1972) and its water supply symbolism. Participants were invited to collect water from the school faucet into a small plastic bag. Then they were instructed to drive to the beach, stopping three times to collect a plastic teaspoon of earth and pour out a small of water until they reached the ocean. There, they emptied the contents of the baggie into the sand, replacing it with seawater, and then began the return trip. Journeying back, they once again replaced water with teaspoons of soil until they returned to the building. The remaining precious fresh water and arable soil were then flushed down the toilet, symbolizing how we continue to treat our natural resources.

The Feminist Art Program wasn't my only focus at CalArts. I continued experimenting with performance modeling as Allan Kaprow's teaching assistant. With Kaprow and other mentors, I engaged in the same kinds of lengthy conversations about modeling solutions, grounded in relational politics, that I had pursued with Marcuse. I thought then that these experiments were politically volatile, and welcomed the shelter of academia.

Access to technology prompted me to stay at CalArts, when the rest of the Feminist Art Program left. Chicago's overarching interest at the time was in immediate social reform. I wanted to connect that process to the environmental problems that remain unresolved today and knew technology would be a key part of that puzzle. However, many feminists then believed, as Chicago did, that only raw emotion could move an agenda of social change. She and others felt technology represented "male-dominated" thinking. It seemed arbitrary to me to divorce the passion of art from the power of technology.

Ecofeminism remained disassociated from technology for several more decades. There were scant examples of women exploring similar means in the seventies and fewer opportunities to pursue my interests after graduation. But the premises and technologies I studied at CalArts prepared me to restore the site of the *Ghost Nets* model, almost two decades after *The Meat Piece* and *Physical Education.*

Stay Wait Look Listen, My Symphony 1970–1974 was a collaboration with the ghost of Beethoven, his *Pathetique,* sonata and letters to his paramour. It was my most extreme modeling experiment. I imagined a relationship across centuries of time. That work taught me to iteratively monitor multiple layers of insight and perception. It served me later to monitor complex environmental fields as an ecological artist. Rehearsing the sonata over and over on school pianos, with guidance from the pianist Leonid Hambro at CalArts, I juxtaposed and mapped that acoustic data in a display of 65 of my personal diaries and sketchbooks, some meticulously mapping the symphonic structure of emotional interactions. Those notebooks were displayed in 1974 at Gallery 707, shortly before my M.F.A. graduation. Auspiciously, the opening was the same night and in the same building as the opening of the new Woman's Building in Los Angeles.

In the late seventies, returning to San Diego, I continued to look for lessons in nature. *Sunsets* (1976–1979)[16] was another experiment in *Stay Wait Look Listen*. Every twilight for three years, I photographed and painted the sunset as the colors sank into the Pacific from my then-ex-husband's Del Mar, California backyard. The view of the ocean horizon encompassed the geologically unstable offshore intercontinental shelf, where Reagan was threatening to install oil wells. With my ex-husband, I worked on the design and illustration of a brochure for Congress to educate them about the dangers, commissioned by the Scripps Institute of Oceanography. My participation in activist resistance and scientific presentations such as the one for Congress contributed towards forestalling those oil wells and taught me the basics of integrating aesthetic form, data, and political effect.

My second site-model was created for rural San Marcos between 1979 and 1985. It was the first one I planned in advance, based on regional studies of the larger patterns of natural resources and patterns of human demographics. This became an experiment in what I would come to define as *Trigger Points*, making analogies between acupuncture and regional planning, the theoretical basis for my present work.

Before purchasing the rural property of the site, I looked for maximum interspecies balance between biodiversity and human infrastructure. Still interested in technology but without ready access, I applied traditional gardening skills, permaculture, and biological research to materialize my vision. The San Marcos site still exists as an oasis of natural preserve of wildlife diversity, in the heart of urban sprawl now surrounding the University of California at San Marcos, which grew up around the site after I left California.

The inspiration for sustainable wildlife management I sought in the eighties, I found retrospectively in the nineties, in the examples of indigenous basket makers. Utilizing sophisticated means to monitor and protect constellations of natural resources, these respected women harvest their raw materials, acting as respected cultural and environmental custodians.

The irrationality of human violence, the elusiveness of healing and giving voice to the voiceless, continued to obsess me. *Floating Worlds* (1979–83),[17] a series of performances about parenting, took place as three years of the *Sunsets* slides dissolved behind participants (representing the first three crucial years of child-raising). As performers read and responded to personal letters from other artists about having children, I painted in eight large posters I had designed, that alternately portrayed women as victims or empowered, trying over and over to decide in real time whether I could care for a child in my studio, whether to bear a child in a violent world. Ambivalence in my audience was expressed in lively discussions after the performances. Many of the as-yet childless women asserted they could have a career and a child without conflict. But since I wasn't so sure, I didn't have a child.

In 1985, an interior mural collaboration with the teenagers at a facility for abused children explored how the residents felt about violence and what they thought healed it.[18] The imagery was realized in the context of inspirations about the natural world from the Native American Medicine Wheel. When the staff found the content of the mural so psychologically alarming that they sandblasted it, it confirmed to me how powerfully provocative a *Stay, Wait, Look, Listen* observation can be. Performing the *REQUIEM* project (1987–1989)[19] and the *Safety* project (1989), subsequently explored grief, happiness, and realistic safety. But by the late eighties, I had accepted that the vulnerability of fear and powerlessness in relational violence was the feminist third train rail that could destroy whomever touched it. It seemed professionally safer to own eroticism, anger, and intellect. The body of my work before 1990 had investigated the dynamics of relationship to place and "other." The next phase of my career applied what I had learned to scientific modeling with scientists.

Historically, the gendered roles of husbandry and housekeeping include care for the surrounding landscape that supports pastoral life. Urbanization still depends on rural sustenance. Press releases for my third site-model, *Ghost Nets*[20] (1990–2000), on Vinalhaven Island, Maine, declared that we had ten years to reverse disastrous environmental policies, calling it: "the decade of global choice." I proclaimed then, as my present e-mail signature still does, that, "what the world needs is a good housekeeper."

Good housekeeping creates a model for sane living. *Ghost Nets*, my first model outside California, set out to restore a degraded two and a half acre former coastal wetlands, the former town dump on Vinalhaven Island, Maine, a fishing village. At this time, as ecofeminist academic writing was becoming more rigorous,[21] my own research also became more systematic.

Choosing the *Ghost Nets* site was as practical as it was symbolic. The title was taken from the term for lost fishing drift nets, that strip-mine the sea, familiar routines can strip-mine us of hope. The two and a half acre site linked seventy acres of open wilderness in Class A migratory bird fly zones for two continents. Guided by readings in Darwinian island biogeography, I knew how systems die from edges inwards, as connections are lost. This site was an ecological edge, a connecting corridor for wildlife in a regional hotspot: a Trigger Point. I speculated that the restoration would reinvigorate the larger landscape. I also speculated that when we were done, we might calculate how many square feet of restored wetlands would generate how many saleable fish. The intent was to promote such restoration amongst coastal landowners.

I imagined the restoration site as an avatar [22] and forecast my own healing. It was a "Trigger Point" to catalyze a larger systemic healing for the Gulf of Maine, even as it would daylight the core of my creative power as an ecological artist.

The salt marsh beneath my dump had been buried for one hundred years by rip rap from the granite mining industry. Native American and Shinto beliefs, that rocks have spirits, inspired me to conceive that those rocks had been violated. Surely the site was experiencing PTSD. My question, that would take a decade to answer, was, had the baseline disruption been so profound and continuous that it would be irredeemable What is the threshold beyond which triage is hopeless? I set out to find ways to re-marry science and art in the service of the natural world, searching for tools of healing change and answers to my questions. Learning about Traditional Environmental Knowledge (TEK) was a major guide. My first action was to bring a Cherokee Elder, Grandfather Thunder Cloud, to the site to inaugurate the restoration of the uplands riparian zone, "The Trigger Point Garden." With Grandfather Thunder Cloud, we performed a traditional Native American Medicine Wheel and dance to inaugurate healing in 1991.

Two collaborators I found in the early nineties,—bioengineer and geologist Wendi Goldsmith, president and founder of the Bioengineering Group in Salem, Massachusetts, and Dr. Michele Dionne, biological ecologist, Director of Research at Wells Natural Estuarine Research Reserve (NERR), Wells, Maine, respectively, pioneered innovative salt marsh restoration work and wetlands research studies. They helped me restore the *Ghost Nets* wetlands in 1997. Working with Goldsmith and in-kind donations, we completed the daylighting, geomorphological shaping and planting in three days. My New Year's Card for 1998 was an image of the restored *Ghost Nets*, salt marsh presided over by Grandfather Thunder Cloud. In the sky the text was, "The environment was lost by increments, it can be restored by increments." I meant that the artfully giving strategic micro-attention, as in *The Pocketbook Piece,*" can have macro-effect.

Estuaries are the most fecund ecologies on earth. In 2000, Dr. Dionne, thanks in part to a grant from the Nancy H. Gray Foundation for Art in the Environment, did the biological productivity analysis for the site. Her studies confirmed that the site had all 18 indicator species for estuarine health.

Thirty-three years after my rape, I thought of the restoration as, “restoring the ultimate (degraded) cunt,” referencing the Old English definition of “cunt” as the site of hallowed fertility. *Ghost Nets* was my first site-model whose conceptual framework explicitly identified rape as a primary metaphor for ecological devastation. I then set out set out to effect further “environmental triage.”

Each site-model developed until then, had emerged a decade apart and resulted from a decade each of research and contemplation. But only *Ghost Nets* was remedial and designed to address larger landscape interpretations of degradation. It was the first site to collaboratively employ sophisticated theory and technologies to analyze and repair problems.

Just as the human body has meridians of electrical energy that can be activated with acupuncture, ecological studies tell us there are Trigger Points, “hot spots” of biological diversity on the global body upon which larger systems depend. That is often where people settle, attracting by the resources but ultimately degrading the original site, as the *Ghost Nets* site had illustrated when I first found it.

I explored this theory further, on a larger scale, in a series of working sessions with scientists, as part of a United Nations mandate on wetlands restoration monitoring protocols in the nineties. Then as a part of the Gulf of Maine Information Exchange (GOMINFOEX)[23] as we turned the century, I continued to *Stay, Wait, Look, Listen* to what I could learn from this research, much based in Geographical Information Systems (GIS).

At the end of *Ghost Nets*, the application of my *Trigger Point* theory of “good housekeeping” had evolved into my current project, *Cities and Oceans of If (C&OI)* (2000–present). *C&OI* has analyzed about 20 degraded sites internationally, as possible suitable sites for “environmental triage,” vastly expanding my applied observation strategies from *Physical Education* (1971).

In 1998, with Susan Steinman and Jo Hanson, founders of WEAD,[24] I initiated a panel for the 1999 College Art Association conference in Los Angeles, on the state of the art of environmental art (Off the Mainstream, Onto the Mainstream). That led in turn to the Ecoart dialog, an invitational listserve of almost one hundred international practitioners of ecological art[25] who over the next seven years, produced a series of shows, essays, books, and conference panels introducing a wide audience to ecological art. This was one more experiment in collaboration and relationships that would lead to a virtual *C&OI* in 2006.

In 2002, my ideas about catalytic events and *Trigger Points* came together as part of *C&OI* and led to the *Blue Rocks* project.[26] That work combined performance, installation and calculated risk. *Blue Rocks* identified another crucial wetlands I had studied on Vinalhaven Island, degraded by a too-narrow culvert. It initiated a model 26-acre salt marsh restoration for the North Eastern governmental agencies involved. As Chair of the Natural Resources Sub-committee for the Vinalhaven Comprehensive Plan, I had observed and had been motivated by how GIS[27] maps revealed the site's abundantly fertile ecological edges (fig. 4-3).

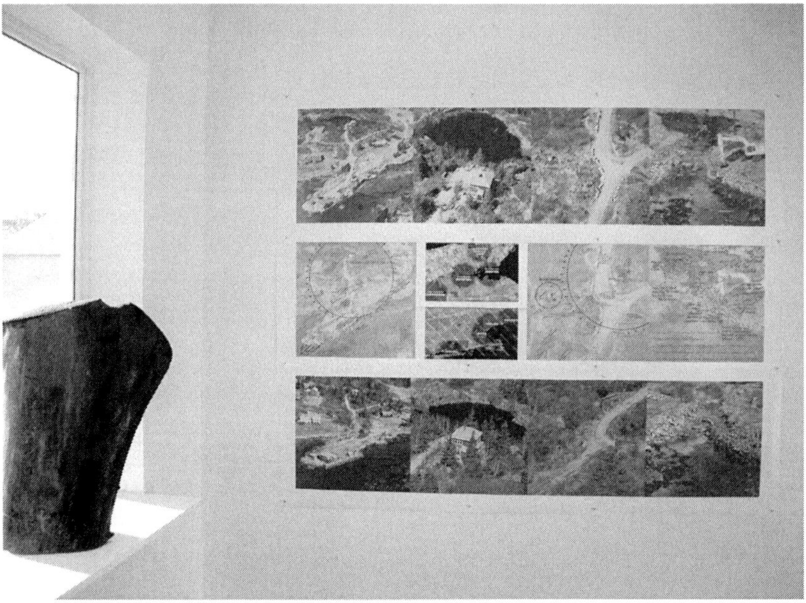

Fig. 4-3
Trigger Points Installation, Called to Action Art Sites Gallery, NY 2007, Aerial Photography under the direction of Aviva Rahmani, photographed by Ben Magro. Center images courtesy of Google Earth. Painted wood stumps and drawings by Aviva Rahmani.

As the locus of *The Meat Piece* was the chambers of a heart, the site of *Blue Rocks* was a place where the island geomorphology mimicked heart chambers surrounded by ocean. *Blue Rocks* consisted of painting seventy large glacial boulders blue, some more than 20 feet in diameter, along the degraded causeway. The local rocks embodied the spirit of the place with as much power as people. The vivid translucent color was a biodegradable slurry of buttermilk, moss, and pigment to grow more mosses, and elicited controversial attention. In the end, $500,000 of regional- and state-funded restoration, primarily from the U.S. Department of Agriculture brought back the wetlands and "flocks" of eagles.

Stay, Wait, Look, Listen also recurred in 2002, flowering in a commission for Arts-In-Transit, in St. Louis, Missouri. St. Louis is built in a floodplain. But most landscaping there eschews local vegetation that might contain floodwaters. The *Confluence* plan, based on indigenous vegetation and rock formations, would have provided serenity and passive education, through out the year for passengers coming and going to the train station at the University of Missouri at St. Louis and provided ecological modeling. Designed as a "Trigger Point" landscape installation, *Confluence* created a continually changing, patterned color display of indigenous paintings and rocky outcroppings. Part of the planned installation was a series of duratrans, graphic displays in the train stations illustrating details of how the plan would evolve. On each poster was one of the four words: "Stay, Wait, Look (or) Listen." The proposal provided space for people to consider different regional land use strategies. Although unrealized, it further expanded my ideas about why, where and how a "Trigger Point" can be chosen and implemented.

Stay, Wait, Look, Listen is a message about nature. As a member of an impatient race, the mantra cautions me to be mindful, teaching me to carefully develop, fulfill, and observe change. Continued monitoring of the *Ghost Nets* site guides the *C&OI.* But as with the consequences of human rape, at any given site, including *Ghost Nets,* it is unclear, once damage has occurred, whether recovery is fully possible.

In the first decade of *C&OI*, I began to question the extensive, exhausting traveling I was doing to achieve "ecological triage." Contemplating the devastating impact of Hurricane Katrina on New Orleans in 2005, provided my answer in 2006. I married technology to relational issues by inaugurating the first "Virtual Residency," as part of *C&OI.*

Katrina was arguably the most frightening recent example of the effects of human degradation to, and poor housekeeping of, our ecology in American history. During the early summer of 2006, uneasy about a plan to physically visit three separate international sites to design environmental interventions, I designed a month-long Virtual Residency.[28] Instead of engaging in jet travel around the globe, adding more carbon emissions to an already over-loaded earth, I stayed on my Maine island. From the *Ghost Nets* site, I studied and corresponded with other artists at the various locations I had planned to visit. I collected data on the problems at each site and compared them to each other. Accounts of that site work in *Ghost Nets*, New Dehli, India, Pescia, Italy, and Geumgang, Korea, and proposed interventions, were written about on my Web site blog. The resulting research, and observations about what was accomplished, including the work of the other on-site artists, was presented in two 16-hour "concerts." The Virtual Residency observed the circumpolar effects of global warming. It explored a model for "environmental triage," that did not spew jet fuel over the earth's waters as I traveled the globe to effect healing. The goal was to create an analog virtual community and culminate that in on-the-ground effects.

My Web site thus became a virtual *Trigger Point*, to engage broad participation in restoration areas, across great geographies. Arguably this was one more extrapolation of *The Pocketbook Piece*, the outgrowth of consciousness-raising more than three decades ago. This is the opposite model for action than that of the heroic individual acting *upon* the land or helpless human body of my girlhood. Rather, it represents a process of discovering experiential parallels and the means for inclusiveness.

My model for the Virtual Residency was in how terrorists have used the internet. If terrorists can use the net to cross boundaries to effect damage, then that tool of warfare can be re-tooled to effect peaceful solutions to ecological threat. The means I developed have continued as a series of "Virtual Concerts" online, conversations with international ecological art practitioners.[29] The same means were then employed to attend conferences, as European Sociological Association (ESA) in Lueneburg, Germany; to establish a collaboration with Dr. Jim White, carbon emissions expert, interim director of the Instaar Institute and chair of the Environmental Studies program at the University of Colorado, Boulder, Colorado, for Lucy Lippard's "Weather Changes" show on global warming at the Boulder Museum of Contemporary Art; and to participate in the 2007 Venice Biennale, as part of the Joseph Beuys' Social Sculpture event, "100 Days of Permanent Conference," with the international group, Cultura21, which emerged from ESA.

The models discussed, applied systems theory, to extrapolate from the experience of rape, a process of healing. Collectively, they represent a series of relational dialogues in time. The term *ecofeminism* has gone out of fashion. But this essay argues for reconsideration in a new light. The continuing rape of the earth horrifies most of us. Concern for this earth, the desire for innovative solutions that sustain her health as part of our own, are stronger than ever. Those concerns are grounded in real world issues. Scientists now project that hundreds of millions of people and countless other whole species of life will be casualties of weather changes by mid-century. We are already seeing that horror unfold. I have argued that we reconsider and recognize the validity of the metaphor of rape and recovery, as a paradigm for present-day ecological damage and repair. That conceptualization and manifestation points to a particular range of action: practical ecofeminism.

---

[1] Rachel Carson, *Silent Spring,* (Boston: Houghton Mifflin; Cambridge, MA: Riverside Press, 1962), 1–3.

[2] Mary Mellon, "Gender and Environment," in *Ecofeminism and Globalization: Exploring Culture, Context,and Religion*, ed. Heather Eaton and Lois Ann Lorentzen, (Lanham, MD: Rowman and Littlefield Publishers, 2003), 11–22.

[3] Veranda Sheva, *Water Wars: Privatization, Pollution and Profit,* (Cambridge, MA: South End Press, 2002).

[4] Wengaari Maathi was a founder of the Green Movement.

[5] Nobel Prize Winner and Founder of the Green Belt Movement in Africa.

[6] My understanding of Marcuse draws upon UCSD Philosophy lecture classes audited, readings and personal conversations: 1968–1972.

[7] See Welton Jones, "Troupe At Synanon Plans Non-smooth Performance," *San Diego Union*, December 29, 1968.

[8] "Nine Women," included Eleanor Antin, Ida Applebroog, Faiya Fredman, Patricia Patterson, Ellen van Fleet, Barbra Strasen, Martha Rosler, Judy Nikolaides, Joyce Cutler Shaw, and Aviva Rahmani.

[9] http://www.ghostnets.com. Access date March 10, 2007.

[10] Carolee Schneemann and Bruce R McPherson, *More than Meat Joy: Performance Works and Selected Writings* (New Paltz, NY: Documentext, 1979).

[11] Alison Knowles, *The House of Dust* (Cologne: Gebr. Konig Verlag., 1968).

[12] Diana Russell, *The Secret Trauma: Incest in the Lives of Girls and Women*, 2nd ed. (New York: Basic Books/Perseus Press, 1999). 117–204.

[13] The leading current author of this premise is Mark D. Bertness, Robert P. Brown Professor of Biology, Brown University. Mark D. Bertness, *Atlantic Shorelines: Natural History and Ecology.* (Princeton, NJ: Princeton University Press, 2007).

[14] Ronald D. Laing, *The Divided Self*, (New York: Pantheon Books, 1969).

[15] For further discussion, see the writings of Carey Lovelace and Vivien Greene Fryd, and art works by Vanessa Beecroft, Annie Sprinkle, and Barbara T. Smith.

[16] Norma Broude, Mary D Garrard, and Judith K Brodsky, *The Power of Feminist Art: The American Movement of the 1970s, history and impact* (New York: H.N. Abrams, 1994). See also Rahmani and Montano, 1979.

[17] See Jill Sebastian, "Review of Floating Worlds Revisited," *New Art Examiner*, November 12, 1982; Aviva Rahmani, "The Floating Worlds Project," *High Performance Magazine*, June 1982, Issue 21, 44–9; Moira Roth, *The Amazing Decade: Women and Performance Art in America, 1970-1980*, (Los Angeles: Astro Artz, 1983); Arlene Raven, *At Home*, ex. cat., (Long Beach. CA: Long Beach Museum of Art, 1983); Aviva Rahmani, *Floating Worlds*, (Del Mar, CA: Internetwork Press, 1982); Elise Miller, "The Reproduction Dilemma," *Artweek*,

(August 1982), 13, No. 27; Elise Miller, "The Artist as Parent," *San Diego Magazine*, July 1982, 96–8.

[18] Informed by studies with Native American Healers and conversations with Barbara T. Smith, then healing from her own rape. See Ruth Wallen. Review: "The Medicine Wheel Murals" .33 (Spring 1986), 84.

[19] Aviva Rahmani, "The Mental Technology of REQUIEM" *The Act* 1989. 64–7.

[20] Joseph Tallmer, "Artist's Ghost is a 9-year Haunt." *New York Post* (December 28, 1990): 44. Sue Spaid, (Sue Spaid and Amy Lipton, curators), *Ecovention: Current Art to Transform Ecologies*. (Cincinnati, OH: Contemporary Arts Center, 2002); A. Sutherland, "Art-Eco on Vinalhaven," *Maine Sunday Telegram*, June 10, 2001, E1-E2; Gloria Orenstein, "The Greening of Gaia: Ecofeminist Artists Revisit the Garden," *Ethics and the Environment* 8 no. 1 (Spring 2003): 103–11; Initiated by Herman Prigann, edited by Heike Strelow in co-operation with Vera David, *Ecological Aesthetics: Art in Environmental Design: Theory and Practice* (Basel: Birkäuser Verlad für Architektur, 2004): 196.

[21] Gloria Orenstein, *The Reflowering of the Goddess*. (New York: Pergamon Press, 1990); Gloria Orenstein and Irene Diamond. *Reweaving the World: the Emergence of Ecofeminism* (San Francisco: Sierra Club Books, 1990); Carolyn Merchant, *Earthcare: Women and the Environment* (New York: Routledge, 1996).

[22] David Joselit, "Do Images Have a Gender?" *Feedback: Television Against Democracy* (Cambridge, MA: MIT Press, 2007).

[23]Aviva Rahmani et al, "The Gulf of Maine Enviromental Information Exchange: participation, observation, conversation," *Environment and Planning B: Planning and Design* 28: 865–887. Online version available at http://www.commoncoordinates.com/papers/2001epbgominfoex.pdf. Access date March 10, 2007.

[24] Women's Environmental Art Directory.

[25] http://www.ecoartnetwork.org/membersLst.html_. Access date March 10, 2007.

[26] Part of the exhibit Site Specific curated by Pat Nick. "Why Blue Rocks?" http://greenmuseum.org/generic_content.php?ct_id=91. Access date March 10, 2007.

[27] GIS is Geographic Information Systems, see http://erg.usgs.gov/isb/pubs/gis_poster/ Access date March 10, 2007.

[28] "Birthing a Virtual Residency," http://greenmuseum.org/generic_content.php?ct_id=268. Access date March 10, 2007.

[29] Aviva Rahmani *Ghost Nets Virtual Concerts*, TalkShoe Chime In http://www.talkshoe.com/talkshoe/web/talkCast.jsp?masterId=1210&cmd=tc. Web site launch date June 15, 2006.

Works Cited

Bertness, Mark D. *Atlantic Shorelines: Natural History and Ecology.* Princeton, NJ: Princeton University Press, 2007.

Broude, Norma, Mary Garrard, and Judith Brodsky. *The Power of Feminist Art: The American Movement of the 1970s, History and Impact*. New York: H.N. Abrams, 2004.

Burnham, Linda and Linda Montano. "Saving the Moment: Aviva Rahmani," *High Performance Magazine* 2 no. 3: p. 68–9

Carson, Rachel. *Silent Spring*. Boston: Houghton Mifflin; Cambridge, MA: Riverside Press, 1962.

Eaton, Heather and Lois Ann Lorentzen. *Ecofeminism and Globalization: Exploring Culture, Context, and Religion.* Lanham, MD: Rowman and Littlefield Publishers, 2003.

Joselit, David. "Do Images Have a Gender?" *Feedback: Television against democracy*. Cambridge, MA: MIT Press, 2007.

Knowles, Alison. *The House of Dust*. Cologne: Gebr. Konig Verlag, 1968.

Laing, Ronald D. *The Divided Self.* New York: Pantheon Books, 1969.

McDonald, Robert. "At the Galleries." *Los Angeles Times* (November 22, 1985)

Merchant, Caroly. *Earthcare: Women and the Environment*. New York: Routledge, 1996.

Ollman, Leah. 1989. "Grief and Joy Unfold in Performance." *Los Angeles Times* (September 8, 1989): p. 21.

Orenstein, Gloria. 2003. "The Greening of Gaia: Ecofeminist Artists Revisit the Garden." *Ethics and the Environment* 8 no. 1 (Spring 2003): 103–11.

——. *The Reflowering of the Goddess*. New York: Pergamon Press, 1990.

Orenstein Gloria and Irene Diamond. *Reweaving the World: the Emergence of Ecofeminism*. San Francisco: Sierra Club Books, 1990.

Prigann, Herman, Heike Strelow, and Vera David. *Aesthetics of Ecology: Art in Environmental Design: Theory and Practice*. Basel: Birkäuser Verlad für Architektur, 2004.

Rahmani, Aviva. "Birthing a Virtual Residency" http://greenmuseum.org/generic_content.php?ct_id=268

——."The Mental Technology of REQUIEM." *The Act*, Vol. 2/No. 1 1989. 64-67.

Rahmani, Aviva, Paul Schroeder, Paul Boudreau, Chris Brehme, Andrew Boyce, and Alison Evans. 2001. "The Gulf of Maine Environmental Information Exchange: Participation, Observation, Conversation." *Environment and Planning B: Planning and Design* 28: 865–87.

Russell, Diana E.H. *The Secret Trauma: Incest in the Lives of Girls and Women*. 2nd ed. New York: Basic Books/Perseus Press, 1999.

Schneemann, Carolee. *More than Meat Joy: Performance Works and Selected Writings*. New Paltz, NY: Documentext, 1979.

Spaid, Sue. (Sue Spaid and Amy Lipton, curators) *Ecovention: Current Art to Transform Ecologies*. Cincinnati, OH: Contemporary Arts Center, 2002.

Sutherland, Ann. "Art-Eco on Vinalhaven," *Maine Sunday Telegram,* June 10, 2001. E1-E2.

Tallmer, Jerry. "Artist's Ghost is a 9-year Haunt." *New York Post*, December 28, 1990. 44.

Wallen, Ruth. "Review: The Medicine Wheel Mural." *High Performance* 33 (1986), 84.

ENACTING RELATIONSHIP: ECOFEMINISM AND THE LOCAL

RUTH WALLEN

I still recall the pride I felt at having my first major professional artistic endeavor, a performative lecture at the Exploratorium,[1] included on the large orange and yellow poster, listing all of the exhibitions of women artists occurring simultaneous to the inaugural exhibition of Judy Chicago's *Dinner Party* in San Francisco, California. As a young artist, the identification of my work as part of a wellspring of feminist art making was most empowering. Initially trained in the sciences, I turned to art to shape the values that inform ecological decision-making. I saw the potential of ecological art as connective—examining, restoring, and re-envisioning ecological relationships between various components of an ecosystem, from the biophysical to the socio-cultural. But though I had a sense that through art I could explore concerns that eluded science, I felt a profound uncertainty about what I could contribute as an artist-in-residence at a predominantly science museum. Feminist art practices and theory, by exploring new terrains of subject matter, artistic media, forms of production, and the interaction with the audience or viewer, offered engaging possibilities for enacting meaningful relationships between the artist and society.

My project for the Exploratorium was titled *The Sea as Sculptress*. The work's title embraced the identification of nature with the feminine. Though essentialism was a topic of hot debate around Chicago's opening, I was more inspired by the ecofeminist position, which as Karen Warren describes, "takes gender as a starting point for providing analyses of and solutions to the unjustified domination of human and nonhuman Others."[2] Val Plumwood writes of the tendency in western culture to identify wilderness as absence. I was motivated by her proposal that the Other could be experienced "as another center, as a fullness or presence."[3] At monthly intervals during a yearlong residency, by means of macrophotography, I recorded growth on wooden forms placed in the San Francisco Bay. Without any pretense of objectivity, I envisioned reciprocity between the observer and observed. Instead of controlled sampling, I photographed growth that delighted me visually. While my results were not strictly scientific, they nonetheless visually displayed a marked decrease in the diversity and abundance of marine life in the industrial, and hence likely more polluted, areas of the bay.

I desired to give marine life standing, generate a sense of wonder, and create a relationship with an environment generally dismissed as a polluted wasteland. While much early feminist work centered on personal story, my stories concerned creating a relationship to place. Sharing these stories can be central to the practice of ecological art, as well as specifically ecofeminist art. In this essay, I would like to discuss my continued exploration of enacting relationship to the local as well as how the strategies I have learned might be applicable to broader ecofeminist concerns.

In his "Environmental Art and the Recovery of Place" essay in a catalogue of a major recent exhibition of collaborative ecological art, *Ground Works*, Andrew Light argues for the importance of place-based work. He writes of a "storied relationship to place," where "the importance of place is always presented from the perspective of a specific individual or community of valuers."[4] Through place, the interrelationships of the biophysical and social, cultural, historical or political aspects of an ecosystem acquire value or meaning. Dolores Hayden defines the "power of place" as "the power of ordinary urban landscapes to nurture citizen's public memory, to compass shared time in the form of shared territory."[5] Though she addresses specifically urban environments, her definition points to the importance of place in fostering community and collective memory. Her definition also emphasizes the temporal dimension, the dynamically changing nature of space encompassing memories of the past, present and future. Lucy Lippard, in her exhaustive survey of art about place, *The Lure of the Local*, suggests that place is in fact a "basic" element in the development of a robust public art or community-based art practice. Place provides a locus for the development of art practices that seek to engage society. These practices can "stimulate people's own ideas about what they would like to see in their environment and empower them to make changes."[6]

But how does one define a place? Does place-based work require long standing familiarity with a locale? Love, or at least respect, for the local? Not long after my work at the Exploratorium, I moved to San Diego, California. Having grown up with a Northern Californian's disdain for the southland, I wondered where I was. How did one identify place in an ever-changing environment? Was championing the local only an excuse for xenophobia? San Diego presented significant opposing challenges to creating a relationship with the local—boundaries that tended to be either too loose or tight—never ending sprawl and an increasingly fortified border fence. Having now lived in San Diego for over 20 years, I would like to use the discussion of several art works that I have created here to examine the challenges of enacting an appropriately bounded relationship to place.

I♥Del Mar

My first project, *I♥Del Mar* was created both as an installation and artist book (fig. 4-4). The installation was exhibited locally and at Franklin Furnace, New York. The work centered on a locale just east of the coastal city of Del Mar, California. Though the area was officially designated as North City West, developers preferred Carmel Del Mar, or Del Mar Highlands. The first chapter, or work, in the larger project consisted of a series of 15 black-and-white photographs showing various stages in the

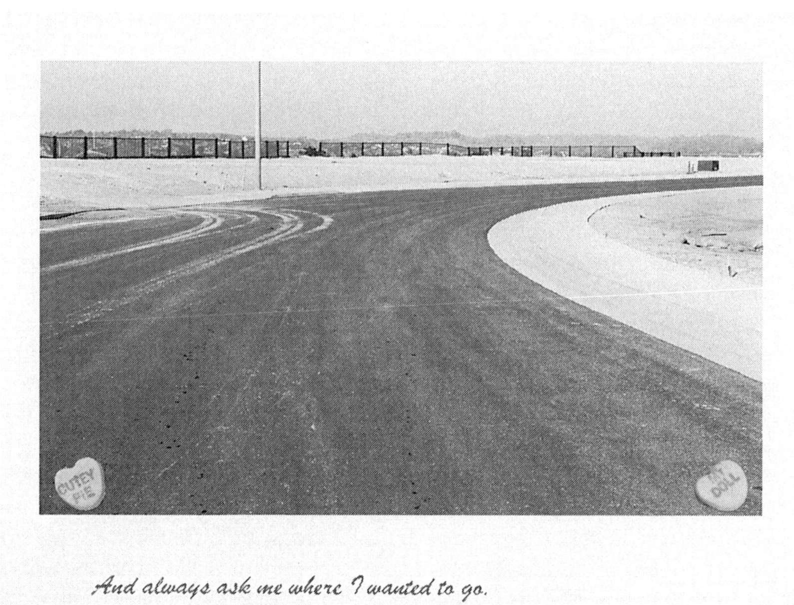

Fig. 4-4
I♥Del Mar, Part of an installation and book, photograph by Ruth Wallen 1986.

construction of new homes, accompanied by a single line of text and candy hearts. The text began with "My father was a transportation engineer," and told of his desire to "build better roads" so that "people could get to places more quickly" and "live better lives." He even dreamed of "going overseas to build roads for the poor" or selling "trains to China." Then the text shifted: "He used to take me out for rides. . . So tell me, what are you dreaming of? Tell me about your friends. Tell me about your boyfriend . . . What position do you sleep with him in? Tell me." And finally, asking about my mother, "Why she is so frigid? . . . Why can't she be more like you. Tell me." The candy hearts added another layer, seductive both metaphorically and textually. Placed over the photographs, they offered sweet nothings from, "Don't tell, " "Why not?" to "Hug me." "Will you?" "Sweetheart." "Be True." "Don't stop."[7]

This incestuous tale, though created as part of a larger whole, was first exhibited in 1986 at the Los Angeles Women's Building, in an exhibition about sexual abuse titled Family Album. Positioned at the beginning of *I♥Del Mar*, the work deliberately suggests the similarities between incestuous relationships and the narcissism and lack of boundaries in the real estate strategies used to market suburbia, strategies that deny local biological or historical legacies in favor of imported, idealized fantasies. As I describe in an article "Memory Politics," the incest victim is a master of dissociation, secrecy, and denial: "Pain felt by the body has been called pleasure. Violation has been called love. . . .Pummeled by the logic of double-speak, intellect has learned to resist sensation, distrust all feelings. Mind has been split from body has been severed from heart."[8] Furthermore, according to psychologist Judith Herman, it is not only the victim, but also the perpetrator and witness that experience the effects of this trauma.[9]

Susan Griffin's essay in an early ecofeminist anthology, *Healing the Wounds: The Promise of Ecofeminism*, is entitled "Split Culture." After describing the process of disassociation and numbness (in similar terms discussed earlier in this section), Griffin laments that, "Long ago we gave up on ourselves. . . We have traded our real feelings for delusions. We deny all evidence at hand that this civilization, which has shaped our minds, is also destroying the earth."[10] She makes a strong and blunt assessment. Likewise, I use the specific analogy of incest not simply to equate the rape of nature to that of women, but to call attention to the similarities between the distortions in sprawling development and those of the incestuous relationship.

At the heart of healing is making relationships, reestablishing connections between that which has been twisted, denied, and severed.

This opening chapter is followed by six others, many of which include interactive elements, including flip cards, or envelopes. After witnessing the trauma, the reader or viewer, is challenged to make the connections within and between each of these multilayered works—to begin to understand the process of denial and initiate one of healing.

To describe some of the other works briefly: a box of chocolate covered tomatoes and a series of actual greeting cards with messages written inside asking what it means to be frigid, refer to the distortion and commoditization of sensuality and desire in western culture. This theme is elaborated in a wall piece of large format sepia-toned hand-colored photographs, in the style of nineteenth-century landscape photography. However, these sumptuous images depict tomatoes rotting on the vine. Text, printed on flip cards mounted on a shelf below, offers two interpretations of the photographs. One side describes my desire to thwart my father's pride in my tomato garden by neglecting it until it dies. The other side explains that clearing the land for tomato farming paved the way for development. Though local residents were poisoned by both the pesticides and fertilizers, the growers declared the chemicals "safe to drink." Nonetheless, the tomatoes were left to rot on the vine, supposedly due to a drop in prices in the Florida crop making harvesting unprofitable. "Now they (the local residents) have experienced the dilemmas and frustrations of the local farmer," declares the grower's general manager.

The final piece includes six large color photographs depicting the differing styles of place settings found on the dining room tables of model homes. Each plate is heaped with tomatoes. These photographs are juxtaposed to sample pages from marketing brochures that include photographs of the homes, text from actual brochures, and information about the history of tomato cultivation and attempts to grow the perfect tomato.

I♥Del Mar presents stories of alienation and denial. Uttering these truths, whether personal familial stories or the experiences of rural residents prior to development, is a first step towards healing. Framing advertising in a larger socio-cultural context is also important. As a whole, the piece is open-ended and layered. It does not give simple answers or prescriptions, but encourages the viewers/readers to make connections, to ascertain the truth for themselves.

Writing of ecofeminism, which she sees as a synthesis of feminist and ecological perspectives, Ynestra King states that these philosophies "embody the revolt against human domination. They demand that we rethink the relationship between humanity and the rest of nature, including our natural, embodied selves."[11] Through the many juxtapositions in this work, I hope that the viewers will be encouraged to rethink their relationship to the local, and ponder the dangers of the seductive commodification of desire involved in the marketing of suburbia.

View Points

The southern periphery of San Diego shares certain similarities to the north. When I began to work there, much of the area, except along the freeway corridors, was rural. Though the city of Tijuana, Mexico, abuts the border, to a large degree the United States-side of the border area was regarded as an impoverished wilderness, with the associations of absence that Plumwood describes. However this wildness was defined by an increasingly fortified fence, designed to keep out a dark, dangerous Other.

My first artistic involvement with the border region was as a member of Las Comadres, a multiethnic, multinational collective of women artists. Initially formed as a reading group, we evolved into an activist artist collaborative. Our major installation was titled *La Vecindad* or *The Neighborhood*. As opposed to seeing the border as protective barrier and the neighbor as the dark, faceless Other, a blank slate for the projection of fear, members of Las Comadres conceived of the border as bridge, as permeable membrane, as place, as neighborhood.

Most influential to our developing notion of border culture was Gloria Anzaldúa's *Borderlands/La Frontera*.[12] In the beginning of the book, she delineates a crucial distinction between a border: "set up to define places that are safe and unsafe, to distinguish *us* from *them*," and a borderland as, "a vague and undetermined place created by the emotional residue of an unnatural boundary." Throughout the book, she celebrates the potential of this place of "*mestiza* consciousness," this previously marginalized zone, where the dualistic thinking of Western culture, the splits between male and female, dark and light, subject and object can be uprooted and healed. Like Anzaldúa, in our work, we wanted to reconceptualize the border from a dividing line to a region, a significant region at that, where the splits of Western culture, most highlighted, could be renegotiated.

Collaborative work is essential to developing new perspectives about the border region. However, here I would like to discuss in more detail a temporary public installation, *View Points*, created in 1995 after Las Comadres disbanded, but informed by my previous experience. *View Points* was an interactive nature walk at the Tijuana River Estuary that abuts the border with Mexico. Largely undeveloped, the area was a sanctuary to rare and endangered plants and birds. At the time the project was created, not only bird watchers, but the border patrol constantly surveyed the area, on the lookout for the daily flow of immigrants who crossed through the estuary attempting to gain entrance into the United States. Directed by public officials to avoid controversy, I tried to create a site for contemplation, a site where viewers could make relationships between the biological and socio-political realities of the preserve. I hoped that my work would at least destabilize, if not begin to dislodge, the many dualities associated with the border fence.

The Claude glass serves as a basic metaphor for *View Points*. This concave lens was used to frame an idealized picturesque landscape before the advent of photography. Accompanied by a replica of a Claude glass, the introductory panel reads:

> Before the advent of photography, a popular pastime was to use a Claude glass to frame the perfect picturesque landscape. The viewer would stand with their back to the vista, moving the glass until the ideal image appeared. Rose, yellow, scarlet—the glasses even came in different colors to simulate the color of light at different times of day.
>
> What is the ideal view of the estuary? At one time, wetlands were viewed as wastelands. Later they glittered with dollar signs and were filled in to make prime shoreline real estate. By the seventies scientists sounded the alarm, claiming that coastal wetlands were among the most productive habitats in the world.
>
> *This work is a proposal in a dozen questions:* Instead of answers it offers a suggestion to think ecologically, to examine relationships. The viewing stations point to phenomena from all parts of the estuary. Viewing scopes both frame and deliberately distort the view. Do we, like the users of the Claude glass, turn our back on nature in search of preconceived or idealized views?
>
> Stop.
> Look.
> Listen.
> What can we learn?[13]

This introduction is followed by 12 viewing stations; each includes a text/image panel and a viewing scope and pertains to some aspect of the local ecology. After describing the blockage of mouth of the estuary in recent years, that panel asks, "What life forms perish when a boundary no longer permits exchange?" The corresponding viewing scope has a divided lens, half clear, half covered with a red filter. Another text panel, "Diversity," describes the challenge of accurate sampling and inquires:

"Since we can't count everything, what, when and how often should we sample to measure diversity?" Several stations explore proposals for an aquaculture park to treat sewage. One panel concludes: "How would we treat our waste if we saw it as a resource instead of something to be discarded?" The picture for the plaque shows *ecoparque* in Tijuana, the only aquaculture park in the region that has actually been built.

The last station describes Heisenberg's uncertainty principle, that what is seen and how it is described depends on the ideals held by the observer. How do our ideals influence our perceptions in this charged location? As the walk points out, an estuary, an area where fresh and salt water mix, is itself a border zone. The work invites viewers to interrogate their preconceptions, to experience the area as a region, as a locus for shifting perception or possibilities, instead of a locus for rigid dichotomies.

In the borderlands, "the unjustified domination of the human," is brought into focus.[14] The borderlands highlight political and economic injustice. The San Diego border, in particular, is said to be the border with the largest economic disparity of anywhere in the world.[15] While *View Points* focuses on the natural environment, it attempts to make connections with human communities that most "nature walks" ignore. The photos include clothing and trash discarded by immigrants; the viewing scopes point to both countries, and the text relates ecological principles to human culture. Framing the many borders, from the estuary to the international boundary, the work prompts one to ask about who or what, is being perceived as Other and why.

Mary Mellor describes her ecofeminist position as one of "deep materialism," combining a desire for social and economic justice, with the insights of deep ecologists regarding a "non-anthropocentric ontology and cosmology."[16] Her work, in particular, highlights the need to focus on the mechanisms creating political and economic injustices, while not discounting that that culture is "embedded" in a larger ecological context. In my work, I try to make a space for the possibility of these many linkages.

Working in the borderlands serves as a reminder that there is a problem with reifying dualities—equating all women with nature and all men with culture, assuming that women are either a unitary category, or unwittingly divided into oppressed third world women and privileged first world women.[17] Fellow Comadre Emily Hicks theorizes that the border crosser exists in a deterritorialized space, a space of contradiction and multiplicity: "The border crosser is both 'self' and 'other.' The border crosser 'subject' emerges from double strings of signifiers of two sets of referential codes, from both sides of the border."[18]

Inhabiting the border region demands that one think in complex terms, employing multiple codes without attempting to unify them. Plumwood cautions about borrowing concepts from deep ecology, privileging sameness and identification with all living things to the point that human differences are subsumed in a collective wholeness.[19] Border culture suggests a very different possibility where difference is not denied and one can hold multiple viewpoints simultaneously.

Preserving Paradise

While border culture epitomizes the potential complexity of human society, the border as bridge holds a myriad of contradictions in relationship. Sprawl behaves as the antithesis, informed by a desire for escape, by lack of container, and by lack of relationship to biological or historical legacies. Despite no-growth rhetoric in city government initiated before I arrived in San Diego, only recently has urban infill been taken seriously. From 1980 to 2000, the population of the metropolitan area increased by one million. One mesa after another met the bulldozer as the real estate development I disparaged in *I♥Del Mar* was repeated throughout the country. How can a society develop a sense of place, or embodiment in the local, when the local is seemingly without limits and constantly being recreated? During the years 2004 to 2006, I returned to the suburbs, knowing that there was more of the story to tell, a story whose relevance stretched well beyond the city limits.

As early as 1970, more Americans lived in suburbs than in urban areas.[20] Since that time the population has increased in only 11 of the 30 largest central cities,[21] yet the developed area of cities has continued to expand. Both new homes and new lots continue to increase steadily in size. I include the following statistics in the work I am about to discuss: In the 1950s, the average size of an American new home was 800 square feet, 2 bedrooms, one bath, sited on a 300 square foot lot. By 1999, the average size for a new house was 2,250 square feet, sited on a 12,910 square foot lot, even though the average family size decreased during this period.[22] Currently, "construction and operation of buildings account for an astounding 40% of the materials entering the world's economy and one third of the global energy consumption."[23]

Preserving Paradise begins in Arroyo Sorrento, California, a small enclave that had been farmed from before the turn of the century. During the eighties, I'd often house-sit there for ecological artists Helen and

Newton Harrison, dear friends and mentors. It was from their home that I photographed both the rotting tomato fields and the construction of North City West. For a long time, Arroyo Sorrento had remained as a small rural haven in a sea of development, but now multimillion dollar, 5,000–6,000 square foot, cookie-cutter estates were overshadowing the older bungalows. Residents had fought hard to keep density down, but the resultant lot size pushed land values up to the point where developers referred to the older homes simply as "tear downs." Returning to the area, I began by interviewing members of the community, both old time residents and recent arrivals, then reaching out to activists, developers, and city officials. Through personal stories, I hoped to find the linkages to place.

Preserving Paradise was created both as an installation of postcards, which included text excerpted from interviews, and as a more complex performative lecture that combined a reading of the postcards with projected images, excerpts from the taped interviews, and stories of my experiences. Beginning with the nostalgia of old timers, I present the competing ideals informing the struggle over the future of the area, from environmentalists' efforts to preserve the last coastal mesa in the county that boasts the most endangered species in the continental United States, to developers' desires to maximize investments while acceding to pressures to offer environmentally friendly construction; and from a master plan envisioning affordable housing, public transportation, and commercial centers, to residents fearful of anything that will lower property values.

The complexity of interwoven narratives is hard to summarize. Old timers reminisce about knowing all their neighbors, all night long poker parties and the plethora of wildlife. Acute observers mourn not only the disappearance of mountain lions, but even the displacement of red ants by black ones and the subsequent loss of horn toads that preyed on them. New residents explain the logic of the market: if you have an acre lot, you build a 5,000 square foot home. Old timers call this "how to own an acre without any yard." Newcomers say that the area will look as it did before, when new trees grow in on land cleared for development. Both appreciate the location convenient to work and shopping. However, the workers in the new office buildings below, or the construction workers adding embellishments to new homes, bemoan the long commutes necessitated by the lack of affordable housing. A caretaker for the local's horses tells of losing all of his belongings when his trailer was bulldozed by developers.

At one point, the performance shifts in tone to a PowerPoint lecture about how to be a successful activist. Carmel Mountain, the last coastal mesa in San Diego, located at the terminus of Arroyo Sorrento, must not be sacrificed to developers: "Organize. Build coalitions. Form non-profit . . ." Local activists were determined to preserve this mesa, though major environmental groups were willing to compromise assuming that development was inevitable: "Raise money. Develop publicity. Research useful legislation." Proposition A[24], which passed despite limited financial backing in 1985, required voter approval for future development. Though city government proved largely ineffective in regulating development, voters proved more difficult to convince: "Don't loose vision." Developers won approval of plans for a larger area further inland after they agreed not only to the preservation of Carmel Mountain, but also to additional conservation easements, the use of sustainable building materials, the first enforceable requirements for affordable housing, and more.

All of these stories are interspersed with my exploration of Carmel Mountain itself. The "puddles" that I'd walked by years before turn out to be vernal pools, home to a host of species including the endangered San Diego fairy shrimp. The more I slowed down and learned to look carefully, searching for this elusive creature, the more I saw, and the more my fascination, indeed love, of this place grew.

The scripted part of the *Preserving Paradise* performance concludes as I sit beside a pool at twilight, listening instead of looking, to both the sounds of frogs and crickets and the many voices churning in my mind. I am filled with questions—from the adequate size of a dwelling, to alternative methods of construction and clustering of homes. I ponder the efficacy of existing mechanisms for political, economic, and community oversight and ask what insight audience members might offer. Extended, penetrating conversations have followed all of the lecture performances that I have presented thus far. In truth, the North City West area is proximate to a university and jobs. If population is to grow, development in this area makes sense. But are there more sustainable, more ecologically conscious patterns of development? Can we provide for greater economic and racial diversity among potential inhabitants? Must development entail the type of numbing described by Susan Griffin? Can we create an embodied relationship to this place?

Envisioning alternatives that are most inclusive and sustainable requires both the multi-voiced discourse learned in the border region and a caring concern for the local. My performances present multiple narratives of place. I hope that this work and resulting conversations will engender greater relationships to the local along with more expansive visions for the future.

My immersion into this local history demanded additional action. In the last year, I have worked with local activists to create interpretive panels for Carmel Mountain, informing residents of local ecology. The panels became the centerpiece of a collaborative effort of the city, environmental activists and various users groups—from mountain bikers, to horse back rides, to joggers—to preserve endangered species habitat and limit use to a defined trail system. The signs themselves depict the vernal pools, the fairy shrimp, and a small, endangered plant. The text is open-ended, providing information while posing questions. The last panel, about Short-leaved Dudleya, asks, "Do you want to live on a mesa by the sea? Some plants and animals can live nowhere else. How can we share the mesa with all species that call it home?"

I pause to ponder the first sentence in Lippard's *Lure of the Local*: "Place for me is the locus of desire."[25] My early explorations into suburbia certainly suggest that desire can be manipulated by the market. Fellow Comadre Margie Waller[26] has written of addiction as a response to trauma. Mindless acquisitiveness, the search for the ever-bigger home, and better life in suburbia can certainly become a type of addiction. Desire itself is part of being human. I hope that my work can serve to ignite a passion arising from embodied relationship, from love of place. This passion can in turn engender an ecological ethic, and with it, a passion to live in sustainable relationships, relationships that honor both the human and the non-human legacies of place.

---

[1] Located in San Francisco, California, United States.

[2] Karen J. Warren, "The Power and the Promise of Ecofeminism, Revisited," in *Environmental Philosophy: From Animal Rights to Radical Ecology*, eds. Michael E. Zimmerman, J. Baird Callicot, Karen J. Warren, Irene Flaver, and John Clark, (25 Upper Saddle River, NJ: Prentice Hall, 2005), 252.

[3] Val Plumwood, "Wilderness Skepticism and Wilderness Dualism," in *The Great New Wilderness Debate*, ed. J. Gaird Callicott and Michael P. Nelson, (Athens: University of Georgia Press, 1998), 680.

[4] Andrew Light, "Environmental Art and the Recovery of Place, in *Ground Works: Environmental Collaboration in Contemporary Art* (Pittsburgh, PA: Carnegie Mellon University, 2005), 54.

[5] Doloras Hayden, *The Power of Place: Urban Landscapes as Public History* (Cambridge, MA: The MIT Press, 1995), 9.

[6] Lucy R. Lippard, The Lure of the Local: Senses of Place in a Multicentered Society (New York: The New Press, 1997), 286.

[7] To see examples of this piece, and others referred to in this essay, please consult the artists Web site: http://communication.ucsd.edu/rwallen

[8] Ruth Wallen, "Memory Politics: The Implications Of Healing From Sexual Abuse" *Tikkun* 9, no. 6 (1994): 38.

[9] Judith Herman, *Trauma and Recovery*. (New York: Basic Books, 1992), 6, 11.

[10] Susan Griffin, "Split Culture," in *Healing The Wounds: The Promise of Ecofeminism*, ed. Judith Plant (Philadelphia: New Society Publishers, 1989), 7

[11] Ynestra King, "Healing the Wounds: Feminism, Ecology, and the Nature/Culture Dualism," in *Reweaving the World: The Emergence of Ecofeminism*, ed. Irene Diamond and Gloria Feman Orenstein, (San Francisco: Sierra Club Books, 1989), 117.
[12] Gloria Anzaldúa, *Borderlands/La Frontera: The New Mestiza* (San Francisco: Spinsters/Aunt Lute Book Company, 1987), 3, 80.
[13] http://communication.ucsd.edu/rwallen/estuary/index.html. Access date June 10, 2007.
[14] Karen J. Warren, "The Power and the Promise of Ecofeminism, Revisited," 252.
[15] Ruth Wallen, "Barrier or Bridge: Photojournalism of the San Diego/Tijuana Border Region." *The Communication Review*, 6 no. 2 (2003): 137-164.
[16] Mary Mellor, "Ecofeminism and Environmental Ethics: A Materialist Ecofeminist Perspective," in *Environmental Philosophy: From Animal Rights to Radical Ecology*, eds. Michael E. Zimmerman, J. Baird Callicot, Karen J. Warren, Irene Flaver, and John Clark (25 Upper Saddle River, NJ: Prentice Hall, 2005), 214.
[17] Chandra Talpade Mohanty, *Feminism Without Borders: Decolonizing Theory, Practicing Solidarity* (Durham: Duke University Press, 2003), 17-43.
[18] D. Emily Hicks, *Border Writing: The Multidimensional Text.* (Minneapolis: The University of Minnesota Press, 1997), xxvi.
[19] Val Plumwood, *Feminism and the Mastery of Nature.* (London: Routledge, 1993) 157-160, 174.
[20] Dolores Hayden, *Building Suburbia: Green Fields and Urban Growth, 1880–2000.* (New York: Pantheon Books, 2003), 10.
[21] Tom Daniels, *When City and Country Collide: Managing Growth in the Metropolitan Fringe* (Washington, DC: Island Press, 1999), 6.
[22] Hayden, *Building Suburbia*, 190.
[23] Timothy Beatley and Kristy Manning, *The Ecology of Place: Planning for Environment, Economy, and Community*. (Washington, DC: Island Press, 1997), 124.
[24] Proposition A was a proposition that appeared on the San Diego city ballot in November of 1985. It required that city land which had previously been designated as "future urbanizing" in the General Plan could not be redesignated for development without the approval of the majority of voters.
[25] Lucy Lippard, *The Lure of the Local: Senses of Place in a Multicentered Society*, 4.
[26] Marguerite Waller, "Addicted to Virtue: The Globalization Policy-Maker," *Social Identities* 12, no. 5 (2006): 575–594.

Works Cited

Anzaldúa, Gloria. *Borderlands/La frontera: The New Mestiza.* San Francisco: Spinsters/Aunt Lute Book Company, 1987.

Beatley, Timothy and Kristy Manning. *The Ecology of Place: Planning for Environment, Economy, and Community*. Washington, DC: Island Press, 1997.

Daniels, Tom. *When City and Country Collide: Managing Growth in the Metropolitan Fringe*. Washington DC: Island Press, 1999.

Griffin, Susan. "Split Culture." In *Healing the Wounds: The Promise of Ecofeminism*, Judith Plant ed., 7–17. Philadelphia: New Society Publishers, 1989.

Hayden, Dolores. *The Power of Place: Urban Landscapes as Public History*. Cambridge, MA: The MIT Press, 1995.

——. *Building Suburbia: Green Fields and Urban Growth, 1880–2000.* New York: Pantheon Books, 2003.

Herman, Judith. *Trauma and Recovery.* New York: Basic Books, 1992.

Hicks, D. Emily. *Border Writing: The Multidimensional Text.* Minneapolis: The University of Minnesota Press, 1997.

King, Ynestra. *Healing the Wounds: Feminism, Ecology, and the Nature/Culture Dualism*. In *Reweaving the World: The Emergence of Ecofeminism,* edited by Irene Diamond and Gloria Feman Orenstein, 106–121. San Francisco: Sierra Club Books, 1989.

Light, Andrew. "Environmental Art and the Recovery of Place." In *Ground Works: Environmental Collaboration in Contemporary Art.* 49-57. Pittsburgh, PA: Carnegie Mellon University, 2005.

Lippard, Lucy R. *The Lure of the Local: Senses of Place in a Multicentered Society*. New York: The New Press, 1997.

Mohanty, Chandra Talpade. *Feminism Without Borders: Decolonizing Theory, Practicing Solidarity.* Durham, NC: Duke University Press, 2003.

Mellor, Mary. "Ecofeminism and Environmental Ethics: A Materialist Ecofeminist Perspective. In *Environmental philosophy: From Animal Rights to Radical Ecology*, Michael E. Zimmerman, J. Baird Callicot, Karen J. Warren, Irene J. Klaver, and John Clark eds., 208–227. 25 Upper Saddle River, NJ: Prentice Hall, 2005.

Plumwood, Val. *Feminism and the Mastery of Nature*. London: Routledge, 1993.

——. "Wilderness Skepticism and Wilderness Dualism." In *The Great New Wilderness Debate*, J. Gaird Callicott and Michael P. Nelson eds. 652-690. Athens: University of Georgia Press, 1998.

Wallen, Ruth. "Memory Politics: The Implications of Healing from Sexual Abuse. *Tikkun* 9, no. 6 (1994): 35–40.

——. "Barrier or Bridge: Photojournalism of the San Diego/Tijuana Border Region." *The Communication Review*, 6 no. 2 (2003): 137-164.

Waller, Marguerite. "Addicted to Virtue: The Globalization Policy-Maker. *Social Identities* 12, no. 5 (2006): 575–594.

Warren, Karen. J. "The Power and the Promise of Ecofeminism, Revisited." In *Environmental Philosophy: From Animal Rights to Radical Ecology*, Michael E. Zimmerman, J. Baird Callicot, Karen J.Warren, Irene J. Klaver, and John Clark eds., 252–279. 25 Upper Saddle River, NJ: Prentice Hall, 2005.

DRAWING THE CIRCLE: FROM THE PRIVATE TO THE PUBLIC TO THE CLASSROOM AND BACK AGAIN

SHARON SISKIN

For more than 25 years I have made work in my studio that addresses my own experiences with gender and ethnic identity, parenting and family, displacement, loss and grief, environmental and other social issues. Personal memory influences how I distill the conceptual and the visual. Social issues become personal matters and private matters become public. I understand social issues by engaging with communities as an artist and then taking social action as a citizen-artist. Social action, community-based research, and engagement inform the studio work. I also take this integration of practice into the classroom in both undergraduate and graduate courses that I teach.

My journey as an artist and teacher might also mirror the trajectory of feminist art practices from the 1970s into the early twenty-first century. Using some aspects of my own work as a case in point, this essay intends to highlight the feminist thread that weaves through and influences my current studio practice, community-based public practice, and teaching—sometimes drawing a straight line with a beginning and an end, sometimes drawing an endless circle, and sometimes stitching the three together in a seamless, richly textured fabric.

From the Private to the Public

In 1987, I saw the Names Project's AIDS Memorial Quilt displayed for the first time in its entirety at the Moscone Convention Center in San Francisco, California. Each panel of this enormous and ever-expanding public art project was made by separately grieving individuals or groups and given to the Names Project for the same reason: to memorialize a person who was loved and who had died of AIDS. The cumulative product of this cathartic creative process—the art—made public and visible what had been mostly private up until then, humanizing the terrible cost of the disease and transforming statistics about those who had died into names with faces and stories. Witnessing this phenomenon—the public connection of art (and, more specifically, a form that had been considered traditional women's craft) made by a community immersed in personal loss and grief to a larger viewing public in order to foster education and encourage compassion and social action—marked a turning point in my art-making and my teaching of art. For much of the time since then I have been most interested in the challenges of making art that comes from the personal needs and voices of a community, making visible to the larger public some of the most important issues we are facing in these often troubled times. This practice has given me the opportunity to share skills of self-representation through the visual arts and also to collaborate with a diverse number of communities: people who are living with AIDS, homeless women and children, older adults who are living in long-term care facilities, HIV-positive California State Correctional Facility inmates, ex-violent offenders in collaboration with victims and survivors of violence, residents of Richmond, California's Iron Triangle, and the social-ecology of my own neighborhood of West Berkeley, California.

From the Classroom to the Community

These projects have informed not only my artwork but also my work as a visual arts professor. Since 1991, I have taught classes at many of the San Francisco Bay Area's art schools and university art departments, developing a curriculum that is focused on teaching students the basic tools, techniques, and best practices involved for working as a community-based activist artist. These include a course called "Beyond the Studio: Community Collaborations A & B," required for graduate students in the MA in Transformative Arts program at John F. Kennedy University in Berkeley, California; and a required undergraduate course called "Arts Outreach: The Artist as Citizen-Part A (Cultural Diversity)" and "Arts Outreach: The Artist as Citizen-Part B (Service Learning)," which I co-teach with my colleague and collaborator Richard Kamler, for upper division students enrolled in the BA in Fine Arts program at the University of San Francisco.

The methodologies, formal strategies, and activist goals of our work set community-based activist art apart from other art with socio-political content and, I believe, connects it to the history of feminist art practices. What follows is a distillation of some of the key principles of our collaborative practice in the classroom and in the street.

Personal Connection

In our experience, the most successful community-based activist public art projects begin when artists and the collaborating community, or community partner, are personally connected. This may occur through a long-term geographic proximity or a shared interest in social or ecological issues. In this principle, which is the seed that gives initial life to our projects, we are intimately tied to the aesthetic form of the credo of 1970s feminism: "the personal is the political." According to Nina Felshin, writing in the introduction to her invaluable 1995 publication, *But Is It Art? The Spirit of Art as Activism*, "the idea guiding much activist art is its examination of the public dimension of our private experience."[1] If an artist doesn't already have a personal connection to the collaborating community, it is important to seek out a person within the community who will be that bridge and help establish mutual trust, dialogue and relationship. In a very explicit way, we need to be welcomed into the community.

Research

There then follows a very crucial period of time for any community-based activist art project, during which she or he is simply there, part of that community, either observing and soaking up information like "sponges," or working as active community members, volunteering labor to help with particular community needs. This early phase of the creative process will be familiar to any artist who does studio-based art projects; this is when we ask questions, search for creative solutions, and imagine how to make the process visual, while also considering how we might frame it. In the classroom we call this part of our process the research phase, and we ask our students to come to the classroom prepared to share their visual and written journal entries, informed by their readings, their on-site experiences and their interactions and research in their chosen communities. Stories from out in the street are shared in the classroom, and the discussions we have about each student's project helps inform all the class members about the need to be a responsible and respectful citizen in that community, as well as the need to remain open and flexible. One of the important lessons is that things do not always proceed as originally conceived and planned in the studio and the classroom—life often gets in the way. This phase of the project involves a substantial, often long-term investment of time by artists, and an openness to see, hear, and fully understand the needs and important issues of the collaborating community.

Collaborative Process

When community-based artists are fully engaged in the creative process we are working collaboratively with our community and beginning to consider our audience. According to Lucy Lippard, feminist art strategies include, "collaboration, dialogue, a constant questioning of aesthetic and social assumptions and a new respect for the audience."[2] The community collaborative process may take many forms. Sometimes the artist may be sharing or teaching studio-based skills, encouraging self-representation from community participants. At other times, the artist may be learning new skills and becoming informed about issues through oral history interviews and community meetings. In any case, we are working together to make the ideas that are important to the community visible and to re-present or to frame them, much like an artist who works in two-dimensional media choosing a particular frame to install their artwork on a wall. As artists we are trained in the imagination and taught to solve problems in the studio. We are also trained to create, or make something that never before existed in the world. We can share these inherent skills as artists with any community and work collaboratively with that community to imagine how to make what seems invisible into something visible to our audiences, who are often the larger public. The collaborative process of community-based activist artists is referred to worldwide by a variety of terms, some of which include social practice, cultural animation, community cultural development, or working for cultural democracy.

Project Proposal

You may have already wondered how community-based art projects are funded and how artists can afford to do this form of cultural work, especially since there is often no final object that can be exhibited and sold in a gallery. This brings us to possibly the most private, time-consuming, and often frustrating part of our work. It is imperative in our process to be able to passionately articulate our rich experiences in the community, both orally and as a formal written project proposal. This can be a crucial part of our effort to raise the money needed to realize the objectives and long-term impact of our projects. No matter where we go and how we obtain financial support—fiscal agents, government granting agencies, community foundations, private foundations, individual donations, in-kind donations of materials, even fundraising events like bake sales—we must be able to communicate to others our vision of what we are hoping to create (even if it is still unresolved or in process) and how much the project might cost.

Public Space

Many community-based artists have one foot in the community and the other foot in the established art world of studio, galleries, and museums. While galleries and museums may sometimes be ideal venues for studio-based art, they may not give us access to the larger audience that we hope to reach with our community-based activist art projects. Also, people tend to go to museums and galleries with certain expectations about what they might encounter; catching people unaware, not in a traditional "art space," may be much more effective (fig. 4-5). Knowing exactly who our audience is and locating the best site for reaching an expanded audience makes our projects visible in the public arena. This visibility is often critical to the project's activist goals and its ultimate success.[3]

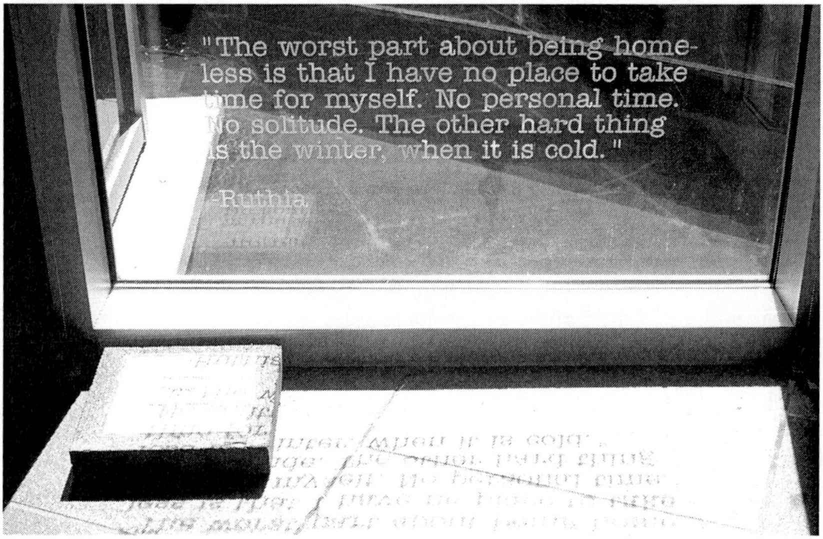

Fig. 4-5
(In)Visible Installation. Ruthia quotation. Photograph copyright Sharon Siskin 2006.

The Media

In Suzanne Lacy's introduction to *Mapping the Terrain: New Genre Public Art* she writes:

> Moving into the public sector, through the use of public space, including the media, was inevitable for artists who sought to inform change. Because of their activist origin, feminist artists were concerned with issues of effectiveness. They had fairly sophisticated conceptions of the nature of an expanded audience, including how to reach it, support its passage through new and often difficult material, and access its transformation or change as a result of the work.[4]

Many of us have discovered that it can be fairly easy for community-based activist artists to get the attention of newspapers, magazines, radio, and television media, though it can be a challenge to get the media to deliver the message that we intend. If our project's objectives include reaching the largest possible audience, it is very important to engage the media and also to be as articulate and clear as possible about our activist and aesthetic objectives in our press releases, in the images we send to the media, and in our verbal interviews.

Documentation

It is important to document our projects—for the artists, for the collaborating community, for our funding supporters, and for sharing with the media. It is often the only tangible object that we can show for our time and our labor after the project ends. Of course, there are always ethical issues to consider when carrying a camera or tape recorder into a community. Like all other aspects of our community-based activist work, it is important that we remain respectful, open, flexible, and that we continue to ask permission.

Long-term Impact

How do we measure the success of a community-based activist art project? Certainly, we can see results along the way, in all the steps of the process I have mentioned above—fundraising, media attention, documentation, and so on. But it is the long-term impact of our projects that can help us to truly evaluate what is very hard to quantify. The social change or environmental remediation that can occur for ourselves and the collaborating community, especially when the collaborating community takes ownership of the project, can often only be observed over time, often after artists have moved on to new projects. Our ability to observe and understand the long-term impact of our projects is what keeps many of us continually involved in this collaborative community-based process. It reaffirms for us that art can be transformative—a powerful catalyst for effecting social and environmental change.

Back Again

Nina Felshin reminds us of the important historical influences of feminist art practices on the process and final presentation of community-based activist art in her introduction to "But Is It Art? The Spirit of Art as Activism:" "Clearly, the art practices of the 1970s that made creative use of feminist methodologies to grapple with issues of self-representation, empowerment and community identity have provided important precedents for activist artists."[5]

My practice as a community-based activist artist and art professor is informed by my own personal history, coming of age in the sixties and early seventies, immersed in the Feminist Movements of the last 40 years. My work as an activist on behalf of the environment, peace, and social justice, and my participation in creative non-violent civil disobedience have also been strong influences on the nature of my creative process and the form and formal presentation of my artwork. Feminist thought has encouraged me to continue to work for equality and social justice as an artist, and environmentalism has taught me to understand the connections—how everything that we do individually and as a culture can affect the whole world, or at least our small part of it. It is from this solid foundation that I am able to take the first step into the street and recognize my connection as an artist and citizen, so that I can begin to draw the circle from the community to the studio to the classroom and return back again.

---

[1] Nina Felshin, *But Is It Art? The Spirit of Art as Activism* (Seattle, Washington: Bay Press, 1995), 18.

[2] Jeff Kelley, "The Body Politics of Suzanne Lacy", in Nina Felshin, *But Is It Art? The Spirit of Art as Activism*, 223–224.

[3] *(In)Visible* artist statement:

> "Tamara Costa, Lauren Devine, Meghan M. Stoll and homeless artist in collaboration with USF student/artists Errica , Charlesetta Frazier, Raven-Hawk, Edward James, Mrs. Brenda J. McIntosh, Sammie L.

Minnieweather, Frances Moore, Antoinette Nichols, Ruthia, Linda Smith, and several anonymous participants.

As part of the "Borders" Crossings exhibition this installation intends to make economic, social and geographic borders apparent. It brings two sides of a boundary together, face to face, hand to hand, and heart to heart. In *(In)Visible*, USF students met with me and we in turn met with homeless people living on the streets of San Francisco and the East Bay. Carrying with us a collaboratively created series of questions, we solicited responses from people rarely seen and voices rarely heard here at USF, although in close proximity, only miles away. The discussions were simply based on basic day–to-day survival without permanent shelter, and larger views of the world as seen by homeless women, men and children. The photographic images were inspired by the objects and tools of survival, that belong to the people we met. These respectfully collected responses and images were selected for their poetry, poignancy and power. They are brought to public view in order to open dialogue about economic inequities and economic injustice in San Francisco, the Bay Area, the United States and globally. The hope of my work as an artist is always to move the viewer to action, with the belief that even the smallest movement of the heart, can plant the seeds for social change. Special thanks to the Women's Daytime Drop-in Center in Berkeley, Poor Magazine in San Francisco and Vital Signs in Berkeley. Additional thanks to Richard Kamler, Pamela Blotner, Glori Simmons and Dean Cannon, for their support of this project.

[4] Suzanne Lacy, Introduction by Nina Felshin, *Mapping the Terrain: New Genre Public Art*. (Seattle, Washington: Bay Press, 1995), 27.
[5] Felshin, *But Is It Art? The Spirit of Art as Activism*, 19.

Works Cited

Felshin, Nina, ed. *But Is It Art? The Spirit of Art as Activism*. Seattle: Bay Press, 1995.

Lacy, Suzanne, ed. *Mapping the Terrain: New Genre Public Art*. Seattle: Bay Press, 1995.

How to Make Waves

Anna Shapiro

> In the creation of new cultures that neither pit humans against nature nor set them above it, but rather situate humans within the cycles of the cosmos and celebrate the interconnectedness of all things, the arts have begun to play a major transformational part."
>
> Gloria Orenstein, 1987[1]

Introduction

The historic, western, patriarchal ethic of estrangement and domination over the "other," fosters a soul-less, mechanistic oppression of race, class, sex, and nature, and has marginalized and subjugated individuals and communities for centuries. Empowerment movements that arose from this oppression include, among others, the Feminist Movement, the labor movement, the civil and equal rights movements, and the ecological movement. Each of these movements embraced empowerment and change as core values.

Any political movement can be defined as waves. In America, the first-wave feminists gained the right to vote. Second-wave feminists gained the right to work as equals, gain control of reproductive rights and the right for women to own property. Third-wave feminists challenge notions of gender and sex, race and class, and subvert paradigms of power and oppression. Ecofeminism[2] extrapolates that patriarchal societies' treatment of the earth is mirrored in the way it treats women. Therefore, ecological concerns are inherently feminist concerns as well.[3] Ecofeminism is a precursor to third-wave feminism. It is sited between the second and third-waves of feminism, at the intersections of gender, race, class, religion, economy, and globalization. Ecofeminism and third-wave feminism are plural and inclusive. They openly embrace related issues as intertwined, not isolated. Social action, political activism, spirituality and capitalist abuse of power all tie into the current ecological condition of the social and natural landscape. Ecofeminism is a "social movement in process," a movement that depends on practice more than theory.[4]

Just as ecofeminism is not an isolated idea but rather a deeply rooted social justice movement that recognizes the interconnectedness of oppressed groups, it must withstand polemic challenges to its own viability from within its own academic circle. Ecofeminism in the past 30 years has been a dynamic discourse between "cultural ecofeminism"[5] and "social ecofeminism."[6] There is a poetic ecofeminism and a theory-driven one, but there does not need to be a separation of the two. They balance and feed off one another, and it is through the arts that they can be simultaneously expressed.

The Wave

I carry around within me a sense of place. I also carry around "a Wave" within my pocket.

The Wave is a participatory and ongoing interactive project that has had three propagations in New York, Boston, and Providence. *The Wave*[7] is a rectangular image of a solitary wave that has been reproduced through video, color photocopy, silkscreen, and printed text; it folds into a three-inch package that fits into my pocket. The folds in the paper create a grid that measures out the image, a visual tension between the fluid and the rigid. The vertical and horizontal rigid structure represents the inflexibility of culture, specifically modernism, where the grid is a measure of time and space.

Reproducibility is inherent in the notion of waves. Mechanical and digital reproductions multiply this print of an individual wave. It is ironic in its real disconnection from nature, dissociating the wave from its location. I rely on contemporary methods of art production to generate illusions of waves. It is through the performative action of making "waves" through social interaction, that I reanimate the ritual use of art, which mechanical reproduction has denied.[8]

Engaging with others in the project is a subversive act to the "art viewer." I invite the viewer in a non-art setting to become an active participant rather than a passive consumer. Stopping people street-side, asking them to unfold the package to find a 7 x 10 inch image of a wave inside, and then documenting the event, brings nature into an urban setting. This slows people down, and creates a momentary community, valuable even if just for a few minutes.

At the 2006 WCA Conference in Boston, I passed around the *Wave III: Instructional* blue three-inch rectangle of folded paper (fig. 4-6). On the top was a title: "How to make waves (please open)." Inside there was a three- color silkscreen of a small New England wave. Printed on the back

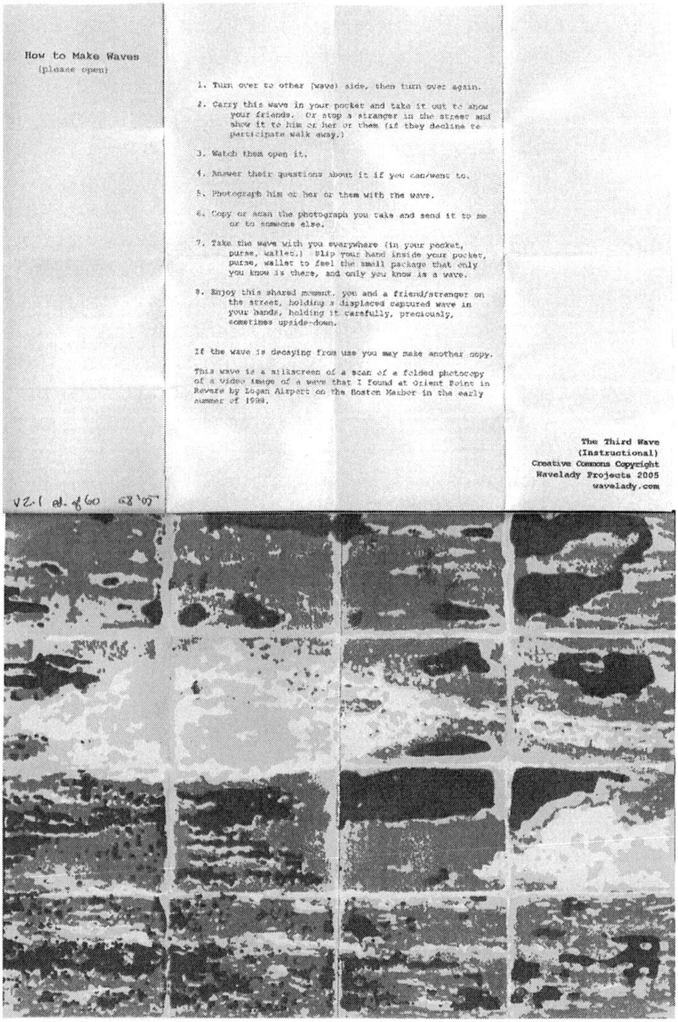

Fig. 4-6
Wave III: Instructional, photograph copyright Anna Shapiro 2006.

was a series of instructions.[9] The instructions included the option to make two-sided reproductions after the session, to make multiple waves, or to distribute them ad infinitum. I invite you, the reader, to do so with the image provided here. This notion of reproducibility and non-ownership of nature and object both echoes contemporary challenges to art and commodity, and embraces the multiplicity of postmodern feminism. Rosalind Krauss speaks of an "aesthetic economy" (specifically referencing minimalism and distinctly applicable here), where there is tension between "originality and repetition… the multiple to the singular, the reproducible to the unique, the fraudulent to the authentic, the copy to the original".[10] Modernism, which can arguably be interchanged with patriarchy, is the power of the singular in opposition to the multiple. Julia Kristeva states that "one must decenter the closed set and elaborate the dialectic of a process within plural and heterogeneous universes."[11]

The act of passing out "waves" in the conference room brought the presence of nature into a space completely devoid of any connection to the natural. I took a photograph of everyone in the conference room holding "Waves III" up, turning the room into a veritable sea: a sea of women, an ecofeminist sea. This connection to nature in a highly manufactured environment is a tongue-in-cheek joke about third-wave feminism using a simple and direct means to make my point.

Conclusion

Artistic traditions have evolved to create emerging practices, which reflect historic changes and document cultural shifts. It is through art that the practical and the spiritual of ecofeminism meet.

While ecofeminism has been marginalized by academia, it takes its place through a ripple outward from the earlier waves of feminisms to challenge the norms of the current patriarchal, capitalist, and consumer society. Rather than a pyramid that builds towards one truth at its apex, ecofeminism and later third-wave inquiries draw from a multiplicity of resources and actions.

The artist as shaman, as mythmaker, as goddess, as scientist, as educator and maker of beauty, is an ecofeminist artist. If ecofeminism is a branch of feminism that has been discounted for spiritual currency, it survives best in the artistic expression of ecofeminist principles. Art that takes part in performative, practical ecofeminism can exist in the realm of the poetic and the spiritual, as well as in academic discourse.

Performative practical ecofeminism, interjected into the every day, reminds people of the lyrical and the absurd. Action and connection can jar people out of a fearful and apathetic position. Political messages expressed through artistic interventions become poetic acts of ecofeminism.

---

[1] Gloria Orenstein quoting herself in "The Greening of Gaia: Ecofeminist Artists Revisit the Garden," *Ethics & the Environment* 8, no. 1 (Spring 2003): 103–11.
[2] The term ecofeminism was coined by Françoise d'Eaubonne in her book Le Feminisme ou la Mort [Feminism or Death] in 1974. I argue that the arts were challenging dominant paradigms of modernity and patriarchy in advance of an academic shift. As found in Peter C. List *Radical Environmentalism.* (California: Wadsworth Publishing Company, 1993), 49, and as part of Carolyn Merchant's essay "Ecofeminism and Feminist Theory"
[3] Merchant, Carolyn. *The Death of Nature: Women, Ecology and the Scientific Revolution.* (New York: Harper Collins 1980, 1983).
[4] Richard T. Twine, *Ecofeminisms in Process,* http://www.lancs.ac.uk/staff/twine/ecofem/ecofem2001.pdf. Access date June 10, 2007. This essay clearly defines the rifts between academic feminism and the more process-oriented ecofeminism.
[5] Ibid. The term is coined from Val Plumwood "Ecofeminism—An Overview and Discussion of Positions and Arguments" 1986, as cited in Twine. Authors who address this cultural ecofeminism would include Alice Walker, Starhawk, and Gloria Orenstein.
[6] Ibid. As cited in Twine, the authors of social ecofeminism would be Susan Griffin and Carolyn Merchant.
[7] Waves represent the natural cyclical movement of the ocean, the feminine connection to the moon, the tides, and sexuality. "Wave" also becomes the language we use in reference to population growth and social movements.
[8] The idea of authenticity in relationship to the art object and its use-value is a major contribution by Walter Benjamin in his article "The Work of Art in the Age of Mechanical Reproduction" in *Illuminations*, (New York, Schoken Books, 1968), 217-242.
[9] The instructions read:

> How to Make Waves (please open)
> 1. Turn over to other (wave) side, then turn over again.
> 2. Carry this wave in your pocket and take it out to show your friends. Or stop a stranger in the street and show it to him or her or them (if they decline to participate walk away.)
> 3. Watch them open it.
> 4. Answer their questions about it if you can/want to.
> 5. Photograph him or her or them with the wave.
> 6. Copy or scan the photograph you take and send it to me or to someone else.
> 7. Take the wave with you everywhere (in your pocket, purse, wallet.) Slip your hand inside your pocket, purse, wallet to feel the small package that only you know is there, and only you know is a wave.
> 8. Enjoy this shared moment, you and a friend/stranger on the street, holding a displaced captured wave in your hands, holding it carefully, preciously, sometimes upside-down.

If the wave is decaying from use you may make another copy.
This wave is a silkscreen of a scan of a folded photocopy of a video image of a wave that I found at Orient Point in Revere by Logan Airport on the Boston Harbor in the early summer of 1999.
The Third Wave (Instructional) Creative Commons Copyright Wavelady Projects 2005 wavelady.com

[10] Rosalind E Krauss, *The Originality of the Avant Garde and Other Modernist Myths*. (Massachussetts: MIT Press, 1986), 151–170.
[11] Julia Kristeva, *Revolution in Poetic Language*. (New York: Columbia University Press, 1984). Later she questions "at what historical moment does social change tolerate or necessitate the signifying process in its 'poetic' or 'esoteric' form…corresponding to socioeconomic change…even to revolution…and under what conditions does it remain a blind ally…," which I feel is particularly relevant in the arguments among ecofeminists.

Works Cited

Benjamin, Walter. *Illuminations: Essays and Reflections*. New York: Schocken Books, 1969.

Krauss, Rosalind E. *The Originality of the Avant Garde and other Modernist Myths*. Massachussetts: MIT Press, 1986.

Kristeva, Julia. *Revolution in Poetic Language*. New York: Columbia University Press, 1984.

List, Peter C. *Radical Environmentalism*. California: Wadsworth Publishing Company, 1993.

Merchant, Carolyn. *The Death of Nature: Women, Ecology and the Scientific Revolution*. New York: Harper Collins. 1980, 1983.

Orenstein, Gloria. "Shamanic Dimensions of an Ecofeminist Narrative," Eve Online (2007) http://eve.enviroweb.org/perspectives/shamanic.html.

Twine, Richard T. *Ecofeminisms in Process,* Ecofem.org 2001. (e-journal) Online at http://www.lancs.ac.uk/staff/twine/ecofem/ecofem2001.pdf

From Fire to Water: Crafting a New American Dream

Ann Rosenthal

Introduction

> We live in times of unprecedented peril and promise. Technological advancements have globalized communications while bringing terrorism to our doorsteps. We have the tools to collectively address hunger, disease, and climate change, working with colleagues around the planet. Yet despite such wonders, we seem more lost than ever. Minute by minute, we are offered up a plethora of consumer goods to fulfill our every desire. Yet there is a deep chasm, a longing we cannot name. Like an invasive species, material desire runs wild with no checks to balance our greed. Material desire has consumed our social desire—to feel connected to a larger whole, to seek out alternatives that do no harm, to live in communities of care and compassion that nurture the magnificent diversity of life, to live in places of beauty and abundance.[1]

Many communities are standing at the precipice of the future—former mill towns that once produced steel, paper, textiles, and lumber, or turned these raw materials into useful goods for the marketplace. Those heady days of hard work and substantive paychecks, building the United States economy and the "American Dream," are over. What is the "American Dream" for the twenty-first century? Is it a "McMansion" in a gated "village" with a Hummer in the driveway?

We have the tools to craft a new "American Dream", but do we have the will, the desire to make that journey? Let's assume that we are willing to take that first tentative step into the unknown. Where do we begin? In indigenous cultures, such journeys have guides—a medicine man or woman, a wise elder, or perhaps a trickster. Of course, we have access to many knowledgeable and wise experts in our towns and cities: professionals, community leaders, and organizers. Yet, how often do we together around the same table and dream a new "American Dream"?

This is the role of the community artist—to listen and look hard for the pieces of a place that make it unique and connect the fragments into a whole; to bring citizens, community leaders, and resources together; to daylight dreams and the imagination; to make the invisible visible; to give voice and image to our social desires; to prepare the soil and facilitate its planting.

This essay will focus on a community arts project that proposed a new identity for a former steel mill town near Pittsburgh, that suggested how a neglected riverfront could be reclaimed to revive a local economy, and that sought to enlist its youth in a new "American Dream." This essay is about that journey, which is not over, a journey that might serve as a model and inspiration for similar communities and the artists who live there.

Envisioning McKeesport: From Fire to Water

> The people of McKeesport rekindled a new optimism from the ashes of the steel industry. While the first industrial revolution brought prosperity, extracting the resources of the earth was finite and eventually depleted the town and its people. The citizens knew they could not give their rivers away twice: a new vision for McKeesport was needed. With faith, courage, and patience, they began to craft a resilient economy that could sustain both the people and their natural resources.[2]

In June 2004, artists Jackie Brookner, Stephanie Flom, and I were invited by the Monongahela Conference, a project of the STUDIO for Creative Inquiry at Carnegie Mellon University, to explore the potential of riverfront public space and ecological restoration in McKeesport, Pennsylvania. Located 10 miles south of Pittsburgh at the confluence of the Monongahela (Mon) and Youghiogheny (Yough) Rivers, this once thriving steel town has lost half of its population since 1940. There are few employment options to attract local youth, who tend to get into trouble or leave the area. The majority of the population is aging and, without retaining their youth, the city will wither and die.

With a support staff of two graduate students (Siobhan Rigg and Priya Krishna) and project coordinator Reiko Goto, our team spent three weeks in residence at the People's Building in downtown McKeesport—a former bank where city offices and services were located. Our "office"—a few desks off the center aisle on the first floor—made us easily accessible to the public. While we were given an open slate about what we might do in McKeesport, our hosts Tim Collins and Reiko Goto encouraged us to focus on the benefits of a proposed McKeesport trail as a critical link in the Great Allegheny Passage (GAP) connecting Pittsburgh to Washington

D.C. The trail could revitalize the city's economy and natural environment by capitalizing on the its strategic location at the confluence of two rivers.[3]

While our interests and expertise focused on ecological revitalization, we did not want to approach the community with a preconceived agenda. Rather, we listened to the people of McKeesport, to understand how they saw the assets, needs, and problems of their town. We strived to work in dialogue with them, and to maximize their participation and guidance.[4] We sought as many points of view and as broad a cross section of people and groups as we could, with the goal of understanding the existing social, economic, and environmental conditions, and their interrelationships. We began with an advisory group that our sponsors and Pittsburgh team member Stephanie Flom had organized before our arrival. Then we spoke with people we met on the street, in city parks, from local organizations and businesses. We learned from trail representatives, teachers, and policy makers, including the Mayor and City Council. We looked for places of possibility where solutions could build upon existing resources. We reflected what we heard and learned back to the community for feedback, and to brainstorm together.

What we found was economic despair; that people are waiting (in vain) for a renewed steel industry; that jobs are scarce and youth leave seeing work elsewhere.[5] We heard nostalgia for a simpler more prosperous time, and we witnessed fear of the poorer, largely African-American housing projects, fear of youth, drugs, and crime that was undermining the town and trail. We recognized vital, but fragmented, social resources—extremely dedicated people who are working hard to make things better, but somewhat in isolation.

To instill local pride about the city's rich natural, social, and historical resources and to enhance the capacity to imagine a positive future, we created a visitor's brochure set in the year 2020, after the City had won the "2018 Urban Conservation Excellence Award." McKeesport has become a thriving town, its successes based in a rich trail and park system that is a regional attraction, and its economy sustained by new "green" industries of the future. The keystone of its success, and the foundation of our vision, is a youth job training program where young people learn and earn as they build the trail and trail structures and restore the riparian ecosystem.[6]

We proposed reuse of two historic buildings—a railroad roundhouse and a water roundhouse—each gateways to the McKeesport section of the trail. Programming of these buildings would include an interpretive and information center for visitors to plan their trail adventures, and an international center for water education and research. A unique park at the confluence of the rivers would attract visitors from the region and beyond, with its unparalleled river views, a Wright-styled restaurant cantilevered over the Point, and a plaza for casual summer encounters, as this excerpt from our 2020 visitor's brochure describes:

> Confluence Park: Where Two Rivers Meet. Bring a picnic basket and soak up the sun in the wildflower meadow, or gather with your friends at McKees Point's Confluence Park. Wandering pathways guide you to river views and diverse indigenous landscapes, or to the European-style plaza where you can savor home-baked treats and refreshing beverages. Looking for a little peace and quiet? Seek out Queen Aliquippa's Grove and consider her words engraved on the historical marker. For a romantic and memorable dining experience, the Riverview Inn provides fresh, local cuisine and stunning views of the confluence. Children of all ages love the Living Watershed Garden. This meandering water feature in the shape of the river system is fed by storm water runoff cleaned by bioremediative plants. . . . Need to repair your bike? OneStop will serve all your needs from bike rentals to repairs. This unique business venture is run by local youth who recycle and repair bikes. People of all ages seem to be active and engaged in this "trail town."[7]

We presented our brochure and a phased action plan to our Advisory Board and the community in November 2004. Key stakeholders turned out from the city, trail groups, the high school, local non-profits, and the business community. To capture the imagination of our audience, we decided to transport them to 2018. While Stephanie gave an introduction to the project, Jackie and I excused ourselves. We doused our hair with white powder and, on cue, hobbled onto the small, school-sized stage. Stephanie proclaimed, "Where have you been? It's 2018!" We replied, "The Foundation for Urban Conservation Excellence asked us to return to McKeesport to deliver their awards to community members who have made the McKeesport vision a reality." We proceeded to give out awards (water bottles with unique "Discover McKeesport" labels) in the areas of Trail Development, Reclamation and Programming of Historic Buildings, the Youth Earn & Learn Program, and the Creation of Confluence Park. Rather than rewarding individual efforts, we awarded teams—people who we thought would work well together and have complementary interests and expertise, such as the director of the Historical Society and the architects who are redesigning the public housing along the river.

Now that we had our audience's attention, we presented the Envisioning McKeesport action plan. Our brochure allowed us to imagine without constraint, but we also recognized the need for concrete plans to realize the vision. We therefore developed a set of one-page sheets in modular format—so that parts of the plan could be tackled individually, or in parallel, by different groups. The sheets describe initial conditions, immediate needs, and long-range opportunities, including guidelines for the Youth Earn & Learn Program. Our proposal was enthusiastically received, and community members pledged to continue our work. Jackie returned to New York, I returned to Massachusetts, and Stephanie began a full-time position as the director of a community center.

As is so often the case with community arts projects, our vision for McKeesport languished without the continuity of our involvement. Two years passed with continued, but fragmented, local efforts. No significant progress was made toward realizing McKeesport as a "trail town."

In 2005, Tim Collins and Reiko Goto launched a comprehensive exhibition, *Groundworks: Environmental Collaboration in Contemporary Art*, curated by Grant Kester. Our project, along with six similar efforts through the Monongahela Conference, was featured within the context of national and international environmentally focused community arts projects at the Regina Gouger Miller Gallery at Carnegie Mellon University, Pittsburgh. We represented our vision of McKeesport through a floor model of the trail, park, and renovated buildings. A timeline from the present to 2020 charted how the vision could be realized. The exhibition and symposium made clear that environmental and social problems are inseparable; community artists around the world are addressing both issues through a process of dialogue, civic engagement, imagination, and creative action.

Youth Earn & Learn Program

Renewed attention on the McKeesport project through the exhibition provided a second chance to reignite our vision by initiating the Youth Earn & Learn Program. I had relocated to Pittsburgh and was ready for the challenge. Prior to the disbanding of our team two years earlier, we had proposed the youth program to the director of the McKeesport Area Technology Center (ATC), a vocational program within the High School. Before I could proceed, I had to ensure that the ATC and City were interested in partnering on such a program. It took a few months to obtain letters of support, but surprisingly, interest had not waned. In less than two months, I raised enough money from local foundations, the Steel Valley Trail Council, and the Redevelopment Authority of the City of McKeesport to run a three-week program in August 2006.[8] The high school assigned me a teacher, Kim Robertson, and we began developing the program. A biology teacher, Jackie Thompson, volunteered as well and participated for two of the three weeks.

What could be accomplished in nine days with ten high school students and two teachers? The vision of students learning job skills working alongside professionals to build the trail was not possible in such a short period with no lead time. Though a new section of the McKeesport trail was on the drawing board, its implementation was delayed. Opportunities for direct student involvement were premature. What I envisioned for this pilot program was to introduce students to the trail and its potential for their own and McKeesport's future, and to give the students a vehicle to communicate their vision to their community.

The first two weeks of the program consisted of learning about the ecology and history of the riverfront and trail from professionals across a range of disciplines: a trail engineer walked us through his blueprints and the complicated process of developing a trail. A Native American from McKeesport and former mill worker told us about the medicinal uses of plants and trees, and he demonstrated a traditional game made from the bark of a willow tree. During a field trip to Pittsburgh, we learned about green roofs and environmental engineering, and we toured an award-winning stream restoration project. We heard about the history of the steel mills from two women steel workers, and learned how the geology and geography of Pennsylvania made Pittsburgh the center of the steel industry. We experienced the Great Allegheny Passage south of McKeesport—a beautiful and well-maintained trail frequented by people of all ages. Along the way, we gathered photographs and sketched images that could represent our view of the trail in preparation for the final week of the program—a banner-making workshop with Connecticut artist JoAnn Moran.[9]

In preparation for the final week of the program, students designed their banner images—steel mills and bicycle wheels, trees and leaves, maps and riverfronts, fish and boats. JoAnn skillfully led the students in a flurry of creative activity, preparing the recycled banners for painting, transferring their designs to the recycled vinyl banners, developing a color scheme to provide continuity to the project as a whole. The back of each banner illustrated a section of the Great Allegheny Passage, with a place name from that section. The maps float in undulating lines suggesting water, together forming a rainbow of color.

The banners are now mounted on light posts connecting City Hall to the riverfront. The first McKeesport Community Trail Day in October 2006 celebrated the creativity and imagination of the students' work while informing citizens about McKeesport's critical location in the larger trail system. In a ceremony to honor the students, McKeesport City Council president Regis McLaughlin announced a major trail development project, and he invited Youth Earn & Learn to be part of that endeavor. Kim Robertson, the teacher with whom I worked closely throughout the program, is now a "trail-convert," as are many of the students who now embark on regular trail bike rides. Partnerships are forming between the City, trail organizations, the National Park Service (Rivers, Trails, and Conservation Assistance Division), and Youth Earn & Learn to realize McKeesport's trail as part of the Great Allegheny Passage and include youth in that process.

Program evaluations indicated that the students enjoyed the activities and learned what we intended. When asked "What do you hope the outcome of the program will be?" they unanimously said they wanted the trail to be valued and used by the public. As student Michael Pollak emphasized in a 2007 *Daily News* interview, "The people don't really know that there's a trail in McKeesport…We're here to help them understand the trail is here, that it can lead to things and go places if they put work into it."[10]

Through a *Community Trail Art Initiative* in partnership with the Steel Valley Trail Council, Youth Earn & Learn ecoliteracy and art programs will continue in communities along the trail, with the goal to connect young people to their local landscapes and inspire pride in the social and environmental legacy embodied in their trail. My vision is that the trail will serve and be served by the youth of today, and stewardship will be passed down to their children and their children's children.

Lessons Learned

As a community artist, I have thought long and hard as to how my work is similar or different from professionals in complementary disciplines. Though I may draw from landscape architecture, urban planning, the social and natural sciences, or communications design, my training and expertise are as an artist. Over the course of our project, I noted how Jackie, Stephanie, and I applied our skills, not to canvas or clay, but to designing and crafting a new identity and dream for a community. Rather than carefully observing a subject to express its essence, or researching an issue to inform a socially relevant work, we carefully listened to people's fears and frustrations, their hopes and dreams. In parallel, we absorbed the built and natural environment that has shaped and been shaped by this community. Over time, we were able to identify the unrecognized strengths and resources of this place and weave these into a comprehensive vision. The people of McKeesport supplied the dots; we connected them. This ability to recognize relationships and patterns, Howard Gardner[11] calls "the Naturalist Intelligence," a skill that artists also share.

When I talk to colleagues and students about community arts practice, I am often asked, "Aren't you an outsider, an intruder, imposing your own vision onto the community?" To the contrary, we found that our interest in the community was a validation, especially coming from such a prestigious institution as Carnegie Mellon. We discovered that being outsiders was an advantage: we entered their domain with open minds and people opened up to us. And we were reminded that as human beings, the dream for a better life and the social desire to create that life, as individuals and as a community, is deep within each of us, longing to be heard and supported. As one person commented after our awards ceremony and community meeting, we were able to suspend cynicism and invite people to dream with us, because that's what artists do.

In retrospect, we realized we were approaching McKeesport as an ecosystem—in the broadest sense, applying ecological and systems thinking to community art practice. The steel industry was an economic monoculture that could not sustain itself over time. The trail town solution could be equally vulnerable. To be successful, it must catalyze economic diversity and revitalize relationships and networks between community members, as well as between the community and their local environment.

Because we placed the needs of the community first and used the trail and tourism as a means to an end, not the end-goal, we hope to distinguish our strategy of developing McKeesport's identity as a trail town from a generic solution for postindustrial communities. We see the trail as a catalyst for helping the community see a future, and for engendering resilience in both social and ecological systems, so that they can be self-healing and self-organizing, with the capacity to adapt to unexpected challenges and to evolve over time.

The seed was planted and the Web site was launched (http://steelvalleytrail.org/YELP).[12] It will take persistence and patience to root this new vision deep into McKeesport's soil and weave the trail into the fabric of their culture. Artists can create change by facilitating communities to re-imagine and re-image their "American Dream." This does not happen in a month. We must commit ourselves to the community for change to be sustained, at least for a period of time. We can act as catalysts, dreamers, planners, facilitators, mediums, and workers—as part of a team effort, lessening our role steadily as others take it up.

The Youth Earn & Learn Program represents a first step: guiding youth to see the interconnections between local nature and local culture, introducing them to environmentally related careers, providing them opportunities to be leaders in their community, owning and crafting their own vision and identity for McKeesport. We hope that partnerships with the City, educational institutions and educators, trail organizations, and regional foundations will catalyze a program that can serve the community, evolving as McKeesport meets its future.

Perhaps the "American Dream" can be refashioned, starting in communities like McKeesport. *From Fire to Water*, out of the ashes of the last industrial revolution a new way of co-existing with non-human nature can emerge, where the diversity of all life is valued and celebrated. Though we can communicate with friends and colleagues around the globe, the next frontier is closer to home. What is most needed is to dialogue with our neighbors to build community and democracy from the inside out, house-by-house, block-by-block, to consider what kind of place we want to inhabit and how we can make it our home.

---

[1] Jackie Brookner, Stephanie Flom, and Ann. Rosenthal, *Discover McKeesport: 2020 Visitor's Brochure* (Pittsburgh: Self-published, 2004), available online at http://jackiebrookner.net/mckeesport.htm.

[2] Ibid.

[3] Argueta J., S. Farber, and S. Hughes. *2002 User Survey for the Pennsylvania Allegheny Trail Alliance.* Pittsburgh: University Center for Social and Urban Research, University of Pittsburgh, 2003. Chapter 3. http://www.atatrail.org/about/reports.cfm. It reported $12,096,285 total spending in Pennsylvania attributable to the trail system, which is not yet complete.

[4] "The Transformation of McKeesport: From Fire to Water," in *Groundworks: Environmental Collaboration in Contemporary Art*, ed. Grant Kester, 161. (Pittsburgh: Regina Gouger Miller Gallery, Carnegie Mellon University, 2005).

[5] Brookner, Flom, and Rosenthal. 2005.

[6] Ibid.

[7] Ibid.

[8] Youth Earn & Learn project partners and funders: City of McKeesport; Grable Foundation; Henry C. Frick Educational Fund of the Buhl Foundation; McKeesport Area Technology Center; Mon Valley Media; Murphy Foundation; Redevelopment Authority of the City of McKeesport; Steel Valley Trail Council, and the STUDIO for Creative Inquiry, Carnegie Mellon University.

[9] http://republicart.org.

[10] J. Vertrullo, "Students Help Bring Attention to Youghiogheny River Trail," *The Daily News*. August 24, 2006.

[11] Howard Gardner, *Intelligence Reframed: Multiple Intelligences for the 21st Century* (New York: Basic Books, 1999), 50.

[12] Inception date December 3, 2006.

Works Cited

Argueta J., S. Farber, and S. Hughes. *2002 User Survey for the Pennsylvania Allegheny Trail Alliance.* Pittsburgh: University Center for Social and Urban Research, University of Pittsburgh, 2003. Chapter 3. http://www.atatrail.org/about/reports.cfm.

Brookner, Jackie, Stephanie Flom, and Ann Rosenthal. *Discover McKeesport: 2020 Visitor's Brochure*. Pittsburgh: Self-published, 2004. http://jackiebrookner.net/mckeesport.htm.

——. "The Transformation of McKeesport: From Fire to Water," in *Groundworks: Environmental Collaboration in Contemporary Art*, ed. Grant Kester, 161. Pittsburgh: Regina Gouger Miller Gallery, Carnegie Mellon University, 2005.

Gardner, Howard. *Intelligence Reframed: Multiple Intelligences for the 21st Century.* New York: Basic Books, 1999.

Vertrullo, J. "Students Help Bring Attention to Youghiogheny River Trail." *The Daily News*. August 24, 2006.

Hello/Hola

Think Again (David John Attayh and S.A. Bachman)

Hello/Hola links the rape and murder of over 300 unidentified women in Ciudad Juarez, Mexico to the structural effects of NAFTA and intergovernmental relations between the United States and Mexico. Of particular interest are the ways that capitalism and misogyny conspire to jeopardize women. Many of the murdered women of Juarez remain unidentified, personifying the anonymous violence that can be precipitated by policy change. In an attempt to acknowledge their lost identities, *Hello/Hola* uses the recurring image of a blank nametag manufactured by Avery, one of the *maquiladora*s operating in Juarez. *Hello/Hola* connects the flow of international capital to the flow of women's lives, from their rural birthplaces to cities where multinational corporations search for cheap labor. The project represents the movement of money and bodies that results in increased danger for young, poor, brown women who are effectively displaced from their homes and exposed to new forms of violence (fig. 4-7).

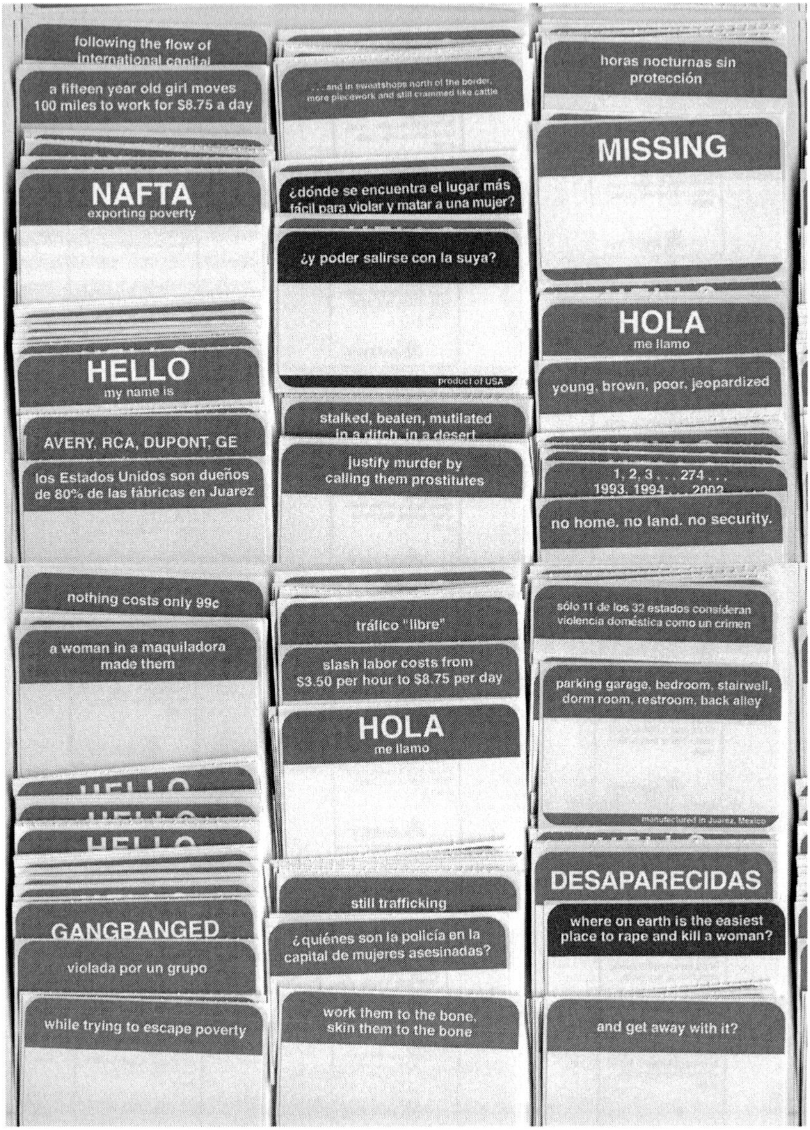

Fig. 4-7
Hello/Hola, photograph copyright THINK AGAIN 2006.

CONTRIBUTORS

Pamela Allara

Associate Professor Emerita, Brandeis University; art historian and author of a monograph on Alice Neel, *Pictures of People: Alice Neel's American Portrait Gallery,* (1998/2000). Recent research has been: activist art in South Africa, including Co-Existence: Contemporary Cultural Production in South Africa, Rose Art Museum at Brandeis, 2003; as well as global feminism, addressed in the exhibition *Geobodies: A Question of Boundaries*, for the Women's Studies Research Center at Brandeis University, (included in a forthcoming new Eastern European feminist anthology).

Simone Alter-Müri

EdD, ATR-BC, LMHC, founder, director, professor of Art Therapy/Art Education Programs at Springfield College, Springfield, Massachusetts. Dr. Alter-Muri has published, presented and exhibited nationally and internationally, and was the 2003 recipient of the Massachusetts Art Educator of the Year in Higher Education. She is a recipient of a Massachusetts Cultural Council Grant and a researcher in art development.

Maria Elena Buszek

Critic, curator, and professor of Modern and Contemporary Art at the Kansas City Art Institute. She is the author of the book *Pin-Up Grrrls: Feminism, Sexuality, Popular Culture,* and her writing has appeared in such journals as *Art in America, Woman's Art Journal, TDR: The Journal of Performance Studies*, and Kansas City's *Review*. Dr. Buszek is also a regular contributor to the popular feminist culture magazine *Bust.*

Laurie Beth Clark

Professor in the Art Department at the University of Wisconsin at Madison for Video, Performance, and Installation. Clark produces large-scale installations and performances as well as single channel videotapes and virtual environments. In addition to the work on the performance of credibility included in this volume, Clark is currently completing a project on the persistence of material culture in the electronic age and will appear as a comparative global study of trauma memorials.

Jennifer Colby

PhD, National President of Women's Caucus for Art, 2006-08; lecturer at the California State University at Monterey Bay; and Founding Director/Owner of Galería Tonantzin, San Juan Bautista, California, a women's art gallery; artist, curator and writer.

Eleanor Dickinson

Professor Emerita at California College of the Arts, painter, and recipient of numerous awards including the 2003 WCA Lifetime Achievement Award. Represented in collections across the United States, Dickinson has been honored in 24 solo museum exhibitions, including Corcoran Gallery of Art and Fine Arts Museums of San Francisco. She has also co-authored many publications, including *Revival!*

Noreen Dean Dresser

MFA, feminist ethicist, addresses global agency and historical experience as in her *Queer Memorial Memory in Nazi Germany* series New York City/Berlin. Dresser directs Parlour153 in Harlem and co-curated Her-Humanity Transformative Agency and Advocacy, Casa Frela, New York. Dresser serves on the College of Art's (CAA) Committee on Women in the Arts 2007 and is a past president of the WCA 2002-04.

Ellen Driscoll

Professor of Sculpture at Rhode Island School of Design. Her installations include The Loophole of Retreat, and Passionate Attitudes; public art projects include As Above, So Below, Catching the Drift, and LUMINA. Recipient of numerous fellowships, including the Guggenheim Foundation and the National Endowment for the Arts fellowships, Driscoll has work represented at the Whitney Museum of Art, and the Metropolitan Museum of Art.

Emily D. Eastridge

School of the Museum of Fine Arts, Boston; "It's not always about the two of us. We work over distance, sometimes a physical distance, but mostly over an isolated cerebral vastness. We play frisbee with thought, throw things back and forth. Eventually, you get it. Sometimes everyone misses despite putting everything out there."

Cynthia Fowler

Received her PhD in Art History from the University of Delaware in 2002. She is currently an associate professor of Art at Emmanuel College in Boston, Massachusetts. Her research consistently focuses on the artist production of twentieth century women artists. Most recently, her research on painter Jaune Quick-To-See Smith (Flathead) was published in the art history journal *Aurora.*

L'Merchie Frazier

Visual/performance artist whose works are informed by cultural, cloth, and mask traditions of Africa and the African Diaspora. She is director of education at the Museum of Afro-American History, Boston, Massachusetts.

Karen Frostig

PhD, visual artist, author, associate professor at Lesley University and Research Associate at the Hadassah-Brandeis Institute. Publications include *Expressive Arts Therapies in Schools* (1998; Korean trans. 2nd ed., 2007), and numerous journal articles. She is a recipient of a Puffin Foundation Grant, a Massachusetts Cultural Council Grant, and several fellowships, is National WCA Board member and co-president of the Boston chapter. Holocaust Legacies will be on exhibition at the University of Vienna Institute for Philosophy of Law, 2008.

Elinor W. Gadon

Cultural historian, author, resident scholar at Brandeis University Women's Studies Research Center and founder of the Women's Spirituality doctoral program at the California Institute of Integral Studies. Co-curator of the exhibit Tiger By The Tail: Women Artists Of India Transforming Culture. Ground-breaking 1989 book *The Once and Future Goddess: A Symbol for Our Time*, and her new book *From Blood to Fire: The Changing Culture of the Village Goddess in India.* She was a 2006 WCA Lifetime Achievement Awardee.

Janet Gillespie

Teacher, anti-racist educator, dancer, and choreographer whose recent work is concerned with the unacknowledged impact of African and African Diaspora dance practices on modern dance.

Ellen S. Ginsburg

Medical anthropologist and associate professor of Anthropology/ Sociology at Massachusetts College of Pharmacy and Health Sciences, Boston, Massachusetts.

Raishad J. Glover

Yale University School of Art: "What inspires me to make my art? Flat simple, it goes back to my mom. I've always have been making art with my mom, trying to please her with art and surprise her at the same time. Since my mom has passed away, I realize the unpredictability of being. With that, I realize the unpredictability of art. Challenging this inspires me."

Jennifer Hall

Information artist and professor at Massachusetts College of Art, and director, *Do While Studio*, Boston, Massachussetts.

Laurie Elizabeth Talbot Hall

MFA, PhD, feminist theoretician; uses the tools of clinical psychology and photography to undermine the patriarchal motifs that subjugate women's lives. Her essays and artworks illuminate and validate from the interpersonal to the eco-feminist, such as chairing "The Art of Being Global" panel CAA 0007. Hall currently is at the Albert Einstein College of Medicine.

Kathy A. Halamka

BA, Stanford University, and MFA, Tufts University/School of the Museum of Fine Arts Boston. She is active as a visual artist, curator, and instructor in Media and Culture at Bentley College, Waltham, Massachusetts. Recent collaborations include: co-president of the WCA Boston chapter; co-chairperson for the 2006 National WCA Conference; National WCA Board member; and regional coordinator of New England for the Feminist Art Project, Rutgers University.

Mags Harries

Professor of Sculpture at the Museum School of Fine Arts in Boston. Harries is a trained sculptor who collaborates with Lajos Héder to create installations and objects in public spaces that address aspects of community, environment, history and memory. The artists work in a wide variety of locations including parks, zoos, museums, libraries, streets, plazas, and public buildings. The two have collaborated on public installations since 1991.

Patricia Hills

Author and professor of Art History, Boston University; has written books and catalogues on nineteenth- and twentieth-century American art, including Alice Neel, Marianna Pineda, and May Stevens. Her *Modern Art in the USA: Issues and Controversies of the Twentieth Century* was published in 2001. Currently she is writing a book *Painting Harlem Modern: The Art of Jacob Lawrence.*

C. M. Judge

Intermedia artist. She holds a MS in Visual Studies from MIT and is a recipient of numerous grants that support collaborative public art projects including a NEA Challenge America grant. Ms. Judge co-curates FemLink: The International Video Collage, with French video artist, Véronique Sapin, and co-founded the Central Massachusetts chapter of the WCA.

Susan King

Chaired the WCA Lifetime Achievement Awards Committee from 2003 to 2006. She is an artist and art historian living and working in Southern California. Two intersecting interests drive her art historical research: the imbrication of twentieth-century modernism, nationalism, and imperialism; and the role of women artists and critics in the formation (and criticism) of modern art.

Cher Krause Knight

Assistant professor of Art History at Emerson College, Boston. She received her PhD from Temple University and her MA from City College. She has published work in various journals and anthologies and authored *Louis Bosa: A Keen Eye and a Kind Heart.* She has been twice awarded the Gemmill Research Fellowship at the Michener Art Museum. Her book *Public Art: Theory Practice and Populism* is forthcoming from Blackwell Publishing.

Christina Lanzl

Project manager at the UrbanArts Institute at Massachusetts College of Art and visual artist; works to promote excellence in public art and design. With degrees in art history, information science, and broad studio training (MA, Boston University; Diploma, FHB Stuttgart, Germany). She has completed over 100 projects of both local and national scope, regularly presents and writes on the arts and culture, and has received numerous awards.

Catherine McGregor

Body-centered performance artist who has worked in Europe and the United States. She is interested in sexual representations of the female body and intersections between s/m practices and performance art.

Denise Malis

Currently enrolled in the PhD in Expressive Therapies and adjunct faculty at Lesley University. She has 15 years of experience in art therapy and has exhibited nationally and internationally since completing her MFA in 1980. Denise is committed to community-based art making, and co-founded the "art-for-all" studio as well as a cooperative gallery in South Boston.

Joan M. Marter

Ph.D. Distinguished Professor of Art History at Rutgers University; co-editor of *Woman's Art Journal.* She writes regularly on women artists and issues in contemporary art. Recent publications include: *Abstract Expressionism, The International Context* (Rutgers University Press, 2007).

Dena Muller

Executive director of ArtTable. She was the director of A.I.R. Gallery from 1999 to 2006. She received her MA from New York University in 1998. She has served on the board of the Women's Caucus for Art since 2000 and was its Board President from 2004 to 2006. Dena also serves on the National Coordinating Committee for the Feminist Art Project.

Mari Novotny-Jones

Faculty, School of the Museum of Fine Arts, Boston, Massachusetts. M.A. Lesley University. Tanne Foundation Artist Award 2001; fellowship from Boston Cultural Council. Member of Boston's Mobius. Recent international credits include Macedonia, Croatia, and Poland; Festival Forfest, Czech Republic; Kicevo Artist Colony, Macedonia; the Harta Festival in Monza, Italy; the 6th Annual Performance Open in Chengdu, China; Eurpto Festival in Transylvania. Recent works include *Shrinekeepers*, 2007 Boston Cyberarts Festival and *Harvest* 2006 Mobius International Festival.

Thea Paneth

Painter, parent, and peace activist. Her work is personal and political. Small-scale landscapes investigate the diversity and fragility of life. Full-reach works depict historical events and/or iconographic historical or cultural figures. Paneth seeks in her work to render a particular moment that resonates with emotional impact.

Jeanne Philipp

Media artist and curator, lecturer in Art History at University of Dayton and adjunct graduate faculty at Antioch University. Philipp developed and taught upper level Art History and Feminism courses. She holds an interdisciplinary M.A. from Antioch University. Her multimedia work has been shown in numerous colleges, universities and museums throughout the United States.

Aviva Rahmani

Aviva Rahmani's work has reflected environmental and social concerns throughout her forty-year career. Projects range from complete landscape restorations to museum venues referencing painting, sound and photography. Rahmani has taught, lectured and performed internationally, and will participate in the 2007 Venice Biennale, as part of the international group: Cultura21. She is the recipient of numerous grants and fellowships including from the Nancy H. Gray Foundation for Art in the Environment in 1999 and 2000.

Patricia Rodríguez

Chicana artist, educator, co-founder of Bay Area art Collective "Mujeres Muralistas," 1970 to 1979. Her artwork is in art history books. She currently serves as the Gallery Curator, for Mission Cultural Center for Latino Arts, San Francisco, California. Exhibitions include: The Museum of Modern Art, New York; the Smithsonian, Washington, DC; Mexican Fine Arts Museum, Chicago, Illinois,; White Gallery, UCLA, Los Angeles, California; Daniel Saxon Gallery, Los Angeles; and De Young Museum, San Francisco.

Ann T. Rosenthal

Twenty-five years of experience as an environmental artist, educator, and writer. Her installations have been featured at the Hudson River Museum, Plymouth State College, Exit Art, Carnegie Mellon, and the Warhol Museum. Her writing appears in critical anthologies and journals. She has developed numerous courses on environmental art and lectures widely on how art can transform post-industrial landscapes and communities.

Joan Ryan

Associate professor of Drawing at the Art Institute of Boston at Lesley University. She is a Boston-based artist, and her work has been exhibited nationally and internationally. She has received grants from the Massachusetts Cultural Council, the Puffin Foundation, and George Sugarman Foundation. Her work has been selected by jurors Ned Rifkin, Donald Kuspit and Olga Viso. She is affiliated with A.I.R. Gallery.

Mira Schor

A painter and writer teaching at Parsons, The New School for Design. Schor is the author of *Wet: On Painting, Feminism, and Art Culture* and co-editor of *M/E/A/N/I/N/G: An Anthology of Artists' Writings, Theory, and* Criticism and of *M/E/A/N/I/N/G* Online at: http://writing.upenn.edu/pepc/meaning/. Two books are forthcoming in 2008-2009: A *Decade of Negative Thinking: Essays on Art, Politics, and Everyday Life* from Duke University Press, and *The Extreme of the Middle: The Writings of Jack Tworkov*, edited by Schor, Yale University Press.

Harriet F. Senie

Director of Museum Studies and professor of Art History at City College and the Graduate Center, City University of New York (CUNY). She is the author of *The 'Tilted Arc' Controversy: Dangerous Precedent?* (2002), *Contemporary Public Sculpture* (1992), and co-editor of *Critical Issues in Public Art* (1992; 1998). Her current book project is titled *Transforming American Memorials: From Symbolic Cemetery to a Light in the Sky: Vietnam to 9/11.*

Anna Shapiro

Interdisciplinary artist concerned with social and ecological issues. MFA from the Maine College of Art 2000 and BS from Tufts University 1996. Her site-specific sculptures, installations, and public works have earned her numerous awards and residencies. In the past she has worked as a National Park Service Park Ranger (environmental educator) and wilderness guide, and is currently the director Firehouse 13, Providence, Rhode Island. She lives and works between New York, Rhode Island, and Maine.

Sharon Siskin

Assistant professor of Studio Art and Art Outreach: The Artist as Citizen in the Visual Arts Department of the University of San Francisco, California, and adjunct professor in the Graduate School of Arts and Consciousness at John F. Kennedy University, Berkeley, California. She is a board member of the Women Environmental Artist Directory, a nationally exhibiting visual artist, and a continually inspired community-based activist artist.

THINK AGAIN (David John Attyah and S.A. Bachman)

A two-person public art collaboration. Exhibitions have been held at Museu d'Art Contemporani de Barcelona, Museum of New Art, Exit Art, and Track 16 Gallery. Collections held at Los Angeles County Museum of Art, Palacio de Bellas Artes, and Center for the Study of Political Graphics. Their work has been featured in *Artforum*, *Ms. Magazine*, *Social Text*, *The Progressive*, *Graphic Agitation 2*, and *Peace Signs: The Anti-War Movement Illustrated.* A monograph of their work *A Brief History of Outrage* was published in 2003. Attyah is an instructor at Glendale College in Los Angeles and Bachman is a senior lecturer at the School of the Museum of Fine Arts in Boston.

Ruth Wallen

Faculty of the interdisciplinary arts MFA program at Goddard College. She is a multimedia artist whose work is dedicated to encouraging dialogue about ecological and social issues. Her multilayered installations and performances have been exhibited at Franklin Furnace, New Langton Arts, the Exploratorium, Sushi Gallery, and CEPA Gallery. Public installations include several interactive "nature walks."

Ruth von Jahnke Waters

BA, Stanford University, 1955; sculptor; founder and director of the 1870 Art Center, Belmont, California (1977); founder and President of Peninsula Museum of Art; co-founder of Peninsula Sculptors' Guild; founder of Peninsula Chapter of Women's Caucus for Art, National Board of WCA; Allied Member of American Institute of Architects; co-founder and board member of Peninsula Arts Council. Has also worked in communications as a technical writer and editor, community college journalism instructor, and department editor for a daily newspaper.

Anna Wexler

Faculty member at Springfield College, Boston, Massachusetts, where she teaches courses on African, Atlantic, and other ritually based healing systems. She is a scholar, teacher and interdisciplinary artist whose recent work reflects the impact of Haitian *Vodou* and other Afro-Caribbean ritual traditions on politically engaged performance art.

APPENDIX

WCA LIFETIME ACHIEVEMENT AWARD HONOREES

Los Angeles 2009
Maren Hassinger
Ester Hernandez
Joyce Kozloff
Margo Machida
Ruth Weisberg

Dallas 2008
Ida Applebroog
Joanna Frueh
Nancy Grossman
Leslie King-Hammond
Yolanda López
Lowery Stokes Sims

New York 2007
Ferris Olin
Judith K. Brodsky
Barbara Chase-Riboud
Wanda Corn
Buffie Johnson
Lucy R. Lippard
Elizabeth Murray

Boston 2006
Eleanor Antin
Marisol Escobar
Elinor Gadon
Yayoi Kusama

Atlanta 2005
Bette Blayton-Taylor
Rosalynn Carter
Mary D. Garrard
Agnes Martin
Yoko Ono
Ann Sutherland Harris

Seattle 2004
Emma Amos
Jo Baer
Michi Itami
Helen Levitt
Yvonne Rainer

New York 2003
Eleanor Dickinson
Suzi Gablik
Grace Glueck
Ronne Hartfield
Eleanor Munro
Nancy Spero

Philadelphia 2002
Camille Billops
Judith K. Brodsky
Muriel Magenta
Linda Nochlin
Marilyn J. Stokstad

Chicago 2001
Joyce Aiken
Marie Johnson Calloway
Dorothy Gillespie
Thalia Gouma-Peterson
Wilhemina Holladay
Ellen Lanyon
Ruth Waddy

Los Angeles 1999
Judy Baca
Judy Chicago
Linda Frye Burnham
Evangeline K. Montgomery
Arlene Raven

Barbara T. Smith

Philadelphia 1997

Jo Hanson
Sadie Krauss Kriebel
Jaune Quick-To-See Smith
Moira Roth
Kay Sekimachi

Boston 1996

Bernice Bing
Alicia Craig Faxon
Elsa Honig Fine
Howardena Pindell
Marianna Pineda
Kay WalkingStick

San Antonio 1995

Irene Clark
Jacqueline Clipsham
Alessandra Comini
Jean Lacy
Amalia Mesa-Bains
Celia Alvarez Muñoz

New York City 1994

Mary Adams
Maria Enriquez de Allen
Beverly Pepper
Faith Ringgold
Rachel Rosenthal
Charlotte Streifer Rubenstein

Seattle 1993

Ruth Asawa
Shifra M. Goldman
Nancy Graves
Gwen Knight
Agueda Salazar Martinez
Emily Waheneka

Chicago 1992

Vera Berdich
Paula Gerard
Lucy Lewis
Louise Noun
Margaret Tafoya
Anna Tate

Washington DC 1991

Theresa Bernstein
Mildred Constantine
Otellie Loloma
Mine Okubo
Delilah Pierce

New York City 1990

Ilse Bing
Elizabeth Layton
Helen Serger
May Stevens
Pablita Velarde

San Francisco 1989

Bernarda Bryson
Margret Shahn
Clare Craver
Betye Leighton
Samella Saa
Lewis Sanders

Houston 1988

Margaret Burroughs
Dorothy Hood
Miriam Schapiro
Edith Standen
Jane Teller

Boston 1987

Grace Hartigan
Agnes Mongan
Maud Morgan
Honoré Sharrer
Elizabeth Talford Scott
Beatrice Wood

New York City 1986

Nell Blaine
Leonora Carrington
Sue Fuller
Lois Mailou Jones
Dorothy Miller

Los Angeles 1985/Toronto 1984

Minna Citron
Clyde Connell
Eleanor Raymond
Joyce Treiman
June Wayne
Rachel Wischnitzer

Philadelphia 1983

Edna Andrade
Dorothy Dehner
Lotte Jacobi
Ellen Johnson

Stella Kramrisch
Lenore Tawney
Pecolia Warner

New York City 1982

Bernice Abbott
Elsie Driggs
Elizabeth Gilmore Holt
Katharine Kuh
Charmion von Wiegand
Claire Zeisler

San Francisco 1981

Ruth Bernhard
Adelyn Breeskin
Elizabeth Catlett
Sari Dienes
Claire Falkenstein
Helen Lundeberg

Washington, DC, 1980 Alternate Awards

Bella Abzug
Sonia Johnson
Sister Theresa Kane
Grace Paley
Rosa Parks
Gloria Steinem

New Orleans 1980

Anni Albers
Louise Bourgeois
Carolyn Durieux
Ida Kohlmeyer
Lee Krasner

Washington, DC, 1979

Isabel Bishop
Selma Burke
Alice Neel
Louise Nevelson
Georgia O'Keeffe

INDEX